MAZZINI

MAZZINI

DENIS MACK SMITH

YALE UNIVERSITY PRESS
NEW HAVEN AND LONDON   1994

Copyright © 1994 by Denis Mack Smith

First published in paperback 1996

Set in Meridien by Best-set Typesetter Ltd., Hong Kong
Printed and bound in Great Britain by Biddles Ltd., Guildford and Kings Lynn

Library of Congress Cataloging-in-Publication Data

Mack Smith, Denis, 1920–
    Mazzini / Denis Mack Smith.
        p.   cm.
    Includes bibliographical references and index.
    ISBN 0–300–05884–5 (hbk.)
    ISBN 0–300–06884–0 (pbk.)
    1. Mazzini, Giuseppe, 1805–1872. 2. Statesmen—Italy—Biography.
3. Revolutionaries—Italy—Biography.   4. Italy—
History—1815—1870.   I. Title.
DG552.8.M3M23   1994
945'.08'092—dc20   93–38313
[B]   CIP

A catalogue record for this book is available from the British Library.

Contents

List of Illustrations

The following illustrations are between pages 118 and 119.

Italy: The Regions

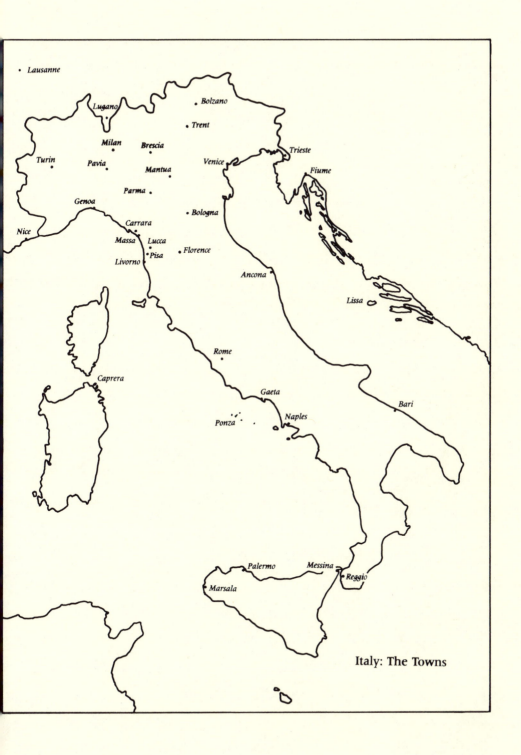

Italy: The Towns

CHAPTER ONE

Beginnings

Apprenticeship

THE CREATION OF a united Italian kingdom was among the more dramatic stories of the nineteenth century, and the new nation was fortunate in its founding fathers, three men who while often disagreeing with each other were people of exceptional ability and fascination. Count Cavour, the first Italian prime minister and one of the finest European politicians of the century, combined liberal beliefs with a talent for diplomacy and political manoeuvring that equalled Bismarck's. Giuseppe Garibaldi, a rebel and legendary master of guerrilla warfare, rose from humble origins to become the best-known and perhaps most admired person anywhere in the world. The third, Giuseppe Mazzini, was the principal theorist and ideologue of patriotic movements in Europe. Though he exercised political power briefly in 1849, nearly all Mazzini's adult life was spent in exile and under sentence of death, organising conspiracies throughout Italy from the shelter of shabby London boarding-houses. This relative obscurity has made it easy to see him as less successful and less interesting than Cavour or Garibaldi, but some contemporaries considered him the most admirable of the three and not the least effective.

Mazzini's name is familiar to many who know little about him. His achievements have always been hard to estimate because, directing an underground and persecuted movement, he had to live inconspicuously and destroy much relevant documentation. Ten thousand letters have been published in the hundred-volume edition of his collected works, but hundreds of thousands have disappeared, and replies had almost always to be destroyed for reasons of security. The governing classes in Italy were solidly ranged against him. So was the Church. So were the socialists. Among the minority of Italians who took an active part in the patriotic Risorgimento, some minimised his contribution for political reasons or out of envy, and in later years some popular histories barely mentioned his name. Cavour's friends, while belatedly accepting Mazzini's ideas about uniting Italy, did so without public acknowledgement because they needed to disparage this revolutionary leader as a dangerous radical who challenged their authority.

Another reason why Mazzini's achievement cannot readily be assessed is that he worked on the minds of men rather than through the more easily studied means of politics, diplomacy or military conquest. Most of his conspiracies failed and could hardly help but fail, yet they exerted a constant pressure which in the long run was highly effective, as his chief opponents sometimes privately admitted. Hard though it might be to quantify, successive generations of Italian youth were inspired by his vision, perseverance, honesty and enthusiasm. His personal magnetism and humanity attracted disciples in each generation and persuaded them to risk their lives under his inspiration. He was an intrepid agitator and effective pamphleteer whose designs were feared by the leading politicians of Europe, despite the fact that he himself and what he wrote were proscribed everywhere except Britain. As well as propagating political revolution and creating the first Italian political party, he was a pioneer in campaigning for social security, suffrage reform and women's liberation. He was an early opponent of Karl Marx and an effective critic of communism. He was also someone of deep religious conviction who questioned the dogmas of all the established Churches. Above all he was a great educator who did more than anyone to formulate the idea of Italian patriotism and stimulate a growing number of people to bring a new nation into being.

One index of his personal charm and reputation was that even far from Italy this impoverished refugee found prominent people to befriend him and intervene on his behalf. In England he was admired by Dickens and Meredith, positively worshipped by Swinburne, and welcomed as an honoured guest by such different people as John Stuart Mill, Jowett the Master of Balliol, Sir John Seeley the historian, and Lord Amberley the son of a prime minister and father of Bertrand Russell. John Morley was not the only eminent Victorian who remembered him as one of the most seductive and morally impressive personalities in the London of his time. Carlyle, while disagreeing with his politics, knew him better than most others and called him a man of genius. Another later admirer was Georges Sorel, the French syndicalist philosopher, who thought that his place in Italian history ranked much higher than that of Cavour, and the same view was held by a celebrated Italian prime minister, Francesco Crispi, who believed that future generations would look back on him as the greatest Italian of his time.

Mazzini lived between 1805 and 1872. He was born in Genoa, at that time part of Napoleon's empire, and keenly resented the humiliation of foreign rule. His father was professor of pathology at Genoa university and as a physician once attended Queen Victoria's father. But the young

Mazzini found dissection distasteful and took his degree in law. From his earliest years he suffered from delicate health and a highly strung temperament. But already at university he was recognised by other students as a quite exceptional person and was much admired for his strength of character, courage and sincerity.

The career he had in mind was that of literary criticism. From his early notebooks we know of his fascinated interest in Vico, Condorcet, Rousseau and Herder. As a boy he read every volume by Walter Scott he could find and copied out poems by Milton, Pope and Shelley. He was among the first Italians to appreciate Burns and Wordsworth, whom he took as exemplars of a new liberal romanticism that would replace the sometimes authoritarian classical stereotypes of the previous century. Literature he regarded as essentially international, cutting across political frontiers and a necessary ingredient in creating the common European consciousness that he himself tried earnestly to promote.[1] His greatest enthusiasm was for Dante; then for the writings of Foscolo and Byron, whom he saw as harbingers of a united Italian republic. Though he also greatly admired Goethe and Shakespeare, he always preferred writers committed to a social and political message. In the years 1828–30 three periodicals published twenty of his literary articles, earning him a considerable reputation.[2] All three magazines were then suppressed by the governments of Piedmont and Tuscany which feared any challenge to accepted ideas.

Piedmont–Sardinia and Tuscany were two of eight Italian states which after the defeat of Napoleon were reinstated in 1815 by the Congress of Vienna. Each had a reactionary and absolutist government. Each was nominally independent while acknowledging a general dependence on Austrian protection. Naples and Sicily were jointly ruled by a Spanish Bourbon dynasty, Parma by Napoleon's widow, Lombardy and Venice by the Austrian Habsburg emperor in Vienna, Modena by another Habsburg duke. A composite state including Piedmont, Savoy and the island of Sardinia was restored to a French-speaking king in Turin allied by marriage to the Austrian Habsburgs, and this Piedmontese sovereign was allowed in 1815 to annex Mazzini's homeland, the once independent republic of Genoa. The pope was also permitted in 1815 to return as temporal sovereign of a state stretching across central Italy from Rome to Bologna and Ancona on the Adriatic coast.

Against this restoration of an authoritarian *ancien régime*, abortive revolutions took place in the years after 1820. These were inspired by the *carbonari*, a quasi-masonic group of secret societies with widespread connections throughout western Europe. Among their objectives were greater personal liberty and independence from foreign rule. They had a vague apprehension of nationality and a desire to replace effete monarchies by a republican regime. Excited by such visionary ideals the young Mazzini enlisted in 1829 as a *carbonaro*, but after being betrayed by a companion in November 1830 was imprisoned by the Piedmontese government which was reputedly the most despotic administration in Italy. Three months later, released for lack of proof, at the age of twenty-six he began a new life in exile. Thenceforward he was dedicated single-mindedly to the cause of political and social revolution.

Apart from two short visits to Tuscany, the only part of Italy he knew at first hand was Genoa, and nearly all of his remaining forty-one years were spent abroad. He had to watch from a distance when, in February 1831, another disjointed rising led to provisional governments being briefly set up in Parma, Modena and the Papal States with a programme of ending the pope's temporal power and bringing the various states of Italy closer together. Hoping to support this revolution he travelled to Corsica with the intention of landing on the mainland with a group of Italian exiles. But the various revolutionary governments were disunited and treated each other almost as potential enemies. This made it easy for Austrian troops to invade and restore order, after which the more promi-nent rebel leaders were tortured and executed.

The lessons to be learnt were obvious enough. First, the Austrian empire was a powerful and incorrigible enemy of liberty and patriotism. Some of the *carbonaro* leaders, notably Michelangelo Buonarroti, had miscalculated in expecting help from France. Most of the others made the mistake of assuming that an Italian revolution needed the backing of only a small group of intellectuals and upper-class liberals without seeking support among the common people. Success in future would evidently require concerted action and a preliminary programme of propaganda and education. The *carbonari* had worked so secretly that Mazzini doubted whether they ever possessed a common programme. But at least they had demonstrated that the existing autocratic governments might be vulner-able if confronted by a better-organised insurrection, and also that some patriots were ready to die for the ideals of personal freedom voiced by Foscolo and Byron.

After returning from Corsica, in March 1831 Mazzini fixed his resi-dence at Marseilles, which had easy communication by sea with Genoa. There he met other émigrés, many of whom disagreed with him in preferring the elderly Buonarroti's socialist and francophile ideas. To-gether they talked about forming a new revolutionary association to cover the whole of Italy and replace the many *carbonari* groups which had a merely local membership. This period was important for his political education, because in enforced idleness he read widely in contemporary literature, especially that of France. Concealed by friendly French repub-licans, almost never in an entire year did he dare to leave his secret lodgings. Day and night he spent writing letters to other active or potential revolutionaries. His reputation was already such that many letters were intercepted by various foreign governments, and the one serious love affair of his life was thereby revealed long after his death by researchers in the archives of the Tuscan and papal police. Giuditta Sidoli was another political exile, a widow with four children. Their short relationship seems to have produced a child who died in infancy,[3] but for the rest of their lives they were forced by circumstances to live apart. Mazzini never married.

His personal ascendancy over many other exiles in southern France was quickly apparent. One of them described him as the 'most beautiful being, male or female', he had ever seen. Another spoke of his 'divine eloquence such as never before shone over Italy' and which in a few months made him 'the heart and soul of the Italian movement'.[4] A few expatriates, however, were ready to accept money to spy on him, and one reported to the Piedmontese government that Mazzini was a truly dangerous person because personally disinterested and ready to give his life for the regeneration of Italy.[5] Such venal spies were a permanent problem throughout his life. Sometimes he had suspicions, but it was always hard for him to be sure, and he occasionally profited from the fact that some of them were sufficiently corrupt or repentant to let him know what information they were selling to foreign governments.

King Charles Albert of Piedmont-Sardinia had in youth been closely associated with the *carbonari*. Some of the patriots therefore took his accession to the throne in 1831 as a good augury and foreign ambassadors in Turin thought he might allow the exiles to return. In June 1831 this monarch received a direct appeal from Mazzini to break free from Austria and create a united Italy; failing which, Tuscany or Naples might forestall Piedmont in claiming a preeminent position in the Italian peninsula. Mazzini said he never expected much from this appeal but needed to explain publicly that many republicans would support any ruler who provided an army to liberate and unify their country. Thirty years later his suggestion would be adopted by another king of Piedmont. But the immediate reaction in 1831 was outrage that a mere subject should presume to advise a sovereign who ruled by divine right. Charles Albert therefore expressed his determination to execute the liberals whom ten years earlier he had encouraged. Far from wanting to fight against Austria, this autocratic and incalculable sovereign made a military treaty of alliance with the Habsburg emperor in Vienna, whom Italian patriots regarded as the chief national enemy.

In July 1831, Mazzini and a group of thirty or forty exiles founded at Marseilles an association called Young Italy. At first this was intended to be less a party than an 'apostolate', a quasi-religious movement calling its members to a life of political conspiracy and self-sacrifice. In practice it became the first organised Italian political party, possessed of a programme, a membership, regular subscriptions, and a service of couriers to keep members from the various Italian regions in touch with each other. People who had learnt from the *carbonari* a vague passion for liberty were now presented with clearer objectives of Italian territorial unification, democracy, greater social equality and self-determination for all the peoples of Europe.

A republican form of government was strongly preferred by most members of the association, though this preference would be left for a future national assembly to accept or repudiate. In Mazzini's vocabulary the word 'republic' stood for *res publica*, a 'commonwealth' or government by the people.[6] If a king offered himself as a patriotic and liberal leader he would be supported, though this was a remote possibility since the rulers of Italy were despots depending on a small privileged class and the support of Austrian troops. Hereditary sovereigns had in 1820–1 defended their absolute power by suppressing revolutions in Naples and Piedmont, and again ten years later in the duchies of central Italy. Another relevant fact was that the rulers of Naples and Tuscany would not readily accept the supremacy of a rival Piedmontese sovereign, and neither would the pope. Divisions and regional jealousies inside Italy were such that an altogether new republican regime might have more general appeal than the prospect of domination by one region over the others.

Though any clandestine movement is impossible to trace in detail, Young Italy enrolled thousands of partisans all over Italy, including younger children of a few aristocratic families,[7] and some future prime ministers of Italy owed their political initiation to the often unrealistic but eloquent propaganda smuggled over the frontier from Marseilles. Mazzini insisted that, although education and persuasion were the main prerequisites of future success, armed rebellion would almost certainly be needed before despotic governments were supplanted. He applauded the example of Belgium, which was ahead of Italy in winning independence by force. He pointed out that Spanish civilian guerrillas helped to defeat Napoleon, whose army in Spain had been very much larger than anything that Austria could now deploy south of the Alps. Such guerrilla risings were ideally suited to the wooded and mountainous territory of many regions in Italy. He therefore gave detailed instructions as to how such warfare should be conducted, creating alarm through small-scale insurrections, taking care to respect property, not to antagonise the clergy, using only a minimum of violence; and especially it was important to befriend the peasants who as 'a volcano ready to erupt' would be an

indispensable element in future victory.[8] Lacking the resources to organise a major revolution, these were the only tactics available to him.

One early plan was for an insurrection to take place at Naples in August
1832 and be supported at once by others in Tuscany and the Papal States,
but the authorities were forewarned and preparations had to be can-
celled. The Grand Duke Leopold, ruler of Tuscany, had intercepted letters
by Mazzini. So had the pope, who was paying at least one of Mazzini's
close associates for information. Reports by papal nuncios throughout
Europe referred to the formidable threat posed by this dangerous young
man, and details of his activity were regularly exchanged with other
governments in Vienna, Paris, St Petersburg and London.[9] The papal and
Neapolitan police sometimes received information two or three times
each week about the 'famous' or 'infamous' Mazzini, learning from
informers about his secret codes and the chemical reagents needed to read
the invisible ink of his messages.[10] In July 1832 the customs authorities at
Genoa discovered his instructions for an armed insurrection hidden in the
false bottom of a trunk addressed to his mother, who was at once placed
under close observation. With alarm Charles Albert noted in his diary that
Young Italy had penetrated every class of society; it had infiltrated the
Piedmontese police, the army and every department of government in
Turin; but he promised he would never make the slightest concession to
any advocate of liberalism and political change.[11]

Nowhere was alarm greater than in Austria, where numerous police
reports described Mazzini as being the most able and threatening of
revolutionaries. Repeated requests were made from Vienna and Turin for
the French authorities to discover his whereabouts and expel him. Austria had once encouraged the Italian patriots when they were needed as
an ally against Napoleon, but Metternich, now chief minister of Austria,
declared the very fact of belonging to Young Italy treasonable and punish-
able by death: with much exaggeration he said it had over one hundred
thousand affiliates among 'the lowest classes of the population and licen-
tious youth'.[12] To apprehend its leader a description was circulated to
Austrian embassies of someone of medium height and olive complexion,
with a fine forehead, noble and energetic bearing, a great talker with a
beautiful and sonorous voice.[13]

To help spread his ideas about nationality, Mazzini started a periodical
called *Young Italy*. It was with difficulty smuggled into Italy, sometimes by
Genoese sailors who concealed copies in cargoes of pumice and pitch.
Most of each issue had to be written by Mazzini because he could not
afford to pay contributors, and his companions lacked his journalistic
talent. Its effectiveness can only be guessed, but Metternich and other
European statesmen were eager to secure copies. The young Piedmontese

aristocrat Count Cavour knew of its existence, and had to agree with other politicians in his native Turin that its editor had recruited many Italian readers. From England to Trieste and Sicily the magazine was avidly devoured, and by more than a few initiates.[14] The young Prince Louis Napoleon was immediately attracted by its message. So was the Abbé Gioberti, subsequently prime minister of Piedmont, who as a young man proclaimed his readiness to die in the cause of rebellion. So was Luigi Carlo Farini, another future premier, as well as others who ended their career in the opposite camp as conservative ministers in the king's service.

There was justifiable panic in Turin over the spread of revolutionary ideas among junior officers in the Piedmontese army. When an attempted military coup early in 1833 was betrayed, Charles Albert intervened personally with the judges to insist that military tribunals hand out exemplary sentences. Twelve conspirators were publicly executed, a hundred more condemned to prison and hundreds had to escape abroad. The fact that these sentences were harsher than those imposed by other Italian governments tarnished Charles Albert's reputation. Even the Austrians claimed to be shocked. Mazzini was condemned to death *in absentia*, the sentence being read publicly outside his family home. What haunted him for the rest of his life was that his closest friend, Jacopo Ruffini, committed suicide in prison to avoid betraying his companions under torture.

Switzerland

Expelled from France, Mazzini set up his headquarters at Geneva in July 1833 and remained in various Swiss cantons for the next three years. Already some of his less committed associates were disillusioned and deserted him, but as always he found new converts attracted by his visionary enthusiasm. One fellow exile in Geneva described him as another Socrates surrounded by eager pupils and as the Voltaire or Rousseau of a new age of national liberation.[15] Giuditta Sidoli was with him for a few days but had to leave in the desperate hope of being allowed by the Duke of Modena to rejoin her children. Her departure was a great sadness, but he could not ask her to share a life of deprivation and persecution for ideas she accepted only in part.[16] Over the next years his letters to her were intercepted and carefully read both by Metternich and the papal authorities, though they can have satisfied only an indecent curiosity.

Because his network of agents and correspondents in Piedmont had been broken, Mazzini again turned his attention to Naples, which to-

gether with Sicily formed the largest state in Italy. Here he quite improb-
ably spoke of having fifty thousand followers ready to start a revolution
that would spread to northern Italy and thence to France, Spain and
Germany. He even spoke of ultimate victory as being certain, because he
was always inclined to accept the most hopeful reports from his local
representatives, and no doubt saw the need to encourage his followers by
exaggerating the chances of success. Possibly he also used such exaggeration to frighten the authorities who, as he knew, were reading his correspondence. But once again his plans for southern Italy were betrayed and
came to nothing.

Nonetheless the rulers of Italy and Austria continued to be frightened
by Young Italy. Informers, perhaps for mercenary reasons of their own,
exaggerated the danger of revolt and some of their information was quite
false. More reliable details came from priests who learnt about them in
the confessional. Also the police could fabricate incriminating documents
to excuse their own incompetence and influence public opinion against
the revolutionaries. At the end of 1833 the Piedmontese government
was employing *agents provocateurs* to entrap Mazzini by trying (in vain)
to persuade his followers into attacking the well-prepared fortress of
Fenestrelle.[17]

He himself justified resort to violence by arguing that governments
used terrorist tactics and were 'waging a war of barbarians, not of civilised
Europeans'; moreover by their refusal to permit political debate in the
press they were preventing any alternative method of peaceful protest.
Charles Albert denounced rebellion as sacrilege, despite having no scru-
ples himself in supporting violent revolution against a brother sovereign
in France. Mazzini was aware that violence would be needed, but had
humanitarian reasons for strongly disliking the punitive cruelty advocated by the *carbonari* and practised by the king. For the same reason he
always condemned the death penalty and duelling. Although frequently
accused of advocating regicide, he regarded assassination as almost always an immoral and useless absurdity,[18] but he admitted that there were
moments in history when individuals – he mentioned Brutus, Charlotte
Corday, William Tell and the biblical Judith – might see the killing of
tyrants as a lesser evil, a view that he knew was supported by many
Catholic authorities. Though he always strongly opposed terrorism,
Mazzini would not deter such individuals if they sincerely and in good
conscience resisted his contrary arguments.[19]

One such missionary zealot was Antonio Gallenga, later in life a British
citizen and a devoutly monarchist member of the Piedmontese parliament. Towards the end of 1833, Gallenga half-heartedly proposed to
assassinate Charles Albert, a plan actively encouraged by Luigi Melegari,
who eventually became a much-respected foreign minister of united

Italy. Mazzini subsequently maintained that he tried to persuade this
would-be assassin that the king's death would not help the cause of
revolution, but when his advice was rejected he provided Gallenga with
money and what was later recalled as being 'a paper-knife'. Gallenga
never carried out his attempt, and when this episode came to light in the
1850s Mazzini minimised his personal involvement. There is no evidence
that he ever ordered any assassination, but he accepted that revolution
was bound to mean loss of life, and the killing of anyone who acted
tyrannically might sometimes help to make success more likely in a
concerted insurrection.[20]

The almost ridiculously ambitious project he had in mind was to start
a revolution in Savoy, which formed part of Charles Albert's kingdom,
and at the same time to instigate a mutiny in the Piedmontese navy.
Giuseppe Garibaldi, a young ship's officer who while sailing in the Black
Sea had been excited to hear about Young Italy, enrolled in the king's
fleet to support this mutiny. Once again the plot was uncovered and
Garibaldi, after escaping abroad, was condemned to 'ignominious death'.
More serious was a plan in February 1834 for volunteers to invade Savoy
in four different places. Mazzini again spoke of success as almost certain.
His intention was to liberate the population, who would then decide by a
free vote whether to break free from Piedmont and join either Switzerland or France. Those contributing the necessary funds insisted that the
military command, despite Mazzini's objections, should be taken by a
former Napoleonic officer, Girolamo Ramorino, but the choice was a poor
one. Synchronisation of such a complex movement proved impossible,
and not enough volunteers could be mobilised at the right places at the
right time. Mazzini himself took an active part but, as often in future, was
incapacitated at the critical moment by illness and had to be carried to
safety. The chief reason for failure was that the authorities knew of his
plans in advance.

Mazzini blamed Ramorino but also admitted to having made mistakes
out of inexperience. He had to accept that Italians were not yet ready to
fight for their nationality; also that too many people preferred to cooperate with foreign governments rather than risk their lives and possessions
in a domestic revolution.[21] He had to rest content with having forced a
new problem on the attention of European diplomats. More of his friends
were captured and some of them executed. Still more were disillusioned
and abandoned him. It was nevertheless an achievement to have formed
a volunteer army containing not only Italians but Poles, French, Swiss
and Germans. He himself was ready to try again and again in the conviction that the death of martyrs would advance the cause by disseminating
a consciousness of *italianità* and forcing governments into unpopular
repression. The important lesson was to keep up the threat of revolution

and never admit defeat. Only by struggling would Italians deserve their freedom and become fitted for it.

The authorities in Switzerland, whose hospitality Mazzini had abused by employing their country as a base for attacking Savoy, came under pressure from Austria as well as from Piedmont and France to expel him, but he managed to hide in Geneva and then at different addresses in the other cantons of Vaud, Berne and Solothurn. He had been obliged in part to finance his attempted invasion by borrowing and now needed still more money to support a group of fugitives who had no chance of gainful employment. His mother responded as generously as she could. He wrote to her that he rarely dared leave the security of his room and spent all his time thinking and reading. He asked her to send him some of his own books including Homer, Vico, Ossian, Lamartine's poetry and a transla- tion of the Koran. History, he said, was his favourite reading when he was living in concealment. For a short time he was lucky to discover lodgings looking out over the Alps, a sight that always gave him the greatest pleasure. Later in 1834 he found a sympathetic family at Grenchen, who protected him together with two brothers of his dead friend Ruffini. In their company he spent the next two years revising and amplifying the ideas of nationality and self-determination that dominated the rest of his life.

Further practical conspiracy was for the moment impossible and he knew he had no right to complain of being exiled as a traitor. Nor would he express any hatred against Charles Albert and Austria, only condem- nation of their cruelty in repression and a quiet confidence that their world was beginning to disintegrate. Metternich was in his view the one politician with the ability to delay that process, though ultimately the Habsburg empire was doomed, since its subject nationalities – Italians, Magyars, Czechs, Southern Slavs and Poles – would in time assert their independence. Metternich had to concede that this lonely exile and his novel ideas about nationality threatened to undermine Austrian imperi- alism, and the greatest severity was therefore needed to deter further insurrections. To coordinate information about the Italian exiles a special Austrian agency was created with a staff of eighty, one third of them Italians, which continued in existence for the next fifteen years.[22]

In the Spring of 1834, while at Berne, Mazzini and a dozen refugees from Italy, Poland and Germany founded a new association with the grandiose name of Young Europe. Its basic and equally grandiose idea was that, as the French Revolution of 1789 had enlarged the concept of individual liberty, another revolution would now be needed for national liberty; and his vision went further because he hoped that in the no doubt distant future free nations might combine to form a loosely federal Europe with some kind of elected assembly to regulate their common interests. Small wonder that the papal government reinforced its surveillance over what it called 'the immense designs of this extraordinary man'.[23] His intention was nothing less than to overturn the European settlement agreed in 1815 by the Congress of Vienna, which had reestablished an oppressive hegemony of a few great powers and blocked the emergence of smaller nations. Since 1815, Greece and Belgium had won a degree of national freedom, which was bound to be seen as an example for Italy and other subject peoples of Europe. He probably did not know that even the governments of Belgium and Holland were alarmed that the propaganda of 'the famous Mazzini' was penetrating their own countries.[24]

Mazzini hoped, but without much confidence, that his vision of a league or society of independent nations would be realised in his own lifetime. In practice Young Europe lacked the money and popular support for more than a short-term existence. Nevertheless he always remained faithful to the ideal of a united continent for which the creation of individual nations would be an indispensable preliminary. Alongside Young Italy, in 1834–5 he tried, with indifferent success, to create similar patriotic organisations for Germany, Greece, Spain, Russia and Poland. Small groups of enthusiasts were found as far away as Constantinople and even South America. Briefly there even existed a Young Bohemia, a Young Ukraine, a Young Argentina, a Young Tyrol and a Young Austria. He would have liked to create a Young England, though the British saw themselves as too distinct from the continental mainland to fit easily into his scheme. He had more success in persuading a group of Swiss to found an association, and himself wrote fifty articles for a bilingual periodical, *La Jeune Suisse*, which succeeded in collecting seven hundred subscribers. Journalism, he wrote, was rapidly becoming one of the great forces in the world;[25] it was the only available method for communicating his ideas about democracy, patriotism and internationalism to a wider public, and for the rest of his life it remained the chief weapon in his armoury.

Politics and religion

Mazzini was a patriot not a nationalist, and indeed condemned nationalism as absolutely wrong. Despite what some critics have said,[26] from as early as 1836 he used the word 'nationalist' in a pejorative sense to denote those chauvinists, xenophobes and imperialists who sought to encroach on the rights of other peoples.[27] Patriotism was not a wider form of selfishness, nor ever an end in itself, but should always serve the wider interests of humanity. He was innocent enough or sufficiently far-sighted to think that the nations of Europe were bound eventually to learn that they had more to gain from cooperation than conflict. Admittedly new nations could come into existence only through fighting or the threat of war, but more destructive and far less justifiable would be any attempt by a belligerent Austria to crush an inevitable process of patriotic liberation. National forces were everywhere laying the foundation of a new Europe; they were 'the ruling principle of the future' and sooner or later their existence would have to be acknowledged by Metternich and the other diplomats of Europe. Yet patriotism must never be allowed to damage 'the brotherhood of peoples which is our one overriding aim'.[28]

National identity, as he knew, admitted no easy definition. It had little or nothing to do with biology or race, and history showed how Greeks, Celts, Goths, Lombards and Arabs had successfully merged inside Italy over the centuries. Sometimes geography was a helpful index of nationality, as the Alps and the sea were important in defining his own country. Language was often another factor, but four languages were spoken in Switzerland and three in Piedmont (together with other distinct dialects), although both countries were politically united. The Italian language was perhaps spoken by less than five per cent of the population in the Italian peninsula. Far more important as ingredients in nationality were historical traditions and a sense of community. The distinct but complementary sense of individualism, excellent up to a point, had been taken to excess by Italians, who spent too much energy quarrelling with each other and needed more public spirit as a counterpoise. A nation was not a mere aggregate of individuals but something more, a community with a positive existence and purpose that went beyond the mere maximising of individual liberty. Language, territory, ethnicity, historical tradition and a sense of belonging together, all these were ingredients or indications that would help to define an elusive concept.[29]

Since he never in his life enjoyed freedom to travel, Mazzini's information about other European countries was indirect and often quite inaccurate. So, inevitably, was his information about Italy itself, most of which he knew only at second hand. This helped him to exaggerate the possibilities of a patriotic revolution. He resented that the existing division of the Italian peninsula into eight sovereign states had been artificially created and preserved by international congresses at which Italian interests had been of very little concern. Each of these Italian states, and even some individual regions within each state, had its own currency and a distinct system of weights and measures. Each had its own commercial and penal legislation, its own customs barriers, all of which made economic nonsense. Existing territorial divisions could be justified only by antiquated ideas of divine right. Hence these separate states continued to exist only by a disregard for self-determination and a repudiation of representative

institutions. Mazzini was convinced that a twenty-million-strong population of the whole Italian peninsula could, if only it worked together,
defeat an Austrian army of occupation that had many other frontiers to
defend. The chief difficulty was that after centuries of foreign occupation
there were too many regional rivalries inside Italy and too many vested
interests hostile to change. The citizens of Austrian-controlled Italy were
sufficiently oppressed by foreign proconsuls and foreign taxation to be on
the verge of revolt, but too many of their potential leaders accepted
domination by Vienna as at least a temporary prophylactic against social
revolution. The magazines *Giovine Italia* and *Jeune Suisse*, which advocated
radical change, were not easily smuggled across the Austrian and Italian
frontiers, and in a predominantly illiterate society could reach only a few
educated intellectuals.

The task was made harder by Mazzini's conviction that to seek armed
help from France would at best lead to exchanging one imperial domination for another. Italians would not deserve liberation unless won by their
own effort and sacrifice. Nor would they gain true independence if they
relied on favours from the very same great powers of Europe that had
shamelessly settled their own private problems by giving Poland to Russia, Venice to Austria, and kept Italy internally divided in the interests of
a European balance of power. Another difficulty was the belief among
perhaps most of his fellow exiles that their best hope of nationhood
was a federal union between existing Italian states. He could agree that
federation might suit a large country such as the United States or a
united Europe, but in Italy it would spell weakness as it obviously did
in Switzerland. Only a single united state would be strong enough to
challenge French and Austrian imperialism, whereas federation would
allow the old autocratic dynasties to continue misgoverning Piedmont,
Naples, Modena and Tuscany. Moreover the Austrians, unless driven out
by force, could claim as rulers of Venice and Lombardy to be included
inside an Italian federation. Such a federal state would not be viable and
would never constitute a nation.

Mazzini's enemies unfairly accused him of equating national unification with a centralised administrative system. On the contrary, he agreed
that local and individual liberties were rightly prized by Italians. A centralised administration not only would create disaffection locally but was
likely either to be ineffective or else lead to an exaggeration of state
controls. He allowed that the islands of Sicily and Sardinia had separate
needs and traditions that would require administrative autonomy, and
elsewhere he envisaged at least a devolution of powers to elected local
authorities as a check on central government.[30] Democratic elections
were needed as a reinforcement of personal freedom. Every citizen
should ideally have a right to vote and so indirectly call local and central

government to account.[31] Liberty was, in his view, as important as, or even more important than, patriotism, but internal liberties would be a vain objective before first winning national independence and ending a system of government by regional despots.[32] If ever an Italian monarch could be found who would agree to fight against Austria, Mazzini would support him, if only as a second best,[33] though he would then do all he could to prevent such a sovereign ruling as a dictator: dictatorship and especially military dictatorship would always be a disaster.[34]

These ideas were formulated over the next few years in a set of general principles. Despite his distrust of France, Mazzini recognised that the right to individual liberty had been enunciated by the French Revolution, for which the world should be truly grateful. But France had regrettably used the revolutionary ideas of 1789 as an excuse to impose her government over other peoples. Moreover, something more than individual liberty was required, because man was a social being and lived in a society where it was necessary to curb the unfettered right of each individual to be egotistic and acquisitive at the expense of his weaker neighbours. Individualism could lead to anarchy unless modified by recognition of social duty. Rights must be matched or purchased by duties, because individualism could lead to disaster if not complemented by a sense of social obligation. This notion of duty towards others and towards society was at the centre of his political creed. Alongside it were the ideas of private initiative and political association, without which Italians and the other submerged nationalities of Europe could never overcome the divine right of individual autocrats to rule as they pleased.

Another unfair criticism was that preoccupation with national unity and international fraternity made him neglect justice between different social classes.[35] Mazzini believed on the contrary that failure to recognise the needs of social justice had been a major reason why the risings of 1820–1 and 1830–1 failed. Now that the Revolution of 1789 had liberated the bourgeoisie, the next move forward for humanity must bring a similar advancement of the common people: 'All revolutions are essentially social revolutions.' Young Italy was therefore given the specific task of reaching workers and peasants with a promise to 'overturn the old system' and end the abysmal poverty which, as well as being a wrong in itself, was a permanent danger to social order. Without greater equality, individual freedom was a fraud that helped only the few. Taxation should therefore be proportional to wealth. There ought to be free and compulsory education for everyone, as well as complete equality of all citizens before the law.[36]

During the 1830s, Mazzini occasionally spoke of himself as being a socialist,[37] but this was before the word changed to mean not a general aspiration but a set or various sets of dogmas. Already he argued against most socialists for their materialism and hostility to religion. While insisting that a better deal for the poor was urgently needed, he also criticised anyone who, by putting economic questions above all others, intensified the conflict between classes, because that would disintegrate rather than unify society. His hope was not to imitate the Revolution of 1789 which had replaced one ruling class by another, but rather to find a wider community of sentiment, and when he spoke of 'the people' he meant 'an aggregate of all classes'. While anxious 'as far as possible' not to damage existing property rights, he thought it important to spread ownership more widely among the generality of citizens; property ought ideally to be earned rather than inherited, and politicians ought to strive their utmost to avoid the divisiveness and bloodshed of class war.[38]

He therefore strongly opposed the communism that he associated with the French revolutionaries Babeuf and Cabet. Robert Owen, whose character he greatly admired, was in his opinion almost equally wrongheaded.[39] Mazzini acknowledged a debt to the French socialist Saint-Simon but rejected the latter's 'tyrannical tendencies',[40] and his own writings referred ten times as often to the dissident French priest Lamennais as to Saint-Simon. Another socialist who helped clarify his ideas was Filippo Buonarroti, though their friendship ended in 1833. Buonarroti, apart from insisting that French leadership was necessary in the next European revolution, was criticised for his readiness to promote dictatorship, even terrorism and a communist agrarian reform.[41]

Mazzini's political and social opinions matured during his three years in Switzerland. He was deeply depressed for part of this period. He was usually in debt and often wondered whether his set task was too much and he might have to please his father by giving up politics altogether. To his mother he wrote of his surprise to find that he possessed no residual ambition for himself and no longer paid much attention to the search for personal happiness or even the approval of other people. One positive experience was finding the Swiss people to be cordial and generous, straightforward and self-reliant. In addition they possessed an admirably democratic sense of social equality that he had rarely found at home. Unfortunately Switzerland was a federation of twenty-two partially autonomous cantons, and hence unable to withstand political pressure from Paris or Vienna, with the result that he had to live in seclusion under constant threat of being expelled.

In his solitude he started learning German so as to translate a book on popular education by the German playwright Gotthold Lessing: the literature of northern Europe, he now found, was more spontaneous than that of Italy and less corrupted. He re-read some of the Latin classics, especially Tacitus.[42] He also tried to locate copies of the *Edinburgh* and *Westminster Reviews* so as to discover articles by Foscolo unknown in Italy. Loneliness led to further introspection and brooding as he thought of the sorrow he had caused not only his parents and Giuditta Sidoli but the families of those he had encouraged to fight in a premature revolution; and he sometimes wondered if his idea of a resurgent Italy was a mere fantasy of imagination and not foreordained by providence. He later referred to having experienced for some months 'a total desolation of the soul' that brought him close to madness and suicide.[43] Little can be said about such an important episode in his life because he was never able to speak to others of the full depth of this depression and was especially anxious to conceal it from Giuditta and his family. He was shocked into sanity only when he suddenly understood the selfishness of excessive introspection, and emerged with a new confidence, a profound religious faith and a sense of duty and mission that never deserted him again.

Although at university Mazzini had gone through a period of atheism when he secretly used to read Condorcet during celebration of the mass, painful years in exile confirmed what became an unshakeable belief in the existence of a benevolent God. His religious and political beliefs became complementary and are sometimes hard to disentangle. One result of this had practical importance, because after he had recovered his hope that the making of an Italian nation was dictated by divine providence, his political convictions could survive any number of setbacks or prudential calculations about what other people might regard as insuperable obstacles. Many of his companions did not share his religious opinions and saw them as unreasonable or even dangerously theocratic. Nevertheless, an important contribution to the success of the Risorgimento was his confident belief that he could see 'the finger of God in the pages of the world's history'.[44]

Now and during the rest of his life he spent much time filling notebooks for a treatise he meant to write on religion, but on his travels he lost many of his manuscripts and never had the necessary leisure to complete the project; or possibly he realised, after many arguments with Lamennais, Carlyle and others, that his ideas were too idiosyncratic and personal for reasoned presentation. He sometimes called himself a deist but sometimes denied it. He occasionally took part in Catholic rituals and used to celebrate Christmas as a sacred day. He believed in the afterlife and purgatory, but while he said he loved Jesus Christ above all mortals he could not believe in his divinity[45] – 'I am not a Christian, or rather I am a Christian plus something more' – and he sought some of the answers in the Talmud, the Koran and the Mahabharata.[46] Though he welcomed Christian morality and the teaching that all men were equal in the sight of God, he felt the Christian Church had deviated from its origins and he thought himself closer to the message of the New Testament than were the 'magnates' of Catholicism: 'I belong to what I believe to be a still purer and higher faith; but its time has not yet come; and until that day, the Christian manifestation remains the most sacred revelation of the ever-onward-progressing spirit of mankind working its way towards an Ideal which must sooner or later be realised.'[47]

One theme of his religious writing, never satisfactorily explained by himself or by others, was the paradox created by the rival claims of conscience and divine authority. He profoundly believed in the rights of individual conscience, always respecting other religious convictions if sincerely held and if not anti-social; and yet individuals could only delay, not prevent, 'the progressive development of humanity'. Everyone had to work out their own salvation but 'only on the conditions prescribed' and not by the anarchic choice that often characterised Protestantism. 'Between good and evil the individual can freely choose and is consequently responsible; but it is not given him by his choice to enthrone evil in the world. God is there to modify its effects and to turn to the benefit of successive generations even the errors and crimes of perverse and mistaken men.'[48] It is nevertheless interesting that he called Shakespeare superior to Aeschylus because, while the latter saw destiny as absolute, Shakespeare allowed that at critical moments his tragic heroes were free and arbiters of their own future.[49]

Already in 1834 Mazzini was hoping that a General Council representing all believers would one day correct the worldliness and authoritarianism which had perverted the papacy. Three years earlier, Pope Gregory XVI, under pressure from the great powers, had undertaken to introduce political reforms at Rome as a means of avoiding revolution, but then refused to carry out his promise. Mazzini was convinced that many junior clergy were eager for such reforms, and yet the pope ruled over Rome as an absolute monarch, censoring books, rejecting popular education or any involvement by the laity in government and forgetting the great civilising mission of the papacy during the Middle Ages. As well as welcoming Austrian military intervention in Italy, the Vatican was so far from evangelical Christianity as to play at power politics in defence of authoritarianism, even supporting anti-Catholic dictatorships in Turkey and Russia. Its worldly materialism was such that a few Italian bishops were by a long way the richest prelates in Europe while most parish clergy remained in absolute poverty. Under such spiritual guidance Italians had become 'the most irreligious people on earth',[50] and this was a scandal which Mazzini was convinced must and would be changed.

His later amplification of these themes convinced Ernesto Buonaiuti, in a massive *History of Christianity*, that he was 'the most eminent religious figure in our national Risorgimento'.[51] But he was no theologian, and his idiosyncratic views offended believers and non-believers alike. Without accepting the doctrine of redemption through divine grace, he thought that God created man as an imperfect being who could by his own effort become better and earn a reward on earth and in heaven. If men failed it was due partly to faults in society and certainly not to any presumed original sin.[52] Social and political revolution would, perhaps in the distant future, be accompanied by a moral and religious revolution. One day a General Council would discuss and explain the common denominators between various religious beliefs, 'the gospel of Christ being one beautiful development of this progressive and infinite revelation'.[53]

CHAPTER TWO

England: 1837–45

First years in England

IN JUNE 1836, responding to continued foreign pressure, the Swiss federal authorities ordered Mazzini's expulsion and resisted his attempt to challenge their decision in a court of law. When the town council at Grenchen tried to protect him by the offer of honorary citizenship, their decision was overruled by the cantonal government, and there was justified resentment against a foreigner who was compromising Swiss neutrality.[1] Spain and America were suggested as possible places of refuge. But despite repeated Austrian protests he remained hidden for six more months, moving from house to house, often with the windows blacked out to conceal his presence. As long as possible he needed to stay near the Italian frontier ready for another attempt at revolution.

Upset at what he called the cowardice of the Swiss government, at the end of the year he very reluctantly decided to leave for England where at least he would no longer have to hide. He wondered if Scotland might be even better, but London offered more chance of earning money, which had been impossible in the past three years. Unrealistically he told his mother that he hoped to be no further financial burden on her because in London he already possessed some contacts. He had known several English families in Genoa, where he began to learn the language so as to correspond with a Marianne Thomas to whom he was greatly attached. The magazine *Young Italy* was admired by a few sympathisers in England, one of whom in 1834 published a book dedicated to its editor.[2] Another contact was a London bookseller who possessed a manuscript by Foscolo that Mazzini was hoping to edit.

He was thirty-one years old when he arrived in England, where he lived for most of his remaining life. After borrowing money for the journey, he took the cheaper route, not by train from Dover but sailing up the Thames to land at the 'indescribably spectacular' London docks. He found lodgings in Goodge Street together with the two Ruffini brothers who accompanied him and lived mostly at his expense; both of them wrote home that he was excellent company, though they no longer sympathised with his talk of revolution and were upset by his weakness in sharing with other importunate exiles the meagre income he received from his parents.[3]

The cost of living in London was more than twice that in Switzerland and he complained that even candles and newspapers were occasionally too much for their budget. Some new acquaintances were kind, but in general he was miserable and knew that this was partly owing to his dislike of social occasions and preference for solitude. He deliberately stayed at home when the rest of London was in the streets watching Queen Victoria's coronation, and did the same to avoid the huge crowds during the Oxford and Cambridge boat race. As an excuse for refusing invitations he said he did not possess the right clothes and it might seem an unwelcome ostentation of republicanism if he called on respectable houses in his everyday dress. Unable to afford a cab, he would also expose his poverty by arriving covered in mud. The dirt in the London streets appalled him. So did the bed bugs, which increased his nostalgia for Switzerland. So did the drunkenness, which seemed to affect half the population – including newspaper editors, he added.

His penury, however, cannot have been as absolute as he later remembered. He kept a maid who brought him breakfast in bed, and also a boy to clean his shoes. He had always believed that servants should be treated as equals[4] but paid them only one pound sterling a month, and perhaps for that reason they never stayed long. He could occasionally afford to eat in cheap restaurants. He sometimes drank punch and even cultivated a new taste for wine and plum pudding. Best of all was light ale, much healthier than the local water which was full of 'worms and insects'. His one incorrigible indulgence was cheap Swiss cigars, despite his father's medical advice that they might cause apoplexy. On the worst days of winter he had a fire in all six rooms of their apartment. He always went to a barber to be shaved; advised to remove his moustache since it was a sign of dangerous continental republicanism, he refused to comply.

Mazzini was not without patrons in London society. Some years earlier he had met a member of parliament, Sir John Bowring, the friend of Jeremy Bentham and a future governor of Hong Kong. He was also persuaded to attend a weekly literary gathering in Berners Street by the distinguished surgeon Joseph Toynbee and his brother George. Thomas Medwin, a friend of Byron, invited him in July 1837 to tour the Lake District and the Highlands, but lacking money he made an excuse to go no further than Edinburgh. Mazzini's father, who had once known the Duke of Kent, fancifully wondered if that casual acquaintanceship might not procure an introduction to Buckingham Palace.[5]

More serious was an introduction to Mrs Eliza Fletcher, who later remembered him as 'a young, slim, dark Italian gentleman of very prepossessing appearance'.[6] She introduced him to the poet Thomas Campbell and tried to bring him out of the melancholy isolation which Mazzini admitted to her was a misguided and self-inflicted punishment. She it was who procured for him a reader's ticket to the library of the British Museum, and though he never liked working in libraries he could save on domestic fuel by attending it three times a week, impressed that the staff were helpful and refused to take tips. There he made the acquaintance of another exile, Antonio Panizzi, who later became a British citizen and the library's most famous director. Panizzi, like Mazzini, was under sentence of death in Italy as a *carbonaro*, but this older expatriate was now trying hard to become accepted as an English gentleman and distanced himself from Mazzini's republican friends. The Italian refugees of the 1820s, who were richer and moved on a higher social plane that those of the 1830s, were slow in using their connections to find jobs for their poorer compatriots.

Some of the luckier newcomers found employment as teachers of Italian or singing, but Italian was beginning to be ousted by German as the smart language to learn. Gallenga and Carlo Pepoli were among a few who solved some of their problems by marrying rich English-women. Exiles who lived in France enjoyed a small subsidy from the authorities; those in England were less fortunate. A few could practise as doctors of medicine, but Mazzini's training in Italian law was no use to him in the English courts. After failing to get employment as a corrector of proofs, he at one point half-seriously thought of working on railway construction.[7] More fanciful was a daydream which recurred in later life that one day he might become the ambassador to England of a united Italian republic.[8]

His one chance of serious employment was as a writer. Because of the language barrier he would have much preferred to write for Italian readers: possibly he could correct their ignorance of European literature by translating into Italian the best books of the previous fifty years. Alternatively he thought of filling another gap by writing on Italian history. He disliked the current fashion in history for being concerned only with individual Italian states and cities, or for dealing with merely the dominant classes without realising that 'the real life of a nation lies in the people as a whole', and almost always omitting such vital topics as agriculture, industry and science.[9] Contemporary historians were too often mere chroniclers who, pretending to impartiality, shied away from interpreting the past, whereas he believed that a true historian had the great responsibility of teaching present-day Italians who they were and how their society had become what it was;[10] for which task chroniclers were of little use.

To remedy these gaps in Italian culture would have required time and money that he lacked. Instead, he was glad to discover that a few periodicals in London would pay one pound a page for contributions. Unfortunately the more serious magazines were unacceptably Tory in politics. One editor even objected on moral grounds to a piece in which he praised Byron: a friend remembered that 'he could never forgive England for her neglect and misappreciation of Byron', a writer whom he placed 'far above Wordsworth and Coleridge whom he calls contemplative poets only, living remote from action amid their mountains and lakes'.[11] In literature as in religion and politics he was too opinionated and self-assured to follow current fashion. He was sure he could have earned a better living had he been ready to write for magazines that catered for a low-brow taste with trivial stories about Italian travel and bandits, but would have despised himself for what he called prostitution.

One immediate source of a small income was a series of fifteen articles he wrote at the request of Lamennais for *Le Monde* in Paris about society and politics in London. These articles appeared between March and June 1837 and to avoid censorship had to appear unsigned. The first dealt with the 'barbaric' penalties of the legal system and the need for law reform in England. Others criticised the system of 'poor relief in workhouses' and the prevalent 'materialism' among intellectuals. In one article he praised the Parliamentary Reform Act of 1832 as a first step in reducing the domination of society by the landed aristocracy. In another he discussed the unrest among the French-speaking population of Canada. In one of the more interesting he examined the reluctance of parliament to confront the extreme poverty in Ireland: the Irish were being treated as colonial dependants of the United Kingdom, and he argued that the Protestant ascendancy could not survive unless some form of local self-government could be devised to help the Catholic majority. Unfortunately a change of editorship put an end to these contributions to *Le Monde*, but they had been a useful means of learning about English politics and society.[12]

Among editors in London there was a slight reluctance to employ someone whose ideas were too 'continental', by which was meant too abstract, 'synthetic' and metaphysical. He made some effort to change in response to this criticism but habits of thought were too deeply rooted. The English, he wrote, were fifty years out of date intellectually. The names of Vico and Hegel were almost unknown to them. The local intellectuals were too 'matter-of-fact' and disliked general ideas or theorising. Their preferred history was narrative; they had not advanced beyond Locke in philosophy, Blackstone in jurisprudence or Adam Smith in economics.[13] The fashion was for utilitarianism, for putting analysis above synthesis or theory, dealing with facts rather than moral principles; and he wondered if this might be a product of Protestant individualism.

British opinions about Italy were conditioned by the fact that Austria appeared to govern Lombardy and Venice with more honesty and efficiency than was found in other regions, and this made magazine readers unwilling to understand his message about the God-given concept of nationality.

In September 1837, John Stuart Mill, who succeeded Bowring as editor of the radical *Westminster Review*, mentioned having just met 'the celebrated Mazzini, the president of *La Jeune Italie*, and the most eminent conspirator and revolutionist now in Europe'. Soon after their meeting, Mill called him 'one of the men I most respect', 'one of the most accomplished and in every way superior men among all the foreigners I have known'.[14] The result was an invitation to write on recent Italian literature, for which the author received £36, far more than he had ever earned hitherto. This article gave him the chance to speak on behalf of 'a people oppressed but not broken' who under Caesars and popes had twice led the rest of Europe in artistic creativity, but now languished in a backwater under Austrian and papal despotism.

Mill described this essay as being full of 'interesting novelties', coming from 'the best school of continental criticism, the only good school of criticism now going'; but another editor pertinently objected that the author condemned some Italian writers merely because of 'their failure to transform art into a patriotic mission'.[15] Mazzini was invited to dinner by Mill and resented having to walk four miles there and four miles back, all 'for a bit of fish or chicken which I do not like'.[16] The *Westminster Review* took another article on Paolo Sarpi in which this seventeenth-century Venetian friar was praised for anticipating the scientific discoveries of Newton and Harvey as well as for criticising the pope's temporal power.[17] A third article appeared on recent Italian painters, but another about Lamennais was rejected on what Mazzini called the quite absurd grounds that its subject was too little known in England.

Further support came from John Kemble's *British and Foreign Review*, which in 1838 paid £33 for an excellent essay on Victor Hugo. The poet was described as an enchanting and powerful writer who nevertheless failed to look deeply into the human heart, and 'when his matter fails him he takes refuge in style and expression'.[18] Kemble kept another essay on Lamartine for a year before publishing it and almost another year before sending payment. *Tait's Magazine* in Edinburgh printed an article on Sismondi and another on Guizot, paying only £7 for each, of which £3 went to a translator; and the same magazine took another on the need for revolution in Europe – its translator was found for him by a new friend, the wife of Thomas Carlyle. A long treatise on 'The State and Prospects of Italy' was held up for a year by a new editor of the *Westminster Review* only to be then rejected for its advocacy of republicanism. Fortunately it found a home in Bulwer Lytton's *Monthly Chronicle*, which then printed further articles on Lamennais, Thiers and George Sand. When financial difficulties compelled this magazine to reduce Mazzini's fee to £1 an article, he accepted out of a wish to prevent the collapse of a vehicle for his opinions. Literary life in London was not easy, but he hoped that he was making a small contribution to correcting an insularity of mind.

One interesting admission was a slight sense of shame that, in order to justify his hopes for Italy, he was ready to pretend in public to greater confidence in his fellow countrymen than he inwardly possessed.[19] He resented that Italians were too often judged by foreigners through the highly coloured novels of Mrs Radcliffe or the memoirs of Casanova; too often tourists saw only hotels and theatres or studied only the paintings and literature of the past. He himself, on the contrary, constantly stressed that Italy should have a leading role in the future because of its leadership in the struggle for nationality and the contest between political progress and reaction.

> Italy, dumb in the hands of the executioner, and discouraged by a series of abortive insurrections, has need of an encouraging voice. Nothing is wanting in my opinion to enable Italy to raise herself to a level with her destiny but the consciousness of her will and of her power. She has been so often told that she is weak, that she ought not to hazard attempts which are called premature, and that she must expect liberation from abroad.

A violent revolution was bound to happen so long as free discussion was forbidden, and would not be by 'the higher classes' alone, as in 1821, but 'by the people', the sole lever of grand revolutions; and the basic elements of a successful revolution were all present and ready for when leaders and direction could appear.[20] In his treatment of Italian culture Mazzini never concealed his instinctive preference for creative artists who had an involvement in politics. 'The world is not a mere spectacle for contemplation but also a field of battle for justice, beauty and holiness.' The immediate need was for writers who saw their work as having an educational function to change society and were not preoccupied by mere entertainment or uncommitted individual inspiration. Manzoni, whom he admired for 'talent of the first order and an exquisite sensibility', partially failed this test because his central political message was resignation.[21] The later poetry of Wordsworth and Coleridge was admirable, but likewise 'incomplete'.[22] Leopardi, admittedly a patriot and fine poet, was too much a literary classicist who discouraged political action: 'he *did* love Italy; but almost delighting, I think, with her own ruins and his own despondency'. Mazzini preferred Dante, Schiller and Byron, who were not content with merely holding a mirror up to nature.[23] For the same reason he continued to feel an especial kinship with Foscolo, an earlier patriotic exile who died in England a few years earlier. In an extraordinary labour of love, without payment and without even having his name on the title-page, Mazzini completed and annotated in four volumes Foscolo's unfinished commentary on Dante's *Divine Comedy*. This, he explained, was a moral duty so that Italians could be helped to understand the heroes of their own culture.[24]

The same criterion of commitment was applied by him to architecture and the visual arts. These always reflected the social context and structure of each successive period; and as an example he talked of a 'distinction between the parallel-terrestrial-rest-lines of the Parthenon and the up-pointed-restless-heaven-to-aspiring curves of Cologne cathedral'. He thought that the finest contemporary English painter was Turner, who took much of his inspiration from Italy. Yet he disliked 'those who would have art floating bubble-like without any support, according to individual inspiration'. What was required was art 'for the world's sake; not art for art's sake'. 'Art for art's sake was an atheistic formula, like the political catch-phrase of every man for himself.'[25]

Music, too, could have 'a social message and lead us to moral regeneration',[26] so he wrote in an earlier article on 'The Philosophy of Music', though he never explained this idea convincingly. He seems to have loved music more than contemporary literature. He himself had a fine voice and used to sing and play the guitar in ensembles of chamber music with the Nathans and Rossellis, his Jewish friends in London. The 'astonishing' Liszt was his favourite executant and he took note that Liszt was a republican. Impressed by Thomas Moore's 'Irish Melodies', he urged people to collect Italian folk songs before they disappeared, because they were a vital part of the national heritage.[27] Once a year he could afford a visit to the opera, though with remorse for spending five shillings that might have saved a poor family from starvation. Subsequently the leading singers at the Italian Opera at Drury Lane gave him a free season ticket and he once confessed that this afforded him his finest pleasure in life. He liked the music of Palestrina and Pergolesi. Not keen on *Il Trovatore*, he was greatly impressed by *Fidelio*, even more by *Don Giovanni*, and was curious about the early Wagner. Rossini he once called the Napoleon of music who effectively broke with classical tradition. His favourite composer, however, remained Meyerbeer, who 'moralised the drama, making it an echo of the world and its eternal vital problem. He is not a votary of the *l'art pour l'art* music; he is the prophet of the music with a mission, the music standing immediately below religion.'[28]

Mazzini's close observation of British society in the late 1830s reinforced and developed his own political views. Although after his Swiss experience he would not become actively involved, he found much to criticise from the sidelines. He was horrified by some episodes of British imperialism in China. He condemned the barbarity of flogging in the army and the death penalty, which was not only immoral but useless as a deterrent to crime. He found the gap between rich and poor far wider than in egalitarian France and was astonished to watch the carriages of the aristocracy with their powdered and liveried servants. He knew that one cause of this gap was the legal tradition of entails and primogeniture which kept property in the hands of a small minority, and he noted that toadying to this minority was the only path to success for other people of talent. In some areas of Britain a fifth of the population lived on charity. Poverty was so extreme that unless action was taken he thought popular unrest would force the government into further repression, which in turn would lead to revolutionary excesses as bad as those of 1793 in France. After serious rioting in Birmingham he wrote an essay entitled 'Is it a Revolt or a Revolution?' He deplored these riots and was sorry that as a foreigner he could not take part alongside friends in the Chartist movement to help avert what he feared was an imminent catastrophe.[29]

These first impressions were gradually modified when, with some surprise, he found that a predominantly aristocratic government never dared violate certain basic liberties which every Briton claimed as a right. Despite his belief that liberty without more equality was an illusion, he was impressed to find that ordinary citizens, though not permitted to vote, could make their views known and possessed a sense of civic responsibility that was entirely lacking in Italy. He was astonished by the degree of popular involvement in both Chartism and the campaign for free trade: every day public meetings took place which the authorities were sensible enough to permit, subscriptions poured in, and petitions with hundreds of thousands of signatures created a pressure that the government could not ignore. For the rest of his life he desperately hoped for something similar in Italy. Evidently revolutions could come about more slowly and surely than he had imagined and with relatively little violence, provided that there was tolerance of controversial opinions and provided poor people had some hope of a better life.[30] Equally impressive was the extraordinary development of local government in England; also the fact that politics were far more moral than in France and were conducted with more decency and mutual respect. There was less venality, less corruption, less calumny against opponents. England had one Walpole while France had a whole generation of Walpoles.[31]

One immorality that he found distasteful was the isolationism which led to non-intervention in continental affairs and to a spurious impartiality between justice and injustice in international politics. He was overjoyed that bystanders in London hissed Tsar Nicholas of Russia who was

on a visit. For different reasons he was equally pleased when taken by the
Carlyles to see Macready act at Drury Lane, where the audience applauded a remark about the great debt owed to the civilisation of Italy.
But despite the fact that England alone in Europe allowed foreign refugees to live in peace and relative security, there were occasional examples
of hostility towards them since they were usually assumed to be French.
A narrow inward-looking patriotism explained the rarity of protests
against the cruelties and injustice of Austrian administration in northern
Italy. Protestants in Britain had no difficulty about criticising persecution
in the Papal States, but usually preferred to keep quiet when Metternich
in Milan and Venice appealed to a fraudulent political legitimacy and
divine right.

Mazzini was not impressed by the House of Commons when Bowring
took him there in June 1837. Like Cavour a few years earlier, he was
scandalised by the casual behaviour of members who talked to each other
through the debates and prevented spectators from hearing. What he
called the really important issues were neglected by speakers concerned
with 'miserable questions of power' rather than principle. Events in
Europe had not much interest for them, nor had the wishes of the great
majority of British citizens who lacked representation in parliament. Long
before Disraeli's famous reference to the 'two nations', Mazzini in April
1837 used this same phrase in reference to the silent majority outside
Westminster and he thought their silence would not last much longer.[32]
The Whigs, so far as he could judge, were little different from Tories.
His main hope for the future lay in fifty radical members of parliament
who were gradually coming to realise that the fundamental problems
were educational reform, free trade, a wider suffrage, the abolition
of primogeniture and reform of the House of Lords. Mazzini used to
attend political meetings to improve his English, but found even these
radicals insufficiently anxious to demand all the social changes he saw as
necessary.

Increasingly he turned against the utilitarian and 'materialist' philosophy which, by stressing personal rights and the search for individual
happiness, depreciated duty, religion and morality. Before leaving Italy
his early writings had contained half a dozen not unfavourable references
to Bentham, and in general principle he agreed with the aim of reconciling 'the maximum of individual liberty with the maximum of social
progress'.[33] But although the utilitarians were individually better than
their doctrines, he felt that by concentrating on the satisfaction of material needs they came close to 'the ignoble and immoral "every man for
himself"'. Bentham was admittedly a remarkable thinker and yet his
ideas could easily lead to 'unbridled competition without any higher
regulating principle'. Liberty, if it merely meant an absence of legal

restraint and compulsion, could justify manufacturers in seeking monopoly, prohibitive tariffs, and the lowest possible wages. Some Benthamites encouraged the idea of the nightwatchman government as 'a necessary inconvenience to which they submit on condition of giving it as little power as possible', but this was misguided.[34] Adam Smith, too, 'has tended by the doctrines of self-interest and material well-being to the enthronement of selfishness in men's hearts': his ideas might have fitted the circumstances of his time, but they should now be revised in response to the changing relationship between different classes.[35]

As this became a constant theme in Mazzini's writings, it should not be forgotten that he admired the champions of individual rights for having won freedom of conscience, freedom of the press and now free trade. But more was now needed, though he feared that only Carlyle and Emerson realised as much. The French Revolutions of 1789 and 1830, though fought in the name of individual rights, had not profited the great majority of citizens. Uncontrolled individualism tended to help the strong, whether the aristocracy in Britain or the upper bourgeoisie in France. Only the superior claims of duty and morality could in Mazzini's opinion resolve controversial questions where the interest of workers and employers differed. He hoped that the future would establish more clearly that society had rights and duties which should modify selfish individualism. In particular an Italian nation would hardly come into existence unless the clash of individual rights was transcended by a readiness for self-sacrifice and a greater assertion of collective responsibility. This would require a revolution in thinking and behaviour. The desire to satisfy material interests might lead to riot or rebellion but never to the real revolution in society that was needed. Only a higher allegiance would produce martyrs ready to die for their faith, and without martyrs the *ancien régime* was in all probability unassailable.[36]

Mazzini's acquaintance with the Carlyles started slowly. Not only did he dislike accepting invitations, but he lacked the money for a bus fare from Holborn to Chelsea and regularly lost his way when he walked. Nevertheless, meeting them was an important experience in his life. Thomas Carlyle, who was ten years older, referred to him in 1838 as 'a man of some talent, but a furious radical, one who has no notion except of pulling down', but soon was recommending him to an influential editor as 'a man of true genius, an honourable, brave and gifted man'. In July 1840 when Mazzini moved to new lodgings in Chelsea with the two Ruffinis, this was at the suggestion of Carlyle who wanted them near his home in Cheyne Row and came with them to find a convenient boarding house, after which he signed the contract as a witness. Six rooms cost them only £30 a year, and here they found peace and quiet away from the bustle of London, with a partial view of sailing vessels on the Thames,

while on the other side was a field with cows and horses which delighted Mazzini. One service he could offer in return was to help choose Italian books for the new London Library which Carlyle and Dickens had
just launched[37] – a library for which he himself could never afford the
subscription.

He was once told that he had a 'strong affinity of nature' with Carlyle,
to which the reply came that he recognised the latter's powerful and
virtuous mind but their ideas were almost diametrically opposed. He
thought Carlyle praiseworthy for lacking many current prejudices but he
'is the sceptic of sceptics; he is grand when he pulls down, but incapable
of reconstructing something fresh'[38] – it is interesting that they had the
same criticism of each other. Both men shared a powerful sense of duty
and mission; both found fault with utilitarianism and the overriding
search for individual happiness. But Mazzini thought that the other's
admiration of force and heroes was horrifying and could easily lead
to despotism, while Carlyle had no patience with Mazzini's belief in
collectivism and 'progress' nor with his 'wild and fanciful theories borrowed from the French republicans'. They therefore argued incessantly,
over capital punishment, over the relative merits of Goethe and Byron,
or over Beethoven's sonatas, which Carlyle provocatively called mere
rubbish.[39]

Despite their friendship, in two published articles, one of them translated by the popular novelist Geraldine Jewsbury, Mazzini made what *The
Times* called the finest criticism of Carlyle's historical method. Mazzini's
personal view was that history should be much more than the biography
of great men, much more than a chronicle uninformed by some higher
principle. Admittedly Carlyle wrote brilliant pages about individual moments of the French Revolution, 'tableaux wonderful in their execution
but . . . without connection'. Preferring to 'derive great events from accidents', he failed to evaluate 'the greatest event of modern times', an event
which 'left the feeling of right, that of liberty, and that of equality
ineffaceably engraven on the souls of men'. Whether the motive forces in
1789 came more from below or from above, whether that Revolution
represented the people or the bourgeoisie, what it accomplished and how
it fitted into 'the progressive development of humanity', these fundamental questions were left unanswered.[40]

Such disagreements were taken in good part by Carlyle. 'No man did he
reverence more than Mazzini,' was the comment of a mutual friend.
Mazzini was 'the most pious living man I now know', wrote Carlyle,
'though entirely unpractical'. He was 'full of sensibilities, of melodies, of
clear intelligence and noble virtues'; 'by nature a lyrical poet, plenty of
quiet fun in him too, and wild emotion rising to a shrill key, with all that
lies between these two extremes'.[41] Reference to Mazzini's sense of fun,

confirmed as it was by other English friends, is worth underlining as it contradicts one legend still current in Italy. Thirty years later, to an American acquaintance, Carlyle added further comments:

> a more beautiful person I never beheld, with his soft flashing eyes, and face full of intelligence. He had great talent, certainly the only acquaintance of mine of anything like equal intellect who ever became entangled in what seemed to me hopeless visions. He was rather silent, spoke chiefly in French, though he spoke good English even then, notwithstanding a strong accent. It was plain he might have taken a high rank in literature. He wrote well as it was; sometimes for the love of it, at others when he wanted a little money; but he never wrote what he might have done had he devoted himself to that kind of work. He had fine tastes, particularly in music. But he gave himself up as a martyr and sacrifice to his aims for Italy. He lived almost in squalor; his health was poor from the first, but he took no care of it. He used to smoke a great deal, and drink coffee with bread crumbled in it, but hardly gave any attention to his food. His mother used to send him money, but he gave it away. When she died she left him as much as two hundred pounds a year, all she had, but it went to Italian beggars.[42]

Two years spent in Chelsea helped to mitigate what Mazzini called the hell of exile, 'that slow, bitter, lingering death which none can know but the exile himself, that consumption of the soul which has only one hope to console it' – to return home. Thomas and Jane Carlyle feared for his health and used to take him on long walks. They tried in vain to persuade him to go with them to Scotland. When Jane accompanied him on a visit to St Paul's Cathedral, he found it more like a dirty stable than a church, but was greatly impressed looking down from above the dome on a sea of smoking chimneys and fires that recalled Dante's purgatory. Accompanied by other friends he also went without much enthusiasm to Westminster Abbey, the Zoo, the Tower of London, and was properly startled by the Chamber of Horrors in the waxworks of Madame Tussaud. He marvelled at seeing the tunnel under the Thames. The British might be a century behind the rest of Europe in moral and intellectual development, but were ahead of the world in building bridges, machines, ships and canals.[43]

Mazzini in England continued to pay interest on debts contracted in Switzerland and still depended on credit for some of his current expenses. He sometimes pawned not only his watch and his mother's present of a diamond ring but his overcoat and boots, occasionally paying forty per cent interest. The full extent of this deprivation he kept secret from his family and feared that without their continued financial support he might end in the debtors' prison at Newgate. Of this family, one sister who became a nun had already died. A second, his favourite, died of consumption in January 1838, and a third married into a Catholic family that disapproved of him. His father, whom he was never to see again, lacked enthusiasm for Italian unification and republican politics, though he was quietly proud of a son 'who made the great powers of Europe tremble',[44] and at the age of seventy postponed his retirement so that he could send occasional gifts of money. His parents hoped that this money would be used to find a good job instead of being given away to other needy expatriates. Some of the other Italians in London knew that the young Mazzini was the only son of a moderately well-off family who one day might leave him an inheritance. Some of them continued insensitively to blame his father for not being more generous.

His mother was a woman of strong character, considerable intelligence, and profound religious faith. She sometimes tried to restrain her son's enthusiasms but took comfort in believing that God had singled him out for great things. After 1831 they met only once, briefly, in 1848. She and his father did not much like what they knew of England and feared that their son would suffer from the philistinism of editors and the arrogant condescension of English aristocrats towards foreigners.[45] She used to send hampers of food and clothing to London, preferably cheap clothes that he would not be tempted to give to his impecunious friends. Many years later she confessed to having kept secret that the remittances sent to London came in part from her own savings without daring to let her husband know.[46]

When occasional journalism proved unrewarding, Mazzini told his somewhat sceptical parents that he would try his hand at trade. Already in Switzerland they had sent him the equivalent of £300 sterling to invest in Swiss railways and ironworks, but most of this investment was lost, if indeed it was not partially spent on organising conspiracy. In London 'the demon of commerce' again briefly took hold of him when he sent lace to be sold in Genoa in return for importing macaroni, truffles and salami. His mother despatched a consignment of olive oil, for which he promised he would 'infallibly' pay her back with interest in three months. He and his friends bottled this oil and were proud to report that some had gone to another distinguished exile, Prince Louis Napoleon, but they lacked the necessary experience and eventually sold at a loss. His health suffered as a result of these difficulties. He mentioned toothache and constipation, but above all complained of lowness of spirits and 'spleen'. Unlike other exiles, he did not blame the English weather: on the contrary he positively enjoyed the rain and cold and subtle colours of an English winter. The London fogs turned the city into a beautiful enchanted world that reminded him of Dante's hell and the witches' scene in *Macbeth*.

Politics: 1838–43

Lacking other occupation, Mazzini in the summer of 1838 turned again towards active politics. Under British law he was free to pursue his mission as a conspirator so long as he acted with discretion and did nothing illegal. In any case the British, as he often reminded them, won their own freedom against the Stuarts by means of conspiracy and revolution. Moreover, in the years before 1815 the British government had enthusiastically encouraged Italian rebellion against Napoleon, only to go into complete reverse when an alliance with Austria seemed more useful. His own aim in the years after 1838 was to keep the rulers of Italy in constant fear of revolt, so driving them into acts of persecution that would help the cause of patriotism and win sympathy in London.[47] Equally important was to revive the enthusiasm of former companions who were losing interest or hope. He wrote of his shame that, while many Polish refugees kept up their patriotic agitation, the Italian exiles rarely did more than talk and usually accepted the Austrian domination of Italy with only verbal protest.

The one notable exception was in South America, where the society of Young Italy continued to enrol recruits among many Italian exiles, and its newspapers were said to have five thousand subscribers in Montevideo and Buenos Aires.[48] Garibaldi wrote from the Rio Grande asking Mazzini, as head of a nominal government in exile, to send letters of marque that would authorise preying on Austrian and Piedmontese shipping. When Garibaldi gave two piratical vessels the names *Mazzini* and *Young Italy*, the news was reported with apprehension by the diplomatic representatives of Austria and Piedmont who were carefully intercepting his correspondence.[49]

In July 1839, Mazzini decided to relaunch Young Italy in London. He had no money, few dedicated companions, no elaborate organisation, and was realistic enough to expect that he might only prepare the way for others to continue the struggle after his death.[50] Nonetheless he was still confident that Italy was 'predestined' to initiate a crusade on behalf of the suppressed nationalities of Europe, a crusade whose ultimate success was assured since it was part of a divine providence, and immense forces were bottled up in readiness for action. Napoleon forty years earlier had demonstrated the possibility of defeating the *ancien régime* and creating a united kingdom in northern Italy. The Dutch in 1609, the French in 1789, Spain in 1808 had all shown that liberating revolutions were sometimes feasible even against long odds, and the Greeks in 1821 had succeeded against an enemy that outnumbered them by ten to one. Conspiracy could fail any number of times, but 'ideas ripen quickly when nourished by the blood of martyrs' and could never be destroyed by cannon or executions.[51]

One lesson learnt in Switzerland was for this revived organisation to be more exclusive and regulated than before. A number of other conspiratorial societies still existed inside Italy, most of them with a purely local allegiance, none with much vitality, and some with atheistic and communist opinions that Mazzini thought reprehensible and divisive. What he now decided was to create a central committee in Paris to discourage this multiplication of local groups and formulate a single policy of action. The committee was headed by Giuseppe Lamberti, with whom he corresponded at least once a week for the next eight years. His desire for greater exclusiveness was regarded by some patriots as evidence of intolerance, an accusation that he greatly resented. Earlier experience had taught that some degree of centralised direction was necessary for success, and although individuals had every right to disagree and stand aside, they would have to move towards positive collaboration before he would accept them as active partners. If no one else could suggest an alternative plan, he admitted that he would try to impose his own views, and if necessary do so dictatorially.[52] This was bound to offend some potential collaborators, though others thought him not dictatorial enough.[53]

Despite withdrawal from active politics in the years 1836–8, his writings and intercepted letters were still being closely read in Turin. King Charles Albert wrote to the Duke of Modena that this dangerous agitator was a second Luther and was plotting another republican revolution in the near future.[54] And yet events would show that Mazzini was not an unqualified antagonist of monarchy: he allowed that some monarchs had, like feudalism itself, served the community well in the past, and he enjoyed more freedom in royalist Britain than in republican Switzerland. In Italy, however, monarchy was 'foreign in its origin, in its institutions, in its policy, grafted on the country in an era of decay, always subordinate to one or other of the great European Powers; it has never done anything to put a period to the ills of the people or to the abasement of the nation.'[55] Once again he repeated that he would support any Italian sovereign who would fight for national unification, provided only that after the Austrians had been expelled a popularly elected assembly was allowed to vote on a constitution; and though he hoped that such a constitution would be republican, it would be accepted by him whatever was decided.[56] But he had little confidence that any existing Italian sovereign wanted either unification or an elected parliament. Hence his personal preference for a republic, not as an end in itself, but as the most effective means for representing popular wishes. He could admit that republican institutions were no guarantee of good government and there was slavery in the republican United States. Yet absolutist monarchies were despotic by nature, whereas his own alternative of a freer society offered the safeguard of internal checks and balances.[57]

King Ferdinand of Naples, as Mazzini knew, ridiculed the idea of a united Italy.[58] In Piedmont, King Charles Albert had recently begun to introduce overdue administrative reforms but was still an autocrat bound by a treaty of alliance to Austria. Moreover, administrative reforms had one major disadvantage, because however welcome in themselves they would perpetuate a despotic regime and lessen recognition of the need for national unity and independence. Mazzini described Charles Albert as 'mentally a kind of political Hamlet . . . despotic in inclination and liberal only through vanity, a prey to remorse, and worn out by terrors inspired by the Jesuits and the patriots by turns'.[59] No free press was allowed at Turin. Popular education was discouraged, while the circulation of books and ideas was far easier in Tuscany and Austrian Milan. Even the aristocratic and respectable Cavour complained of the great obstacles to publishing books in Piedmont, and the list of banned authors included Boccaccio, Leopardi and Voltaire. Among words forbidden by the censorship were 'Italy', 'nation', 'constitutional liberty' and even 'railways'. Mazzini's own writings were banned, including his edition of Foscolo's *Dante*, which the censors admitted was politically unobjectionable.[60]

The lack of freedom to publish and discuss was, according to Mazzini, the main reason why Italy was falling further behind other countries where political criticism was permitted; and without peaceful change there was ultimately no alternative to revolution with all its dangers. Violent protest would be 'crazy and harmful' in any free society, but wherever free speech was prevented by censorship and torture he hoped that the fellow countrymen of Pym and Hampden would not deny the legitimacy of violence as a last resort. Rebellion should never be motivated by hatred and should always aim to avoid useless bloodshed. But even if it failed, rebellion was more easily justified than the arbitrary cruelties of absolutist repression.[61] He admitted in an article of 1839 that any advocate of revolution

> may be deceived as to the remedy to be applied; he may anticipate too much from the future and substitute his individual intuitions for the common sense of the masses. But . . . with the revolutionist every question resolves itself into a question of principle: he takes up his position decidedly, proceeds in a straight line, neglects what are called tactics, renounces many elements of success, trusts to the power of truth, commits a thousand petty errors, but redeems them by the proclamation of some general maxims sooner or later useful. . . . The man of revolutions prefers to invoke duty, the man of reaction invokes right. . . . The men of the first class, accustomed as they are to count sacrifices as little, labour less for the

generation that lives around them than for generations to come; the triumph of the ideas that they cast on the world is more slow, but assured and decisive.[62]

He felt sure that such ideas would find some acceptance in England, but elsewhere had to defend them against public opinion which continued to believe that kings had a divine right to rule as they thought fit. In other countries he also had to fight against those who fabricated documents to depict him as a bloodthirsty enemy of all organised society. In 1841, with financial support from his family, he took legal action in Paris against a French police officer who accused him of encouraging assassination, and obtained a withdrawal of the accusation. While accepting that people would be killed in war or revolution, he himself would never countenance terrorism, and he consistently condemned the killing of enemies as wrong and inexpedient except in the context of international or civil wars fought for liberty.[63]

Mazzini was already able to identify in Italy a potentially rival force in the 'Moderates', a miscellaneous group of upper-class intellectuals and conservative liberals who criticised not only his republicanism but also his advocacy of conspiracy and his refusal to recognise the advantage of gradual reforms and constitutional monarchy. Like him, most of these Moderates were eager for greater Italian independence against Austria. Some of them had learnt about Italian patriotism from his articles in *Young Italy* and a few frankly acknowledged the fact.[64] But none of them believed in a united Italian state, thinking instead that the most to hope for would be a loose and not extensive federal union between a few Italian states. For various reasons they all strongly disliked and feared his democratic ideas. They also took for granted that national independence would never be won by Italians on their own, so that it was better to remain quiet and submissive until they could obtain foreign diplomatic help and a French or British army to push the Austrians back over the Alps.

These views were not unreasonable, but Mazzini had equally reasonable arguments for disagreeing, however much he admired some of the Moderates as individuals. He praised Manzoni and Silvio Pellico as writers and for their sense of religion, but was appalled by their pessimism and political resignation. The Marquis Massimo d'Azeglio was also admirable as a writer and patriot despite his aristocratic disdain for democracy. Gioberti and Farini, who succeeded Azeglio as prime ministers under the monarchy, had once been close to Young Italy, if not actually members, but now tried to cover up their youthful indiscretions by eulogising Charles Albert and speaking of Mazzini as some kind of monster who did more harm to Italy than all the despots of Europe put together.[65] Arguably Gioberti's idea of the 'primacy of Italy' – he published a famous book with that title in 1843 – had been learnt from Mazzini.[66] But Gioberti thought it expedient to conceal his own more extreme opinions so as to evade the censorship; federalism was a safer immediate objective, and seeking national unification by violent means was said by him to be immoral. As well as defending the temporal power of the papacy, Gioberti even found words of praise for the King of Naples, and carefully avoided any criticism of Austria.[67]

Count Cesare Balbo, another Piedmontese Moderate and future prime minister, shared the hope of winning independence from Austria, but strongly criticised most of Mazzini's other ideas in a famous book that called Italian unification an impossible absurdity.[68] Balbo flattered Charles Albert by writing that national independence was something to be left entirely in the hands of the various sovereigns of Italy, and even argued that the concession of greater internal liberty was likely to impede that process; yet ironically the author had to complain that his book could be much more freely discussed in England than in his own country.[69] Though admitting Balbo's honesty and good intentions, Mazzini was nauseated by such a disregard for liberty and nationality. His own primary goal was to defeat Austria, and by the method of popular insurrection in alliance with the other subject nationalities of the Balkans; whereas Balbo had the very different and totally immoral idea of sacrificing those nationalities to Austrian conquest as an inducement to make Metternich surrender Lombardy and Venice in exchange.[70]

For Balbo, the wishes of ordinary people were almost irrelevant.[71] Mazzini on the contrary, despite over-optimism in interpreting popular wishes, was sure that 'the labouring classes' could not be held down much longer, and thought it far better to welcome them as partners than to drive them into a class war that might ruin the Italian cause. To him the advance of democracy was, like nationality, something inevitable, and resisting it by force would be immensely damaging. Any opposition to democracy, he felt, would play into the hands of communists whose hostility to private property and individual initiative spelt economic disaster.[72] Equally disastrous, however, was the threat posed by 'feudal servitude' in the countryside and the 'concentration of territorial property in a few hands'. The peasants who made up three-quarters of the population of Europe were sometimes dying of hunger despite a possible overproduction of food: they must somehow be given a stake in society and persuaded that greater liberty would help them as well as the middle and upper classes. Mazzini in London had no direct personal contact with these peasants, yet the frequent accusation that he ignored their revolutionary potential is untrue.[73] Long before Marx's communist manifesto he called their subjection morally wrong and a disastrous brake on economic development.

In 1840 he started a mutual aid society among Italian artisans in

London as a branch of Young Italy. The initiative came from these same working men who, stimulated by the example set by Chartism and the Polish exiles, promised to pay a small sum each week to start a newspaper and an adult school. The first issue of the *Apostolato Popolare* appeared in November as the official publication of Young Italy and was written almost entirely by Mazzini himself. Its message included a demand for greater social equality as the best defence against communism. Workers should organise so as to be able to bargain with their employers.[74] But instead of a war between different classes, rich and poor should work together to create a nation as the first step towards a just society. The national language ought to be learnt by everyone in addition to the mutually unintelligible regional dialects in almost universal use, and no longer should individuals think of themselves primarily as Genoese, Piedmontese or Neapolitans. Two thousand copies were printed of the first issue of this paper and a reprint had to be ordered after a request for another five hundred arrived from the United States. At least one batch was burnt in France, but copies reached Turin, Venice, Naples, Calabria and Rome. Subscribers were eventually found in Algeria, Egypt, Tunisia and Asia Minor. Copies were regularly acquired and studied by government officials in Rome, Turin and Vienna.[75]

In November 1841, Mazzini accompanied this initiative by opening a free school in Hatton Garden where there was a sizeable Italian population. It was partly for adults but mainly for the juvenile street musicians and trinket-sellers brought from Italy by not very scrupulous Italian entrepreneurs. These children had been sold by their families into virtual slavery through fraudulent contracts, and over a thousand were living in London under the most appalling conditions.[76] He had been warned that none of them would voluntarily attend a school after their long working hours, but fifty came the first day, sixty-five the second day, and eventually over two hundred, ten of whom were girls. His first aim was to rescue them from illiteracy. Each day there were evening classes in Italian language, Italian geography and arithmetic, on Sunday morning a class in drawing, and Sunday evening a more general lecture, perhaps on morality or patriotic history. Later by popular request he introduced the teaching of English, chemistry and elementary mechanics.

Mazzini at first kept in the background so as not to deter potential benefactors to his school who might disapprove of his politics, and most of the richer Italian exiles in fact refused his invitation to subscribe.[77] Among those who gave small sums were Lord Shaftesbury, Lord Radnor, the Carlyles, Harriet Martineau, Sir Edwin Landseer, Thomas Campbell, the widow of Lord Byron, J. S. Mill, Erasmus Darwin and several of the Wedgwood family. Queen Victoria's personal physician contributed a guinea. The teachers were generally unpaid: they included Joseph and

George Toynbee. In 1842 the school encountered opposition from the Piedmontese embassy and employers of the 'organ boys'. There were even attempts to disrupt classes by violence, especially after the ambassador's chaplain issued notice of excommunication to all pupils who attended. Supported by the London press, Mazzini was able to secure police protection, and members of his 'Union of Italian Working Men' were eager to stand guard and protect someone 'whose life belongs to Italy'.[78] A happier result was that the Catholics were shamed into starting a rival school a few doors away. A third school was also opened by the Methodists, because Mazzini refused when they offered material help in return for introducing anti-Catholic teaching into his own curriculum.

Another incidental result of this charitable enterprise was that Mazzini's name became widely known and respected. A British ambassador came to ask his views about Russia. A prominent solicitor, working with Lord Shaftesbury a leading Tory, helped him in legal action to repatriate some of the organ boys and bring their employers before the courts for brutality.[79] A number of English ladies used to visit the school on Sundays to show their support, and so did a famous American visitor, Margaret Fuller, who more than once gave the children a moving address. Dickens was another interested participant – the slums round Hatton Garden were familiar territory to Fagin and Oliver Twist. Its most active patron, Arethusa Milner-Gibson, was the wife of a well-known privy councillor, the same lady who caused a sensation when she defied the Genoese police by appearing in a box at the opera dressed in the colours of the Italian flag.[80]

Few events in his life gave Mazzini more pleasure than the annual prize-giving ceremony when adult and young pupils were invited to a dinner by their teachers. Gabriele Rossetti, father of the more celebrated poet, presided at the first prize-giving in November 1842. Though Mazzini hated speaking in public, he later agreed to give some of the Sunday lectures, choosing to talk on patriotism and morality but also on geography and elementary physics. In September 1843 he moved his lodgings from Chelsea to Camden so as to be nearer the school. Each year, to cover its annual expenses of nearly £200, he made an appeal to the British public. Each year too he organised a concert for the same purpose, finding performers and selling the tickets himself: 'I never saw a mortal man who so completely made himself into "minced meat for the universe",' wrote Jane Carlyle when she discovered how much work was involved. Among celebrities who performed without fee in these concerts were Sabilla and Vincent Novello, Julius Benedict, John Parry, and the famous couple Mario and Grisi of the Italian opera who broke their professional contract when they accepted his invitation.

Conspiracies in Italy

By 1844 Mazzini was once again regarded as being the most influential revolutionary in Europe, and Metternich had cause to fear that his incessant agitation was frightening the sovereigns of Italy into conceding reforms they would otherwise have resisted.[81] But not all of Mazzini's former companions were enthusiastic over the re-launching of Young Italy. In 1840, Agostino Ruffini departed from their joint household to take a teaching post in Edinburgh, so establishing a better claim to *gentlemanismo*, and eventually moving away to become a much respected member of the Turin parliament. Giovanni Ruffini, equally disillusioned with what he called Mazzini's lack of measure and judgement, left to become a celebrated novelist and to write the libretto for Donizetti's *Don Pasquale*. Donizetti's Paris house continued to be used by Mazzini as a cover address for some of his secret correspondence.[82]

While some earlier followers deserted the revolution, others wanted more forceful conspiratorial activity, among them Nicola Fabrizi, who was planning in the British dependencies of Malta and Corfu to start a revolution in Sicily and Naples. Mazzini tried to persuade an at first unwilling Fabrizi that unified direction was absolutely necessary and that they should avoid local insurrections unless part of a concerted plan. He himself would never advocate 'a hopeless civil war', though he did not deny the need sometimes to act with only an outside chance of success. Even failures could help to diffuse a sense of discontent and create alarm, apart from persuading the rest of Europe that an Italian problem existed and had to be resolved.[83] But decisions should be taken with deliberation and only after counting the cost. In particular he feared Sicilian separatism and was afraid that most of the potential rebels in Sicily wanted to break free from Naples rather than unite Italy.

Mazzini was a visionary who often appeared to take little account of realistic considerations, but sometimes his apparent lack of realism was a calculated tactic and he could be more prudent than his critics assumed. Although he was automatically blamed for insurrections after they had failed, some unsuccessful revolts were in fact instigated by the same Moderates who liked to accuse him of imprudence while copying his practice, whereas he himself knew nothing about such risings, or else counselled caution, or helped only after his advice was rejected.[84] Another invented accusation was that he was intending to murder Charles Albert; yet another depicted him as a communist, an enemy of religion, and a coward who sent others to their death while himself enjoying the comfortable safety of London. It did not suit many people to admit that he was a brave man who, living in penury, was a dedicated opponent of communism and atheism. Others repeatedly accused him of believing that the end always justified the means, though this was a maxim he categorically rejected.[85]

One episode for which he was excessively blamed was a rising in southern Italy that led to the execution of Attilio and Emilio Bandiera in July 1844. These two brothers were officers in the Austrian navy, a fleet which, because Austria was land-locked, had to be largely manned by Italians from Venice and Dalmatia. After being inspired by reading one of Mazzini's newspapers at Smyrna they let him know of their plan to start an insurrection in Naples and the Papal States. Mazzini was ready to discuss such a project and knew the importance of creating disaffection inside the Austrian navy. Believing also that the papal authorities had 'the wretched supremacy of Italy in misery and misgovernment', he saw some chance that monarchists and republicans could join forces to start a movement in central Italy. Such a revolution might then spread to Austrian-controlled territory and compel Charles Albert to support it.[86]

This idea would to most people have seemed wildly optimistic, but so were later local movements in 1848 and 1860 that proved astonishingly successful. Mazzini's initial attitude in 1844 was 'better act and fail than do absolutely nothing', if only to show the rest of Europe that Italians were more than boasters or cowards and they deserved support.[87] But on reconsideration he and Fabrizi did their best to dissuade the Bandiera brothers and had reason to think that this advice was accepted.[88] Once again, however, several renegade Italians among Mazzini's close collaborators kept the Viennese and Neapolitan governments secretly informed about what was afoot – adding, as usual, some fabricated facts to enhance the price of their services.[89] The two conspirators, when they learnt of this betrayal, deserted their ship and fled to Corfu. They knew the risk involved in acting on their own, but believed that 'Italy will never live until Italians learn to die.' In June they walked into a trap which led to their capture in Calabria. Mazzini was automatically blamed for their execution even though, as was known in Vienna from intercepted letters, he had tried to deter them.[90]

Some degree of responsibility lay with the British government, in particular with Lord Aberdeen and Sir James Graham, who had authorised the interception of Mazzini's private letters in London and were passing information to Vienna. They took this action in response to a request from Metternich, who had protested that Corfu was a British protectorate and such piratical expeditions would endanger European peace. Mazzini knew that his correspondence was being read by governments in Paris, Vienna and Turin, but did not know that Metternich was fabricating stories about another presumed plot to assassinate Charles Albert.[91] He took for granted that the British never interfered with private letters, until an article in The Times led him to suspect that his own were read and information was being leaked to the press. With the help of two Chartist friends, William Linton and William Lovett, he confirmed this, checking that two letters posted simultaneously to his address arrived always at different times if only one of them bore his name, and also that the seals and postmarks had been altered. After receiving corroboration from a friend in the Post Office, he took legal advice and made a formal protest to parliament against what he called this 'disgracefully un-English behaviour'.[92]

The resulting furore, as he hoped and intended,[93] gave enormous publicity to the cause of Italian patriotism and to his own name as a victim of political persecution. Investigating committees were appointed by both Houses of Parliament in London, their members hand-picked by Graham, and both committees did their best to whitewash the whole affair, though they strangely omitted to call on the petitioner to give evidence, and the eventual discrepancies between their two reports gave clear indication of a cover-up. Parliamentary debates on the matter filled 550 pages of the record in Hansard. Graham was reluctantly forced to confess that a secret warrant had been issued on 1 March and this evidently legalised the interception, but before that date there seems to have been an illegal intelligence operation and the forging of seals and postmarks was another evident misdemeanour.

A further scandal that emerged from the inquiry was that the despatches of foreign ambassadors were occasionally being tapped by the British government as well as letters by members of parliament. Yet the same government was hypocritical enough to protest at similar action by Charles Albert in Piedmont.[94] Aberdeen with equal hypocrisy denied in parliament that information from these letters was given to any foreign power, and subsequently had to confess that this was a lie. Graham made matters worse when, under protection of parliamentary privilege, he bolstered his case by calling Mazzini a convicted assassin, and then was forced to withdraw this gratuitous and shabby remark[95] – but never apologised personally to his victim.

Information had in fact been given by Aberdeen to Austria, and Metternich thanked him before sending selected details to the pope and the King of Naples: almost certainly this had no direct part in the capture of the Bandieras but it may have helped to secure the death of other patriots.[96] The Duke of Wellington, who many years earlier had promised positive assistance for the liberation of Italy, now stood behind his Tory friends who saw it as a British interest to defend despotic governments against individuals agitating for free speech and liberty of conscience. Yet Mazzini had broken no British law or else he would certainly have been prosecuted. The propagation of liberal opinions was no crime in Britain: on the contrary, there was by general consent a national interest in defending the country's reputation as a haven for political refugees.[97]

These protracted discussions in parliament and press did a great deal to publicise and win sympathy for Italian patriotism. One cabinet minister confessed that the parliamentary debate had been 'one of the most disagreeable and painful he had ever heard'.[98] According to Aberdeen, 'this Mazzini affair has been the most unpleasant in which I have ever been engaged', and he deeply regretted his part in it, while according to Lord Macaulay 'the turning of the Post Office into an engine of the police was utterly abhorrent to the public feeling'.[99]

Other personal testimonials to Mazzini are evidence of this same sentiment. Support came from Robert Browning, from Dickens and from Lord John Russell, who shortly afterwards became prime minister in a cabinet which included other supporters of Mazzini.[100] Popular sympathy was such that pictures of this arch-conspirator were sold in London by the thousand.[101] Sir John Bowring assured parliament that everyone who knew Mazzini 'testified to his high intellect and pure and unspotted morality'.[102] The *Westminster Review* wrote that 'Mazzini enjoys the confidence and respect of many Englishmen of the first rank, and stands for public character and private worth upon as high moral ground as any distinguished foreigner who had visited English shores'.[103] Carlyle wrote to *The Times* that reading someone's private correspondence was like picking his pocket, and to aid despots by doing so was doubly a crime:

> I have had the honour of knowing Mr Mazzini for a series of years; and, whatever I may think of his practical insight and skill in worldly affairs, I can with great freedom testify to all men that he, if I have ever seen one such, is a man of genius and virtue, a man of sterling veracity, humanity, and nobleness of mind, one of those rare men, numerable unfortunately but as units in this world, who are worthy to be called martyr souls, who, in silence, piously in their daily life, understand and practise what is meant by that.

Carlyle followed this testimonial by sending to Mazzini 'with my kind regards' a copy of his new book on Cromwell.[104]

In May 1845, Mazzini published at his own expense a pamphlet criticising Aberdeen's argument that repression and despotism were needed to keep Italy peaceful and quiet. On the contrary, repression had led to revolutionary outbreaks almost every year since 1820, and until Italians could enjoy greater freedom their only protest would continue to be violent revolt – as Englishmen had discovered for themselves in the seventeenth century. The British government condemned black slavery in the Americas, yet tolerated or encouraged white slavery in Europe. Its practice of non-intervention in continental affairs was a hypocritical fiction if improperly obtained and incriminating information was given to the Austrian police. Non-intervention was immoral if it meant indifference to persecution and was inexpedient if it diminished the reputation of Britain among liberals in Europe. Nor would it do anything to reduce the likelihood of further revolution and civil war.[105]

This pamphlet received praise for its 'intellectual power' from Leigh Hunt, the friend of Byron and Shelley,[106] but being privately published was not widely circulated. It cost its author £60 to produce, almost a third of his annual income. He could no longer borrow from his Jewish friends in London, the Rosselli family, whose financial affairs had gone badly wrong. Also the collapse of a Genoese banking house left his parents in difficulties and he had been borrowing on the expectation of their fairly regular remittances. He was rescued temporarily when several richer exiles in Paris lent him money to pay off the exorbitant demands of London moneylenders – whom he called his salvation but also his ruin. Incompetence in worldly matters had been correctly diagnosed by Carlyle as one aspect of his character. Jane Carlyle mentioned as an instance of his 'usual impracticality' that, when travelling the short distance to Oxford in 1845, he let the train take him sixty miles in a different direction.[107] Nor was this an isolated example of its kind.

After seven years in England he felt less of a stranger and had found good friends in the world of culture and politics. By now he also had a more informed curiosity about social behaviour in London, for instance about the mixture of extreme prudery and mass prostitution. His youthful study of the physical sciences led him to an interest in the current fashion for mesmerism as 'possibly containing some germ of a profound truth that one day may be discovered': after several experiments, however, he found that hypnotism would not work with someone so averse as himself to an irrational suspension of disbelief. In Switzerland he had already observed some experiments in acupuncture, but was sceptical about the confidence of his English friends in homoeopathy.[108]

There are various indications of his increasing sociability. Without doubt he had some influence on individual Chartist leaders, and vice versa. One of these, William Linton, knew him as well as anyone in the 1840s and commented on his cheerfulness, joviality and good nature:

> on whatever subject he spoke, political, social or literary (English literature included) there was always something to be learned from him. . . . He was a man who had not only the faculty of loving but also the faculty of inspiring love. Few came under his magnetic influence without becoming attached to him; even those who were unable to comprehend his highest thoughts.[109]

Lady Harriet Baring called him 'a man well worth seeing and not at all specially anxious to be seen'. Professor Masson of Edinburgh, who did not meet him until 1847, disagreed with some of his political views but found him 'simple, kindly, affectionate' and his conversation full of 'whim and laughter'. His was 'one of the friendships of my life for which I thank fate and which I shall ponder till I die'.[110] As well as casual meetings with Robert Browning, he attended the *soirées* of Macready, the Shakespearean actor whose wife helped at his school. He was invited to the legendary breakfasts of the poet Samuel Rogers, whom he greatly admired. He became one of the thousand members of the Whittington Club founded by Douglas Jerrold and, in recognition of his campaign for civic freedoms, was elected one of the club's vice-presidents.

Mazzini shone best in female society and would hardly have joined the Whittington if it had been for men only. 'Despite my lack of social graces,' he wrote to his mother, 'I get on well with almost every woman who knows me because I much prefer them to men'; and he never understood why many Italians preferred their children to be boys.[111] He criticised the education currently given to women and the presumption of their supposed intellectual inferiority, as he also criticised the organisation of society that left them dependent on men.[112] He even succeeded in liking the formidable Harriet Martineau, and she at first admired him before losing patience with his 'unreason' and political utopianism.[113] His own intellectual admiration went above all to the French writer George Sand, with whom he corresponded for some years until her socialist opinions came between them. She translated one of his articles into French and called him 'a great intelligence, a great writer . . . one of the leading characters of our age'.[114]

During the years 1844–6 he usually kept one day a week for a visit to the Carlyles in Chelsea, and though some of his verbal contests with Thomas reduced him almost to tears, in 1844 he wrote that Jane was the woman he esteemed most in England. When for six months he suffered from a facial ulcer and suspected cancer, she found him a leading surgeon who operated without fee. To her he confided about a number of 'declarations of love' he had lately received and which forced him to take refuge in Oxford. Though impatient with his 'absurd' revolutionary projects, she treated him as an affectionate and valued companion; in a wise and sympathetic letter he tried to answer the doubts she had about her own marriage.[115] Mazzini's many messages of consolation over sickness, bereavement or personal despair are among the most attractive and impressive letters he wrote.

In 1845 he met the family of William Ashurst, who became his closest friends in England. Ashurst was an under-sheriff of London, a champion of Chartism, anti-slavery and the penny post, who had acted as lawyer for George Holyoake when he was prosecuted for blasphemy. Mazzini was soon spending most Sundays with this family at Muswell Hill and wrote of never having met such sympathetic people. Besides a son, also named William, there were four daughters, all sufficiently liberated that they could visit him unchaperoned to take tea and bring him flowers. It particularly appealed to him that they smoked cigarettes because he himself, though an incorrigible smoker, always abstained in the presence of people to whom it caused offence. Eliza, the eldest, asked him almost at once to use her Christian name, something he never presumed to do with Mrs Carlyle. Matilda, who was thought by some to be the most remarkable of the four, married Joseph Biggs, a manufacturer from Leicester and noted philanthropist. Caroline married James Stansfeld, a minister in several governments. Emilie became perhaps the closest friend to him of them all and in 1847 was already trying to persuade him to let her publish a collected edition of his writings. These quite exceptional people provided him with the comfort and encouragement of a surrogate family. Without the fifteen hundred letters to them which have survived, his personal history would be hard to write.

In later retrospect Mazzini remembered 1845 as the year when he began the campaign of serious propaganda which he believed was the fundamental factor in creating a united Italy. His privately printed pamphlet against Lord Aberdeen reminded British readers of the anomaly that Italy was still eight separate countries, each with an expensive court to maintain, with no 'common market' linking them but separated by customs barriers that were an absurd hindrance to trade: 'Eight different systems of currency, of weights and measures, of civil, commercial and penal legislation, of administrative organisation and of police restriction, divide us and render us as much as possible strangers to each other.' Additional internal barriers inside each state were an extra anomaly. In the diminutive Duchy of Parma a traveller could encounter seven customs stations in the thirty-kilometre journey from Guastalla to the capital city, and one Englishman counted forty-three different scales of weights and measures in the single territory of Lombardo-Venetia. All eight states were still ruled despotically and all of them, except to a lesser extent Tuscany, by governments hostile to free speech, hostile to the diffusion of education and to the introduction of foreign books and newspapers. Their main link with each other was being tied by treaty or family relationship to Austria. A quarter of the Italian population was in fact ruled by foreigners speaking an alien language, who exported from Italy much of what they gathered in tax revenue and imposed an educational system that deliberately excluded or denigrated the achievements of Italian culture.[116]

Against these governments he regarded himself as having been personally in a state of war since 1831, but since then the chances of victory had improved because the rest of Europe had an increasing awareness that there existed an Italian problem to which old solutions might no longer apply. He hoped that before becoming too old he could return home, if only in secret, where he could conspire more actively. But Giuseppe Lamberti, who in Paris headed his organisation Young Italy, told him that a commander's job was to devise and coordinate strategy, so that he should remain in the one country that allowed him freedom of movement and action.[117] Mazzini admitted that success was no more than 'possible and still full of difficulty'. He had learnt from experience that in public he always ought to express confidence, but in private used to repeat that victory might not come in his lifetime. For the moment his task was to organise propaganda and find the money to prepare something bigger than another merely local operation.[118]

In September 1845 there was another local rising in the papal Romagna for which he was unfairly blamed. Some of his followers were involved against his wishes, but so were some of the Moderates, who had the different objective of winning constitutional reforms rather than national unification.[119] In some despair he tried once more to secure greater agreement on a programme of action, 'to begin all over again like a spider whose web has been ruined by some troublesome flies'. He was corresponding with at least a hundred people, writing perhaps twenty letters a day, and regretted not having the help of trusted subordinates who could assume some of this secretarial burden.[120]

Italians, he wrote, were shamefully passive about contributing money. Garibaldi and his remarkably successful Italian Legion in Uruguay and Southern Brazil were proving that some patriots were ready to fight for freedom, and he did his best to encourage them by informing the outside world about their exploits.[121] But inside Italy, though often full of good intentions, people had been taught in three centuries of foreign rule to lack self-confidence and the will to fight or risk committing themselves to the cause of political change. When a subscription was opened in Tuscany to present Garibaldi with a sword of honour, the Piedmontese government discouraged it and some Italian states forbade it altogether.[122]

One reason for Mazzini's pessimism, as Cavour realised with delight,[123] was that the political radicals in Italy were mainly middle- and upper-class people who had property to defend and feared that revolution might become social as well as political. Another reason for discouragement was that the Moderates, in particular Gioberti, Balbo and Azeglio, were allowed freer circulation of their books by the various Italian censorships; and this put him at a great disadvantage. Though he welcomed the fact that such books helped the diffusion of patriotic sentiment, he was also glad to think that his own propaganda was pushing these Moderates faster towards nationality than they intended. Nevertheless, their support for constitutional change was suspect because local and partial reforms encouraged the perpetuation of existing territorial divisions and so were a positive obstacle in the path of national unity. Individual acts of reform, however desirable, gave people the comfortable illusion of being able to stand back and wait for governments to do all that was necessary. Such reforms might 'only prove a fresh stimulant to egotism and a narcotic for all truly great and decisive national feeling'. He would support them only if any one sovereign went further and became a champion of Italian patriotism.[124]

CHAPTER THREE

The Revolution: 1846–9

Prelude to revolution

IN 1846 THE election of Pius IX, a reforming pope, gave a dramatic and unexpected stimulus to all Italians hoping for change. Metternich was appalled when modest political reforms in the capital city of Catholicism indicated that the *ancien régime* was beginning to crack. Mazzini at first hardly knew what to think. He had been a fierce critic of papal administration which, in his opinion, after its great contribution to civilisation in the past, had become a corrupt oligarchy and was chiefly responsible for the atheism and agnosticism prevalent among all classes in contemporary Italy.[1] Rome before 1846 had been recognised by many or most foreign visitors as the most impervious to change of all Italian states: liberalism was condemned there as sinful as well as seditious, and even the inoffensive word 'liberty' had been changed by the papal censors to 'loyalty' in Bellini's opera *I Puritani*.[2] Mazzini welcomed the new pope's piety and good intentions, but above all hoped that, like the sorcerer's apprentice of Goethe's story, Pius might be evoking a spirit he could not control. A new papal amnesty could be used to assist the return to Rome of exiled republican sympathisers, and the republicans correctly foresaw that the spread of liberal ideas might then provoke Austrian intervention in central Italy, which in turn would do more than anything to arouse feelings of patriotism.[3]

Rumours were beginning to circulate that Charles Albert of Piedmont, possibly influenced indirectly by Mazzini himself,[4] was beginning to speak in private of wanting to end fifteen years of virtual vassalage under Austria and to champion the cause of Italian independence. But this king had changed his political opinions so often that he could hardly be trusted. Moreover, his family had regularly intermarried with the Austrian Habsburgs. In any case Charles Albert had absolutely no objective of Italian unification or of imitating the pope in yielding to popular pressure for constitutional, as distinct from merely administrative, reforms.[5] At most this monarch thought of extending the frontier of Piedmont by annexing Lombardy, and such a move might hinder unification by antagonising the governments of Tuscany, Rome and Naples, which feared him as a rival and possible enemy. Nevertheless Mazzini, while never wavering in his belief that the ideal form of government was a republic, repeated again and again in the years 1846–8 that he stood by his previous appeal to Charles Albert in 1831, an appeal that was now reprinted and freely on sale in Florence and Rome. He would enthusiastically fight against the Austrians in support of a truly national king or pope. Yet the Piedmontese monarch refused to let such a dangerous man return from exile, despite Balbo's advice that this might be helpful.[6]

Meanwhile there were other signs that the institution of absolute monarchy was under threat. Mazzini wrote that 'the democratic tendency of our times, the upward movement of the popular classes who desire to have their share in political life (hitherto a life of privilege) is henceforth no utopian dream, no doubtful anticipation: it is a fact, a great European fact which occupies every mind, influences the proceedings of governments, defies all opposition.'[7] Reports came from conservatives as well as radicals that the propaganda of Young Italy was still eagerly read by students and intellectuals south of the Alps,[8] and Gallenga, before long one of Mazzini's opponents, thought that most Italians would vote for creating a united Italian republic if given the chance.[9] Fear of republicanism, while it was pushing some governments towards introducing political reforms as an antidote to liberalism, was making other governments react by harsh repression that could only make revolution more likely. The new pope paid Mazzini the compliment of referring to him by name as a serious enemy.[10] Such was the alarm aroused by this mysterious conspirator that false rumours told of his being seen in Germany, Switzerland, Italy and Malta.

Of all governments it was the Austrian that had most to lose, as it suspected this one man of keeping the rest of Italy in expectation of some dramatic revolutionary initiative. Metternich now guessed that the active Italian republicans were fewer than a thousand, but thought that with widespread passive support they constituted a greater threat to his system than all the Italian governments put together. In Vienna until now there had been a general assumption that the politically conscious classes in Italy were the last people to be attracted by liberal ideas or notions about nationality. Metternich also believed that, since Piedmont had a tradition of joining the probable victor in any war, she would remain a subservient ally. But as the balance of power in Europe showed signs of shifting, Charles Albert's subservience might no longer be guaranteed.[11]

A dramatic example of this shift was when Metternich, by annexing the Polish republic of Cracow in November 1846, took a bold step which set him against the public law of Europe, and no longer thereafter could he invoke 'legitimism' and the settlement of 1815 as an absolute bar against territorial alterations in Italy. Moreover, his action aroused patriotic feeling among the Slav populations of eastern Europe. Mazzini was among the first to realise the importance of the fact that three such groups, Poles, Czechoslovaks and Southern Slavs, which together made up half the population of the Austrian empire, were potential nationalities in their own right. Since they would be natural allies of Italy in defeating the Habsburgs they should be given every encouragement to win their national freedom. The Austrian empire, he repeated, though it seemed formidable, was a house of cards that would collapse as soon as these subject populations combined to replace the Holy Alliance of sovereigns by a new union of peoples.[12]

Metternich in 1847 called Italy a mere geographical expression and nationality 'a meaningless word'. But this was less a confident assertion than a recognition of the urgent need to eradicate the very opposite ideas that he knew were gaining ground. Although he still took for granted that the various states of Italy feared and disliked each other too much to form a political union, in private he was apprehensive that local revolutions were on the point of breaking out in Rome and Tuscany. To convince others of this danger he sent to London one of Mazzini's letters that he had intercepted, hoping that the British government would join Austria in guaranteeing the existing frontiers inside Italy.[13] Mazzini on the contrary was convinced that public opinion in London not only supported the different idea of Italian independence against Austria, but was even beginning to consider national unification as a possibility.[14]

All his life he had tried to work upon public opinion in the hope that change would come peaceably and violence could be avoided or at least minimised.[15] But in July 1847 this hope faded when the Austrian government made yet another provocative gesture by despatching troops into the papal city of Ferrara, and soon afterwards sent arms to help the minority of Catholic cantons start a civil war in Switzerland. These actions, in defiance of formal treaties, antagonised Palmerston, who already knew that a widespread boycott was in operation in Milan against the Austrian occupation forces. Mazzini concluded, and Palmerston feared, that at any moment a spark might ignite a European war between what were now called the forces of progress and reaction; and war, however horrible, would be the only resort for a rebellious population if peaceful demonstrations were put down by brute force.[16] When a minor rising took place at Messina in September, Mazzini turned his attention again to southern Italy, and wrote to ask Garibaldi about bringing his Italian Legion from Montevideo to Sicily or Naples when the moment for concerted action arrived.[17]

On 8 September he also wrote a long letter to the pope begging Pius to unite Italy under papal leadership. Unification would come anyway because it was part of God's providence, but better if under papal patronage because 'with you at its head our struggle will take on a religious aspect and liberate us from many risks of reaction and civil war'.[18] Mazzini subsequently said that he never had much hope that this letter would produce results, but at the time he confirmed in private that he was ready to recognise Pius as life president of a united Italy, and the sincerity of this admission has been widely admitted,[19] though he must have known it would upset many of his supporters on the radical and anticlerical left.

Earlier in 1847, after discussion with various friends, he had inaugurated in London a People's International League

> to enlighten the British public as to the political condition and relations of foreign countries; to disseminate the principles of national freedom and progress; to embody and manifest an efficient public opinion in favour of the right of every people to self-government and the maintenance of their own nationality; to promote a good understanding between the peoples of every country.[20]

He hoped to convert this League into a larger European Convention with representatives from other European countries, though such a hope proved too ambitious. The League had Bowring as president. Its secretary was Linton, the Chartist and noted wood engraver with whom Mazzini used to go on long country walks. Its regulating committee included three members of parliament as well as Ashurst, Jerrold, Dickens, and Peter Taylor of the Courtauld family who was to be of great assistance in future years. Opposition came from *The Times*, which referred to 'tiresome quackery', but after a few months the League had four hundred members and a thousand active sympathisers.[21]

This association was overtaken by the revolution of 1848 before there was time to win a substantial public, but until then its meetings were well attended. In July 1847 it published a tract on the dangerous prospect of civil war in Switzerland, and its weekly seminars were called deeply interesting by Thomas Cooper the poet, who recorded that its founder's 'eloquence and sincerity had a marvellous effect upon us'.[22] Mazzini's central message to its members was, first of all, that new nations were ready to appear which were identifiable by 'language, tendencies, traditions, geographical characteristics'. Secondly, the nations of Europe should eventually become 'one vast market, in which no one member could suffer or be fettered in developing its powers without inconvenience to the others. . . . Europe is marching by the common consent of her populations towards a new era of union . . . all contributing to one work, whose fruits are to enlarge and strengthen the life of all.' The League abstained from any concern with the domestic politics of other countries. Nor was there any suggestion that Britain should intervene by armed force on the continent. On the contrary, it is emphatically for peace that the League is founded. Not the pretence of peace now existing, but peace founded upon right and ensured by justice ... peace for the free growth of national peculiarities of character ... ; that the world's goods may readily be exchanged, that every man may have the opportunity of placing himself in that sphere in which his energies may be turned to the best account for the public service; and that each country may thus be the gainer, not only by the immigration of useful members from other countries, but also by the emigration of such of her own members as cannot find at home a profitable investment of their faculties; for a constant intercommunication of ideas and information for the benefit of all countries; and for that free trade, the unrestrained interchange of natural products and manufactures by which alone the material wants of nations can be supplied.[23]

This vision of a European common market was unusual among contemporaries. Mazzini's complete absence of any narrow nationalism helped to consolidate the admiration felt for him by a select circle of friends. The American writer Margaret Fuller, as well as finding him 'the most beauteous person I have seen', remarked that he was 'far above the stature of other men', with 'a mind far in advance of his times', and better company than her other friend Carlyle.[24] Lloyd Garrison, the champion of anti-slavery, was another American who met him in 1846 at the Ashursts' and admired 'the brilliancy of his mind, the modesty of his deportment, the urbanity of his spirit, and the fascination of his conversational powers'. Garrison noticed no trace of the fanatic or the mere visionary and 'felt drawn to him by an irresistible magnetism; in him there was not discoverable one spark of self-inflation, one atom of worldly ambition'; he was 'a sublime idealist, but never transcending the bounds of reason. . . . Of immense physical and moral courage, he was grave in deliberation and eminently circumspect in all his movements'; and moreover was 'as far removed from bigotry and superstition as any living man'.[25]

Another casual acquaintance was Giuseppe Verdi, like Donizetti by repute something of a Mazzinian in politics, who came to London in 1847 for a performance of *I Masnadieri*. A few months later, when Mazzini asked the composer to produce an Italian *Marseillaise*, Verdi wrote a national hymn to verses by Goffredo Mameli, of which both music and text remained Mazzini's property.[26]

Money was still his greatest problem and continuing debts left him exposed to occasional depression and 'the blue devils'. Every other day he had to find a few shillings to help other impoverished exiles. After her Italian husband deserted her, his one-time servant Susanna Faulkner remained a permanent charge on his purse for decades, though few

people knew it; so did the education of her children; so did his wayward
Danish friend Harro Harring. Organising revolution was expensive. Even
postage was costly and writing letters still took up half of his time. The
other half was in part spent earning a pittance from translating and proof-
correcting. His one self-indulgence was still that of smoking cheap cigars,
'perhaps looking unconsciously for a symbol, alas, to my thoughts and
schemes ending in smoke'.[27] He knew of a hundred Italians who could
afford £50 without noticing the expense, and with one contribution of
£50 the Bandiera brothers might in his view have been well enough
armed to defeat their captors. But he had to admit that the failure of that
particular enterprise discouraged contributors. Enrico Mayer of Livorno
helped to settle his debts and contributed £10 to his school. Another rich
Italian, Adriano Lemmi, now made the first of many providential donations. The operatic soprano Grisi, another companion in his country
walks, offered him £10 for action in Italy but prudently made it payable
only when the revolution had begun.

English and Scottish friends continued to keep his school from closure,
though he felt reluctance in asking them to back revolution when Italian
financial support was so insufficient. Dickens and Cobden both contributed small sums to an impostor who claimed to be collecting on behalf of
Mazzini, and Dickens gave evidence in court when this man was convicted of fraud.[28] Inevitably there was envy when very substantial funds
were available for other political and charitable associations in London.
One example was the Anti-Corn Law League, which was thought to have
have collected hundreds of thousands of pounds. Even poor working men
obtained thousands of pounds for Chartism by a penny-a-head subscription. If the impoverished Irish were reputed to have collected £100,000 to
force concessions from the British parliament, surely Italians could and
should do as much.

To accompany his International League, Mazzini therefore launched a
National Association and a National Fund in 1847, George Grote the
historian agreeing to act as its treasurer. One Italian gave £50. Other
Londoners opened a penny subscription, for which the stockbroker
Meyer Nathan collected sixteen shillings in one day. A degree of subterfuge was necessary, because some people would contribute only to the
school, while others might be ready to help fund political propaganda,
and bolder spirits would assist a revolution if only they could be shown
that Italians felt strongly enough to risk their money and lives.[29] To
minimise any cause of offence Mazzini took care to remove the name
Young Italy from the subscription list, but disingenuously intended to
hold some of the proceeds back 'for any operation, peaceful or warlike,
that will promote success'. One covert project was to charter a ship to

bring Garibaldi and his 'Italian Legion' back from South America when the revolution began.[30]

By the end of 1847 a council of Italian patriots representing many different shades of opinion existed in London under Mazzini's presidency.[31] In October, after almost eleven years in England, he travelled briefly to France for consultation with Lamberti and other organisers of Young Italy. There he met Lamennais and Gioberti and spent several days with George Sand. The French police were warned by informers in London and kept him under close surveillance, but took no hostile action. Among Italian exiles in Paris, even those who disagreed with his politics, his reception was extraordinary. He did not much enjoy this visit but everywhere was greeted with ovations and almost adoration by people who knew him only by repute.[32]

Clearly his quiet work of propaganda had not been fruitless. The word 'Italy', hitherto forbidden by the various censorships in his own country, could now be heard everywhere, and he had the stimulus of rediscovering that he personally continued to inspire fear in the governments of Austria and Piedmont.[33] A collected edition of his writings appeared in three volumes at Lugano in 1847 and was not without its effect.[34] Under popular pressure, not only Charles Albert but the Grand Duke of Tuscany were forced into political reforms, thereby showing the power of public opinion, and the London *Spectator* hoped that this process would before very long make Italy into the sixth great power of Europe.[35] One report explained that almost all the students at Pavia University were enthusiastic supporters of Mazzini. Cavour in Turin was trying to find a copy of his recent articles. In a letter to Jane Carlyle, Mazzini wrote, 'I feel hopeful, I could say confident, that before long I shall be enabled to die in and for my country, the best thing that can befall to me.'[36]

His expectation was that the great European revolution might break out in three or four months' time. He therefore went back in December to London where he would have greater freedom to observe events. To prepare for his return to Italy he asked a friend to procure a forged American passport, and he also sent money to Malta so that Fabrizi could be ready to start a movement in southern Italy when the right moment arrived. The aim should be quite straightforward, to chase out the Austrians and unify Italy. The revolution should have no truck with communism or with the terrorism that had blighted the French Revolution in 1793.[37] So long as there was some chance that the royalists in Turin would cooperate, he urged people to avoid any call for a republic. Republicanism would in any case remain a side issue: discussion of such constitutional matters would eventually depend on how the existing sovereigns of Italy reacted in face of the common enemy, and 'we shall not try to

impose our own views'. His earlier organisation, Young Italy, was therefore dissolved in order to unite all patriots in a common front.[38]

The Revolution of 1848

The year 1848 produced revolutionary outbreaks all over Europe and
Mazzini took pride from the fact that they started in Italy. In January
there were serious disturbances throughout much of the country, not
directly instigated by him though his friends and followers took an active
part, and they were all examples of the kind of spontaneous popular
movements that he consistently advocated – but which the Moderates
usually discouraged. In Milan a refusal to pay taxes led to forcible repression by the Austrian Marshal Radetzky, with many casualties. In Venice
the police were warned that Mazzini was planning 'a national enterprise',
and Daniele Manin was imprisoned by the Austrian authorities after
presenting a demand for Venetian home rule. In Tuscany there was
rioting in Livorno against the Grand Duke, and in Genoa an impressive
popular demonstration was attributed by Charles Albert to Mazzini's
influence.[39]

The motivation behind these disturbances was diverse. In Sicily, where
a successful rising took place at Palermo against Naples and its Bourbon
king, some insurgents flew the yellow and red flag of Sicilian separatism
while others raised the tricolour flag that was the symbol of Italian union.
As important, though patriotic historians could admit the fact only in
private, were *mafioso* gang-leaders with less idealistic objectives – one
future restaurant-owner in London's Soho recalled how he marched with
a hundred villagers into Palermo searching for plunder and carrying the
head of a policeman impaled on a stick.[40] Mazzini at first regarded this
Sicilian rising as premature and knew that it might easily be exploited by
separatists or reactionaries, but was nevertheless not displeased that some
of his own followers participated: they were setting an example to other
regions of what could be done by popular agitation wherever people
possessed enough self-confidence.

One dramatic result of the Sicilian revolt was to frighten King
Ferdinand into granting to his subjects an 'irrevocable' constitution with
a representative assembly, an example followed reluctantly by the Grand
Duke Leopold of Tuscany, and in March, with equal reluctance, by Pope
Pius and Charles Albert, who had sworn on oath to do no such thing.
These were extraordinary developments after so many years of political
stagnation and were another indication that public opinion could no
longer be ignored. Mazzini was nevertheless worried that such constitu-

tional reforms might result in weakening revolutionary sentiment: 'I fear them, not because I am a republican, but because I want a single Italian nation.' Yet he welcomed the advantage that the grant of press freedom would give to his own political propaganda, and equally welcome was the possibility that Austria might be provoked into armed intervention, which could only encourage national consciousness and the desire for independence from foreign interference. Another unexpected if unpublished bonus was that the British, hostile as ever to revolution, warned Austria that they might conceivably fight on the Italian side if Metternich continued to provoke revolution by using force against peaceful demonstrations of opinion.[41]

Metternich, by now old and ailing, complained to the British that Young Italy had been one inspiration behind the unrest in Milan, and debates in the French assembly showed that Mazzini was widely recognised in other countries as a threat to the establishment. But almost everyone was caught by surprise when at the end of February a republican revolution in Paris brought the French monarchy to a final and unhappy conclusion. Two days later, Mazzini said he hoped to follow this example by starting a similar insurrection in Milan.[42] Lamberti begged him to return to Paris for urgent consultations, and on 2 March he arrived there with Linton to represent the People's International League. His suggestion was at once adopted to ally with the Italian Moderates in a much more broadly based association to replace the republican Young Italy. At a meeting of some two hundred Italian exiles he was elected in preference to Gioberti as president of this association, after which he issued an appeal to support Charles Albert in winning Lombardy from the Austrians.[43] This astonished and upset some of his republican companions, but realistically he recognised that support from the royal army would make any war far easier to win. Less realistically he hoped that, if others dropped their talk of a republic, the king's supporters would accept a political truce and would not make internal politics an issue until after the war was won.

On 13 March an even more unexpected insurrection took place, this time in Vienna, the capital city of the *ancien régime*, and Metternich was forced into exile. The emperor saved his throne only by renouncing his absolute power. This exciting news, when on 17 March it reached Milan, triggered off five days of rebellion by the civilian populace which forced Radetzky's sixteen thousand soldiers to withdraw from the city. Soon afterwards Venice too declared itself independent. Such an astonishing success surprised almost everyone, but Mazzini had always assumed that this would be how a nationwide revolution would begin. Although he had no direct part in starting the Milanese rising, his propaganda had reached not only the Lombard intellectuals but also some of the shopkeepers and artisans in the city population.[44] His main regret was that, once the Austrians left Milan, they were replaced by a provisional government dominated by the patrician classes: these men had mostly been prudent enough to hold aloof from the actual fighting and now begged Charles Albert to save them from what looked like becoming a much more dangerous nationwide revolution inspired by republicans.[45]

Nor was Charles Albert a friend of revolution – not at least unless it was the kind of rebellion he had secretly instigated against the federal government in Switzerland and against a rival dynasty in France. Monarchist or republican France was in the king's opinion as great an enemy to Piedmont as was imperial Austria, and as late as 22 March, at the same time as the Austrians were suffering defeat by the civilian population of Milan, he was making friendly overtures to the Austrian emperor.[46] But the next day he suddenly ordered his army to intervene in support of the Milanese. One motive for this dramatic change was his desire to claim leadership in the movement for Italian independence, just as Mazzini had urged him to do in 1831. He also saw his chance of annexing Lombardy. And another urgent motive was that, without his intervention, the republicans might take power in Milan. His ministers warned him that failure to act might encourage Genoa to secede from Piedmont and possibly lead to a republican insurrection in Turin itself.[47]

This last reason could not be openly confessed. In public the king promised not to impose his monarchist regime on Lombardy but to leave the 'institutional question' open for future decision by a free popular vote.[48] In private, however, he said the opposite.[49] Far from accepting Mazzini's offer of a political truce, he intended to act as decisively against republicanism as against Austria. He was warned that this would make the war much harder to win[50] but the risk seemed worth taking, especially when reports in April indicated that other more extreme republicans in Genoa and Milan were working independently of Mazzini and might be close to seizing power.[51] The British vice-consul in Milan reported that

> the greatest union had prevailed among all classes; but since His Majesty the King of Sardinia has entered Lombardy, two parties have sprung up: one, the high aristocratic party, is desirous that Lombardy and Piedmont should be united with His Majesty Carlo Alberto for their sovereign; the other, the middle class, in which I must distinguish the commercial and literary people together with all the promising youth, are for a republic.[52]

This second group found leaders in Giuseppe Ferrari and Carlo Cattaneo, two of the more interesting thinkers of the Risorgimento, both of them republicans who feared that the king would exploit Mazzini's political truce in order to crush the revolution. Cattaneo, who had taken a leading part in the street fighting of March, admired Mazzini as 'the precursor of the Risorgimento' whose patriotic propaganda had been one inspiration of this civic revolt.[53] But Cattaneo saw more clearly than Mazzini that Piedmontese intervention was designed to paralyse the popular forces in Milan. He looked on Charles Albert's government as more tyrannical than the Austrian, more dominated by a reactionary clergy in Piedmont and a semi-feudal aristocracy. Ferrari, too, had been an admirer of Mazzini,[54] but like Cattaneo had reservations about complete Italian unification as something that might produce an overcentralised state and an exaggerated nationalism. Both men assumed that personal liberties and a pluralist society would be better guaranteed by a federation of Italian states in which the different interests of each region could be met by concessions to local self-government.

This conflict of opinion inside the republican ranks confronted Mazzini when on 7 April he arrived in Italy after seventeen years of exile. His journey was a triumphal progress. At the Italian frontier he was greeted by customs officials who knew his writings, and at Milan by musical bands to accompany an enthusiastic popular demonstration outside his hotel. Here he met, for the last time in his life, his mother and sister. But despite the excitement he was depressed at arriving too late to consolidate the political truce that he believed necessary if the war was to be won.

At once both main parties sought his alliance. When local republicans asked him to join them in opposition to the king, he tried to persuade them that such internal dissension could only help Austria.[55] From the royalist camp, on 11 April he received a message from Charles Albert in which a hint was dropped that he might conceivably be given a ministerial post at Turin if only he openly accepted the monarchy,[56] and at the very least his advice would be sought in drawing up a truly democratic constitution for a new state of northern Italy. In reply he said he would try to make his friends support the king but only if the latter issued a public statement to confirm this offer and only if the objective was complete unification for the whole of Italy.[57] This the king refused to accept.

Mazzini had made a substantial concession, and although some people questioned his sincerity, he constantly offered this same concession from 1831 to the end of his life – never concealing his personal republican preferences while always ready to subordinate them to any monarchist regime that would undertake a truly patriotic revolution. James Stansfeld, who thought he knew Mazzini better than anyone, was quite sure that his readiness to support a patriotic kingship was absolutely sincere.[58] Indeed for the next month after 11 April, Mazzini continued to observe a political truce[59] even though the royalists refused to do likewise. Despite their initial promise in March to postpone questions of internal politics, the ministers in Turin were determined to impose a monarchist system on Lombardy as the price of their military support.[60] To justify

this intention they invented the excuse that Mazzini was actively working for a republic. Their secret hope, according to one observer at the
king's headquarters, was for the republicans to help the monarchists
by encouraging a further popular movement against the Austrian
army, after which this movement could be exploited to persuade Britain
to back Charles Albert in 'restoring order' by suppressing any republican
opposition.[61]

Because of his momentary negotiations with the royalists, Mazzini was
subjected to much criticism from Ferrari and other republicans. They
even accused him of being a traitor to the revolution, an ally of Austria,
an enemy of the poor, a Moderate, a defender of royalty and the Catholic
priesthood.[62] Other people on the contrary welcomed his evident desire
for reconciliation, his refusal to call for a republic, and his presence
alongside the archbishop in celebrating the feast of Corpus Christi.[63] At
the end of April, Ferrari and Cattaneo tried vainly to persuade him to help
them overturn the provisional government in Milan and obtain French
military support to set up a separate Milanese republic. Cattaneo repeated
that, between Austria and Piedmont, he himself preferred the former;
and Cattaneo was quoted as hinting in a moment of anger that Mazzini
must have accepted a bribe from Turin.[64]

The king's ministers cannot have known, or pretended not to know,
about the extent of this split inside the radical opposition. They inaccurately protested that 'everyone in Milan speaks of wanting a republic and
even of trying to make Genoa secede from Piedmont'.[65] This was their
justification for demanding the immediate annexation of Lombardy and
for threatening otherwise to withdraw from the war.[66] Faced by such a
threat, the provisional government on 12 May was glad to give way: a
plebiscite would be held, but not to choose between annexation or
independence, only on whether annexation should be immediate or
delayed. To defuse any opposition, and as a concession to popular pressure, a promise was made that a constituent assembly would meet after
the war to discuss any necessary changes in the existing constitution of
Piedmont.

This proposal for a constituent assembly was accepted at Turin, albeit
with the greatest reluctance, and acceptance no doubt helped to win an
overwhelming vote for annexation, though as Mazzini now realised there
was no serious intention by the royalists of ever letting such an assembly
meet. He was also correct in judging that the war against Austria would
be greatly weakened as soon as Tuscany, Rome and Naples had this
confirmation that a movement for national independence was being
perverted into an excuse for the 'aggrandisement of Piedmont'. Military
contingents had been sent by the papacy and other Italian states to help
fight against Austria, but were now withdrawn. In any case a plebiscite

held during a war and in the presence of Piedmontese troops was hardly a genuine test of popular wishes. Manin, at the head of a revolutionary government in Venice, agreed with Cattaneo and Mazzini that the king's divisive demand for annexation was the main reason why the patriotic movement of 1848 eventually collapsed.[67]

Mazzini had to admit that he had been ingenuous and outmanoeuvred. There was even an attempt by the monarchists to have him arrested and he received threats of assassination.[68] His political truce had been accepted by the politicians in Turin as a ruse to keep him quiet, not as a means towards military success. On 20 May, to explain his own opinions, he started in Milan his first daily newspaper, the *Italia del Popolo*, which in its brief life became one of the better examples of contemporary journalism in Italy. In its columns he deplored this breach in the patriotic front, but without useless resentment and without picking further quarrels that might undermine the war effort. Though urged again by Cattaneo to help overthrow the Milanese provisional government, he decided instead that annexation could no longer be prevented and rather expressed gratitude to the Piedmontese soldiers who were risking their lives in fighting for the common cause. To push the Austrians back over the Alps and expel them from Venice and Lombardy was his one overriding objective.[69]

His editorials gave him for the first time a chance to explain his opinions to Italians without fear of censorship. His long-term aim was still that of creating a single Italian republic, though he allowed that there was room for discussion with those who thought monarchy or a federal Italy to be a more feasible solution.[70] He could write this in all sincerity because he hoped that the logic of his own republican beliefs would eventually prevail in any free debate. He also reasserted his idea that Europe was a single entity with many basic interests in common, and repeated his hope that one day there would exist a European Congress representing a federation between free and equal nations.[71] Such a congress in his opinion presupposed a new concept of morality in international affairs – morality, not expediency. Rivalry between states posed a permanent threat to peace so long as each country pursued its individual interests without recognising a wider responsibility to the community of nations. In other articles he restated his view that freedom of conscience and of public discussion should be inviolable. Any country that denied such basic rights should be called to account by the international community.[72] By now he had learnt more about the difficulty of reconciling liberty of conscience with the requirements of civil authority, but he innocently hoped that a solution would be easier now that divine right was everywhere giving way to what he called the irresistible rise of democracy.[73]

This public appeal for discussion of constitutional issues was a novel fact in Italian history, but meanwhile the war was going disastrously for the Piedmontese. In June the British government persuaded the Austrians to agree to Charles Albert acquiring Lombardy, and Palmerston was even ready to let him annex Parma, Modena and Tuscany as well; but the king decided to try for still more by risking an attack on Venice, and at the end of July, despite superior numbers, he suffered a major military reverse at Custoza. According to Charles Albert this defeat was due in part to the fact that the army lacked enthusiasm for a war against Austria. This excuse was true among many senior officers, who had been taught to look on Austria as a military ally whereas the Lombards had often been seen as a potential enemy.[74] But another reason for defeat was that the general staff, out of professional rivalry as well as political intolerance, was openly contemptuous of the volunteer units that tried to join the fighting in Lombardy. Political considerations thus took precedence over military common sense. When Garibaldi arrived with a well-trained body of volunteers, his offer of help was rejected by the king on the grounds that collaboration with civilians led by such a soldier of fortune would be dishonourable.[75] Yet at the same time the royalists resented that the civilian population in Lombardy was generally lukewarm and apprehensive about the king's intentions. In Turin it was hard to realise that the Milanese, after defeating Radetzky on their own, were disheartened and suspicious when Charles Albert demanded immediate annexation as the price of his help. One result was that many farmers and peasants of the Lombard countryside preferred to assist the Austrians rather than the invading Italian army.[76]

After defeat at Custoza the king fell back on Milan, hoping to defuse local opposition by promising to defend the city with his life if necessary, but immediately sued for an armistice and fled to Turin amid general derision. His generals caused a further scandal by accusing their own troops of deserting *en masse* out of cowardice.[77] Other more disinterested observers, including Garibaldi, praised the soldiers and rather blamed the total military incompetence of Charles Albert and his staff.[78] Apart from the fact that the king was almost incapacitated by illness, he was a complete amateur in military matters yet refused the request of his ministers to hand over effective command to a professional soldier.[79]

Everyone tried to find a scapegoat for this apparently incomprehensible military reverse. Many Piedmontese backed the king in criticising Mazzini and 'the so-called Italian patriots' for contributing to defeat by their lack of enthusiasm for annexation.[80] Mazzini on the other hand agreed with Manin that 'the fatal idea of aggrandisement on the part of the monarchy had destroyed the Italian revolution'. Many people in Milan were ready to continue the fight under Mazzini's leadership and he thought that with their backing, the war might still have been won,[81] but Charles Albert was determined to prevent any popular participation in the war. Balbo,

Cavour and other politicians in Turin were interested less in creating an Italian nation than in saving the monarchic principle from being swamped by democracy.[82] What Mazzini did not know was that these same royal ministers were all admitting in private that the king's insistence on acting as commander-in-chief was 'the primary cause of this military defeat'. Nor did anyone know that the ministers' request for an official investigation was vetoed by royal command: in military matters the king was still an autocrat and not responsible to parliament. Charles Albert was even told by his own prime minister that the armistice was illegal, unconstitutional and an indication that the monarch saw republicanism rather than Austria as his chief enemy.[83]

Cattaneo was among those who almost welcomed the Piedmontese defeat in the hope that it would restore power to the democratic opposition.[84] On 3 August, Mazzini took a musket and left Milan to join a small group of volunteers under Garibaldi who fiercely criticised the king and refused to accept the royal armistice. For a few days he served in the ranks, enduring long marches under torrential rain before escaping over the frontier into Switzerland. A number of people later recalled his courage and inspiration at this desperate moment.[85] Unfortunately a disagreement arose between him and Garibaldi over what should or could be done to continue the fight, a disagreement that Garibaldi never forgave but in which friends of both men thought Mazzini might well have been in the right.[86] Garibaldi was an experienced fighter who felt that there was little more they could do. Mazzini, however, still believed that a small local insurrection might trigger off another major revolution as the Milanese had shown in March. Determined to keep up the revolutionary momentum, he tried to organise a small expedition from across the Swiss frontier, but Garibaldi refused to take part and it ended badly.

Until the end of the year Mazzini remained in Switzerland, once again isolated and unable to set foot outside his room, spending much of his time reading Gibbon. Yet in Piedmont the semi-official press continued to invent stories about him living luxuriously in the best hotels, sending other people to fight and die while always himself remaining well away from danger.[87] Though his friends protested against such slanders, he himself always disdained to contradict personal criticism. He hoped that his own party would never copy its adversaries by such intolerance. Nor did he deny that there were true patriots among the Moderates in Turin. If together they could unite Italy, even if it was a second-best federal and monarchist Italy, he would accept this and disappear to end his life as an exile in England.[88]

The year 1848 ended with the news of his father's death, 'a man who has been virtuous and thoroughly good', who eventually seems to have shared some of his son's views.[89] The year had brought Mazzini much personal sadness and political disillusionment. The Austrians re-established their control over Lombardy, persecuting, taxing, conscripting a people who in his view were superior to their alien masters in intellect and culture.[90] The downtrodden subject nationalities of Europe, instead of fraternising, had often treated each other as enemies, Croats siding with Austria against Hungary, Hungarians and Germans siding with Austria against Italy. The Italians were internally divided as always, their different regions unwilling to combine, the populace often distrustful of liberal patriotism or at best indifferent. Moreover, some among the patriots were more nationalistic than liberal, while others backed away from action as soon as their class privileges came under threat. Mazzini's vision had proved defective or at least premature.

On the positive side, Venice under Manin was still an independent republic. Also Louis Napoleon was in December elected president of a new French republic. This enigmatic adventurer had in youth been an active revolutionary in Italy, and Mazzini, who had known him slightly in Switzerland and London, was at first cautiously hopeful that he might become a new Washington to lead a 'Holy Alliance of Peoples' against their joint Austrian enemy.[91] A third sensational development was that Pope Pius took sanctuary in Neapolitan territory after his chief minister in Rome was assassinated – a death for which Mazzini was quite unfairly blamed.[92] The papal authorities were still intercepting come of Mazzini's correspondence[93] and knew that their own problems in Rome came not so much from republicans as from liberal Moderates who wanted not revolution but constitutional government. When Pius refused repeated appeals by these Moderates for his return to Rome, a decision was taken by the civic authorities to summon a constituent assembly and install a provisional government to save the papal state from anarchy. Mazzini could have hoped for nothing better.

The Roman Republic

Early in February 1849, the elected assembly in Rome, confronted by the pope's refusal of repeated requests for his return, opted to constitute a new republic and declared the temporal power of the papacy to be at an end. A few days later a revolution in Florence dethroned the grand duke. Mazzini hurried back to Italy hoping to unite Tuscany and Rome as the nucleus of an independent Italian nation. Landing in the Tuscan port of Livorno, though known only by reputation, he received a spontaneous and enthusiastic popular reception. Even people who strongly disagreed with his republican views admitted that he was now the most prominent person on the Italian political scene.[94]

At Florence he was overjoyed to find Giuditta Sidoli after many years of enforced separation. But he was unhappy to find that the republican administration, headed by a former companion, Francesco Guerrazzi, wanted to keep Tuscany independent. Guerrazzi, while admiring the patriotism of a man 'who disturbed the sleep of kings and terrified the great powers of Europe',[95] was envious and distrustful when his one-time friend was welcomed by huge popular demonstrations. Mazzini addressed the Florentine crowds in surprisingly moderate terms, urging them to support Guerrazzi[96] but also to merge their own regional loyalties into a nationwide movement. He was disturbed to find inter-regional rivalries still strong all over Italy, and almost as strong were territorial divisions inside Tuscany itself, yet he correctly judged that an independent Tuscan republic could hardly survive unless all patriotic Italians put minor differences aside. He gambled on using popular pressure to influence the provisional government, and it was a cruel disappointment when Guerrazzi refused to give way.[97]

He therefore moved to Rome, where a unanimous vote of the elected assembly had granted him honorary citizenship. This was his first visit to the city, but it had always been at the centre of his political dreams and was the only conceivable capital for his idealised Italy. Arriving early in March he met another welcoming crowd and was immediately invited to address the assembly. In his speech he called on Romans to take this chance of showing how patriotism was not hostile to religion. They should also prove to the outside world that freedom and equality could coexist in their republic. Liberty of conscience and speech were rights to be enjoyed by everyone, and there should be no intolerance, no hatred of political opponents, only a united effort to win national independence. Quoting Cromwell he urged his hearers to 'put your trust in God and keep your powder dry'. They should invite monarchist Piedmont as well as republican Venice and Florence to unite in a joint effort to end the Austrian occupation of Italy.[98]

Foreign diplomats confirmed the current opinion that the two outstanding personalities in Italian politics were Mazzini and Charles Albert, and the former was the real leader of the national movement.[99] But another attempt by the republicans to join forces with the king was rebuffed. Gioberti, who for several months had been prime minister of Piedmont, repeated the accusation that Mazzini was a greater enemy of Italy than the Austrians, as well as being a puerile politician, a coward, a mystic whose name would be abhorred by posterity.[100] Far from accepting republican help, the Piedmontese government was determined to reassert its leadership in Italy by invading Tuscany and Rome to defeat the republicans and restore papal and grand-ducal authority.

Among other politicans in Turin, Cavour backed Gioberti in wanting to use force against the two central Italian republics that had hoisted the tricolour flag of Italian patriotism.[101] Cavour also supported Charles Albert's desperate decision to renew war against Austria, hoping that such a war would diminish Mazzini's influence and recapture prestige for the monarchy by the annexation of Lombardy; and Cavour added that any Lombards who resisted such annexation should be executed without pity. He expected that the Austrians would be defeated, but even their victory would be preferable if the alternative was Piedmontese acceptance of help from the republicans.[102]

A very different opinion was held by the Austrian commander Radetzky, who judged that Charles Albert by renewing the war would unwittingly be assisting the diffusion of republican sentiment, and indeed that the king would unintentionally be acting as 'the chief agent of Mazzini'.[103] When war was declared by Piedmont against Austria in mid-March, Charles Albert felt sure of a quick success that would let him impose his own terms on the Lombards before they had time to raise objections.[104] But after three days he suffered another military defeat at Novara and at once abdicated. Nor was there any consolation in knowing that some Italian regiments in the Austrian army again fought well and contributed to Radetzky's success.[105] Gioberti's egocentric comment was that 'the Italian Risorgimento, begun by myself, is now at an end'.[106]

Such pessimism was not shared by Mazzini. Though dismayed by the defeat, he was not surprised. He had been hoping that the war would not begin until other Italian states and Garibaldi's volunteers could contribute to helping Charles Albert expel Radetzky's army, and he had little idea that this union of forces, as during the war of 1848, was precisely what the king was again hoping to avoid. One of Mazzini's first actions in Rome was to overcome opposition from the extreme republicans and persuade the assembly to send ten thousand troops to assist the royal army. But far from welcoming his offer of help, the Piedmontese generals did not so much as acknowledge it but denounced him as the root cause of a national catastrophe. Among moderate politicians in Turin, the new prime minister, Massimo d'Azeglio, agreed with Gioberti in calling Mazzini a cowardly terrorist who instead of helping the Italian cause had done it nothing but harm, and other monarchists denounced him as 'a bloodthirsty criminal'.[107]

The object of this intemperate accusation was kinder than some Piedmontese politicians in finding excuses for the royalists who, if they had once more led the country to disaster, were acting from miscalculation and weakness of resolve rather than perversity. He acknowledged that the rank and file in the royal army had done their best, but the absence of public accountability allowed the king to appoint incompetent generals by favouritism and nepotism;[108] and most of Charles Albert's ministers shared the same opinion.[109] But the military commanders in Turin continued to repeat that Mazzini was a greater enemy than Radetzky, and some of them still thought of their war as being fought less against Austria than against republicans among the population of Lombardy. This scornful attitude towards other patriotic Italians was one reason for the defeat of Novara.[110]

Mazzini in Rome revived *Italia del Popolo* as the newspaper of his National Association and used it to repeat his demand for a political truce among all parties who wanted Italian independence inside a new international order. This call for a united front met little response from other regions, especially after the defeated Piedmontese army bombarded and sacked Genoa to defeat those of his friends who were hoping to continue the war. He was not keen to take part personally in the government of Rome,[111] not at least until the assembly voted overwhelmingly for him to change his mind. Some members wanted to make him dictator.[112] His own proposal was to appoint a governing triumvirate to work with the assembly and he suggested the names of Aurelio Saffi and Carlo Armellini, to which he eventually agreed that his own name be added.[113] So began the hundred days that were the one period in his life when he had practical experience of government, during which he and Garibaldi became the chief actors in what G. M. Trevelyan called 'one of the great scenes of history'.

The desperate situation of Rome would have daunted anyone lacking belief in providence and the ultimate triumph of nationality. Most rich people had fled the city before Mazzini's arrival, and their absence was causing serious unemployment. A new constitution and legal system were needed to replace papal autocracy and had to be devised at a time when the pope summoned the leading Catholic powers of Europe to restore autocratic clerical government by force of arms. Pius had dissociated himself from the war against Austria by arguing that the papacy 'must embrace with equal paternal earnestness of love all tribes, peoples and nations', but three countries now sent armies at the pope's urgent request to fight against a small republic which lacked soldiers and money and had a large unfortified city to defend.

Inside the Roman assembly were a dozen critics of the republican government but no effective opposition to what soon became virtual rule by a single man; and even some critics admitted that, in difficult circumstances, Mazzini governed with wisdom, moderation and unexpected administrative capacity, so increasing Italy's reputation in the rest of Europe.[114] Unlike the cardinals whose government he replaced, he lived without pomp or ceremony in a single room, unguarded, eating in a nearby *trattoria*, allowing free access to any citizen.[115] Among foreigners who visited him, the poet Arthur Hugh Clough was full of admiration for his 'wonderful courage and a glorious generosity'; the American diplomatic representative Lewis Cass found him 'a man of great integrity of character and of extensive intellectual acquirements'. The American writer Margaret Fuller, who was now in Rome, confirmed her opinion that he was 'a man of genius, an elevated thinker . . . the only great Italian . . . in action decisive and full of resource as Caesar', to whom 'only the next age can do justice'.[116]

If Mazzini's government survived until July it was because he was seen to be an honest man who could be trusted. His survival was the more remarkable since it defied a papal excommunication of all members of the assembly and the hundreds of thousands who had voted for them. From outside Rome a sustained attack was mounted against him by moderate Italian liberals as well as loyal papalists who invented stories about a reign of terror in Rome characterised by cruelties, wanton spoliation and even people being buried alive. Witnesses among the inhabitants of Rome, including some not friendly to the revolution, testified that these stories were quite untrue and, despite lack of police, public security was far more effective than under the previous ecclesiastical administration.[117] Although Mazzini is still sometimes accused of having used his position to attack religion,[118] the new republican constitution declared Catholicism to be the official state religion and guaranteed the pope's spiritual authority. Mazzini risked offending the anticlerical Garibaldi by encouraging the regular continuance of religious observances. On Easter day he joined foreign diplomats in attending mass in St Peter's, and the papalists were outraged with him for doing so, at the same time as criticising his supposed hostility to religion.

His principles and conduct were in fact far removed from the anticlericalism that his critics alleged. Some of the local clergy rallied to the revolution and a foreign Catholic journalist who was present reported unanimous 'dismay and protest' at the prospect of a return to papal rule.[119] Admittedly the Inquisition was abolished and some of its property used to house the poor – which led some people to accuse the republican government of advocating communism.[120] But confiscation of Church possessions was effected by Catholic governments elsewhere in Italy where it benefited the rich, and Cavour himself, whose newspaper depicted Mazzini as another Robespierre,[121] owed much of his family's wealth to this same source. The clerical monopoly in university teaching was ended and popular education was at long last positively encouraged. Also the removal of clerical censorship led for the first time to dozens of newspapers being published, something unheard of under the previous regime. Among other practical changes the death penalty was abolished; so were protective duties that hindered trade and agriculture; the secret ecclesiastical courts lost their monopoly of justice and were replaced by a lay judiciary; taxes were adjusted to help poorer citizens; and, most challenging of all, there was to be religious toleration. Mazzini had little time to apply these reforms and they were abrogated as soon as papal government was restored, but the memory survived as a bench-mark to guide later generations.

An even more valuable memory was of how Rome proceeded to defend its independence in some of the most successful and heroic military engagements of the Risorgimento. Mazzini was assisted in Rome by a group of patriots who became important in his later life and who now helped to create an enduring legend for posterity. Apart from Garibaldi and Giacomo Medici whom he already knew, there were Count Saffi and Maurizio Quadrio who subsequently became his closest disciples. Among other notable figures were Carlo Pisacane, a professional soldier, and Giovanni Nicotera, both from the minor Neapolitan aristocracy. The Milanese doctor Agostino Bertani helped the Princess Belgiojoso and Margaret Fuller with ambulance and hospital services. None of these people had much confidence in victory against the combined forces of conservative Europe, but they agreed with Mazzini over creating a 'myth of Rome' for the future. Such a myth confirmed the right of this town to become in course of time the national capital to which the other regional capitals could, without loss of self-respect, concede priority; and in such a divided nation this was an immense achievement. The heroism of Italian volunteers drawn from all over Italy and fighting against foreign invaders was another powerful factor in convincing the rest of Europe that an Italian nation should exist in fact as well as theory. Restoration of the pope's temporal sovereignty could take place only as a result of foreign military imposition, and its survival after 1849 would require martial law and a permanent foreign military presence in Rome,[122] which meant that it was artificial and could not last.

In response to an appeal from Pius, armies were sent by Austria, Spain and Naples to restore him to his throne. France in April sent a fourth, despite the fact that the French republican constitution of 1848 enjoined respect for other nationalities and forbad using force against the liberties of other peoples. Louis Napoleon, the new French president, needed Catholic support for his plan to establish a personal dictatorship and therefore needed to crush democratic republicanism in Rome. French national interests also required the occupation of Rome so as to prevent the Austrians from overrunning central Italy. Napoleon's use of force to suppress the Roman republic was positively welcomed by many of the Moderates in Turin. The new King Victor Emanuel even wanted to join

the other conservative powers and regain prestige for his recently conquered army by helping to defeat the republic.[123]

General Oudinot, when he landed near Rome with a French expedi-
tionary force on 24 April, met no initial resistance because he deceitfully
promised to respect the wishes of the Roman population, but his secret
orders were to reimpose papal rule, if necessary by force.[124] He never
doubted that the Romans would welcome deliverance from the communists, atheists and mercenary soldiers who, according to his information,
were governing their republic. He did not know, or pretended not to
know, that even many devout Catholics in Rome were anxious not to
restore a corrupt and tyrannical papal regime that invited foreign powers
to make war on Roman territory.[125] Local indignation was only increased
when an envoy from Oudinot made the tactless remark that 'Italians
are too cowardly to fight'.[126] The French commander was the more
astonished when on 30 April his attack on Rome was repulsed with heavy
casualties. What was almost worse, Mazzini then released hundreds of
captured French soldiers as a goodwill gesture, which was regarded in
Paris as an insufferable insult.[127]

The triumvirs were never forgiven by Garibaldi for not letting him
chase the retreating French, but the decision was politically justifiable,
especially as many French politicians were strongly opposed to Napoleon's war policy. There were risks either way. The republican force defending Rome consisted of fewer than twenty thousand men, including
many volunteers from different Italian regions and not yet welded into an
army. Not only did they lack an offensive capacity, but the French were
far better armed. Garibaldi, the one outstanding republican general, was
headstrong and sometimes had difficulty in obeying orders: never happy
in a subordinate role, he thought he should be made commander-in-chief
of the Roman forces, and one account says that Mazzini proposed this
appointment. But many Romans distrusted Garibaldi as a 'foreigner' from
northern Italy. Moreover other staff officers, notably Pisacane, on whom
Mazzini relied as the main organiser of defence, thought him a defective
tactician and instead supported the appointment of a Roman, Pietro
Roselli.[128] Whether or not this choice of commander was justifiable, it
rankled with Garibaldi for the rest of his life.

Mazzini correctly calculated that the one, perhaps remote, chance of
survival was if the republican government in France changed sides to help
him against an alliance of European monarchies, and he therefore played
for time until the French elections at the end of May. If those elections
produced a government that sanctioned Napoleon's invasion, there was
no hope of any long-term resistance. He first tried to obtain help from the
other revolutionary governments in Venice, Tuscany and Sicily, but each
region was fully occupied in fighting for its own independence. Bologna

and Florence were both captured by Austrian forces during May. In Turin some politicians felt ashamed at leaving the Romans to fight on their own, but others agreed with Cavour in resenting Mazzini's success and hoped that the French would assist the Piedmontese Moderates by showing even more vigour in suppressing the Roman revolution.[129] Garibaldi, again with inferior numbers, after scoring two minor victories over the Neapolitans would have liked to pursue them across their frontier and again blamed Mazzini for holding him back. Pisacane and Roselli, however, thought that Garibaldi's disobedience on this occasion prevented what might have become a greater military success.[130]

Not even that success, however, could conceivably have won the war without a change of heart in France. The triumvirs continued to hope that Napoleon's rivalry with Austria would eventually persuade the French to support the Roman republic, and were encouraged when Ferdinand De Lesseps was sent from Paris to negotiate a settlement. This young diplomat, the future architect of the Suez Canal, had orders to avoid any formal recognition of the Roman republic, but nevertheless was authorised to repeat Oudinot's assurance that the French would not thwart any clearly expressed wishes of the local population. What no one, not even De Lesseps, knew was that General Oudinot had secret orders to act much more aggressively if the Romans did not capitulate.[131]

Mazzini's negotiating ability on this occasion was much praised except by those who favoured capitulation. During a truce of two weeks he was conciliatory. De Lesseps had assumed from what he was told in Paris that he would be dealing with a terrorist, 'a modern Nero' who was no better than a vulgar and deceitful braggart,[132] and was surprised to find someone trustworthy and moderate. In reporting to Paris, the French envoy praised Mazzini for 'the nobility of his feelings, the honesty of his principles, his great capacity, integrity and courage'; and the local correspondent of *The Times* agreed that 'so far as style and matter go' the triumvir 'reduced his diplomatic adversary to very small dimensions indeed'.[133] De Lesseps was astonished to find that 'there was universal opposition in Rome to any return to clerical administration'. Not only had the republican assembly been voted into existence by universal suffrage, but the Frenchman had to admit that it enjoyed a great deal of enthusiastic popular support and was much less in need of the repressive police action formerly employed by the pope.[134]

Negotiations were concluded on 31 May when the triumvirs signed an agreement with the French welcoming them as an ally in defending the city against Austria. De Lesseps was observed embracing Mazzini and promising that Paris would now support the republic,[135] but the next day a message from Paris refused to ratify his signed agreement. Napoleon, after winning the elections in France, had no further need to negotiate.

Meanwhile Oudinot had taken advantage of a truce to occupy a commanding position on one of the hills dominating Rome, and by another ruse cleverly caught the defenders off-guard by resuming his attack more than twenty-four hours before the truce was due to expire. Garibaldi again led a brilliant resistance that saved the republic for another month but threatened resignation unless given dictatorial powers; or, failing that, he wanted Mazzini to take personal responsibility for directing the war instead of leaving decisions to Pisacane and Roselli. But Mazzini insisted that he himself was incompetent to take military decisions on his own.[136]

Some of the Moderates in Piedmont continued to have mixed feelings about the fighting in Rome, recognising that it was honourable for Italian volunteers to resist a large regular army; but there was also resentment that, whereas the royal army had been humiliated by defeats at Custoza and Novara, Garibaldi and his irregular forces enjoyed the prestige of military victories. Balbo was contemptuous of what was happening in Rome.[137] Azeglio, the new prime minister, looked forward with pleasure to Garibaldi's defeat and disdainfully spoke of the Roman republic as a comic interlude in a grand opera. Azeglio and Farini were as anxious as Gioberti to restore the pope and the grand duke to their thrones where they would support the cause of conservatism against the threat from republicanism and democracy.[138] Likewise Cavour, not yet a minister, deplored the enthusiasm generated by Garibaldi and continued to hope for victory by the French, because he thought that Mazzini, by continuing to fight, 'was doing more harm than anyone to the cause of Italy'.[139]

The French commander wanted to avoid fighting in the streets of Rome against a master of guerrilla warfare. He preferred to shell the city and cut off water and food. The foreign consuls in Rome made a collective protest against his artillery bombardment that lasted throughout June. Pius IX was equally dismayed by the destruction and spoke sympathetically of the courage shown by the defenders, but his secretary of state, Cardinal Antonelli, protested that the bombardment was insufficiently intense.[140] The French foreign minister, Alexis De Tocqueville, fearing that the rest of Europe would see this method of fighting as barbaric, decided to replace Oudinot by another less Fabian general who could bring this unfortunate war to a speedy end. He must have been encouraged when some inhabitants of Rome made secret overtures to the attacking force.[141]

Mazzini had been hoping for one final battle. He needed to show the world that, though monarchies might capitulate, republicans would never voluntarily renounce a mandate given to them by a popular vote. His military commanders, who attended a council of war on 30 June, retained confused memories of what was said, but most agreed that they should refuse surrender and either fight in the streets or else move into the countryside further north to continue the war against Austria. Mazzini was ready to adopt either plan but accepted Garibaldi's insistence on the latter. When he summoned the assembly into secret session, an acrimonious discussion revealed that public opinion lacked his apocalyptic vision and, perhaps sensibly, preferred to avoid further loss of life. He accordingly resigned his office. Others could sign a capitulation, but he himself would never impugn a myth that was needed for the next stage in the Risorgimento.[142]

At the beginning of July, when Garibaldi led a remnant of his volunteers into the hills of the Abruzzi, Mazzini decided not to join them. Apart from his recent disagreement with Garibaldi, he needed to demonstrate that the Roman population would not turn against him in defeat, and in fact he remained unmolested for over a week after French troops occupied the city. De Tocqueville was anxious to help anyone to escape from papal reprisals.[143] The United States legation offered the ex-triumvir a passport in the name of George Moore, and the British consulate earned a reproach from Lord Palmerston by issuing five hundred passports to other refugees. Eventually, after preparing for the future by organising a secret resistance movement in the city, Mazzini was helped by a friendly French ship's captain to reach safety. The ship stopped briefly at Genoa, but he dared not go ashore to see his family or he would have been imprisoned as a convicted criminal. Gladstone, passing through Genoa, saw pictures of Mazzini and Garibaldi proudly displayed in shop windows, but few of Charles Albert and none of the pope.[144] Proceeding to Marseilles, Mazzini again had to be smuggled ashore to hide in what he called a 'madhouse' until he found the means for escaping to Switzerland.

The Roman republic had been so short-lived that a balanced judgement is not easily formulated, but one relevant comparison is with what followed. Louis Napoleon may or may not have been sincere in persuading himself that the Romans eagerly awaited restoration of the old regime, and De Tocqueville promised to restore freedom to a city ravaged by 'the tyranny of Mazzini' whose 'reign of terror' had been universally hated.[145] The French minister even claimed in public that the Roman population greeted the occupying forces with joy, though in private admitted that this was untrue, as many foreigners in Rome confirmed.[146] French soldiers with fixed bayonets prevented the elected members from entering the assembly and proceeded to suppress any criticism by banning all newspapers. Perhaps at first they believed the accusations against Mazzini of financial corruption and introducing communism. What their auditors later discovered was that management of government finance, despite enormous difficulties, had been more scrupulous and efficient under the republicans than previously by the papal curia.[147]

The French had known from the first that they were in a false position. They wanted to restore the temporal sovereignty of the pope but only in the expectation that he would permit another elected assembly and some degree of public financial accountability. Pius, however, refused any concessions at all and his refusal was known before the French reached Rome. De Tocqueville's new information, confirmed by other observers, was that the 'detestable' and secretive system of ecclesiastical law courts made priestly government universally abhorred in Rome so that only a permanent presence of foreign troops would prevent another insurrection.[148] According to Azeglio, the pope unintentionally 'was working on behalf of Mazzini and for the destruction of religious belief in Italy'.[149]

Pius in July 1849 was still living as a refugee in southern Italy and read the situation differently. Far from showing any gratitude to the French he was annoyed that Mazzini and Garibaldi had not been captured by them and brought to justice. He confessed that his reforms of 1846–7 had been a tragic mistake and demanded that the French, being in Rome by his invitation, should resist any demand for political freedom. Almost at once the Inquisition was brought back; so were public floggings and the guillotine; executions became frequent though there had been not one under the republic. Moderate conservatives in Rome, who had been left in peace by the republic despite their opposition, were sent into exile. Once again the Jews, liberated by the republicans, were confined in the ghetto, and priests were sometimes punished for having continued their ministry under the republic.[150] Foreign visitors to Rome in the next few months were startled by the corruption and lack of security. Unlike what *The Times* of London and the conservative *Quarterly Review* had led people to imagine, 'Rome was never so well governed as under the republic'.[151]

Despite Mazzini's apparent failure, his reputation was greatly enhanced in other countries as well as over much of Italy. His defeat was described by Stansfeld as 'the brightest and saddest page in the history of the Italian movement'. The historian Michelet wrote with envy of what he had done, and his considerable talent as a politician was admitted even by Radetzky's chief of staff.[152] Gladstone reached Rome a few days after the republic collapsed, and though no friend of revolution was impressed by the lack of popular feeling against Mazzini or in favour of the pope's return. Walter Bagehot, celebrated editor of the *Economist*, recalled being thrilled by the sincerity and disinterestedness of someone who had shown himself 'a perfect marvel of sagacity and moderation' with 'a very rare administrative power'. Dickens wrote that Mazzini must at once be brought 'home' to England, 'for the world cannot well afford to lose such men'. Bulwer Lytton, the novelist, confessed to never having known such heroism in so noble but hopeless a cause. The great hero-worshipper Thomas Carlyle was still something of a sceptic but noted in his diary that

Mazzini was now among the select band of heroes, having 'one element of noble perennial truth that pervaded him wholly', which one day might rouse Italy into a new period of greatness.[153] These were private opinions but not without importance as an indication of support for the Italian revolution.

The republican leader was himself convinced that the spirited defence of Rome had been an immense moral success on the road to national unification and to ending the pope's temporal power. Inside Italy, as well as making Garibaldi into a celebrity, the siege of Rome won more widespread support for Mazzini than he enjoyed at any other time in his life.[154] But because of their popularity these two patriots were regarded with all the more suspicion by the Moderates in Piedmont. Cavour once more called them fatal enemies of Italy and liberty.[155] Gioberti, who had agreed with Cavour in wanting to send Piedmontese troops to destroy the Roman republic, now inexplicably blamed Mazzini for letting that republic collapse and again called him a greater national enemy than the Austrians who without his interference would by now have been defeated.[156] Others agreed with this bizarre criticism, and quite as unfairly ridiculed his escape to Switzerland as another typical example of a cowardly retreat to comfort and security. Some Piedmontese even offered to help the Austrians in their fight against this dangerous patriotic revolutionary.[157]

Massimo d'Azeglio, one of the more moderate and honourable of contemporary Italian politicians, agreed that a republic might be the ideal form of government, but thought that Italians lacked the requisite sense of civic duty and moral responsibility. He regarded Mazzini as well-intentioned but also as a major obstacle in the way of Piedmont's claim to leadership in Italy.[158] As head of government, Azeglio generously offered refuge to exiles from other parts of Italy provided they renounced politics, but refused entry to those whom he contemptuously called the italianissimi, the radical patriots who had done so much to arouse the admiration of Europe. He protested to the British against their new enthusiasm for Mazzini. He also refused to let Garibaldi return home to rejoin his family. Having fought for the Roman republic, Garibaldi was deemed to have forfeited civic rights in his homeland, and when a majority in the Piedmontese parliament passed a vote of censure on the prime minister for what was called a violation of the constitution as well as a lack of human charity, the government paid no attention to this parliamentary vote and was supported by Cavour and Balbo.[159] These leading politicians in Turin knew that the Piedmontese monarchy had suffered in reputation after two lost wars and could not afford to make concessions to such a potentially dangerous popular hero.

Charles Albert's successor, his son Victor Emanuel, was in later years given an accolade by the Moderates for saving liberal government and championing Italian nationality, but in 1849 was coldly received when he arrived in Turin to swear allegiance to the constitution.[160] He had been brought up a dedicated enemy of liberalism and, in private, now told the Austrians about wanting to use his army to crush the hostile majority in parliament.[161] His ministers tactfully persuaded him that any such action would produce the opposite result to what he intended. They preferred to mount a propaganda campaign against the *italianissimi*, trying to persuade public opinion in Turin that Mazzini was not only a coward but an anarchist and communist; worse still, that he was plotting to assassinate Louis Napoleon and was working in close alliance with Palmerston to convert Italy to Protestantism.[162] And some people perhaps believed these fanciful accusations.

CHAPTER FOUR

Further Conspiracies after 1850

Back to the drawing board

FOR SIX MONTHS after leaving Rome, Mazzini remained in the relative security of Switzerland. His mother sent £100 for living expenses, much of which was used to help fifty other refugees from Rome while he tried to reassemble his revolutionary organisation. He asked his family to send more of his books, including Adam Smith's *Wealth of Nations* and Wordsworth's poems. Unable to move freely, he read and sometimes played chess. He was in fairly good health, 'only a little tormented with face-ache'. To his sorrow he had lost most of his few personal possessions in his clandestine flight from Rome, including what he thought his most important manuscript writing and notes for his proposed book on the religious question. Hiding near Lausanne he began to translate the New Testament into Italian.[1]

Sometimes he was depressed and avoided company, but Saffi recalled much laughter as Mazzini 'spread joviality around him'.[2] After his experience in Rome he had a great reputation among the other exiles in Switzerland. To the Romanian, Nicholae Balcescu, he was without doubt the leading revolutionary in Europe.[3] According to the distinguished Russian exile Alexander Herzen, he was the finest politician of them all, though insufficiently aware of the need for social as well as political revolution: he was 'simple and amiable in his manner, but the habit of ruling is apparent, especially in argument; he can scarcely conceal his annoyance at contradiction'. Herzen noted some indication of fanaticism and asceticism. 'An active concentrated intelligence sparkled in his melancholy eyes', but also 'an infinity of persistence and strength of will'. His network of secret conspiracy was truly astonishing: 'there has never been such a revolutionary organisation anywhere'.[4]

The details of this organisation are impossible to trace because a by now practised conspirator preferred to use inconspicuous couriers and warned his friends not to trust the secrecy of the postal services; but the network was less extensive and reliable than his friends or enemies imagined. Another lesson he had learnt was to postpone any plans for another insurrection while he made a careful calculation of resources and feasible objectives.[5] His chief hope as always was that at some point another European crisis would provide another opportunity for action, and next time he thought he might rely on strong support in the United States and England. For the present his task was to spread the word, to obtain new recruits and prevent too many defections. For this purpose he again revived his paper *Italia del Popolo* at Lausanne. It now had a print run of four thousand copies, a large circulation by contemporary standards. The first issue had to be reprinted when many copies went astray or were confiscated by the police and postal authorities.

The chief target of his newspaper articles remained the Austrian domination over Italy, but he also criticised the Piedmontese Moderates. Throughout 1850, according to Cavour, the 'deplorable influence' of this rebel continued to spread almost everywhere, and very numerous diplomatic documents testify to the fear he inspired.[6] Azeglio, who was much travelled and knew the rest of Italy far better than either Cavour or Mazzini, was convinced that patriotism and national independence meant nothing at all to the vast majority of Italians; nor could this prime minister accept Mazzini's belief that Italians possessed the qualities needed for self-government. Nor even did Azeglio think that the small political class in Piedmont had much aptitude for the constitutional regime that an absolutist sovereign had unenthusiastically conceded in 1848.[7]

Politicians in Turin continued to look on Mazzinian propaganda as no less a threat than either Austrian imperialism or Catholic fundamentalism. They even copied the Austrians by setting up a small bureau of espionage at Geneva with the aim of inducing some republican exiles to defect and become informers. One spy was arrested by the Swiss after confessing, whether truthfully or not, that he had orders to kidnap Mazzini and bring him to justice in Turin.[8] Azeglio not only arrested Garibaldi and sent him again into exile, but in a moment of panic planned to deport twenty thousand other dangerous democrats to America, and tried to persuade Austria and France to help pay for this mass exodus. He also threatened to take reprisals against the Swiss if they failed to expel Mazzini and his small group of companions. An order of expulsion had already been signed in Berne, but the Swiss protested against foreign interference in their affairs. The police in Switzerland had in any case learnt how hard it was to discover the many hiding-places of this elusive refugee, who in fact was protected by the cantonal authorities in Geneva, Vaud and Ticino so that he successfully remained in concealment until May 1850.[9]

He then went at some risk to spend three weeks in France. Among his French contacts were Jules Michelet, his great admirer George Sand, and the political philosopher Edgar Quinet. In Paris he had talks with others representing a wide range of opinion, including Daniele Manin, the recently ousted governor of republican Venice, as well as the recusant Catholic priest Lamennais. He met the socialist Louis Blanc and also the president's cousin, Prince Jerome Napoleon. Disappointed at finding little encouragement he then returned briefly to England, where exiles were now gathered from all the main European countries. Here he was involved in organising two benefit concerts to help other refugees and, most unusually, took two days' holiday by the sea in Sussex. But he felt remorse at being so far away from Italy where he hoped to start another insurrection before the end of the year. Moving back secretly to Geneva in September he thought that this might be his last winter before return-ing home finally to Genoa, but it was a forlorn expectation. As an illegal immigrant in Switzerland he again had to live in hiding, frequently changing his address, and renewed protests arrived from the Austrian and French governments. When inaccurate reports again circulated about his being seen in Genoa and in Germany, he wished he could have been 'endowed with that power of ubiquity which is attributed to me by the reactionary papers'. In February 1851 he travelled again to London for what he assumed would be a month at most, though for the rest of his life it remained his one sure refuge and base of operations.

One permanent reason for being disheartened was finance. Lack of money was, he thought, the main reason why the Roman republic had failed to extend its influence into other regions. Only if Italians backed him financially could he with self-respect appeal to foreign generosity.[10] One of the last acts of the Roman assembly had been to announce a 'national loan' of ten million lire (£40,000) in bonds redeem-able when the revolution succeeded. This was a hazardous procedure because failure would publicly expose his lack of support. No balance sheet of the proceeds, perhaps for this reason, was ever produced, though Mazzini reported that collection started well and it certainly caused alarm in Vienna, Rome and Tuscany.[11] Subscriptions in Piedmont could not be prevented and this must have given him useful publicity. Among prominent Frenchmen who subscribed were Victor Hugo, Jules Favre, Quinet and Eugène Sue, but subscribers in Austrian Lombardy and Ven-ice could be executed if caught with bonds in their possession.[12] Cattaneo warned that rich Italians would never contribute to such a risky fund, and some of Mazzini's disillusioned friends refused to help, while a good deal of the money seems to have disappeared before he could receive and bank it in London.[13] Mazzini had hoped that the Rothschilds as good businessmen would see the advantage of hedging their bets by speculat-ing on revolution, but they were accustomed to calculating risks and preferred lending to the pope and the Austrians, who offered far better security.

Naples, Sicily and Sardinia were the Italian regions where Mazzini had fewest contacts. The high rate of illiteracy was one barrier to his propaganda in the south, but even educated southern exiles were reluctant to subscribe to his national fund.[14] Politicians in Turin were nevertheless alarmed by the extent of his influence in Sardinia.[15] Also the Neapolitan police in dozens of private reports revealed how they were frightened of 'the notorious Mazzini', 'that infernal monster', and estimated that a group of his followers could be found in almost every Italian town.[16] The Sicilian revolutionaries of 1848–9 had left two ships in London together with £4,000 in cash which Mazzini hoped to inherit, but the British courts awarded them to the restored Bourbon monarchy after King Ferdinand renounced his 'irrevocable constitution' and resumed authoritarian power.

Mazzini's closest Sicilian associates were Francesco Crispi and Rosolino Pilo. Ten years later these two men prepared the way for Garibaldi and a thousand volunteers to land at Marsala and conquer Sicily. But already in 1850–1 they were both encouraged by Mazzini to work out a very similar plan for landing a thousand volunteers, possibly at Marsala. If successful they were planning to cooperate with armed bands from the Sicilian interior to defeat the Bourbon army and constitute a firm base for a wider Italian revolution. They were in touch with a network of local committees in the island, and Mazzini's central committee hoped to find £1,000 and provide arms from Malta. He realised that 'a rising in Sicily might be of vital importance' and wrote in vain to ask Garibaldi in New York if he would lead such an expedition.[17]

To reassure those Sicilians who had reservations about absorption into a united Italy, Mazzini repeated his earlier promise that they could be certain of enjoying regional autonomy with an elected Sicilian assembly and separate civil service.[18] He knew that a similar anxiety was shared in other regions, not excluding Piedmont itself. The fact that 'municipalism' and local loyalties were still much stronger than Italian patriotism was the reason why most of the leading Moderates called territorial unification impossible as well as undesirable.[19] Even inside Victor Emanuel's small kingdom there were marked regional and linguistic differences between Piedmont, Liguria, Sardinia and Savoy. In the capital city, Turin, use of the Italian language (instead of the more usual French or local dialects) sometimes caused offence. Inside the single region of Tuscany, internal divisions were such that an English visitor was informed that 'Florence, Lucca, Siena and Pisa all hate one another even more than they hate Austria'.[20] Exaggerated or not, this comment shows the size of the problem facing the patriotic movement, what Mazzini often referred to as 'rolling the stone of Sisyphus'. One British ambassador in Italy commented that 'the advocates of L'Unità Italiana forget not only that the favourite aversion of an Italian citizen is the inhabitant of the nearest neighbouring city, but that from one end of the peninsula to the other there is a marked separation between the rural and the town popula- tion.'[21] Mazzini's lack of information about this rural population no doubt helped to boost his confidence in ultimate victory, whereas many Moder- ates were landowners more in touch with local feeling; and yet his confidence and optimism, however apparently unrealistic, were a neces- sary factor in the next stage of making a united nation.

In the autumn of 1850, he was able to announce the existence of a National Italian Committee in London to organise a campaign of propa- ganda for Italian unification: this committee, he said, represented the 'National Party', what he later called the 'Party of Action', and it drew its notional authorisation from a quorum of representatives elected by uni- versal suffrage to the Roman assembly in 1849. His intention was for this party to affiliate groups of like-minded expatriates in Paris, Geneva, Malta, Tunis, Athens and elsewhere. It was itself affiliated to a Central Committee for Democratic Europe composed of himself representing Italy, Ledru Rollin for France, Arnold Ruge for Germany, and Albert Darasz for Poland. A manifesto was then drawn up by Mazzini which extolled the idea of popular sovereignty in a democratic 'Europe of peoples'. Robert Browning, who owned several other writings by Mazzini, lent a copy of this manifesto to his American friend Charles Eliot Norton, who described it as 'extravagant'.[22] Mazzini, however, care- fully avoided including any advocacy of republicanism. Although he still thought it unlikely that any monarchists would initiate a national revolution, in 1848 a successful insurrection by the citizens of Milan had forced Charles Albert into giving his support, and if only this could be repeated the monarchists would make an invaluable contribution to success.

For the next year he therefore revived his appeal for a political truce. Not for the first or last time he made clear that the only objective on which he could not compromise was that of an independent and united nation. He was ready to sacrifice his belief in republicanism[23] and accept a federal union of Italian states if that was the general wish.[24] Republican- ism, as he repeated, was no guarantee of good government. Nor was monarchy always bad, and the British had no need of a republic because 'you are blessed with loyal sovereigns'.[25]

But Italians since the sixteenth century had been governed by dynasties and viceroys who almost all came from France, Austria and Spain, not one of whom could be expected to have the interests of Italy as his chief concern. In 1848 the sovereign rulers of Naples, Rome and Tuscany had under extreme pressure promised reforms to meet local wishes, but had then seized the first chance to abjure them and make peace with the national enemy. Charles Albert in Piedmont had briefly shown that he wanted Italian independence from an intrusive Austria, but then had allowed dynastic and family interests to take precedence over the national cause; and his son, Victor Emanuel, had the inherent disadvantage that his wife and mother were German-speaking Austrian Habsburgs. All monarchs had another fundamental flaw, that they ruled not because of ability, nor because they knew how to act in the national interest, but by heredity and divine right. The Piedmontese monarchists possessed the resources to emancipate the country if only, unlike Charles Albert, they would combine forces with the *italianissimi*; but in 1848–9 their determination to create only an expanded Piedmont had antagonised other regions and parties, leaving Italy as divided and disillusioned as ever.[26]

There was nevertheless one good reason for gratitude to Piedmont. Whereas the rulers of Rome, Naples and Tuscany repudiated their constitutions as soon as they felt strong enough, Victor Emanuel in 1849 retained the *statuto* granted by his father, even though without enthusiasm.[27] Since this constitution theoretically guaranteed freedom of the press, Mazzini's friends in Genoa launched a new paper in May 1851, the *Italia e Popolo*. But on various pretexts this newspaper was regularly harassed by the authorities to bring about its collapse: copies were sequestrated even for merely pointing out that freedom of the press was frequently violated. Successive editors and printers were imprisoned despite repeated acquittal by juries. Azeglio, Cavour and the Moderates needed the reputation for liberalism but preferably without its attendant inconveniences. Mazzini was thought by them to be too dangerous for his views to be read by the public, and hence his hopes for a political truce proved as excessive as in previous years.

More important than a repeatedly censored newspaper in keeping his organisation alive were private communications through couriers of whom little record has survived. Mazzini wrote in January 1851 that his life so far had consisted of sending 'one or two millions of letters, notes, instructions, forgotten, lost, burnt'.[28] Little has survived of his correspondence with Germany or Spain, of the letters he said he wrote to Eastern Europe, and only a few of the letters to North Africa. He spoke of actively working to keep in touch with the whole of Europe as well as the United States and South America. Inside Italy he was in correspondence with groups in Lombardy and the Papal States. In Turin, despite official persecution, we hear of printed appeals surreptitiously posted by his organisation in all the main streets.[29] In Tuscany, where the grand duke had been welcomed back into power by Baron Ricasoli and other Moderates whose social position had suffered during the revolution, every village was said to contain a group of dissidents, and a private printing press in the house of Lord Aldborough was found to be disseminating Mazzinian propaganda: this Irish peer, together with his brother who worked in the British consulate, was immediately arrested.[30] Another English visitor to central Italy in June 1851 reported, no doubt with exaggeration, that Mazzini's network was strong everywhere, almost as 'an invisible government with its own police and system of taxation', and even among the peasantry there was an unlimited confidence in this one man. Everywhere young people were said to have lost confidence in the Moderates and were abandoning frivolous pursuits to prepare for revolutionary action.[31]

If the activity of couriers and the extent of Mazzini's influence is hard to estimate or document, almost as hard to quantify is the growing tendency among some former friends to abandon or criticise him. Criticisms were, paradoxically, one index of at least partial success, as more and more people learnt from him as much as from anyone that there existed an Italian problem for which different solutions might be available. The *italianissimi* were all of them individualists of strong character and usually possessed heterogeneous views of their own. Some, if not actual atheists, were irritated by the prominent place he accorded to religious faith. Many gradually turned to put their trust for the future in Piedmont as the one relatively liberal Italian state, and such people particularly disliked his creating disaffection inside the Piedmontese army on which future success might depend. Others were simply disillusioned over his belief in the capacity of Italians to revolt. Some were even ready for Italy to become a satellite of Napoleonic France as the price of moving one step forward towards becoming a nation. Not a few republicans saw him as tactically at fault in seeking a political truce with the monarchy, while others on the contrary considered him too intransigent and unwilling to compromise. Many thought it unrealistic for him to organise revolution from far away in England, especially since, like Cavour, he had too little direct experience of public opinion in the centre and south of Italy. Others continued to want a federal Italian state and feared that his idea of national unification would result only in Piedmont imposing its own system on other regions, at some cost in individual liberty.

One of the criticisms that still most discomposed him was of acting dictatorially, of being so sure of his opinions and of the need for central direction that he behaved without sufficient consultation. According to Giovanni Ruffini he saw himself as an 'infallible antipope'. Giuseppe Sirtori, until 1851 a loyal friend, began to think that Mazzini's ideal government must be some kind of theocracy with himself at the pinnacle. To Gallenga he was the 'tsar of democrats'; to Felice Orsini and Giorgio Pallavicino he was 'a new Mahomet'.[32] And these men had themselves been rebels against the conservative establishment, and sometimes remained so. Their criticisms may have been excessive but were not un-founded and they pinpoint one of his limitations as a practical politician.

His reply to them, sincere certainly, self-deceiving according to his critics, was that he intensely disliked the exercise of political power and longed for the day when he could return to private life and his writing.[33] He argued correctly that consultation with people far away from London was possible only on general issues, not on precise details of tactics or timing; also that his critics inside Italy discussed endlessly without being prepared to lead or to risk action, and most of them were equally entrenched in their own individual dogmas. No revolution could be competently managed by entirely democratic means or by a committee representing many different shades of opinion: revolutions needed some-one to decide and command at critical moments, who would give way to elected representatives only when success was assured.[34] The fact that decisions were taken in London was an unfortunate necessity because nowhere else did anyone have the freedom to set up an effective organisation. Mazzini believed quite genuinely in popular sovereignty and in what in 1851, long before Abraham Lincoln, he called government 'of the people, by the people, and for the people'.[35] Individuals of what-ever creed or colour were free and equal in the eyes of God, but real freedom 'here below' had to wait until the revolution succeeded and made possible the popular consultation that he regarded as indispensable.

In mid-1851 some of the Italian exiles in Paris formed a rival group, most disagreeing with him by preferring a federal republic for Italy and under French patronage. This 'Latin Committee' included French and Spanish representatives to offset the Anglo-Saxon element associated with the London organisation. Its existence delighted Karl Marx as well as the Vatican because it divided and weakened the 'bourgeois republi-cans'.[36] But it had only a short, tenuous existence and this fact, coupled with its own internal divisions, gave some justification for Mazzini's refusal to give way. One of its leading members, Enrico Cernuschi, shocked patriotic Italians when heard to say what Mazzini could never have said, that he would prefer to see Austrians occupying Turin rather than the Piedmontese reaching Milan.[37] Such remarks may explain why Agostino Depretis, a distinguished prime minister of Italy many years later, received a poor impression of the Latin Committee while he was visiting Paris. Depretis reported that nearly all the exiles in France contin-ued to regard Mazzini as the one great contemporary Italian.[38]

This schism is nevertheless a symptom of how other republicans, espe-cially those of intelligence and strong character, could find Mazzini a difficult associate. Some were exasperated by his apocalyptic vision, oth-ers by his utopian impracticality and apparent self-righteousness. Often they continued to admire him and remain friends at a personal level, but there was a recurrent pattern in the desertion by many disciples in each generation, leaving a new group of younger people to catch fire from his inspiration. Garibaldi had not forgotten their differences during the defence of Rome and did not visit him when passing through England in 1850. Giuseppe Ferrari was affronted by Mazzini's religious zeal, his dislike of federalism and distrust of France. Giuseppe Montanelli, a good Catholic who had been prominent in the Tuscan revolution of 1848–9, continued to admire his courage and determination and subscribed to his National Loan in 1850, but regarded him as too dictatorial and too little a dedicated republican. Sirtori, an ex-priest expelled from Piedmont after fighting against the Austrians in Venice, agreed in thinking him dictatorial but differed from Ferrari in seeing Mazzini's republicanism as excessive and divisive.

The National Party in London and the Latin Committee were both caught by surprise in December 1851 when Louis Napoleon staged a successful military *coup d'état* with enormous loss of life among civilians on the streets of Paris, and in the following year proclaimed himself emperor with the title of Napoleon III. Mazzini had been collecting arms in the hope of helping the republicans in France to collaborate in another European-wide revolution like that of 1848, and Gioberti agreed with the previous French government that such a project had a fair chance of success.[39] Napoleon's coup therefore came as a devastating blow, especially when the new emperor, far from continuing his youthful enthusiasm for a patriotic Italy, gave indications of pursuing his uncle's very different claim to French hegemony over continental Europe. Mazzini's one consolation was that the British might therefore want a stronger Italy as a counterpoise. Politicians in Turin, on the contrary, were not particularly displeased that the victory of authoritarianism in France would reduce Mazzini's influence in Europe and enable Piedmont to resume its expansionist policy as a junior partner of French imperialism.[40]

Another result of Napoleon's coup was a sharp accentuation of Mazzini's polemic against socialism, in particular against the French socialists who in his view (and that of the German socialist Lassalle)[41] could and should have fought in defence of liberty against this palace revolution. Their mistake was to stand aside on the assumption that Napoleon's dictatorship would create favourable conditions for their kind of social revolution, whereas in effect they merely frightened the French middle classes into supporting that dictatorship.[42] Mazzini had warmly supported the Chartist movement in England and until now had occasionally continued to think of himself as some kind of socialist,[43] but his own ideas of social democracy were far removed from what he called the current perversion of socialism that advocated a war between classes and devalued ideals of personal liberty and patriotism. The distinction is important, because it suited many people to continue calling him a communist and this accusation was exploited to deprive him of middle-class support.[44]

He was in fact far more consistently hostile to the leading champions of socialism than to the institution of monarchy, and was treated by all of them as a dangerous enemy. Louis Blanc, Blanqui and Proudhon referred to him as a counter-revolutionary, a charlatan, and also as a major encumbrance to their kind of socialist revolution.[45] One former collaborator, Benedetto Musolino, in an extraordinary piece of vituperation, called him a corrupt and sinister figure insensitive to the needs of the poor, who put personal interest before Italian regeneration and was in politics only to make himself rich.[46] Karl Marx was no less abusive. Mazzini referred to Marx for the first time in an article of 1852, but before then there were dozens of uncomplimentary references to 'the ultra-reactionary' Mazzini in correspondence between Marx and Friedrich Engels. This correspondence referred condescendingly to 'the platitudinous parodies of his cosmopolitan-neo-Catholic-ideological manifestos'. Marx accused him of 'licking the arse of the English liberal bourgeoisie' and blamed him for helping the Austrians by defending the existing social order instead of stirring up a major peasants' revolt.[47]

Mazzini had invited this opposition by his own perceptive criticism of communism between 1846 and 1851. He was astonished that the papacy condemned socialism as virtually synonymous with communism whereas they were different and in some ways contradictory. He knew that there were also differences of opinion and emphasis inside communism, but basically it stood for government being 'at once proprietor, possessor and distributor of all that exists', organising society 'after the manner of beavers'. Communism, he wrote, not only 'animalised man' but precisely reproduced 'the position of the masters of slaves in olden times', because ambitious and unscrupulous people would realise how to exploit communist ideas and use the gullibility of the masses to create another dictatorship as illiberal, cruel and inefficient as the *ancien régime*.

This prophetic vision was ignored by many of Mazzini's critics. Communism, he explained, signified community of property. It meant government controls that would depress initiative and depreciate stimulus to individual effort. The phrase 'to all according to their needs' sounded plausible but left unclear what those needs were, and in practice everyone would be tempted to exaggerate his own needs, leaving governments to decide between conflicting demands, which spelt tyranny. In such a system there could be no economic progress fostered by competition and emulation. Each man would become a machine for production in the service of a new and equally exploiting dominant class. A communist state would be 'a monastic convent without religion'. 'The community will become a community of suffering', 'a society petrified, regulated in every particular, allowing no place for the individual'. In any case the system was based on a false prospectus because inequality would surely reappear under the scarcely disguised pretence of a new and perhaps even less enlightened governing elite.[48]

Mazzini showed some sympathy with socialist thinkers who stopped short of this extreme position. Yet most of them were tainted by a materialist heresy that he found deeply distasteful. He continued to criticise Robert Owen for this, even though there was something to appreciate in the humanitarianism of 'a gentle, inoffensive, rose-water kind of communism'.[49] Though he saw some good in François Fourier, this French socialist thinker was blamed for considering only 'the kitchen of humanity' and prescribing 'pills-for-universal-happiness' as a strict utilitarian lacking any sense of religion.[50]

Another distinguished socialist, Saint-Simon, deserved credit for 'the boldest and sincerest attempt ever made hitherto to realise in practice the fundamental principle of Bentham's idea to organise a society from the point of view of utility'; but the attempt would fail because it ran against some of mankind's deepest aspirations. Individualism and 'collective association', both of them praiseworthy, could both be disastrous if taken to extremes. By putting collective interest way above that of the individual, Saint-Simon's ideas led logically to 'the despotism of authority and the negation of human liberty'.[51] A more practical objection was that Saint-Simon and other theorists of socialism 'antagonised potential friends and created ferocious enemies among the petty bourgeoisie; they turned peoples' minds away from urgent problems of individual liberty and so fragmented the democratic movement'. Above all, they thereby weakened the primary struggle for national identity without which there could be no self-determination and hence no lasting improvement for all classes in society.[52]

The seriousness with which Mazzini treated these socialist thinkers indicates that he feared them as rivals because of what he called their specious appeal to the masses. More than ever he too needed popular support since the revolution of 1848 had been 'falsified by the middle classes' who too often saw the *ancien régime* as the best guarantee of their social position. And yet, as the socialists were quick to point out, he would find difficulty in reaching 'the people' so long as he paid too little attention to the 'kitchen of humanity'. Furthermore, his philosophical and religious ideas were far too novel and abstract for any mass appeal. Censorship in any case ensured that his own audience was much smaller than that enjoyed by Gioberti. Yet it was not in his nature to lose faith in the persuasiveness of his personal message. His task in the early 1850s was to compete with the socialists and appeal to as broad a front as possible by emphasising the need for liberating social reforms. As well as the masses, he had to convince the middle classes that they too would gain from national unification and could also gain from recognising that democracy was not the same as red revolution. In time they would surely learn that they could defeat socialism only by first redressing the inequalities in society.

The class war, as he knew, was a reality in history, but unlike Marx he strove to diminish rather than exploit it. He now wrote more unambiguously than before about his reluctance to subvert the social order or the right to wealth and property.[53] But more then ever he believed that, for moral as well as practical reasons, social reforms were urgently needed. 'To the emancipation of the slaves has succeeded that of the serf; that of the serf must be followed by that of the workman.' Just as the aristocracy had once helped to reduce the power of monarchies, just as the middle classes subsequently helped to weaken the authority of the nobles, so ordinary citizens would one day end the near monopoly of power held by the landowning and capitalist bourgeoisie, and this was far better done by timely concession instead of by violence. The 'democratic tendency' was now a fact of life, and so one day would be 'the co-partnership of labour with intelligence and capital'. In his ideal state there should be compulsory education for everyone and encouragement for voluntary associations of workers in cooperatives and trade unions. There had to be a 'more just distribution of the fruits of labour', 'a more equitable relation between peasants and landowners'; and a 'progressive civilising process in the countryside' might eventually 'abolish the concept of a proletariat'.[54]

Mazzini continued to be accused by Azeglio, Farini and other Moderates of being a dangerous socialist,[55] while others made the opposite criticism that he was a dangerous enemy of socialism, in particular by his not wanting any fundamental change in the relations between landowners and labourers.[56] More correct would be to say that, cut off in exile, he had no chance to learn more at first hand about agrarian Italy and this perhaps strengthened his aversion to stirring up social revolution by the peasantry. Marx wrote of him that he 'knows only the towns with their liberal nobility and their *citoyens éclairés*'. In any case Mazzini's main weapon was written propaganda that could with difficulty reach beyond the towns, and there was not much point in writing for an illiterate rural population that he was prevented from addressing more directly.

Marx, unlike later Marxists, could admit that Mazzini deserved credit for advocating 'the emancipation of the peasants and the transformation of their *métayage* system of sharecropping into bourgeois freeholdings'.[57] Other people even thought that Mazzini went too far in encouraging the rural proletariat.[58] He recognised an imperative moral obligation to improve their standards of living, and continued to do so despite evidence that the peasants regularly backed throne and altar in preference to a liberal patriotism that meant little to them. The Marxists looked on social revolution as their best hope of winning personal power, whereas Mazzini, while he wanted radical social change, knew that the terror of 1793 had produced Bonapartism, and feared that an agrarian revolution might once again lead to absolutist and clerical reaction. Local *jacqueries* and 'occupation of the land' had in 1848–9 had been a divisive element that weakened the patriotic revolution.

Friends in Britain

How far Mazzini helped after 1850 to change British attitudes is impossible to determine. Eventually even most Tory politicians accepted his idea of Italian national unification as inevitable and beneficent, but their fear of revolution and preference for constitutional government meant that they mistrusted him and gave the benefit of any doubt to Piedmont. The conservative *Quarterly Review* once printed an article that nevertheless called him more honest, more courageous and more able than Gioberti and the Moderates.[59] The object of this commendation felt fairly sure that Britain would at some point realise the advantage to herself in helping to create a united Italian state as 'a counterbalancing power against France and Austria'. But British traditional isolationism was delaying any change of heart, and he took this as his theme when George Eliot asked him to write again for the *Westminster Review*. 'England, the country of Elizabeth and Cromwell, has not a word to say in favour of the principle to which she owes her existence': if only she were less hesitant in championing liberty and nationality she could become the leading influence in a future Europe; otherwise she might be shut out of the continent by a coalition of illiberal governments and 'find herself some day a third-rate power'.[60]

What none of the conservatives in London or elsewhere could dispute was that insurrections had taken place in Italy almost every year for a generation and were likely to continue; which allowed Mazzini to argue that here was a danger to European peace since France and Austria might use this permanent unrest as a pretext to intervene again on the plains of Lombardy and fight each other for supremacy in Europe. Whig and Tory politicians agreed in fearing such a possibility and many welcomed Mazzini's alternative idea that Italian nationality might be a matter of self-determination rather than dynastic ambition. They also usually agreed that the cruelty, tyranny and violence in Naples and the Papal States was 'a disgrace to modern Europe'. Above all, after what Leigh

Hunt called Mazzini's 'noble experiment' in Rome, the papal state had gone back to being 'the real plague-spot of Europe', 'the worst and most anomalous government in the civilised world' – where one visitor persuaded himself that more people were executed than in 'all other governments in Europe put together'.[61]

Formal protests by the pope against Mazzini's continued presence in London arrived during 1851, and further protests came from Austria, Russia and Prussia, none of whom objected to the fact that the British gave equal hospitality to Metternich and other exiled defenders of . Louis Napoleon was another who asked for Mazzini's expulsion – despite the fact that the French president had himself been protected as a refugee in England and used that country as a base for planning his own far more violent and illiberal revolution. Napoleon was told in reply that this greatly feared reprobate had broken no British laws and would be no threat to anyone if only foreign governments were less oppressive. Mazzini was even asked by Palmerston's secretary for helpful introductions to use on a visit to Italy. To Elizabeth Barrett Browning he was a noble if unwise man 'who personally has my sympathies always'. Articles in the British press continued to praise him as an honoured guest, as an elected representative of the Roman population, as someone whose cause was that of Italy and who was himself a power in Europe to be reckoned with. 'All who were fortunate enough to know him in England loved him most enthusiastically,' wrote the *Illustrated London News*. He had demonstrated that 'the Italians have a right to choose their own government', wrote the *Spectator*. According to the *British Quarterly Review*, 'of those that knew him intimately we never met one that did not speak of him as a noble and true man; a man of irreproachable rectitude and the most exquisite sensibilities, the very soul of chivalry and honour. Even those who disagreed with him . . . admired his indestructible magnanimity and his heroic perseverance.'[62]

Some forty other refugees had come to London from Rome, for whom he felt personally responsible. Most depended on charity and so did the families of others who suffered the atrocious hardship of Italian prisons. To help them he organised concerts and ran up further personal debts. A committee was formed to collect money for this cause and included Thackeray, Landor, Cobden and Joseph Hume; its published appeal was written by Dickens, who once again expressed admiration for this distinguished refugee.[63]

Among those who failed to share such admiration was Queen Victoria, who could not endure her ministers' growing sympathy for Italian nationality and independence. Similar objections came from some Tories. Lord Brougham, under the cover of parliamentary privilege, called Mazzini 'the head of the assassination department at Rome', but other members of parliament confused the names Mazzini and Manzoni. The celebrated novelist Harrison Ainsworth wrote that he disliked Mazzini almost as much as he disliked Garibaldi. Articles in *The Times*, which relied on hand-outs from the Piedmontese embassy, were full of sarcasm against 'the new saviour of the world' who was one of 'the worst enemies of Italian freedom'; and the same paper was inveigled into publishing fabricated evidence to prove such accusations.[64] Some of its criticisms, however, were well-founded, for instance that the mass of the Italian population had so far shown little interest in patriotism, and also that Mazzini's radical views were bound to antagonise conservative liberals whose sympathy would surely be needed to create a united Italy.

The object of these reproaches, though he lived quietly and unobtrusively in London after 1850, created a striking and much more favourable impression on those who went out of their way to seek his company. His old friend Mrs Fletcher found him far happier than before 1848: 'he is now a man full of experience, patience and hope, one fitted to inspire that confidence which he himself feels, and infuse life and hope into his country'.[65] Emily Shaen, the wife of a friendly and devoted lawyer who helped in his school for Italian children, wrote after meeting him for the first time that she 'had never seen genius before'; she found him full of fun as well as spirituality and passion, 'simply the most wonderful-looking man I ever saw in my life . . . so thoroughly manly-looking', 'the sort of man that everybody around him can't help obeying'.[66]

The effect he made on many very different individuals gives useful indications that help to explain his achievements and also his shortcomings. The intelligent and perceptive Herzen, who often saw him in London, could not accept all his opinions but remained an admirer.

> Such men do not give in, do not yield; the worse things go with them, the higher they hold the flag. If today Mazzini loses friends and money and barely escapes from chains and the gallows, he takes his stand tomorrow more obstinately and resolutely than ever, collects fresh money, seeks fresh friends, denies himself everything, even sleep and food, ponders for whole nights over new resources and every time actually creates them, flings himself once more into the conflict and, beaten again, sets to work once more with feverish ardour. In this inflexible steadfastness, in this faith which goes forward in defiance of facts, in this inexhaustible activity which failure only challenges and provokes, there is something of grandeur and, if you like, something of madness. Often it is just that grain of madness which is the essential condition of success.[67]

Among Germans who saw much of him in London, Karl Blind remembered the unique magnetism of his personality. The orientalist scholar Adolf von Schack regarded him as 'one of the noblest and purest people who ever lived' as well as a delightful companion and conversationalist. Professor Masson, who later edited *Macmillan's Magazine*, commented on the 'absolute fascination' that made people worship him with almost religious fervour; yet Masson also recalled that in private society he was straightforward, unaffected and a most attractive friend.[68] The editor of the *Examiner*, John Forster, remembered him as an unassuming, mild-mannered, kind-hearted man whose views were 'no more inflammatory than a middle of the road liberal'. Goldwin Smith, later Regius Professor of History in Oxford, met him often and was mainly impressed with his nobility of character, his humanity, and the fact that his patriotism was always 'subservient to the general good of mankind'.[69] The Austrian writer Moritz Hartmann knew him in 1850 and was surprised to encounter someone of such simplicity, without a trace of pretentiousness but with a bewitching personality that explained why people followed him to their death.[70] The same response of almost reverential awe was felt in 1851 by Carl Schurz, later secretary of the interior in Washington, who saw him as 'the embodied genius of revolutionary action' without the least element of cynicism, charlatanism or affectation. Mazzini ranked with Bismarck and Oliver Wendell Holmes as one of the three finest talkers Schurz knew in his life, and 'it was difficult to resist such a power of fascination'.[71]

Among former friends, Carlyle was delighted to see the returned exile safely back from the dangers and triumphs of the Roman revolution. Their relations had cooled before 1848 because of a realist's impatience with revolutionary utopianism, but once again became as close as ever, and Mazzini rarely missed his Friday visits to Cheyne Row, though the journey took several hours on foot. There he met Robert Browning, who made a great fuss over him.[72] Carlyle wrote to a curious Emerson that 'the Roman revolution had made a man of him', though providentially the 'Quack-President of France' saved the life of this indomitable conspirator by relieving him of power just in time. Massimo d'Azeglio, when in 1853 after resigning as prime minister he came to London to sell some of his paintings, spoke slightingly to Carlyle about Mazzini and was surprised to earn a sharp reproof for talking nonsense.[73]

Jane Carlyle found him in excellent spirits, 'the same affectionate, simple-hearted, high-souled creature', but more communicative and speaking with much more authority than before. Some of his schemes still seemed laughably unrealistic, and she criticised the fact that his normally generous character 'was greatly spoiled by a spirit of intrigue', because he was always thinking of how he could gain 'advantage for his cause by methods such a man should scorn'. Jane noted that Mazzini now had a greyish beard instead of just a moustache, because during the revolution he had little time to visit a barber. She once again procured him an apartment to share with Saffi and Quadrio, and also helped Saffi find a teaching post in the Wedgwood family until 1853, when this former triumvir of the Roman republic obtained a lectureship at Oxford university.[74]

English and Scottish friends became more important to Mazzini after the death of his mother, who even at a distance had been his closest friend and greatest comfort. Her funeral at Genoa in 1852 took place by public subscription to which the civic authorities contributed, though it offended the clergy because the cortège turned into a great popular tribute to her son: thousands followed the bier, tens of thousands lined the streets, while British and American ships in the harbour flew their flags at half-mast.[75] After recovering from the shock of this loss, Mazzini came closer to Bessie Ashurst until her death two years later, and the Ashurst house became the centre for what he called 'the clan' to meet one evening a week. The Stansfelds, the Shaens and sometimes David Masson belonged to this group, together with Saffi, Quadrio and for a time Medici. Lack of public transport meant that late at night they used to return together on foot from Muswell Hill to Islington, where they could find cabs or an omnibus. After 1854 the preferred rendezvous was the Stansfeld house in Thurloe Square which was much more accessible.

The four Ashurst daughters had by now become an important part of Mazzini's life. He suffered another sad loss when Eliza died in childbirth towards the end of 1850, and to him fell the unpleasant task of acting as intermediary in squaring accounts with her importunate French husband. Matilda, the most intellectual, remained a close friend and helper, though never sharing his religious ideals. Caroline, too, retained some intellectual reservations, yet people sometimes thought she was his favourite.[76] Emilie was less of a pragmatic Benthamite than her sisters. She used to translate some of his articles and acted as a courier to Italy, sometimes carrying large sums of money sewn into her clothes. More than a thousand letters written to his parents were given by his mother to Emilie for her to write a book about his life in exile; and he said he was glad of this, though wondering if such letters would not be better destroyed because he had protected his family from knowing the full story of the dangers and hardships he had suffered.[77] Emilie it was who later discovered his mother's coffin lying untended, even unmarked except for a number, and bought a plot of land for a proper burial.[78]

Rumours were circulated by hostile Italian critics that Mazzini lived luxuriously in one of the more aristocratic quarters of London where he kept a harem of women and lived off their immoral earnings.[79] He certainly continued to value the friendship of many women, among them the Nathan family, the Craufurds, Garibaldi's fiancée Emma Roberts, Clementia Taylor, Daniel Stern, George Sand, Malvida von Meysenbug,

Mathilde Blind, Fanny Wedgwood, Arethusa Milner-Gibson, and Linda White who married Pasquale Villari, the celebrated historian. He never succeeded in meeting Mrs Gaskell but was close to her friends the Winkworth sisters.[80]

Male friends, who saw him to best advantage in mixed company,[81] were more important for his political life. Chief among these was James Stansfeld, who married Caroline Ashurst and owned a brewery in Fulham. Stansfeld gave his son the name Joseph, the anglicised version of Giuseppe. Another benefactor was Peter Stuart, a shipowner in Liverpool who chose for his own son the forename 'Mazzini', as also did John McAdam of Glasgow; and this choice of name was encouraged by George Holyoake the secularist, who used his newspaper the *Reasoner* to collect money for Italy.[82] The unitarian Peter Taylor, a vice-president of Courtaulds' textiles, was a discriminating but very generous supporter. Another munificent source of funds was the industrialist Joseph Cowen of Newcastle, whose ceramic retorts and fireclay utensils were exported throughout Europe and sometimes concealed smuggled messages from Mazzini.

Some of these benefactors gave very large sums to help the National Party. Smaller amounts were more readily forthcoming for Mazzini's school in Hatton Garden. This school is sometimes said to have closed in 1848 when he went to Italy but in fact was kept alive in his absence by Stansfeld and Mrs Milner-Gibson, one of the occasional teachers being Dr Conneau, the personal physician of Louis Napoleon.[83] After Mazzini returned to London it was revitalised because the 'organ boys' were arriving in increasing numbers from Italy and, to the embarrassment of the Piedmontese ambassador, found their greatest protector in Mazzini.[84] When costs mounted, more than once it had to close, and there was a permanent problem in finding 'shilling-a-month' subscribers among the ten thousand Italians residing in London. To combat its influence the pope now offered a special indulgence to subscribers for a new school offering a more orthodox Catholic education. Mazzini himself frequently gave a lecture on Sundays, and other speakers included Taylor, Harriet Martineau, and Mazzini's friends Saffi, Quadrio and Campanella.[85]

British interest in Italy's political troubles, after being kindled by the defence of Rome and Venice in 1849, received a great boost in 1851 from Gladstone's famous denunciation of the horrors of Neapolitan prisons in a pamphlet that went through eleven editions in the next few years. The British government even sent copies to its foreign embassies in hope of arousing public indignation throughout Europe. An important fact was that this highly polemical work was written by a conservative who until now had had little sympathy with the idea of Italian nationality.[86] Gladstone had been led to believe that Mazzini must be an anarchist and an 'apostle of irreligion'. Indeed the pamphlet was published in the expectation that, by forcing governments to intervene, it might forestall or prevent another Mazzinian revolution.[87] Only later did Gladstone desert the Tories and, though never becoming an enthusiast, admit that Mazzini, a man of 'great talents and force of character and the most perfect truth and honesty', had been correct in arguing that national unification was a necessary prerequisite for liberty and good government in Italy.[88] In 1851, Gladstone's moral indignation against King Ferdinand of Naples greatly assisted the cause of Italian patriotism. One irony, not lost on Mazzini or others, was that only the accident of a daughter's bad health brought Gladstone to Naples, and the prisons in Piedmont, while containing fewer political prisoners, were no more salubrious.[89]

In May 1851, largely at Mazzini's instigation, a society called the 'Friends of Italy' was formed in London. Apart from campaigning for Italian independence it had no political affiliation. Its eight hundred members, a quarter of them from Scotland, represented widely different opinions, Protestant clergy alongside secularists, monarchists together with lifelong republicans such as Landor. Its central committee included half a dozen members of parliament, as well as other eminent Victorian luminaries including Samuel Smiles, William Forster the educationist, the historian Froude, G. H. Lewes, Samuel Courtauld, Leigh Hunt, Professor Newman the cardinal's brother, Lord Dudley Stuart, and the editors of the *Daily News*, the *Illustrated London News* and the *Encyclopedia Britannica*.[90] In case they should ever try to visit Italy, the names of these people were sent by the Rome police to all guards at the papal frontier.[91] The society published a monthly record and a number of pamphlets, one of these criticising the British government for non-intervention on the continent, another defending the Roman republic of 1849 against misinformed allegations by *The Times*.

Mazzini was shy of speaking in public but reluctantly addressed three of its meetings. He told a packed and distinguished audience about the aims of the Italian National Party. Minor reforms, he admitted, might be obtained by peaceful means, but even the constitutional reforms in Piedmont had been wrested from an unwilling sovereign and only by threatening revolution. Such a threat, as he admitted, was a method best avoided where possible, but peaceful protests had failed to produce anything resembling a free society in Italy. Political and ecclesiastical censorship was such that prison or even execution were used against those 'circulating a copy of the Bible or teaching a few children to read', and there were said to be more than ten thousand political prisoners among the three million inhabitants of the Papal States – Azeglio thought there were as many as twenty-five thousand, and others said even more, but any request to the papal authorities for a correct figure was met by silence. In Italy, according to Mazzini, 'we are ripe for liberty and independence. Before 1848 and 1849 I would have uttered these words with hesitation: not now. Thank God we have proved to all Europe that liberty is with us the watchword of a whole people and that we could fight and bleed and not despair for it' – whereas not a single person had been ready 'to encounter martyrdom for the pope when we, first in 1831, then in 1849, decreed the abolition of the temporal power'.[92]

Anti-papal feeling in Protestant Britain was an important motive with many members of this society, but politics and human sympathy were equally important, and more money seems to have been forthcoming to help Catholic Polish refugees.[93] The precise amount collected for Italy cannot be estimated, though Mazzini was disappointed and the more glamorous Garibaldi received a larger amount in subsequent years. Herzen contributed £200, one tenth of his income and a very large sum for those days; John Epps, the well-known homoeopathist, gave £100 and William Ashurst a similar sum. A shilling-a-head subscription organised by Cowen and Viscount Goderich found ten thousand subscribers in Newcastle, and another nine thousand contributed through Holyoake, many of them workers in mines and textile mills. According to the British government as much as £20,000 had been collected before the end of 1852.[94]

Mazzini's personal finances had meanwhile improved, first with a small legacy from an aunt in 1850, then at his mother's death he inherited another small capital sum and an annuity of about £180 which she wisely left in trust for him with a Genoese banker so that he would not give it all away at once. Half of his money still went to other refugees, but at least he now had a regular income for basic living expenses and was no longer permanently in debt.[95]

Insurrections: 1853

The Austrians continued with patchy success to watch Mazzini's steps. They could again read some of his secret ciphers. In the five years after 1849, twice a week on average the police in Vienna continued to draw up reports about this 'demon' who, though with limited money and no organised base of operations, was a potential threat to their control over northern Italy.[96] The usual passivity of the Lombard population after 1848 had given the Austrian authorities a false sense of security and a hope that the severity of martial law was enough to paralyse the *italianissimi*.[97] But memories of 1848 were latent as an encouragement to rebelliousness. Hundreds of victims suffered the terrible and sometimes mortal *bastinado*, sometimes their only offence being to possess one of Mazzini's letters or publications. Some of those tortured and executed were priests to whom Christian burial was then refused.[98]

In France and Britain such provocative and short-sighted behaviour caused astonishment. De Tocqueville could not find words to express his contempt for it. If a movement inspired by one lone exile could create such a general panic, here was ample evidence that the Austrian hold over Italy was more fragile than might appear. If Mazzini was correct in thinking that many parish clergy sympathised with patriotism, this was another ominous sign because under their guidance public opinion would increasingly favour resistance and possibly revolution.[99]

Likewise in other parts of Italy the old regime showed signs of disintegrating, and it was significant that prisons sometimes housed as many political prisoners as ordinary criminals. The statistics were largely guesswork and almost certainly exaggerated, but twenty thousand political prisoners were thought to be incarcerated in Naples. In Tuscany there were an estimated four thousand and twice as many in enforced exile, while the government in Florence referred to the existence of secret patriotic committees at work in every village throughout the peninsula.[100]

In the small Duchy of Parma, where the prime minister Thomas Ward was a retired jockey from Yorkshire, centres of higher education were forcibly closed so as to impede the spread of subversive ideas, and three hundred people were publicly flogged to mark the duke's return after the 1848–9 revolution. In the Papal States, dozens of executions took place during a single week in the autumn of 1852, and torture as well as the guillotine continued in regular use – Robert Browning stumbled by accident on one gruesome scene. Many other people were imprisoned for long periods without being brought to trial and on mere suspicion of holding incorrect opinions.[101] One notable victim in Lombardy was the priest Enrico Tazzoli, who in December 1852 was executed at Mantua with four famous 'martyrs of Belfiore' after the fact that he was collecting money for Mazzini was revealed by another priest under torture: the expenses of trial and execution were, as customary, charged to his relatives.

Some republicans blamed Mazzini for what they called this useless sacrifice of lives. He himself, while deploring the death of anyone, saw it as no more useless or deplorable than that of the incomparably greater number who died in the unsuccessful wars of 1848–9 or as victims of Napoleon's police in Paris. Tazzoli, whom he never met, testified that there was a price to pay for freedom and Mazzini's voice was a great inspiration for all who wanted a better future. Nor is it irrelevant that the very same Moderates who criticised Mazzini's failures were simultaneously ready to court certain defeat in war for the opposite reason that it would frustrate Mazzini's agitation for a republic.[102] Others in the republican camp were disheartened, among them Manin who now earned a precarious living in Paris teaching Italian – to Gladstone's daughter among others. Manin confessed to Mazzini that, since popular uprisings were apparently ineffective, the patriots should change tactics and hope for King Victor Emanuel to become a champion of Italian nationality; though Manin admitted that such a possibility might be a long time away in the future.[103]

A less radical change of policy was advocated by other republicans in Genoa who by the middle of 1852 were becoming convinced that the committee in London was too distant to direct the next revolutionary initiative. One of this group, Antonio Mordini, was sent to London to discuss their doubts. This Tuscan exile admitted that Mazzini was irreplaceable: as well as being the most prominent and admired among the republican patriots, he was needed as a collector of arms and funds and to mobilise support in the Anglo-Saxon world. But Mordini suspected that success would be far easier with a broader front that included federalists, atheists, even socialists, without wasting energy in debilitating attacks against each other. Moreover there was need for a better military organisation based nearer the scene of action in Genoa. Revolutions could not be won without resort to arms and required commanders who were not journalists or lawyers but experienced professional soldiers: preferably Garibaldi if he returned to Italy, or Pisacane, or else Garibaldi's lieutenants, Medici, Sirtori and Enrico Cosenz.[104]

Despite these representations from Genoa, or perhaps partly because of them, Mazzini decided to precipitate matters and use his organisation to help another insurrection which he heard was in preparation by some individuals in Milan. This was in origin a spontaneous initiative outside the direct control of his National Party, but although he let some people know of his doubts about possible success, it accorded with his belief that action alone would end disabling divisions among the patriots. There was at least a chance that other regions, as in March 1848, would rally in support once the first shot was fired.[105]

In retrospect it is clear that the odds were greatly against success, but so they had been in the triumphant rebellion of 1848 by the same city. At first he urged the Milanese to wait until Austria was more isolated in Europe, but then agreed to assist when this advice was rejected.[106] He was personally in touch with small revolutionary groups in Pavia, Bologna, Tuscany, Umbria and Sicily which, with his usual optimism, he hoped would all rise at the first news of an outbreak in Milan. He gave the Hungarian patriot Lajos Kossuth £500, all borrowed from English friends, and was told that Hungarian regiments inside the Austrian army would mutiny once the revolt commenced.[107] Nor was it out of the question that success in Milan might again force the Piedmontese to give open or covert military support. One encouraging sign was that Depretis, a leading member of the 'constitutional opposition' in Turin, secretly sent financial help[108] and Mazzini claimed to have received a further hint that cabinet ministers in Turin were not entirely unsympathetic.[109]

To prepare the ground, he left England early in January 1853, travelling via Antwerp and Cologne so as to avoid the French police. His friends in the 'clan' procured him another forged passport and Mrs Ashurst provided a woollen waistcoat against cold weather in the Alps. Arriving in Switzerland, whence he had twice been expelled, he found friendly houses in which to lie hidden – 'though I feel more "Englishman" than ever', he wrote to the Ashursts from Lugano.

One untimely occurrence in January was an abortive attempt on the life of Napoleon, which without any direct evidence was attributed to Mazzini's instigation. He had heard, without disapproval, that some people were planning an insurrection in Paris, and may have hoped that the two movements would help each other.[110] His own plans concentrated upon Lombardy. They involved him in his usual frantic activity, writing messages and orders all day and much of each night. The outbreak was eventually timed for 6 February to profit from the distractions and crowded streets of Milan on a Sunday during carnival. The local ringleaders were intending to proclaim a republic, but he persuaded them to desist in the hope of receiving help from monarchist Piedmont.[111] They in turn persuaded him not to come in person to Milan, preferring that he should remain on the Swiss-Italian frontier until it was known what support could be forthcoming. His private hope was that Cosenz, a professional soldier exiled from Naples, would lead the rising and, if successful, the Lombard, Marquis Visconti Venosta, would then head a provisional government.

On 23 January a council of war met for two days of discussions at Locarno. Some of the Milanese participants were in favour of proceeding at once with their plan. Medici and Cosenz, the two military experts, disagreed. Depretis and Sirtori were not present and could not be consulted. Even inside Milan there was a fatal division of opinion: the middle and upper classes represented by Visconti Venosta were reluctant to lend support until clear signs emerged of a probable victory, whereas leaders of the popular classes were determined to act immediately even without Mazzini's assistance and made quite clear that they 'do not want to be led by the gentlemen'.[112]

This disagreement marked a significant development in the division between Moderates and the National Party, between gradualists and active revolutionaries, the former preferring the objective of peacefully winning more liberties from the Austrians, the latter seeing national unification as a prerequisite of internal liberty. This split was now aggravated by a class division and the fear or hope that a political rising might turn into social revolution: 'better the Austrians or the Russians than another Mazzinian republic' was a sentiment voiced by some middle-class liberals.[113] Moreover, some of the 'gentlemen' in Milan resented that Mazzinians from other regions were trying to convert a local rising with limited objectives into something wider and less welcome.[114]

Mazzini realised from the disagreements at Locarno that the insurrection might have to be called off at the last moment and assumed that the new fact of telegraphic communication would make this possible, without realising that a complex and partly spontaneous rising had a momentum outside anyone's control.[115] The Austrians, who had plenty of money for bribing informers, knew weeks earlier that an insurrection was being planned, and police reports confirm that they thought Mazzini's involvement not particularly important.[116] The Piedmontese government was also forewarned and at the very last moment, as well as arresting some participants, gave information to the Austrians.[117]

The new prime minister in Turin, Count Cavour, was a liberal reformer but also a dedicated opponent of any conspiracy that might result in giving Mazzini political power, and on this occasion saw clear advantage in siding with Austria. Victor Emanuel went further and even congratulated the government of Vienna on the success of its counter-revolutionary repression. The king again criticised the British for giving sanctuary to Mazzini and promised the Austrian emperor that Piedmont could be relied on to 'exterminate' such 'vermin', especially as he believed or pretended that they aimed to assassinate all the monarchs of Europe.[118]

A dozen Austrian soldiers were killed when the rising broke out, but it failed, and sixteen insurgents were executed. Mazzini either deluded himself (or at least tried to convince others) that there were nine chances out of ten for success and failed to allow for the possibility that one single failure in synchronisation of a complicated movement involving several thousand people might be fatal.[119] He took much of the blame on himself, but even more blamed Medici and the 'gentlemen' who had spread distrust and scepticism among the other rebels. Such painful thoughts were kept secret so as not to divide his party still further. He had desperately hoped that 'twenty-four hours of resistance at Milan would have been everything: the kindling of a universal fire throughout Italy'. Success, in his opinion, had been prevented by 'trifling circumstances'.[120]

This was by now a familiar story. He had sent in advance some hundreds of grenade cases with a formula for making explosive, and a model for manufacturing mortars had been smuggled past the frontier guards labelled as a musical instrument; but these munitions were not assembled in time and many guns brought out of hiding were too rusty to use.[121] A great deal of the money he had sent to Milan was stolen by one of the conspirators who absconded. Worst of all was 'the fatal dissent of the middle class, the guilty behaviour of our best republicans belonging to that class. They denied to the last that the "people" could or would initiate.' On the other hand, many humble citizens took an active part and were abandoned by those who had been expected to lead them. Having based his plan on the assumption that groups in other cities were waiting upon events in Milan, Mazzini found that without one immediate local success the whole project collapsed. Some of the Milanese aristocracy, following Victor Emanuel's example, quickly sent an abject address of loyalty to Vienna in gratitude for an Austrian victory over the revolutionaries.[122]

In an ill-considered reprisal, Marshal Radetzky sequestrated the property of many richer Lombards who lived in Piedmont, some of whom were now naturalised Piedmontese subjects. This breach of natural justice and international law had the unforeseen effect of antagonising many who until now had been loyal Austrian subjects. It also permitted the Moderates to protest against Austrian bullying. Cavour made a formal complaint and withdrew his ambassador from Vienna, though he balanced this bold action by imprisoning more of Mazzini's followers without trial and transporting others on a naval frigate to the United States. Cavour also ordered the suspension of any newspapers that carried 'dishonest patriotic writings'. When a rumour circulated that the revolutionary leader was hiding near Genoa his arrest was ordered, and if he tried to escape he was to be shot.[123] Mazzini had to admit that the Piedmontese had at little cost scored a double victory against both Austrians and republicans. In vain he challenged the ministers in Turin to explain publicly whether they genuinely opposed Austria and whether they agreed with the national enemy that Italy was merely a geographical expression. But he himself was now far more vulnerable to criticism. Not only did the expulsions seriously weaken his organisation in Italy: he was accused by officially inspired propaganda of being no patriot, of being a greater scourge than the barbarians who had once attacked the ancient Roman empire, of being 'prepared to immolate the whole population of the country to satisfy his relentless vanity'.[124]

The failure of this revolt in Milan did more than anything since the invasion of Savoy in 1834 to cause desertion among his more level-headed colleagues and was as damaging to republicanism as the military defeat of Novara had been to the monarchists. In Britain some of the 'Friends of Italy' disliked what had taken place, though the society's official record concluded that the rising proved the strength of national feeling and to that extent reinforced the patriotic movement. One well-founded fear in London was that Italian patriots might drag other countries into a European war. *The Times* was predictably hostile at the thought that 'somewhere in the purlieus of Somerstown or Bayswater a small party of madmen were dreaming of the universal empire of democracy'.[125] Lord Clarendon told the Queen that he privately apologised to the Austrians for 'the disgraceful abuse of the protection afforded to these refugees', though he had to agree with *The Times* that until Mazzini broke some British law he could not be arrested. The minister's unsolicited but strong advice to Vienna was that only timely political reforms in Lombardy would avert another much more serious disaster.[126] When a cache of arms was discovered at Woolwich there was an almost automatic suspicion that it belonged to Mazzini. But he appealed as he had done before to what he called the British sense of 'fair play': so long as nowhere in Italy could he enjoy freedom to write and speak, regrettably 'we must be conspirators, purchase grenades, have false passports, smuggle, and rise with daggers if we can get nothing else'.[127]

After hiding for three months in a single room with the curtains permanently drawn, Mazzini returned from Switzerland to England in May 1853. There were reports that people had been hired to assassinate him,[128] but he travelled through France by public transport and through Paris in an open carriage. On such occasions the police excused their failure to catch him by spreading stories about him being a master of disguise, though he insisted that, apart from two occasions in 1831, he never did more than remove his beard and wear spectacles or speak Italian and French with an English accent.[129] 'The more you seek him, the more he eludes you,' wrote an official in Genoa.[130] Yet it cannot be entirely excluded, however improbable, that politicians or police feared to catch him and carry the odium of executing a recognised patriot. Nor is it impossible, however unlikely and despite the obvious risk, that some responsible Italian politicians preferred him to remain at liberty as a useful reagent or scarecrow for their manipulation of Napoleon and of public opinion in Europe.

Frustrated and ashamed of his failure, Mazzini wrote to Caroline Stansfeld that he felt like Othello 'whose occupation is gone'. He even thought of handing to others the burden of organising his party while he tried 'to regularise my own political suicide', convinced that ten years after his death no one would remember his name, yet still hoping that 'what I cannot achieve, others will'.[131] By the end of March he was nevertheless despising himself for such defeatism. 'I felt and feel perfectly convinced that the rising of Italy was the rising of Europe. And I felt and feel convinced that the rising of Italy is a comparatively easy fact, the idea having now reached the multitudes.' Every three or six months there ought to be another attempt because sooner or later a rising was bound to succeed.[132] The Milanese insurrection might have failed in appearance but had also shown that active resistance could be mobilised. The subsequent imposition of martial law in Milan damaged the reputation of the Austrians and widened the gap between them and the Lombard population. In Naples, hundreds of suspected liberals were sent to join others already in prison, and since anyone with a beard or wearing a hat was assumed to be an adherent of Mazzini, innocent Neapolitan citizens were forcibly shaved by the police and their hats cut to ribbons in the open street.[133] Another positive result was to have 'unmasked the Piedmontese government' and shown it to be more interested in foiling the republicans than in making an Italian nation. Even better, the insurrection might make Cavour understand that by outdoing the republicans in patriotic zeal he could weaken their claims on popular sympathy.[134]

Mazzini's extraordinary optimism and pertinacity continued throughout the 1850s to be an essential ingredient in the Risorgimento. Liberals as well as reactionaries found it convenient to censure him for a sequence of failed insurrections and assumed that he was therefore no longer a significant figure in politics, but others have judged that his conduct and contribution were more admirable after 1850 than before, and no less effective. His name continued to inspire people, some with affection and admiration, some with hatred, others with envy and a sense of rivalry. Lord Macaulay thought it 'highly probable that, in a few years, Italy will be on fire'. While criticising Mazzini's tactics, Marx had to agree that 'Austrian brutality has turned the Milanese failure into the real commencement of a national revolution' – and Marx could speak about revolution with some authority.[135]

Opinions were inevitably diverse. Most Piedmontese politicians, despite their own repeated failures in war, thought it unfortunate that he did not give up and leave them to continue what he had begun. One Prussian diplomat, while acknowledging his honesty and intelligence, thought that no one else posed such a threat to governments in Europe.[136] For socialists, on the other hand, the tragedy was rather that no leader on the left existed who could supplant him with a yet more extremist programme for undermining Italian society,[137] though he himself had good reason to believe that the socialist policy of social revolution would spell disaster for the national cause. The Moderates eventually made that cause their own, for which they continued to require his assistance even if without open avowal. They needed him as a constant stimulus; or alternatively as a useful scapegoat and alibi for their own occasional inadequacies; but also as someone who continued to preach an ideal of *italianità* which, after many misgivings, they ultimately came to recognise as feasible; and not least they needed his threat of a nationwide republican revolution to frighten Napoleon into supporting their own alternative of 'Piedmontese expansion'.

This was a role that Mazzini consciously played and exploited for different reasons of his own. Already in April 1853, to keep up the tension, he was planning another revolt. With astonishing persistence he argued that recent events in Milan made ultimate success more, not less, likely.[138] In reply to Medici, Sirtori and Visconti Venosta, who complained that these continued risings were useless, he insisted that the alternative was a disheartening and dishonourable submission to torture and executions. Even another reverse would be better than remaining quiescent, because without constant agitation the belief in nationality would wilt and the Austrians could consolidate their hold on Italy; whereas failures, by hastening the day of reckoning, would at least widen the division between governments and governed. The outside world had to be shown that Italians were ready to die for their liberty. If another local insurrection should ever succeed for a few days like that of March 1848, or indeed like that which eventually took place in May 1860, success might again prove infectious and capture people's imagination.

He now wanted the National Party to call itself the Party of Action, since only by the constant pin-pricks of insurgent action would the momentum towards nationality be maintained. Only thus would the Piedmontese monarchy be compelled to choose whether to risk standing aloof, or to side with the reactionaries, or to play unequivocally for leadership in a patriotic revolution. Victor Emanuel would understandably be unwilling to initiate any revolution and for that reason the Party of Action should retain its freedom to act independently. But Mazzini needed to keep open the likelihood of alliance with those moderate liberals, perhaps the majority of this small but important faction, who were ready to declare their support at the first sign of success; and he therefore again advocated a programme of consensus and a 'neutral flag', leaving constitutional differences for subsequent decision by a national assembly.[139] He continued to hope that such an assembly would opt for a republic, but knew that the Piedmontese monarchy had far greater resources and authority to influence a popular vote in a different direction, and that was an outcome he could accept.

His immediate plan was to concentrate on the Papal States where, according to foreign visitors and informed Italian Moderates, misgovernment and financial corruption were worse than anywhere else and all classes were 'disgusted and discontented'.[140] He had very little money for this purpose. At Rome, however, one of his most trusted agents, Giuseppe Petroni, lived in hiding with his own clandestine printing press for publishing Mazzini's propaganda. A Belgian diplomat at Rome reported in March 1853 that proclamations issuing from this press were plastered all over the city walls.[141] But a fatal division opened among the Roman patriots after they received messages from Turin promising help if they severed relations with Mazzini. Tempted by this offer, Petroni's chief assistant, secretary to the British consul, led a breakaway faction which published counter-proclamations and was thought, perhaps unfairly, to have betrayed ciphers and a list of compromised names to the papal police. Several priests were among those arrested in August 1853, and Petroni remained in prison for the next seventeen years. This was another damaging blow to the new Party of Action.[142]

A month later there was an attempt at revolt in Lunigiana, a much-favoured territory for revolutionary action because strategically well-placed on the border between Piedmont, Parma, Lucca and Modena, and where widespread smuggling provided useful recruits for any war against organised society. In particular the workers in the marble mines of Carrara had a long tradition of collective organisation and lawlessness. Mazzini, perhaps because unwell, left details of this operation to another trusted lieutenant, Felice Orsini, whose plans were betrayed to the Piedmontese police. Cavour was able to place this future national hero under temporary arrest before any serious damage was done.

In October, when the Crimean War seemed about to break out between Russia and the western powers, Mazzini hoped that a general European conflict would almost certainly provide another occasion for insurrections in Italy. Best of all would be if Austria put herself in the wrong by siding with autocratic Russia, or failing that if she tried to invade Serbia and Bosnia leaving her Italian frontier poorly defended. If he could then start another rising in Lombardy, the Piedmontese monarchists might be coerced by public opinion to side with the revolution.[143] He also hoped that Fabrizi, who had been collecting an armoury of weapons in Malta, would simultaneously promote a revolt in Naples and Sicily. The idea of Garibaldi landing with a volunteer force in Sicily was still very much in Mazzini's mind.[144]

CHAPTER FIVE

Marking Time: 1854–8

Garibaldi and Cavour: 1854–5

AFTER AGAIN BEING exiled from Piedmont in 1849, Garibaldi earned a livelihood commanding tramp ships between North and South America and the Far East. Only in the spring of 1854, conditional on renouncing active republican politics, was he allowed home and forgiven for his defence of the Roman republic. On his way, passing through the port of London, he invited Mazzini and Herzen to a meal on board ship. This was a friendly meeting but Mazzini's proposal for an expedition to Sicily was once again rejected. Though still a republican at heart, Garibaldi tried to persuade his guests that further revolutionary action would merely provoke resistance from the government and army leaders in Turin. He preferred the alternative of waiting for such people to become less regional and more Italian in loyalty. He knew this might fail and at best would take time. But, as he told Herzen, 'I know the Italian masses better than Mazzini for I have lived with them and lived their life. Mazzini knows the educated classes of Italy and sways their intellects; but there is no making an army from such people to drive out the Austrians and the pope.'[1]

This was fair comment. Equally justified, however, was Mazzini's rejoinder that neither the Moderates nor Garibaldi would ever initiate a war of national independence unless strongly pressed from below or from outside. He himself could provide such pressure. What he called 'popular movements' were a prerequisite without which nothing was likely to happen. First of all, such movements might convince the Piedmontese that a truly national war would attract widespread support; secondly, they would carry the threat that hesitation at Turin might increase the attractiveness of the republican alternative; and thirdly, they would suggest that the first region to adopt a policy of national unification in alliance with the revolutionaries would establish its claim to primacy over other regional capitals.[2] Such arguments, he hoped, would carry weight with Piedmontese politicians who until now had derided the idea of Italian unification as a utopian dream.

Garibaldi and Mazzini were both invited by the American consul in London to celebrate Washington's birthday. A memorable dinner was attended by the ambassador, James Buchanan, soon to be president of the United States, and the other leading revolutionary exiles in London were invited at Mazzini's particular request – the Hungarians Kossuth and Pulszky, Ruge the German, Herzen the Russian, Ledru-Rollin from France and Worcell from Poland. When after dinner the consul proposed that his guests should join in singing the *Marseillaise*, unfortunately no one knew the tune, so instead they drank a toast to 'the alliance between America and the future federation of free European peoples'.[3] This opened an exciting prospect, especially as it was known that Daniel Webster, a former secretary of state, was calling for an Anglo-American alliance to support the cause of European freedom. Mazzini was also in touch with Buchanan's predecessor as president, from whom he hoped to obtain support for the Italian revolution. But he disliked the way that both men, General Pierce and Buchanan, tried to justify slavery, and the same issue came between him and Kossuth, because the Italian republicans strongly objected to racial prejudice of any kind.[4] Nevertheless this dinner, though it created embarrassment for Buchanan in Washington, gave Mazzini the confidence of enjoying moral support from America. He came away from it hoping that American naval units in the Mediterranean might become 'our best allies' and provide arms for his next insurrection in Italy.[5]

Garibaldi's arrival in London caused quite a stir, though the conservative press regarded him with disfavour as 'a sort of Guy Faux' and he was still seen as being no more than a coadjutor of Mazzini.[6] Both names were now frequently mentioned in other British newspapers, usually with approval, though the hope was voiced that they might eventually cooperate with the Turinese government. According to one authoritative journalist, nine-tenths of those in Britain with an active interest in foreign policy were already convinced of the need to create a powerful, homogeneous Italy, and this was said to be largely Mazzini's handiwork. 'Europe holds few men of finer intellect, of a more pure and spotless moral character, or of a richer, tenderer, more genial nature.' Mazzini was described as being no disappointed intriguer, no vain and shallow egotist, and his distrust of the monarchy might be unfortunate but was understandable. Other people in England were convinced that his continual insurrections might no longer be what Italy needed, though Cardinal Newman's brother was sure that they were not merely justifiable but indispensable. According to Professor Francis Newman, this 'man of sorrows' would ultimately triumph because he preached 'a nobler practice and a higher faith than our routine statesmen dream of'. There was 'no doubt of his sincerity when he says, often, that he would sacrifice his republican views in the cause of unity. . . . He has provided a perennial crop of ever-ready martyrs whose number and devotion, we confess, fill us with wonder and respect. But as yet he has done no more. He has been unable to consolidate anything.' Yet the government in Turin was no longer seen in London as the 'stupid and leaden despotism' of Charles Albert. Under Cavour's guidance this small sub-Alpine kingdom, alone in Italy, was a society in process of gradual modernisation. Gladstone on another visit to Genoa was impressed to find much less censorship and some of Mazzini's writings at last freely on sale.[7]

Mazzini on the contrary continued to deplore that, despite introducing liberal reforms, Cavour and most politicians in Turin continued to suspect or dislike the objective of national unification. The Party of Action feared, correctly, that these politicians with their narrow idea of patriotism were still preoccupied by the ambition of dominating an enlarged state in northern Italy. Mazzini's own idea in February 1854 had been to broaden the movement by organising an expedition to Sicily. After this had been vetoed by Garibaldi, he left England in April, hoping to start another insurrection at Massa in the Duchy of Modena which had a garrison of Austrian troops. Surviving an alarming collision by his channel steamer off Dover he reached Switzerland a week later, despondent, 'rather permanently unwell', even wondering once again if he should not give up politics and return to his true métier of 'writing, printing, educating'.[8] Money was, as always, the chief problem and he was again relying on pawnbrokers. What made him envious was that the Greeks in London had recently collected £14,000 to support their national rebellion against the Turks, while his own begging letters to Italians produced almost nothing. A sum of £1,000 reached him from America and Peter Taylor lent £400, but this was not much when a single rifle cost nearly £1.

The rising at Massa proved to be another disappointment. In Switzerland he was too far away to influence Orsini, who had been released from prison and once again was in command. After one boat ran aground, a second was delayed at sea by contrary winds and failed to land at the agreed destination where arms were in store. In any case the Piedmontese government learnt in advance of what was intended and informed the Austrians as well as arresting most of those involved. A separate rising in the Duchy of Parma, about which Mazzini knew nothing, was equally unsuccessful. Then in August he tried to provoke a movement in Austrian territory where he planned to capture four steamers on Lake Como, but it was another fiasco.

This series of failures was further proof that he had again misjudged the readiness of Italians to support a rebellion. The educated classes, he said, were 'rotten to the core': they continued to allow themselves to be arrested by the hundred without reacting. Those in Lombardo-Venetia supinely paid a hundred million lire each year in taxation to Vienna and yet hardly a single rich Italian responded to his own appeal for funds.

Everywhere there were small groups of less affluent enthusiasts who, after promising him they were ready to rise, in practice waited for others to begin. 'The fact is that we are no party at all: we are a miserable set of boasters and hypocrites living on a certain number of commonplaces about fraternity, regeneration, *amour du peuple* and so on; but full of vanity, selfism, envy, revenge, sophism and pedantry, like our enemies: therefore we do not conquer: why should we?'[9]

Garibaldi instead blamed Mazzini's excessive belief in revolution; and Cavour who was intercepting their letters sent information to London about differences between these two revolutionary leaders.[10] Garibaldi was greatly upset that Pisacane and General Roselli were now publicly criticising his behaviour during the defence of Rome in 1849, and among other criticisms a rumour was even circulated that he might have accepted a monetary allowance from King Victor Emanuel. According to Mazzini, 'Garibaldi is good: he loves his country and hates the Austrians; but Garibaldi is *weak*. Therefore changeable. I believe that he has been really ensnared by the Piedmontese Ministry.' Such a man, though a brilliant guerrilla leader, would never initiate a rebellion; his great, indeed indispensable, contribution would lie in using his talents and prestige to support either conservatives or republicans, whichever succeeded in launching a successful action; but the one great lack was someone to start such a movement and demonstrate to other potential revolutionaries that it could succeed.[11]

Mazzini's low spirits were aggravated by the fact that he had to spend another six months isolated in a single room, first in Geneva and then in a remote hut in the mountains above Zürich, with no one to help in the painstaking labour of transcribing letters into cipher. Under pressure from neighbouring countries the Swiss once more issued an expulsion order and put a price on his capture, so incurring a protest from an American diplomat.[12] They also sent a physical description of this outlaw to Turin – where Cavour had been trying to obtain a daguerreotype so that frontier guards could recognise his features. He was described as dressing always in black, smoking cigars incessantly and possessing 'a noble demeanour as though accustomed to aristocratic society'.[13] But the fugitive was hard to locate even though he managed to keep up a large correspondence. Police agents by mistake once arrested someone sitting in a carriage next to their intended victim. Nostalgically he thought of fog-ridden London and at the end of October returned to the relative freedom of England.

Cavour, after three years as prime minister, was becoming recognised as among the ablest politicians in Europe, though his pragmatic 'Machiavellian diplomacy' was something that the idealist Mazzini could never abide. Both men were conspirators in very different ways. Cavour, too, as a young man had looked with some sympathy on the French Revolution and occasionally meditated on the possibility of changing the character of Italians to permit the regeneration of their country after centuries of submission to foreign rule. Defeating Austria and annexing Lombardo-Venetia were objectives that he called more immediately important than defending individual liberties. More than once he spoke of wanting to create a kingdom of Italy,[14] though until 1859 what he had in mind was to reconstitute the kingdom created by the first Napoleon in 1805, an expanded Piedmont north of the Apennines.[15]

In unrecorded private conversation Cavour often spoke of Mazzini,[16] a fact made more interesting by his almost never mentioning in public the name of his adversary. In 1852 he had again called Mazzini as dangerous an enemy as Austria.[17] He could acknowledge that the ardent patriotism of Young Italy had 'won over a large section of politically conscious youth',[18] but Mazzini's patriotic insurrections were a threat not only to liberal conservatism, but to Italy's international reputation and to what the prime minister continued to describe as 'the expansion of Piedmont'. 'I honour his personal honesty and disinterestedness; I believe his intentions are good and that he sincerely loves the cause of liberty and national independence; nor can I deny his skill as a writer and his extraordinary ability in devising plots and conspiracies. . . . What he entirely lacks is any capacity for leadership. . . . He lacks moral courage in the face of danger and the readiness to risk being killed.'[19] Mazzini could have replied that he risked death far more often than Cavour did, but on principle never answered gratuitous personal recrimination.

In politics these two distinguished Italians differed over other material points. Cavour for instance learnt from the events of 1848–9 the sad lesson that Italians would never win independence on their own; or, perhaps more accurately, that Italians by themselves could win only by a dangerous *levée en masse* which, by playing into the hands of the republicans, might destroy Piedmont's conservative constitution and her dominant position in Italy. In his view, far better and less costly would be to ally with imperialist France and connive at the hegemony of Napoleon III over Europe in return for French military help against the Austrians. He therefore did everything possible to convince Napoleon that Piedmont would have no truck with the revolutionaries. A degree of guile and concealment was required because in great secrecy he also tried to keep in touch with some of Mazzini's party, even giving them occasional encouragement so that he could discover their plans and exploit any success they might achieve.[20] Some of his cabinet colleagues would have been astonished and probably appalled to know that, in February 1854, he briefly contemplated sending Piedmontese soldiers to start a revolution in Neapolitan territory.[21] Cavour found it useful to call the republicans utopian and reckless but was himself no less so on occasion.

More realistically he employed scholars and journalists to cast discredit on Mazzini. This sometimes involved falsifying documents from the archives to which, most unusually, a few official historians were therefore given access.[22] Political considerations justified this at the time, but the archives were then closed for the next hundred years so that falsifications could not be corrected, and Mazzini has thus been held responsible for some actions with which he had nothing to do. Once again this rebel was labelled as a communist and vulgar assassin even when many documents told a different story. The fact that he repeatedly pledged conditional support for King Victor Emanuel had if possible to be concealed because it was politically inexpedient for it to be known, and of course no one was aware that Mazzini subscribed to the Piedmontese loan floated on the London market in 1854.[23] The Moderates managed to convince Gladstone and others that he was an enemy of religion,[24] whereas Mazzini's ecclesiastical policy as triumvir in Rome had not been greatly different from Cavour's in Turin. Another inaccurate legend propagated by the official historians was that the victory over Radetzky in March 1848 was due to King Charles Albert, not to a popular insurrection. Other invented stories were that Mazzini had rejoiced over the military defeat at Novara and was now sending agitators all over Italy to enlist criminals with lavish monetary bribes. One way and another the newspaper-reading public was led to regard Mazzini as the chief cause of Austrian military victories and of Italy's discomfiture.[25]

When Mazzini returned to England in November 1854, one reason was that he felt better understood in 'my second fatherland' and much safer. An Englishman living in Piedmont, with no particular axe to grind, was astonished at the 'disgraceful and bitter' comments made in Turin about the man who was regarded by many foreigners as 'the great Italian of this century': the writer admitted that this persecuted exile had made mistakes, but with slender resources he had done far more than the Moderates to keep the Italian idea alive, whereas 'the Piedmontese speak with disdain of Genoese, Lombards, Venetians, and dispose of them all contemptuously as "Italians"'.[26] Even the anti-revolutionary *Times*, in an article written by another Englishman resident in Italy, praised Mazzini's 'restraint' and the unselfish willingness with which, though denied by official propaganda, he was willing to accept a patriotic monarchy. The same article admitted the effectiveness of insurrections that, even when apparently failing, produced a hundred proselytes for every martyr who died.[27]

Another immediate reason for returning to England was the illness of Mrs Ashurst. Mazzini also once again intended to put his philosophy of life and politics into a book, but now made an interesting admission of how hard it was to find 'a proper shape for ideas which begin to lie too

deep and rather confused in my mind'.[28] To avoid wasting time, and perhaps also for security reasons, he kept secret his London address and lived
under an assumed name, never leaving his apartment in the daytime lest
his presence became generally known. Most evenings after dark he would
go to the Ashursts or Stansfelds for company. Members of 'the clan' later
remembered the enchantment of his conversation over a wide range of
subjects, above all religion, but also equal rights for women, American
slavery, and the injustice of British colonialism in China and the West
Indies. Another favoured topic was the need for cooperative societies in
Italy whereby workers could share the profits of their industry.[29]

One member of the Piedmontese parliament who managed to locate
him wrote of never before having met such a sympathetic and attractive
person: nor was there anyone in Italy with a finer intelligence or who
possessed a better idea of how to win Italian independence.[30] Another
Italian visitor was Francesco Crispi, who later in the century had a
brilliant career in politics. This young exile was encouraged by Mazzini to
make a serious investigation of contemporary culture in Britain and the
growing influence of continental, especially German, ideas. Crispi was
advised to study Carlyle and Mill above all; in poetry he should read
Tennyson and the Brownings; and should also learn about Charles
Kingsley, Landseer, Ruskin and the Pre-Raphaelites.[31]

Politics intruded again once war broke out in the Crimea and put paid
to any hope of peaceful writing and study. Mazzini had always looked on
tsarist Russia as a major danger to Europe but was appalled by the 'paltry,
hateful programme of expediency' that led Britain to fight Russia in
defence of the decrepit Turkish empire. 'War is for me the greatest of
crimes when it is not waged for the benefit of mankind, for a great Truth
to enthrone or a great Lie to entomb.'[32] Initially he hoped that there
might be a clear issue of principle in fighting for liberty and nationality
against the tyrannical governments of Russia, Turkey and Austria. Unfortunately Austria and Piedmont found reasons to support Britain in defending the 'galvanised corpse' of Turkey, so ending any chance of a rising
by the Greeks and Slavs to destroy the Austrian and Turkish empires. The
British championed liberty but only at home; abroad they backed an
immoral war to preserve the unjust territorial settlement of 1815 at the
expense of Italians, Poles and Hungarians who sought freedom to exist as
nations.[33]

Mazzini's remaining hope was that some Italians would take advantage
of the Crimean War and rebel. But the onset of hostilities caught him
unprepared, 'gnawing my teeth, biting my own heart, burning with
shame for my country, despising all my late friends; and grieving to
death'.[34] In a moment of desperation he hinted that only his profound
religious faith and the love of friends kept him from suicide.[35] Each week

he used to meet Kossuth in St John's Wood to discuss the course of the war and whether they could profit from it.[36] He caused great offence by appealing to Piedmontese soldiers to desert rather than fight in the Crimea for such a disreputable cause, and even suggested offering money as an inducement.[37] Not surprisingly he was sometimes accused of being a Russian agent. At one point he was presented with the chance of enlisting Russian help for a revolution in Italy when an offer was made from Moscow of as large a subsidy as he ever received in his lifetime, but it was refused.[38] Having already spent as much as he could lay his hands on of his mother's inheritance, he could afford only nine pence a day for food and talked of possibly having to pass his remaining years in a poorhouse. He could have appealed once more to his friends in Britain, but was ashamed to ask foreigners for still more money so long as Italians were reluctant to contribute.[39]

Foreign ambassadors in the various Italian capitals nevertheless testified to the continued alarm generated by his ongoing encouragement of popular agitation.[40] Everywhere in court circles there was moral outrage against someone who presumed to question the legitimacy of government authority. In 1854 he was automatically accused, though quite inaccurately, of being responsible for the assassination of Duke Charles III of Parma – a sovereign who incidentally was once quoted as having expressed admiration for Mazzini.[41] Chimerical allegations were made of how he continued to send assassination squads to Europe. The following year Giovanni Pianori, an Italian executed in France for trying to kill Napoleon III, denied that he had any accomplices, but many people including Queen Victoria blamed Mazzini, who at least seems to have known that some such attempt was being planned.[42]

In reply to this type of accusation he once again explained his views. He denied categorically that he ever ordered any assassination, for the same reason that he fought strenuously against the death penalty in England and elsewhere. But he was no pacifist so long as many Italians considered themselves in a state of war against Austria and against the French who were occupying Rome by armed force. He again quoted the authority of popes and moderate liberals who as a last resort justified tyrannicide as sometimes the lesser of two evils.[43] According to Panizzi, who investigated the matter, more than twenty thousand civilians may have been killed in Paris by Louis Napoleon when he seized power in 1851 against another 'legitimate authority', yet this usurper had been immediately recognised by Britain as a lawful sovereign. It was pure hypocrisy when Napoleon or moralistic conservatives in Britain condemned retaliation by

> an enslaved population, armed with daggers through want of better arms, upon their foreign oppressors. I do not understand the logic, nor believe in

the sincerity of men who train their children to admire Judith, Brutus or
William Tell, and still shout in horror of any man who, appealing to God
and his own conscience, rises solitary against the oppressor of his country
and saves perhaps hundreds of lives and millions of souls by crushing that
single, defaced, abnormal, impious life away. I believe in the justness of
battles for a holy cause, in the sacredness of revolt for freedom and
justice. . . . I believe this sorrowfully, and *only* when every chance of re-
enthroning right, justice, security through peace has fled, when merely
brutal physical force stands immovable between mankind and progression;
when both life and the aim of the good and brave can be saved only by
cancelling the life of the wicked.[44]

The sharp distinction that Mazzini drew between vulgar assassination
and conscientious armed rebellion has sometimes been called hypocritical, but the argument of hypocrisy might equally be directed against
Gladstone and Palmerston who in 1855 approached Mazzini's republican
friends Bertani and Pisacane for help in launching an armed raid on
Neapolitan territory to liberate King Ferdinand's political prisoners. This
extraordinary enterprise was organised by the British ambassador at
Naples acting under cover of his diplomatic immunity. The attempt failed,
but only because of accidents to a chartered vessel in which several
English sailors lost their lives and without anyone being brought to
court.[45] Cavour, too, who claimed to be morally outraged by Mazzini,
tried in 1856 to persuade the British to support another attempt to defy
international law by stirring up revolution in southern Italy,[46] and in later
years this much respected politician organised successive and secret
armed insurrections against legitimate sovereigns with whom he was
technically at peace. Cavour ridiculed Mazzini's lack of success and dep-
recated his 'immorality', but his own numerous attempts at encouraging
rebellion were no less questionable – and no more successful despite
using incomparably greater resources of money and men.

Further setbacks: 1856–7

Cavour in 1856 admitted privately that he might need the republicans
because they alone by their constant agitation could show that Italy was
dangerously combustible, and furthermore their illegalities might frighten
France into supporting the Piedmontese as a barrier against revolution.[47]
He was moving towards the idea that Italy would become more politically
united – a change of mind in which Mazzini's agitation may have been
instrumental. He was even prepared to admit that republicanism might

one day become an acceptable goal. But in the foreseeable future he did not see this as a serious objective.[48] Moreover a united Italy might mean the triumph of inexperienced and immoderate democrats who had little sympathy with conservative and monarchist Piedmont. In any case complete national unity would be vetoed by Napoleon, who did not want a strong Italy on his southern frontier, and Napoleon's military support remained an essential element in Piedmontese policy – despite Cavour's attempt in strictest privacy to convince Garibaldi that France was his greatest enemy. When hints came that the government in Paris had French candidates for the thrones of Tuscany and Naples, Cavour prudently refused to take a stand against this denial of Italian nationality. A completely united Italy, so the prime minister told Manin when they met in Paris, was in the circumstances a nonsensical dream.[49]

By the beginning of 1856 a group of more moderate republicans was looking for ways to bridge the gap between Cavour and Mazzini. Eventually they formed themselves into what they called the National Society, distinct from Mazzini's Party of Action. Their leader, in Paris, was the Venetian Manin, who until now had admired Mazzini and strongly criticised the Piedmontese Moderates. In Turin its chief members were the Lombard, Marquis Giorgio Pallavicino, and the Sicilian, Giuseppe La Farina. Pallavicino knew Cavour well and, like Gioberti earlier, had doubts about the sincerity of the minister's patriotic credentials.[50] Manin, too, continued to criticise politicians in Turin for talking rarely about Italy and far more about 'the aggrandisement of Piedmont'.[51] But both men disagreed with Mazzini in believing Cavour to be a pragmatic and malleable diplomat who, alone in Italy, had the ability and just possibly the wish to make the rest of Europe accept the existence of an Italian nation. Although Cavour still called Italian unification nonsensical, he recognised at least that the National Society was worth backing if it helped to rally support for Piedmont and isolate Mazzini from some former friends.

Manin contributed to Mazzini's isolation when in May 1856 he wrote to an English newspaper admitting that some Italians regrettably believed in 'the doctrine of political assassination and the theory of the dagger': by implication he was referring to Mazzini. Many dedicated patriots took it ill that this highly prejudicial remark was made public, let alone published in a foreign country, and an angry Mazzini demanded to know which of their fellow countrymen were foolish enough to propound any such theory. He himself repudiated it. Furthermore, despite what the Moderates continued to pretend, he had always promised that he would at once rally to Victor Emanuel in a truly patriotic war, whereas the monarchists since 1849 had consistently preferred to fight actively against the *italianissimi*. What he did not know was that Victor Emanuel, though speaking to some people about wanting war against Austria, could also talk of being quite ready to fight in alliance with the Austrians. The king sometimes admitted that his only pleasure was in fighting, especially since war would give him an excuse to modify the constitution and restore royal authority.[52] He also spoke of Mazzini as an enemy of the state who would be executed if caught.[53] Cavour confided to Pallavicino that Mazzini was a criminal who ought to be 'executed without pity', and the same intention of executing this troublesome opponent was admitted by other politicians including Cavour's immediate predecessor, the elder statesman Massimo d'Azeglio. To Azeglio as well as Balbo the word *italianissimi* was a pejorative expression implying ignominy and contempt.[54]

The authorities in Turin claimed to be confident that Mazzini was too cowardly to risk execution by returning to Italy.[55] But at the end of June, while they assumed he was safely in London, he secretly passed through Turin to see Giuditta Sidoli, and then returned to his home town of Genoa after an absence of twenty-five years. To evade the police he had to hide in one house after another with friendly guards posted to give the alarm. He never even dared to visit his mother's grave.[56] But at some point the government learnt of his presence, probably through an indiscretion by his sister.[57] Instead of arresting him, however, they indirectly let him know that, provided he remained concealed and kept silent about any connivance, they would secretly facilitate preparation for another insurrection against the Duke of Modena.

Mazzini promised he would never reveal any details about this strange episode and kept his word until, in self-defence against accusations by ministers, he had to explain that the initiative came not from himself but from them. He assumed correctly that, as on other occasions, the royal ministers wanted him to trigger off a popular insurrection as a pretext for their own armed intervention, though in retrospect he wondered whether they also meant to entrap him into an action for which Cavour could gain credit by arresting all those involved.[58] Other evidence confirms Cavour's active connivance,[59] whether the motive was entrapment, or more likely to appropriate and exploit any success, or merely as an excuse for suggesting to other countries that only by their helping to enlarge the kingdom of Victor Emanuel could a major revolution be averted. Whatever the reason, a hundred volunteers including monarchists as well as republicans crossed into Modena during the night of 25–26 July. When they were halted by lack of local support, Cavour claimed to be surprised by their action and arrested the participants as well as telling Modena and Tuscany what he knew of their plans.[60]

And yet Mazzini was not arrested but remained at Genoa in some kind of touch with the authorities. On 8 August he wrote to Peter Taylor that the Piedmontese government are a plague. I am indirectly in contact with them and trying all sort of concessions, but it is of no use: they will just try to avail themselves of a victory should we have one; meanwhile do nothing except spoiling our own attempts, and persecute when they fail. . . . I have now sent a sort of ultimatum to the Ministry which will compromise them if accepted, or leaves me free if not.[61]

Ten days later, in another surreptitious visit to Turin, he continued to look for common ground with the government, and the embarrassing fact of his presence in the capital city could not be kept secret. Some of the most intelligent and responsible Italians were continuing to hope, however implausibly, in the creation of a united front led by either Mazzini or Cavour, whichever of the two could present the more credible programme for the future of their country.[62]

The prime minister was in a quandary. His long-term plan was to annex Lombardy and Venice from the Austrians, for which he needed to stimulate popular unrest and appeal for that reason to at least some of the despised *italianissimi*. But far more important in his judgement was the need for French military support, and hence he could not afford to let anyone know that he was in touch with the Mazzinians. In public speeches he promised that in no circumstances would he ever countenance revolutionary methods.[63] In July he supported a public subscription to purchase a hundred cannon, but only for national defence. When Mazzini countered with a rival appeal to buy ten thousand muskets as a reward for the first province that rose in active rebellion against Austria, Cavour made a half-hearted effort to treat this second appeal as aggressive and illegal; but many Piedmontese, as well as Garibaldi and Manin, contributed to both subscriptions without difficulty.

In November 1856, bewildered and disgusted by such apparent prevarication, Mazzini returned to his winter quarters in London to replenish his war chest through a new organisation for the 'Emancipation of Italy'.[64] *The Times* condemned him as 'the prince of democrats', repeating that he was a socialist, an enemy of religion and an advocate of 'brutal rapine'; but on further investigation was honest enough to print a partial retraction.[65] Other British newspapers positively supported him, one of them quoting official statistics that listed as many as 6,701 summary executions since 1852 by the various Italian governments.[66] Surely, he argued, such figures justified rebellion, and if daggers were the only affordable weapon, so be it. He added that the Austrians were far more vulnerable than might seem, because not only did they have many frontiers to defend, but four-fifths of their soldiers south of the Alps were Italians, Slavs and Magyars whose loyalty was suspect. He did not expect the Piedmontese to take the risk of starting a new war, but a spontaneous

rising in one Italian province might be enough to induce them to cooperate and renounce Cavour's alternative policy – a policy that was
bound to result in replacing Austrian by French domination of the Italian
peninsula.

Mazzini's instinctive belief as always was that any insurrection that
failed should be followed as soon as possible by another in order to keep
morale from flagging and maintain a constant state of alarm. After each
failure he quickly set to work like a spider patching the holes in his web,
as he put it. To avoid the hazards of Cavour's double-dealing he decided
to concentrate for his next move on southern Italy, where help might also
be forthcoming from Manin's National Society. Such an enterprise would
help to mobilise resistance against Napoleon's intention to put the French
prince Lucien Murat on the throne of Naples. It might well appeal to the
British, since Palmerston had recently encouraged a similar attempt to
subvert the Neapolitan Bourbons and prevent a French take-over. It
should also appeal to those politically conscious southerners who, without being republicans, were disaffected and critical of the Bourbon regime. Crispi was therefore sent more than once to investigate the
situation in his native Sicily.[67] In November, Baron Bentivegna attempted
to lead a march on Palermo, but the populace was suspicious or indifferent and this brave man was betrayed and executed. Another execution a
few days later was that of Agesilao Milano, a soldier in the Neapolitan
army who tried and failed to kill King Ferdinand. Neither attempt was
organised by Mazzini, though both victims considered themselves his
disciples.

He himself still had less contact with Naples than with the centre and
north of Italy, but now found great encouragement from his former chief
of staff in 1849, the Neapolitan Carlo Pisacane, who had been hoping to
exploit any success by Bentivegna in Sicily. Pisacane had no sympathy
with Mazzini's religious convictions and antisocialism, but greatly admired the intelligence, magnanimity and nobility of someone who had
sacrificed more than anyone in the cause of Italian patriotism and was
incontestably its leading figure.[68] In the early months of 1857 the two
men decided to reactivate Palmerston's project and go one step further by
effecting an armed landing near Naples. Adriano Lemmi, a rich business-
man in Constantinople, sent £1,000 for it, but other money, to Mazzini's
embarrassment, had to be provided by his English and Scottish friends.

In May, to organise this expedition, Mazzini left England with what
funds he had collected, travelling secretly to Turin, then to Genoa where
he remained in hiding for the next three months. The Stansfelds saw him
off at the station in London, and he later wrote back to what he called his
'adoptive family' with news of his safe arrival. He knew the risks he was
running and asked them to think kindly of him 'on account of my being

1 Mazzini: pencil drawing by Giuseppe Isola, Genoa 1830.

2   Lithograph of Mazzini with the other two triumvirs of the Roman republic, Carlo Armellini and Aurelio Saffi.

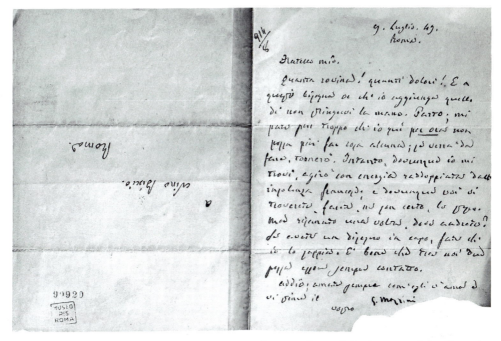

3 Unpublished letter to Nino Bixio, written on the eve of Mazzini's departure from Rome in July 1849: 'I can do no more here *for the moment,* but I will return if anything changes.'

Morale

Dei Doveri dell'Uomo.

n.170 Agli Operai Italiani

XIV.

Conclusione

Ed è questo, Operai Italiani, il vostro avvenire.
Voi potete affrettarlo. Conquistate la Patria. Con:
quistatele un Governo popolare che ne rappresenti
la vita collettiva, la missione, il concetto. Ordinatevi
tra voi in una capital universale Lega di Popolo,
tanto che la vostra voce sia voce di milioni e non
di pochi individui. Avrete il Vero e la Giustizia per
voi: la Nazione v'ascolterà.

Ma badate e credete alla parola d'un uomo
che studia da trent'anni l'andamento delle
cose in Europa e ha veduto fallire a buon porto
per immoralità d'uomini le più sante ed utili im:
prese. Non riescirete se non migliorando, non con:
quisterete l'esercizio del vostro diritto se non me:
ritandolo, col sacrificio coll'attività coll'amore.
Cercando in nome d'un dovere compito o da com:
pirsi, otterrete; cercando in nome dell'egoismo, in
nome di non so quale diritto al benessere che gli
uomini del materialismo v'insegnano, non otter:
rete se non trionfi d'un ora seguiti da delusioni
tremende. Quei che vi parlano in nome del ben:
essere, della felicità materiale vi tradiranno. Cer:

---

4 Draft of 'I Doveri dell'Uomo' written in 1860, dedicated to 'the workers of Italy'.

5   Mazzini in London, from a photograph of 1865.

6   Mazzini, depicted in a caricature of March 1865 as a fanatic, has his left foot on Trinacria, the symbol of Sicily, and his right foot on a bull ('tauro', indicating 'Turin', where a mob rioted against the monarchy for agreeing to the Convention of September of 1864 which replaced Turin with Florence as the Italian capital city).

7　A sample of Mazzini's handwriting, actual size, reproduced by kind permission of Mr James Stansfeld. It is in French and deals with his religious views.

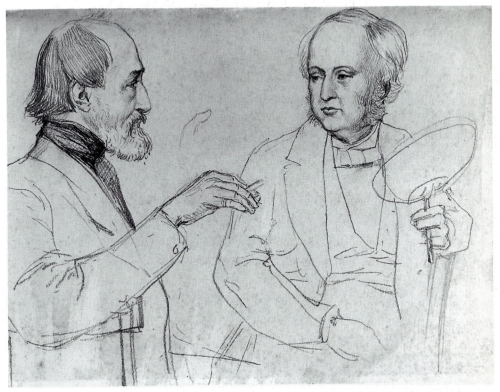

8　Mazzini talking to Benjamin Jowett, Master of Balliol: a drawing by the Earl of Carlisle.

9 Mazzini on his deathbed, sketched by Silvestro Lega of the Macchiaioli school: the finished picture is in the Museum of Art, Rhode Island.

10 Garibaldi, after his death, is welcomed into the pantheon of national heroes by Mazzini, Victor Emanuel and Cavour. At the bottom is a reproduction of Garibaldi's famous appeal of July 1849 offering blood, sweat and tears to anyone who volunteered to join him in his retreat from Rome. At the top, an anonymous writer sarcastically criticises Mazzini, 'the apostle of sacrifice', who refused to risk his own life at Milan in February 1853.

such an Englishman'; theirs was 'the country of my soul, the only and last spot on which I like to rest'; he would make one more attempt in Italy and then retire to die in England.[69]

Once again, despite official denials, the government in Turin knew something of his intentions and did nothing to stop him. Ministers apparently did not know where he was living but were intercepting some of his letters and were told by police informers that he was in or near Genoa.[70] His friends were nevertheless able to visit him without too much difficulty. Nor can the police have failed to know that large quantities of arms were being brought into the city and stored. The French urgently warned Cavour about his presence and in reply received a formal undertaking that the ministers in Turin would never have any dealings with such a dangerous revolutionary;[71] but this had been said before and people close to the prime minister knew that he was again playing a double game.[72] When allegations of duplicity were made in public the minister replied with what he called an indignant silence, and the assumption must be that Cavour was once again waiting for some revolutionary action that he could either exploit if successful, or else ingratiate himself with Napoleon by helping to crush if it looked like failing.[73] This was a highly risky procedure but could be thought justified if successful.

The odds were all against Mazzini succeeding, especially as Garibaldi was prudent enough to remain aloof. The plan was for Pisacane with a small group of friends to seize a packet-boat and sail to the island of Ponza where he would release prisoners of the Bourbon government and then land south of Naples. Like Bentivegna and the Bandieras, this brave man felt that even his death would advance the cause. His attempt, planned for 10 June, was postponed when the main supply of arms had to be jettisoned into the sea during a storm. Pisacane then went secretly to investigate in Naples and returned to Genoa with a deliberately exaggerated report about how everything was ready for an insurrection. Mazzini was not so sure, but agreed after some hesitation to support another attempt at the end of June. Once again a vessel loaded with muskets failed to reach the appointed rendezvous at sea in the Gulf of Genoa, but the intrepid Pisacane continued his journey and, after releasing the prisoners from Ponza, landed on the mainland at Sapri. Meanwhile Mazzini organised an elaborate and hazardous scheme to seize arms from government stores in Genoa. This forced Cavour to take repressive action, which led Mazzini to abort the operation; but his order failed to arrive before one soldier in Genoa was killed. Nor did the promised insurrection break out in Naples, and Pisacane was slaughtered with most of his companions.

Cavour was caught by surprise at the extent of Genoese support behind an 'excessively skilful conspirator'[74] and acted to distance himself from any suspicion of collusion. Not only did he give the Neapolitans information about Mazzini's plans[75] but he begged the French to send policemen to help locate him, and then tried to convince Napoleon of the implausible allegation that this elusive intruder was financed by the Austrian police as well as by Britain. When caught he would be publicly hanged, said the minister, and the same undertaking was repeated to a number of people.[76] If not caught, Cavour hoped the British could be persuaded to prosecute him, especially as the French claimed to have evidence of his involvement in a plot by Paolo Tibaldi to assassinate the emperor. When Lord Clarendon asked to see the evidence for this particular allegation he was told only that the two men knew each other, and other evidence produced in court seems to have been forged. When Mazzini *in absentia* was sentenced to transportation, *The Times*, which at first had automatically assumed his guilt, was compelled to admit that no English court would have convicted.[77]

Mazzini knew at least something about Tibaldi's intentions and not impossibly may have hoped that a simultaneous insurrection in Paris would make Pisacane's success more likely, but he firmly rejected any action motivated by the desire for revenge, punishment or expiation. Prostrate with grief over the death of his friend, he remained seriously ill for the next few months: he spoke of asthma, deafness and a disfiguring attack of what may have been eczema or psoriasis. 'I am weaker and gloomier than I have ever been,' he wrote to Emily Ashurst, and wondered if it was his fate to be 'a perennial source of mischief'.[78] For ten days he managed to hide in or near Genoa. The police once searched the house of Ernesto Pareto, whose Irish wife succeeded in concealing him under a mattress, and the next day after shaving his beard he passed unrecognised through a police cordon, allegedly asking one officer to light his cigar.[79] Many of his companions were arrested and the Marquis Pareto remained in prison for the next six months. If Mazzini succeeded until 8 August in continuing to live just outside Genoa, the explanation may be merely that no one betrayed his whereabouts; or possibly that Cavour feared to have his own collusion exposed in a legal trial; or else, if this is not too far-fetched, that Cavour positively needed Mazzini to remain at large as a bugbear to win outside support for Piedmont;[80] or else, most probable of all, that the police were simply inefficient. Victor Emanuel thought that his own private agents were much better informed than the *carabinieri*, and Cavour used to express incredulity about how this elusive fugitive managed to baffle all the police forces of Europe.[81]

Mazzini had just passed his fifty-second birthday. Failure confirmed once again that, though discontent was widespread, Italians would be hesitant to rebel until they could envisage genuine signs of probable success. Yet he was sure that recent failures had not been fruitless if they helped to give the impression that Austrian domination was being progressively undermined.[82] This was no time to cry halt. 'I am thirsting, raving for action and sick of everything else concerning Italy or Europe. Without a good sweeping storm there is no hope; the air is polluted; words have lost their meaning. . . . Every rule of political truthfulness and morality is lost.'[83]

He readily confessed to Quinet that it was not in his nature to use the artifice and guile needed by a successful politician.[84] Nevertheless the refusal to be what others called 'realistic' was in his opinion sometimes justified even on grounds of practicality and expedience; and many others agreed.[85] *Politiques* were necessary in any political movement, but so were idealists who refused to compromise on at least some issues of principle. Governments ought to be confronted squarely with the problem of nationality, a problem that could not be resolved by half-measures or compromise. Resolute and principled action would eventually persuade Italians that political unification would diminish some of the tensions and instability in their society. Only a large national market would create the prosperity needed to solve their fundamental economic and social problems.[86] Yet such considerations of expediency, just like discussion about beneficial political reforms, were a minor matter.

> The question of Italy is not one of more or less personal security or administrative improvement in one or another corner of our country; it is a question of *nationality*; a question of independence, liberty, and unity for the *whole* of Italy; a question of a common bond, of a common flag, of a common life and law for the twenty-five millions of men belonging – between the Alps and the sea – to the same race, tradition, and aspiration.[87]

Nor should Italians ever forget that their Risorgimento must not be inward-looking, not the 'narrow nationalism' that had been disastrous in the European revolutions of 1848. Only by heralding a wider movement for nationality throughout Europe would it be morally justified and attract general support.[88]

Orsini and Plombières

On 14 January 1858, Napoleon was fortunate to escape when bombs were thrown at his carriage killing eight bystanders. Felice Orsini and Giuseppe Pieri were guillotined for this outrage, and the fact that both these Italians had once been associated with Mazzini gave a pretext for further recrimination against his Party of Action. But Orsini, for personal as well as political reasons, had some months earlier become a bitter enemy of Mazzini and indeed was hoping by such a horrific action to supplant his former leader with a more extreme and violent policy for the patriotic revolution.[89] Mazzini deplored Orsini's attempt, unlike some far less revolutionary and more respectable politicians.[90] The Turin government also deplored it and blamed Mazzini despite possessing evidence that he was innocent.[91] Fortunately no one knew that Cavour, fully aware that the two would-be assassins were enemies of Mazzini, had actually been subsidising Orsini and Pieri from his secret service funds, and subsequently paid a pension to Orsini's widow.[92]

These facts are puzzling in retrospect; and so is the fact that Orsini at once became a national hero in Turin whereas Mazzini was again sentenced to death by the high court in Genoa. This sentence was demanded by Napoleon, who supported the demand by threatening the loss of French assistance. Cavour, too, realised the usefulness of stigmatising Mazzini as a criminal who not only was damaging his country's reputation but was a socialist who was said to have loved revolution more than he loved Italy. The Turin parliament was even informed by Cavour that he had proof of Mazzini's involvement in a further plot to kill Victor Emanuel;[93] though not the slightest evidence of such an improbable plot has ever been found. The object of this damaging allegation felt entitled to explain in self-defence that the government had secretly connived at insurrections by the Party of Action.[94] But radical newspapers were prosecuted when they printed this revelation, and when juries absolved them, Cavour brought political pressure on the judges to convict and sentence with severity. The minister authorised bribery of opposition journalists as well as frequent confiscation of the opposition press 'without bothering too much about legal niceties' so as to drive such troublesome newspapers out of existence; and over a hundred sequestrations eventually forced the *Italia e Popolo* into bankruptcy.[95]

Here was another recognition that this impoverished exile was still considered a rival whose influence was too great and had to be demolished. Both men, minister and refugee, were sincere patriots. Both were revolutionary in their different ways and admitted as much. By foreign diplomats Cavour was sometimes called a 'Mazzini in miniature' and a covert ally of the republicans,[96] but this was a reputation he urgently needed to disprove so as to consolidate his alliance with France. One among his closest colleagues admitted to having learnt patriotism from Mazzini and to be grateful for the fact,[97] but Cavour himself could concede nothing now that he recognised the difficulty of mobilising enough support behind an alternative monarchist programme for an expanded Piedmont.

Nevertheless both men, enemies though they remained, continued to need each other for their own different objectives. Despite his great gifts as a parliamentarian and diplomatist, Cavour required the help of others more persuasive than himself in patriotic propaganda; he also needed them to promote the hazardous insurrections that one day would trigger the European war that was now his chief objective in foreign policy; and of course he continued to need the republicans as a threat with which to frighten Napoleon into underwriting an extension of the Piedmontese frontier in northern Italy.

Mazzini on the other hand was rather hoping to educate politicians in a larger vision of *italianità*. He sometimes could welcome the fact that the government in Turin was increasingly recognised in other European capitals as speaking for Italy, in particular when the Piedmontese were allowed to attend the Congress of Paris in 1856 on terms of almost equality with the other great powers. His personal role would be to provide the armed initiative that he hoped might enable Cavour to declare his support for political unification, so contributing an army and finance that the republicans lacked. If that happened he now thought it 'probable' that Italians would eventually vote to accept Victor Emanuel as their national king; and he repeated that democratic republicans would loyally if unenthusiastically accept such a decision.[98] He himself would resist any attempt to impose a republican regime against a popular vote.[99] Nevertheless republicans knew that they had an essential part to play.

What would Italy be without the Party of Action?. . . . Had nothing revealed Italy's life since 1848, would Europe believe that soon or late her nationality must triumph? Had nobody stirred, would Piedmont itself pretend to hope?. . . . And how, and by whom, and through what has the popular element, now visibly at work, been conquered? And how did the religious reform succeed in Europe except through a series of attempts which were leading to the scaffold, or to fire?

Like the Protestant Reformation, the Risorgimento needed martyrs and insurrections as one means of persuading public opinion that national unification was possible and desirable.[100] Cavour needed what Mazzini called a 'gadfly' and a 'bugbear' to frighten the rest of Europe, a role that the republicans were ready to accept consciously, even gladly.

Orsini's enterprise, though Mazzini thought it wrong, turned out to be an example of just such a successful martyrdom. People close to Napoleon were sure that an almost paralysing fear of assassination by Italian malcontents was important in now making the emperor agree to help Cavour expel Austria from Italy.[101] The French decision was put to Cavour when he was summoned to a meeting at Plombières in July 1858. Here the two men agreed that secret preparations should at once begin for a major war to commence in the following spring. The Italian minister's task would be to create a *casus belli* by provoking a popular insurrection against the Duke of Modena, precisely the place and the objective that Mazzini had repeatedly suggested in 1854–6. Austria would then be compelled to defend her supremacy in Italy and, after her defeat, Savoy and Nice would be ceded to France in payment for Piedmont being allowed to annex the rest of northern Italy. Any idea of unifying the whole peninsula was not mentioned at Plombières and had no place in Napoleon's calculations. The intention was that Tuscany would remain independent but under French instead of Austrian influence. Naples would also come into the orbit of French domination after replacing Ferdinand by Lucien Murat as a puppet king. Napoleon also proposed to make all the states of Italy into a loose confederation, with the pope acting as its nominal president; and Cavour at once saw that, if not an ideal solution, this would be an immense diplomatic victory for himself and his country.

Mazzini learnt more quickly than perhaps any European cabinet about the details of these secret decisions at Plombières. He mentioned having three well-placed informers close to the authorities in Paris and Turin:[102] some people suspected that one of these was a friend of his former collaborator Dr Conneau, the emperor's physician who was notoriously indiscreet. Cavour claimed to be simultaneously paying large sums of money in return for information from 'one of the leaders of Mazzini's party', but had to admit that somehow a single isolated refugee in a humble London boarding house had the means of knowing more and sooner than almost anyone in Europe about the secrets of continental diplomacy, a fact also acknowledged by an envious Karl Marx.[103] What Mazzini realised at once was that a military alliance with France was designed by the monarchists in Turin as a first step towards imposing on Italy a far more restrictive programme than his own plans for a completely unified nation. Such an alliance had the further grave disadvantage that it would antagonise public opinion in Britain which feared French imperial domination in Naples and Tuscany. What he found additionally offensive was that reliance on the French army for winning Lombardy would show the world that Italians lacked the strength and will to achieve nationhood by their own effort. The new state of northern Italy was bound to become a satellite of an authoritarian and militaristic France, a junior partner in another imperialist domination of Europe that repudiated his own vision of a brotherhood between nations. Such an outcome would be shameful and humiliating. It would be the handiwork of a foreign autocrat who presumed to call his enemies assassins but was himself 'the worst assassin of all', a man who had won power in France by wholesale slaughter and subsequently sending many thousands of his political opponents to die of disease in the penal settlements of French Guiana.[104]

How to react to this imminent war was an issue discussed by a committee of exiles that met regularly at Mazzini's free school in Hatton Garden. To propagate their ideas a bi-monthly paper, *Pensiero ed Azione*, was launched by the school managers in September 1858. Not many copies of this paper managed to penetrate the frontier defences of Piedmont or Lombardy, but it found eager readers as far away as Egypt and Malta. Each issue of a thousand copies cost £15 to produce, almost all provided by Mazzini. To begin with it was almost entirely written by him, and subsequently he had to translate other articles by Herzen, Blind, Kossuth and others. The paper's chief concern was with how to promote the emergent European nationalities in their struggle against the four empires of France, Austria, Turkey and Russia. Its hope was that Piedmont might one day assume a mission of leadership in Italy, but there was regret that Cavour and the monarchists never referred to Italian unification as desirable or possible. 'We are against monarchy not because we are republicans, but because we believe in unification': this, once again, was Mazzini's considered opinion. All his life he had maintained that republicanism was a means, not an end in itself;[105] but monarchy would have to justify itself before it deserved support.

Most of his British friends, even pacifists, secularists and socialists who did not always agree with him, continued to give moral and material help to assist his Italian ambitions. A Newcastle paper referred to £27 collected at Hawick and £100 at Paisley; but only a laborious searching through the provincial press would reveal the extent of such fund-raising. When some people, alarmed for his safety, offered to pay for a bodyguard, he refused as he always on principle refused any gift for his personal benefit, but was finally persuaded to take £100 from Taylor and the Ashurst family to provide secretarial help for his newspaper and for propaganda. To protect himself he sometimes carried a swordstick. For further protection a dozen or more well-wishers in London provided him with cover addresses for correspondence, and other friends continued to walk him home at night from their meetings. Peter Taylor's niece later remembered, perhaps not quite accurately, that her uncle prepared 'a cunning little chamber of cupboard size' in case he needed to hide from French or Austrian agents.[106]

While awaiting the outbreak of war he put aside any idea of further insurrection and for the two years 1857-9 remained quietly in London. Cavour's ambassador in July 1857 had reported with regret that Mazzini was thought in England to be the only person with a clear and plausible answer to Italy's problems.[107] Many new acquaintances sought his company, one of them being Charles Bradlaugh the social reformer and secularist, who found him to be one of those rare politicians characterised by 'thorough truthfulness and incorruptibility'.[108] Mazzini made another friend in John Nichol, the Regius Professor of Astronomy in Glasgow, all of whose writings he claimed to have read;[109] and Nichol's son, who became professor of literature in Glasgow, described him in 1858 as someone who, though too much of a poet and idealist to be a successful politician, 'gained the affections of all who really knew him' and would 'long outlive his critics'. In one week he received four invitations to dinner, yet was always too busy to enjoy social occasions with people he did not know well. One of the Winkworth sisters remembered an evening when he 'talked so much it would take me hours to write it down'.[110] Among the usual themes of his conversation were 'duty before rights', the need for religious belief and for everyone to possess a consciousness of nationhood; also to possess an awareness of European brotherhood. His hosts recalled his anxiety to rebut accusations that Italians submitted apathetically to tyranny. Another subject of conversation was the hypocrisy of British politicians who talked of 'fair play' and claimed to believe in liberty while doing little to defend it over most of Europe. But appreciative comments were now sometimes made by him about the beneficent influence of British colonisation in India and Australia.[111]

Conversation between friends is rarely recorded accurately and is easily forgotten. But long afterwards James Stansfeld, MP, told an American friend how

> Mazzini naturally took his place at the centre of our circle, and we continued from that day to the end to grow around him, almost as his own flesh and blood. . . . His entrance into the room every Sunday was eagerly awaited, and our conversation hesitated until his arrival. He used always to withdraw when the hour for his visit to the Hatton Street School for poor Italians approached, and some of us generally went with him to bring him back. His conversation was then, as always, rich, brilliant, his manner modest and winning. He never uttered an idle word.[112]

Other foreign residents in London remembered attending meetings of 'the clan'. Mathilde Blind wrote that

> those who have heard Mazzini will never forget the eloquence, originality, and range of his talk. . . . In fact to have known Mazzini is to understand those mythical and historical figures who, from Buddha to Savonarola, have infused a new spirit into the outworn religious thought of their age. . . . All the writings of Mazzini, however powerful, are but a pale reflection of his own impressive and apostolic individuality. . . . His quenchless faith in the progress of the race, in the duty of the individual to modify and transform the social medium, and in the intrinsic oneness of all human life, gave it a deeper reality by connecting our temporary

passage here with all the generations that have gone before and are coming after.[113]

Malvida von Meysenbug, later a friend of Wagner and Nietzsche, saw him often at this period because she lodged in the same street and he used to send her several books each week as a member of a small book club that he organised. One author she recalled him selecting was De Tocqueville. She described his diminutive bed-sitting-room where he lived 'like an anchorite' with a sofa that converted into a bed. She confirmed that despite his poverty he continued to give half his scanty income to other exiles. 'He was the noblest person I have ever known.'[114] His natural temper was described by her as far from that of a conspirator: indeed 'he profoundly disliked the methods of conspiracy that were imposed on him by circumstances'. And yet beneath his idealism and humanity she, like Jane Carlyle, discerned 'something of Machiavelli' and a readiness to adopt 'furtive methods' when open protest was impossible. She was another who mentioned the magic of his personality and a bewitching voice that kept animated conversations alive far into the night.

> Without wanting to do so he dominated these occasions as someone whose superiority is immediately recognisable, but his domination was very different from the pretentiousness of Kossuth. No one who saw Mazzini for the first time would think that this small, delicate person dressed in black timidly entering the room was a famous agitator. Only when he took up his place by the fireside, where others spontaneously gathered around him, would you recognise him as a quite extraordinary person.[115]

Cavour was upset to hear of large sums of money being given in London to the republicans and was perplexed by the equally inaccurate information that Mazzini had become a British subject. There were even malicious stories of money being extracted by threats of assassination on behalf of this 'cowardly atheist' who was 'the most sanguinary of men'.[116] Conservative newspapers in London sometimes accepted such stories as true, and *The Times* with unconscious irony compared him unfavourably to the more 'gentlemanly' Orsini.[117] On the other hand the far from radical *Daily Telegraph*, with a bigger circulation than *The Times*, caused offence in Turin by an article praising this condemned criminal as 'the greatest Italian of these times'. The author questioned the extremism and impracticality of someone whose ideas were 'far too advanced for the present state of Italian development', but admired the courage and self-sacrifice with which until now he had borne the brunt of Italy's patriotic revolution. Though the article praised constitutional monarchy as in general preferable to a republic, Mazzini's party was said to be 'in every respect' more patriotic than its monarchist opponents. By persecuting this party, by refusing to recognise their debt to it, and instead by narrow-mindedly resorting to 'vulgar scurrility' which the republicans refused to emulate, the constitutionalists were delaying 'the consummation which liberal minds look forward to with so much anxiety, the emancipation of the Italian peninsula'.[118]

The Making of Italy: 1859–61

The war of 1859

IN JANUARY 1859, politicians in Paris and Turin were continuing prepa-rations for the major European war they had carefully timed to break out in April when the rainy season was over. Cavour was secretly hoping that the war would allow him to annex Venice, Lombardy and possibly smaller areas in central Italy. But Napoleon insisted that Piedmont must not think of becoming one of the great powers. Indeed Mazzini received 'positive information' that the French would permit no more than the annexation of Lombardy,[1] and this was one reason why he himself wanted an entirely different war, not one designed by Napoleon to make a still divided Italy into a French dependency. To frustrate the 'anti-Italian policy' of Cavour he therefore encouraged the Party of Action to be ready for local insurrections in order to persuade the Piedmontese that they had more to gain from defying the French and aiming at nothing less than national unification.[2] This alternative objective, so he hoped, might be supported by the British, who could never approve of Cavour's submis-sive acquiescence in another Napoleonic domination of Europe.

A different view was taken by other leading republicans, especially soldiers such as Garibaldi and Medici who felt that only the French army had the capacity to defeat Austria. Mazzini was depressed by this differ-ence of opinion, but gave way in deference to the probability that 'the immense majority' of Italians would support Cavour and Garibaldi rather than himself.[3] To explain the dissenting views of his London committee he nevertheless published a long manifesto, to which he appended 143 signatures of other exiles, sometimes without their prior consent since he had to move quickly – one example of what Meysenbug had referred to as 'dunklen Mittel' and 'etwas von Machiavell'. These were its main points:

the unity and liberty of an oppressed and dismembered people cannot be attained as a concession or gift of others, but must be conquered by the effort and sacrifice of those who desire unity and liberty. . . . Our party believes that without Unity there is no Country; that without national sovereignty there is no Nation; that without liberty, true liberty for all, there can be no real national Independence. . . . We also believe that any war fought by Italians for national independence disjoined from that of liberty would lead to tremendous disillusionment and the mere substitution of new masters for old. . . . We believe that Louis Napoleon Bonaparte cannot without self-destruction establish by force of arms in Italy the liberty that at home he has drowned in French blood. For us to ally with despotism would be to deny those principles which justify and render sacred the Italian cause. . . . We think that an alliance between the Piedmontese monarchy and Napoleon would render inevitable a European coalition against what would be seen as a war of conquest, and this prospect has already deprived Italy of much of the favour she has hitherto received in Europe. . . .

We republicans reserve our right of vote and peaceful propaganda, but now as ever will sacrifice the immediate triumph of our own beliefs to the opinion of the majority. We will therefore follow the Piedmontese monarchy into the field and use our every endeavour to promote military victory provided that the explicit aim is National Italian Unity. . . . We regard Piedmont with affection as a most noble province of Italy called by fortune to a glorious initiative and we hail the Piedmontese people as a people of brothers. . . . Nevertheless our conviction is that not Piedmont but the whole Italian people must one day accept the duty of freely and loyally establishing the form of government of our new nation. . . . Whether our voice is listened to or no, by this declaration we are fulfilling our solemn duty as Italians.[4]

This manifesto alarmed the French emperor, who warned Cavour that Mazzini must have mysteriously discovered their plans for an aggressive war and was using this information to turn the rest of Europe against them.[5] To allay such fears the Piedmontese premier replied that Mazzini was the one person whose offer of support would be rejected out of hand and who would be executed if he tried to interfere with their plans.[6] Cavour explained that for ten years he had been striving to erode the popular backing enjoyed by Mazzini, whose malign influence now threatened to split the patriotic front and pervert to his own advantage their victory against Austria. This reassurance was coupled with an implicit threat that only if Napoleon kept his promise to defeat the Austrians would Mazzini's influence be eradicated; and a similar threat was sent to persuade Prussia not to take Austria's part.[7]

Cavour was shrewdly playing on French fears and ambitions. He knew he could not openly accept Mazzini's offer of support without destroying the alliance made with Napoleon at Plombières. His difficulty was that he needed a war in which the French army would do most of the fighting, yet secretly was hoping for a more revolutionary war than the French wanted, indeed a Mazzini-style war without the unwelcome presence of Mazzini himself. He had to preserve his own reputation as a dedicated enemy of revolution, but privily intended to deceive Napoleon by stirring up insurrections inside Italy wherever he could prevent them being taken over by the radical revolutionaries. In great secrecy he also sent large consignments of arms to Romania and Hungary to start insurrections throughout the Balkans when war began,[8] which was a project quite as unrealistic as anything proposed by the republicans. To promote what he continued to call 'the expansion of Piedmont' he told friends that he was ready 'to set fire to the whole of Europe'. If it could help to defeat Austria he would start a civil war in Switzerland. Even more strange was an attempt to involve the British on his side in the war, and when this met with a rebuff, he talked wildly of fighting not only against Austria but against Britain as well; and for that purpose fancifully envisaged obtaining military help from Russia, Greece and even the United States.[9]

Cavour became increasingly excited as he pursued this extravagant and badly miscalculated vision. In public he pledged his unalterable respect for treaties – which in fact would have obliged him to accept Austrian rule in Lombardy. But in secret his instructions were that, at the end of April, a 'spontaneous' insurrection should be manufactured at Massa to give him an excuse to invade the duchies of Modena and Tuscany; and he was confident that such an insurrection would easily succeed.[10] But the results were negligible, partly because the French vetoed any action in Tuscany, and partly because he feared that any truly spontaneous movement or enrolment of volunteers might favour Mazzini and the democrats.[11] Cavour had to confess, no doubt with regret, that he would prefer the grand duke to remain as ruler of Tuscany rather than let him be deposed by the radical patriots. Better have a divided than a democratic Italy. As a last resort he might even defy the patriots and import from Prussia a Hohenzollern princeling to govern Tuscany as a separate state.[12] For similar reasons Mazzini was the single person he excluded from an amnesty granted in April.

But the prime minister scored a brilliant success when he made Austria put herself in the wrong by being the first to declare war, and Mazzini thereupon overcame initial doubts and promised his full support. Though the intervention of French troops was in his opinion a disaster, war might inadvertently release the pent-up forces of popular revolution, and trusted friends were therefore despatched to prepare for a simultaneous insurrection in Sicily. Day by day, as in 1848, he eagerly followed the course of hostilities on a large wall-map of Lombardy and was delighted to think that the world would now be forced to recognise Italians as able and willing to fight for their independence.

What greatly alarmed him after a few weeks was that the Piedmontese army proved almost as defective as in 1848. Other disillusioning revelations were that many of the Lombard peasants were once again hostile, or at least unenthusiastic about being delivered from Austria, and also that the many Italian soldiers in the Austrian army, while some deserted, again fought valiantly on the wrong side.[13] Equally disturbing was that support from popular risings was positively discouraged by Cavour as soon as he realised that they might be excessively 'patriotic'. The prime minister was eager to promote revolution in the distant Balkans but not nearer home: he preferred the great expense of arming shadowy, nameless figures in Belgrade and Bucharest who in practice did nothing to help him, at the same time as he denied these arms to Garibaldi's volunteers in Lombardy who fought well but were politically dangerous. What he wanted in Lombardy was not Mazzini's idea of popular insurrection but rather a military conquest to justify Piedmontese annexation, and the sad result was that city after city waited to see whether Napoleon's army was winning or losing. Cavour remembered that the insurrections of 1848 had been almost too successful because they encouraged the Lombards to demand a say in their own affairs by calling for a new national constitution, and he was determined that this should not be allowed to happen again. Public statements of welcome by the population would be appreciated, but 'absolutely no street demonstrations' was his order, and only too late did he realise that passive inactivity would reduce the chances of victory.[14]

Lack of popular enthusiasm in Lombardy and insufficient support from the Piedmontese army were two reasons given by the emperor when in July, without so much as consulting his ally and before proceeding to attack Venice, he unexpectedly signed an armistice. The settlement he proposed, again without consulting Cavour, was his favourite programme of making Italy a loose confederation under the pope. He also intended the Austrians, by virtue of ruling Venice, to be part of this confederation; also the rulers of Tuscany, Modena and Parma, who had absconded during the war, should be restored to their separate thrones; and most of Lombardy would be ceded by Austria but only to the French, who could then give it to Piedmont if they wished. Cavour was affronted and humiliated. He resigned and in a moment of anger spoke of defying Napoleon by supporting Mazzini's call for a national revolution.[15] But a few hours later he recovered his equipoise. He still hoped one day to annex Tuscany and Modena, for which, since the alternative of civic risings was too 'Mazzinian', he would be absolutely dependent upon the emperor's continued patronage.

Mazzini's reaction was entirely different. Unlike Cavour he was not at all surprised by Napoleon's desertion, and indeed had precisely foretold it many months earlier. He at once urged Victor Emanuel to seize the crown of a united Italy by rejecting the armistice, repudiating the policy of Napoleon, and putting his trust in the forces of revolution. Mazzini insisted that the republicans, 'as we have said thousands of times', were more than ready to fight for a king who accepted national unification. To encourage a change of heart in Turin he hoped that the people of Tuscany, Modena and Parma would refuse to accept Napoleon's armistice and vote to unite with a still reluctant Piedmont.[16] Sicily and Naples should rebel against their Bourbon sovereign and also vote for union. The French would of course object, but not by force because that would risk war against Britain – this was Mazzini's shrewd and entirely correct judgement. In London a new Whig administration under Palmerston and Russell was strongly against French aggressive ambitions and was able to recognise the advantage to British interests if twenty-five million Italians formed a single independent state.[17] An active interventionist policy by Britain was also advocated by other public figures in London, for instance Mill, Fitzjames Stephen and Matthew Arnold.[18]

To exploit this favourable conjuncture, Mazzini consulted with other exiles and hurriedly left England – 'my real *home* if I have any'. With a passport in the name of Smith, early in August he reached Florence where he remained in hiding for six weeks. The head of government in Tuscany was Baron Ricasoli, a Moderate and a patriot, who was annoyed when he heard rumours of Mazzini's presence but then realised that the republicans were correct in wanting to overturn Napoleon's armistice settlement. Ricasoli, no friend of Cavour, had few of the latter's inhibitions against collaboration with the Party of Action so long as it accepted a subordinate role and did not renege on its conditional acceptance of monarchy. Unlike many of the other Moderates, he had come round to accepting Mazzini's idea of a united Italy,[19] partly because the alternative was Cavour's idea of 'annexation' by Piedmont. As a proud Tuscan, Ricasoli not only resented the condescending attitude at Turin towards what Cavour called the decadent 'Etruscan race', but objected to 'Piedmontese aggrandisement' when all Italians ought to be working together in support of Mazzini's aim to create an entirely new nation.[20] He also disapproved of Cavour's refusal to cancel the sentence of death imposed on Mazzini in 1858, and a request from Turin to hand the returned exile over to possible execution was rejected. Meanwhile, in a personal letter, Mazzini appealed to King Victor Emanuel to support Ricasoli's policy of completing the process of national unification, and once again pledged his own support.[21]

But Ricasoli had an aristocratic disdain for democracy and was by temperament an autocrat. He allowed Mazzini to remain at Florence but in hiding, and this made effective conspiracy difficult. Another problem for the republicans was that Garibaldi, who alone had much chance of captaining a successful revolution, was surrounded by monarchists who encouraged him to continue trusting Victor Emanuel. Garibaldi in August wrote a forthright letter to a bookseller in Newcastle who asked his opinion about Mazzini, and it reveals the persistence of a personality clash that remained a fundamental factor in influencing the course of the Risorgimento.

> Mazzini has been for a long period the representative of the liberal opinions in Italy, and for this reason every man loving his country considered him as his chief. Had Mazzini shown courage enough to lead his friends in the danger, had Mazzini shown that noble feeling which puts the cause of his own oppressed country above every selfish consideration, Mazzini might have been a great man. But Mazzini having been without those two qualifications fell necessarily in the contempt of every man of heart and has been ever since committing faults. Mazzini by his obstinacy and his unaccountable *amour propre* has made democracy impossible in our country and has obliged us to resort to monarchy in order to find what we want above all in Italy, our independence.[22]

Garibaldi in September 1859 commanded a substantial force near the papal frontier, and Mazzini sent him money hoping that despite personal differences they could agree on an invasion of central Italy to coincide with an insurrection in Sicily. Garibaldi gave tentative approval, but before launching an attack felt bound to consult Victor Emanuel, who at first made no objection to letting an army of volunteers act on its own responsibility.[23] But when another veto arrived from a greatly alarmed Napoleon, the king changed his mind and Garibaldi backed down. Mazzini in December returned to London, disconsolate over another splendid chance lost. He spoke of Garibaldi as 'weakness incarnate' because of such a strange deference to royalty, but also as someone with an immense following in Italy who had the ability to act independently of Turin if only he could be persuaded that a popular revolution had good chances of success, and this was a reassurance that only the Party of Action could provide.

Cavour lacked the king's tolerant attitude towards the plebeian Garibaldi. For six months after July this former minister had leisure to rethink his opinions. Hitherto his long-term ambition had been to enlarge Piedmont by annexing other north Italian states. He distrusted any idea of a full Italian union, partly because he still saw this as being a federation whose members would never agree over choosing a single ruling dynasty, so that a federal Italy would 'inevitably' be a republic.[24] Since July, however, Ricasoli and other central Italian politicians had shown the existence of what Cavour had to admit was an 'irresistible' desire for national unification, and this new fact persuaded the Piedmontese Moderates to adapt their own policy and not leave Mazzini with a monopoly of revolutionary patriotism.[25] Cavour tried hard to appease those inspired by regional loyalty and admitted that Naples, Tuscany and the Papal States should remain separate identities, but speaking to others he agreed that nationality was acceptable as a general concept so long as it could be captured from the republicans and dissociated from democracy.[26] His new proposal, as Cattaneo described it, was to appropriate the substance of Mazzini's policy but without making this too obvious. So doing he might win over some of the *italianissimi*, while at the same time continuing to persecute this condemned rebel so as to prevent Napoleon taking alarm.[27] Such a change in policy was in part due to Mazzini's obstinate refusal to accept anything less. This 'reckless agitator' was now recognised by at least some British conservatives as someone who had miraculously changed public opinion and inside Italy had even won for himself a personal loyalty that a king himself might envy.[28]

Garibaldi and 'The Thousand'

As the year 1860 opened, Mazzini was again hoping to cooperate with the monarchists. He recognised Victor Emanuel as not only more open-minded than his ministers but also a far better sovereign than Napoleon, because 'there is an immense difference between a liberal king and a destroyer through violence of the liberty of his own country'.[29] Where Mazzini chiefly differed from the monarchists was in his uncompromising rejection of 'bonapartism' and French ambitions in Italy. As a convinced democrat he believed that nationhood should be won by popular action, not imposed by royal fiat or as a diplomatic device, and certainly not as something that would help French territorial expansion. He therefore surprised the Moderates by his enthusiasm when the populations of Tuscany, Modena, Parma and Bologna voted to join Piedmont in forming a new kingdom of northern Italy. Cavour, on the other hand, after the king in January 1860 reluctantly reappointed him as prime minister, hesitated to accept such a popular vote because he feared Napoleon's disapproval – and incidentally feared that the precedent of universal suffrage might later be used or misused for electing Mazzini and Cattaneo to parliament.[30] But the Party of Action strongly supported the annexation of central Italy for the very opposite reasons: first because it was by popular vote, secondly because it would weaken French influence in Italy, and thirdly because it might help to drag Piedmont into more confident leadership of the patriotic movement.[31] To allay residual fears,

Mazzini again gave explicit reassurances to Garibaldi and others that he had no intention of campaigning for a republic. Nor, contrary to general belief, was he hostile to Piedmont. On the contrary, though he greatly distrusted Cavour, his admiration and liking for the Piedmontese was noted with alarm by other republicans who held a very different opinion.[32]

His private sources of information in both Turin and Paris continued to be remarkably correct. He knew, as did few others, that the king not only disliked Cavour but was much more open than the cabinet to cooperation with the radical revolutionaries.[33] He knew that the French emperor was contemplating another aggressive war to conquer a frontier on the Rhine, which was bound to unite the rest of Europe against both himself and his Piedmontese ally, so putting the whole Risorgimento in jeopardy.[34] In Mazzini's opinion, one of Cavour's reasons for allying with France was a determination to avoid the alternative of having to rely on popular involvement and Garibaldi's volunteers. When Cavour now decided to seal that alliance by ceding to France the king's hereditary possessions of Nice and Savoy, this revealed the minister in his true colours as a diplomat of the *ancien régime*, a 'second-hand Machiavelli' who believed in the 'anti-national' practice of bartering peoples and territories.[35] Cavour would thereby alienate the British government which had asked for, and indeed already received from him, a formal promise that he would in no circumstances surrender these two regions of national territory – though in fact, as was known in London, their surrender had been already agreed. Nice, moreover, was the birthplace of Garibaldi, who reacted by becoming an inveterate enemy of Cavour and reverted back to his former friendship with Mazzini. Both revolutionary leaders now joined forces to impose another fundamental change of policy on the government. Both had an indispensable part to play in the Sicilian insurrection which led to the union of southern Italy with the north.

Mazzini had twice tried ten years earlier to persuade Garibaldi to land with a small force in western Sicily, and once again in the summer of 1859 had attempted to start a Sicilian revolution. His two close companions, Crispi and Pilo, had again been sent a number of times to the island with money and arms provided by himself, but this plan had to be postponed when their over-optimistic appeal to Turin for assistance met no response.[36] Nevertheless, so much was at stake that the Party of Action decided to try yet again. The Bourbon ruler of Naples and Sicily possessed a substantial army and the largest navy of any Italian state. A revolution against him had only an outside chance of success, but if victorious would greatly increase the military forces available to the patriots in frustrating Napoleon's plan to keep Italy a divided and client state. Nor would Napoleon dare to send troops against such a revolution, because Britain could never let Naples fall into a French sphere of influence. Success in Sicily might also compel the Piedmontese to lend passive or active support as the best hope of consolidating their paramount position in Italy.[37]

Early in 1860, Karl Blind was present at meetings in London where the decision was taken. Blind described how this had to be kept secret from Garibaldi lest he should once again warn the king prematurely and so invite another veto from France.[38] Such secrecy reflects the difference between Garibaldi, with his soldier's caution in not wanting to commit himself until there were clear signs of success, and Mazzini, who rather saw the imperative need to start movement after movement in the conviction that one day a small success would attract general support. Garibaldi's contribution would eventually be indispensable but only after the cession of Nice made him lose patience with Cavour. Until that moment the idea, the organisation and resources had to be provided by Mazzini[39] – an important and well-attested fact that in later years was ignored or even categorically denied.

First, money had to be found, and a useful £500 arrived from John McAdam and his friends in Glasgow. Arms were assembled in Malta and Sicily. 'Orsini bombs' were secretly made near Genoa at a factory managed by the Orlando brothers, three Sicilians from the Party of Action. Garibaldi in March was at last informed about the operation and invited to command it, but refused.[40] To take his place and prepare the ground, Pilo and Giovanni Corrao set out for Sicily on 24 March in a small fishing vessel rented with money from Mazzini. Because of atrocious weather their journey took two weeks and they arrived only after the hoped-for uprising had started on 4 April. Under great difficulties they then helped to keep alive the spark of revolt for another six weeks, and although Garibaldi as late as 28 April refused once again to take part, their success finally convinced him. On 5 May, armed with rusty muskets and little else, he set out with a relief expedition of a thousand volunteers in their support.

Mazzini had wanted to go in person to Sicily but for some weeks was completely immobilised by what his doctor diagnosed as acute lumbago. He left England at the beginning of May hoping to join the expedition and arrived in Genoa only a few hours too late. But he had great reason for satisfaction when this small civilian force, most of it drawn from his own party and sympathisers,[41] defeated the Neapolitan army and set up a revolutionary dictatorship in Palermo. Pilo was among those killed in this astonishing victory. One immediate problem was Garibaldi's decision to offer the crown of a united Italy to Victor Emanuel, because some republicans preferred to fight under a 'neutral flag'.[42] Mazzini, too, believed that ideally they should avoid the divisive mention of either republic or monarchy until there was time to consult the population in a general vote,[43] but was realistic enough to recognise the pragmatic reasons for attracting Piedmontese support, even claiming that 'I prevailed on Garibaldi to act *for* the king *without* the king's permission'.[44] Only half a dozen diehard republicans rejected his advice and refused to fight for a monarchist programme, but Mazzini was not among them.

Cavour regarded this expedition to Sicily as a 'crazy enterprise' as well as a dangerous reverse for his own policy. Although he no longer ridiculed the idea of a united Italy, he still could not imagine a union with Naples and Sicily except as some years away in the future.[45] Nor in any circumstances would he welcome unification as a gift from his democratic opponents. At first he therefore offered the king of Naples a formal alliance and suggested that they frustrate the revolutionaries by dividing Italy between them. Probably he also imagined that, when Mazzini and Garibaldi promised to accept the monarchy, they were as deceitful as he thought quite justified in his own political behaviour, and certainly he saw in Garibaldi's expedition a dangerous threat to his alternative plans for a less radical Risorgimento.[46] He was further alarmed when the self-elected dictator of Sicily followed Mazzini's precept by ordering the distribution of smallholdings to landless peasants, a decision that was of great importance in winning popular support among the local population. Horrified by this 'socialist' measure the Sicilian landowners appealed to Piedmont and Britain for assistance against 'the baleful influence of the Mazzinian faction'.[47] Unable to locate Mazzini's whereabouts, Cavour again asked for French police to aid in the search and sent an urgent request for his arrest, first to Ricasoli in Florence, then to officials in Sardinia, and then with uncharacteristic impercipience to Garibaldi in Palermo. Admiral Persano was told that Mazzini's capture 'will be one of the greatest services you can contribute to your country';[48] but the intended victim had never moved from his various hiding-places in Genoa.

One good reason for Cavour's embarrassment over the expedition was a fear that the immediate objective was not Sicily but Rome, where French influence was paramount. Indeed for the next two months there continued to be ample evidence that Garibaldi intended to defy Napoleon's veto and organise a simultaneous attack on the Papal States from the north. Mazzini had from the first intended to organise such an attack. He was oddly, indeed almost incredibly, confident that Garibaldi would without much difficulty overrun Sicily and Naples, after which Cavour should be asked to assist or at least connive at a pincer movement through Umbria to occupy the rest of central Italy. Even though Mazzini specified that the city of Rome should be avoided so as not to provoke French intervention, this ambitious proposal was an embarrassing challenge to ministers in Turin, who had to be especially careful about French susceptibilities.[49]

Cavour eventually admitted that Garibaldi's capture of Palermo, as well as arousing immense enthusiasm in public opinion, was further proof that the Mazzinian idea of national unification might no longer be a utopian dream. It was therefore more urgent than ever to expropriate this idea on behalf of the monarchy. The minister first attempted a take-over by trying to force Garibaldi to accept the annexation of Sicily by Turin and so bring the revolution to a halt. When this failed, secret orders demanded that the victorious revolutionaries must 'at all costs' be prevented by the Piedmontese navy from proceeding further to land on the mainland of southern Italy. Cavour understandably feared that a private army of volunteers, should it succeed in crossing the Straits of Messina, might advance up the peninsula to liberate Naples and the radical democrats would then rule half of Italy. As an additional insurance against this danger, two million lire and a large quantity of arms were urgently sent from Turin to start a rival 'spontaneous' revolution in Naples and seize power before Garibaldi had time to arrive. Some of the Neapolitan generals were also bribed to desert their king, and Piedmontese troops were secretly sent in August to wait on a naval vessel in the Bay of Naples ready to take over the city and prevent its being captured by the revolutionaries. Instead of openly declaring war against the Bourbon sovereign, Cavour was here trying to do something which, when attempted by Mazzini, he had condemned as 'demented' and immoral. Furthermore, despite using more money and arms than Mazzini employed in a whole lifetime of conspiracy, the attempt was a complete failure. Garibaldi evaded the Neapolitan and Piedmontese navies and landed in Calabria, after which he entered Naples in triumph and, demonstrating his desire to cooperate, shamed Cavour by handing over to him the large Neapolitan fleet, thus doubling the size of the Piedmontese navy.

Mazzini by this time had left Genoa for Florence. His intention in doing so was to assist in preparing an attack on papal Umbria to coincide with Garibaldi's occupation of Naples. This project was supported by Ricasoli, who once again refused a request from Turin to arrest Cavour's 'mortal enemy'[50] and contributed arms and money to equip two thousand volunteers at a camp outside Florence. Mazzini hoped that the Piedmontese too would recognise the advantages of invading papal territory and he therefore sent friends to reassure Victor Emanuel that republicanism was not an issue: monarchy, he explained, was evidently 'the wish of the Italian people, to whom we feel bound to bow on account of the very dogma of national sovereignty which is at the root of the republican belief', and he promised that any of his followers who disagreed would be overruled.[51]

The king was not unsympathetic to this appeal, but Cavour foiled it by suggesting a far more daring plan: he would adopt Mazzini's project and himself invade Umbria, not in collaboration with these volunteers but against them. In consultation with Napoleon it was agreed at the end of August that the best way to reassert governmental authority was for the royal army to fight its way through the Papal States in order to hold Garibaldi on the Neapolitan frontier and prevent him marching on Rome. Cavour won approval from the French by assuring them that if necessary he would use force against the greatly enlarged army of forty thousand Italian volunteers now assembled in Naples. He said he was not afraid of breaching international law or of civil war against Garibaldi.[52] Here at last was his chance to defeat the 'red republicans' and 'Mazzinists' by 'throwing them into the sea'.[53] Best of all would be if Napoleon would also let Piedmont annex some papal territory *en passant*, and for this purpose Cavour offered the artful pretext that annexing Umbria and the Marches would better enable him to defend the pope against the revolutionaries.

Mazzini noted the irony of the Moderates' carrying out the same invasion of papal territory that had so frightened them a few days earlier. His own threat to invade had evidently been justified if it now forced others to carry out this act of revolution with much greater strength than he himself could mobilise. The ministers in Turin went even further and adopted not only his own carefully prepared invasion plans but precisely the same tactics they had always condemned him for using. Without daring to declare war against the pope, they sent muskets and 'Orsini bombs' in the hope of precipitating yet another 'spontaneous' insurrection inside papal territory to provide a few useful casualties and hence a pretext to invade and 'restore order'. One further irony was that this insurrection, though backed by the resources of the state just like that planned in Naples, was equally unsuccessful.[54] Cavour nonetheless proceeded with his invasion, so giving the revolutionaries the satisfaction of knowing that they had provoked another major step towards national unification. Mazzini's immediate reaction was that, since the papal state would now be incorporated into Italy, he himself could now withdraw into private life. He would be delighted to retire from permanent agitation and conspiracy so as to enjoy 'one year, before dying, of Walham Green or Eastbourne, long silences, a few affectionate words to smooth the ways, plenty of sea-gulls, and sad dozing'.[55]

On second thoughts, however, 'with a chance for Rome I could not leave Italy yet'; so he took a French steamer from Tuscany and reached Naples on 17 September, ten days after Garibaldi's arrival. The first vision of Naples from the sea was more magnificent than anything he had ever experienced. So large was the influx of people celebrating the revolutionary victory that he tried six hotels before finding a vacancy. His arrival caused considerable panic in conservative newspapers, especially when the next day he met Garibaldi and was overjoyed to hear 'that he will go very soon to Rome. If he goes, I shall go *en amateur*. We shall most likely find the Piedmontese there: they will hasten if they hear that Garibaldi marches. In that case, *servitore umilissimo*, I shall go away. In the other case, we shall fight the French out of the city and then, when Victor Emanuel is proclaimed, I shall be free.'[56] This was an immensely exciting prospect. But the expectation lasted no more than two days. To Garibaldi, unlike Cavour, the possibility of civil war between radicals and moderates was quite unthinkable. When it became obvious that the Piedmontese regarded the volunteers as not an ally but an enemy to be crushed by force, a march on Rome was out of the question.

Mazzini nevertheless remained for the next two months in Naples. Francesco de Sanctis, who as well as being Italy's best literary critic was the most intelligent of Garibaldi's ministers, called Mazzini the real power behind the revolutionary government,[57] but in actual fact he was for the most part a passive observer of events. Apart from a few months in 1848–9 this was the only time in thirty years that he had been able to live openly in Italy. From morning to night his hotel room was full of visitors, some out of curiosity to see a living legend, others hoping he was someone of influence who could recommend them for jobs in the new administration. 'I am sometimes nearly crying through exhaustion and discouragement', yet 'it was necessary to our party that I should see and be seen'. When he could escape he climbed Vesuvius and endured the pestering of guides in the museums. He visited the dead city of Pompeii, 'the loveliest spot on earth', and 'wished myself there with the rest since 2,000 years'. Some more extreme republicans regretted his disengagement from active politics, but he now knew that further rebellion was useless and 'there is nothing bad in bowing to the national will'.[58]

Some of his visitors in Naples recorded their impressions. Giorgio Asproni, an ex-priest and radical member of the Turin parliament, wrote that

> Mazzini lives by himself, aloof from everything, a spectator of what is going on. Not only does he not put forward his republican ideas, but he restrains the haste of the more impatient and preaches that it is imperative to subordinate every sentiment to unity. He has aged considerably and his face shows how much he has suffered. I think this man has a gigantic spirit and an intellect above everyone's.[59]

Foreign journalists on the spot were astonished at the terror he inspired. They also commented on the admirable abnegation with which he subordinated his republican opinions to patriotism.[60] Another visitor was Giuseppe Bandi, a young Tuscan volunteer with Garibaldi's forces, who recorded my own overwhelming desire to set eyes on this man who as a lonely and defenceless exile made all the tyrants of Europe tremble on their thrones. For so many years I had waited to hear that voice which had so stirred my heart and brought tears of sadness and tenderness to my eyes; the voice that had comforted us with hope in the triumph of a sacred cause while other people despaired or were cowed into living as slaves.[61]

A senior English naval officer in Naples wrote more prosaically that this so-called rebel 'has done more for Italy than any living man save Garibaldi'; moreover, despite what was alleged in the conservative press, he was positively supporting the monarchy, whereas the Piedmontese ministers were deliberately fomenting anarchy in Naples and inventing a non-existent threat of republicanism so as to take from this one brave man the credit for a revolution he had initiated.[62]

Garibaldi would have agreed with this comment and tried to convince the king that, since Mazzini's followers had risked their lives for a monarchist triumph, they should be accepted as comrades instead of antagonising them by gratuitously perpetuating needless divisions.[63] Victor Emanuel, who had once boasted to Queen Victoria that he would execute Mazzini if caught, was tempted to take Garibaldi's advice: 'if we succeed in creating Italy,' he sensibly remarked, 'Mazzini will be no trouble; if we fail, then we ought to applaud if he succeeds.'[64] But the prime minister threatened to resign unless Mazzini and his friends were 'crushed' without pity or consideration. Cavour was so disdainful and out of touch that he referred to Garibaldi as an indifferent soldier who had won his battles more by luck than by courage and skill.[65] As well as trying to persuade the king that public opinion in Piedmont was 'ferociously against Garibaldi', the minister chose with carefully deliberate provocation to send Garibaldi's two chief personal enemies, Farini and La Farina, to replace him as governors of Naples and Sicily. Such men could be relied on to impose a settlement by force, and their orders were that anyone who resisted should be 'exterminated to the last man'.[66] This mention of extermination was one of many unfortunate phrases that had to be removed from the published edition of Cavour's letters – like his other remark about Neapolitans being so corrupt that they would have to be held down by military force.

At the beginning of October, unaware of such savage orders, Garibaldi was absent from Naples fighting the retreating Bourbon army in the most difficult battle of his whole career. While he was away some of the Neapolitan conservatives enlisted a mob demonstration to cry 'Death to Mazzini', though its leaders confessed they would as readily cry 'long live Mazzini' if paid the same money. Garibaldi angrily commented that those responsible must be lacking any sense of patriotism or gratitude. Cavour's

government, so Garibaldi wrote, had in May tried to stop the volunteers
from conquering Sicily; then in August and September the same government tried to prevent them from liberating Naples; and now, as well as
threatening civil war, its representatives were blatantly repudiating the
freedom of speech and opinion guaranteed by the Piedmontese constitution. Such a government was not worthy of respect, whereas Mazzini was
an honoured fellow countryman whose rights as a citizen should and
would be protected.[67]

On 18 October, Mazzini started another newspaper in Naples, *Il Popolo
d'Italia*, to discuss the difficult problems involved in consolidating the
union between northern and southern Italy. Three days later, Garibaldi
held a plebiscite by universal suffrage in which an overwhelming vote
was registered in Naples and Sicily for joining a new and united Italy.
Northerners pretended that this vote was by implication directed against
Mazzini and Garibaldi,[68] but in fact both men encouraged people to give
a massive affirmative vote. Mazzini would have liked to precede the
plebiscite by public discussion in an elected assembly, but knew that there
was no time and discussion might well have produced a divisive debate
about federalism and regional autonomy. Cavour on the other hand
objected to the terms of the plebiscite because it referred not to annexation by Piedmont but to the unacceptable idea of uniting the southern
provinces inside an altogether new and fully united kingdom of Italy.
Such matters were for governments and not ordinary citizens to decide,
and he therefore instructed officials to treat the vote as a straightforward
request for annexation.[69] Yet this public vote, however falsified by such
an instruction, represented a great success for Mazzini's main ambition in
life and could not be argued out of existence. The goal of a united Italy to
include Rome and Venice had thus been written into public law and
accepted in Turin, albeit with reservations. Moreover, even if unenthusiastically, Victor Emanuel would henceforward be king 'by will of the
people', not merely 'by grace of God'. This was a substantial victory for
the two principles of democracy and nationality that Mazzini for the past
thirty years had consistently championed.

Cavour's final victory

Early in November 1860, Garibaldi had another friendly talk with
Mazzini and accepted in principle a plan to win Venice by provoking war
against Austria in the following spring, which was precisely what King
Victor Emanuel also intended.[70] Garibaldi then withdrew for the winter to
await events in his island home of Caprera, while Mazzini remained at

Naples for a few weeks after Victor Emanuel arrived in person to put a seal on the process of annexation. The monarch would have preferred to begin his new reign with an act of generosity that included this former rebel in another general amnesty and was prevented only when ministers again threatened to resign.[71] Cavour enigmatically explained that he would gladly sacrifice his private opinions in the cause of Italy but never his sense of personal dignity. Orders from Turin were that this enemy of the state should be imprisoned, but the king objected that the republicans were too strong and reconciliation was the major priority at such a delicate moment.[72]

Cavour, far away in Turin, had little appreciation of the immense difficulties he would face in governing Naples. He assumed that efficient northern administrators would quickly bring prosperity to the south, forgetting that, after more than a century of rule by Turin, Sardinia was still the most neglected and backward region in Italy. Nor had Cavour any idea at all that his own administration in the south might be less popular and even less effective than that of the much despised Garibaldi, nor that it might appear to be less well-intentioned. Against his own liberal instincts he was forced to advise using martial law and press censorship when he was told that almost no local support could be found for his policy of annexation.[73] According to his personal secretary, the *carabinieri* were at one point instructed to kidnap Mazzini. A police officer recalled that there was even loose talk of having him assassinated, and Victor Emanuel claimed that only royal intervention prevented such an atrocity.[74] These stories may well have been exaggerated, but the animosity that inspired Cavour was real enough. Even *The Times* of London, no friend to 'Mazzini and the Red Republic', agreed with some British diplomats in criticising the provocative attitude of the 'Piedmontese race' who not only displaced Garibaldi after he had done all the serious work on their behalf, but who also seemed to prefer that Frenchmen and Austrians should remain as occupying forces in Rome and Venice rather than 'that Italy should be freed by others than themselves'.[75]

The *annus mirabilis* of the Risorgimento ended with radicals and conservatives more divided than ever instead of rejoicing in their joint success. The former prime minister Azeglio, contemptuous of both Garibaldi and Mazzini, was equally critical of Cavour for having been forced into appropriating so much of Mazzini's programme; and Azeglio also blamed ministers for risking rebellion in Naples by imposing Piedmontese laws and taxes before parliament could meet – moreover without even a pretence of local consultation. The annexation of Naples, in Azeglio's opinion, was unlikely to last long and could be justified as a temporary expedient only if it prevented the influence of Mazzini's ill-bred vulgarians spreading into northern Italy.[76] Other future prime ministers – Rattazzi, La Marmora and Menabrea – were equally unhappy that the revolutionaries had forced the government at Turin into premature annexation of the south, and it is noteworthy that similar doubts were expressed in private by both Cavour and Victor Emanuel.[77]

Mazzini might have been proud at this recognition of his success. Nevertheless he was mainly regretful that the Piedmontese arrived in Naples not as partners in a noble venture but as would-be conquerors, even oppressors, and in practice a substantial army of occupation was needed for the next few years to hold down an annexed and rebellious southern population. He himself, still under sentence of death, was eventually chased into exile once again. Yet at least he had the satisfaction of knowing that his idea of popular initiative, so derided by the Moderates, had in 1860 been more effective that the contrivances of diplomacy or a subservient alliance with French imperialism. After a long succession of minor failures he had finally demonstrated that revolution and honest faith in a principle could sometimes succeed better than nice calculations of what seemed merely expedient. Whereas the royal army had no serious victories to celebrate, his own preference for voluntary action had been vindicated when a hastily recruited force of untrained volunteers covered itself with glory. Italians had thereby gained a new self-confidence and a much clearer consciousness of nationhood.

This was the story that Mazzini spelt out to a Scottish friend after he returned to London in December.

> We have constantly acted as the spur: we worked, fought, and bled for Italy, the Cavour cabinet constantly opposing, then reaping the results as soon as won or unavoidable. And all this took place in the name of monarchical unity without a single voice speaking for the republic, or even democracy or liberty; the only thing we claim being to be allowed to work for others and go on until we have Venice and Rome. . . . Since thirty years I began working for Italian unity, when the possibility was laughed at everywhere, and I was styled a frantic, insane agitator![78]

He also could claim that his propaganda had helped to convert British public opinion to enthusiastic support for the making of an Italian nation.[79] Gladstone and Disraeli both recognised, if reluctantly, the extent of his influence, and other members of the British parliament did so with enthusiasm.[80] Newspapers in England compared him to Washington and Franklin, as Scottish newspapers did to Bruce and Wallace.[81] The *London Review* went so far as to call him 'the man who has set his stamp upon Europe, a stamp such as none has set since Loyola': and this paper added that Cavour's policy would have made Italy into a dependency or satellite of France whereas Mazzini in thirty years of struggle and deprivation made it 'a European necessity'; and 'no man ever won more ardent love, more thorough trust and following'.[82]

Other newspapers had equal or greater admiration for Cavour, who had succeeded brilliantly in inheriting the success of the Italian revolution; but historians were correct in also stressing that the derided *italianissimi* had finally compelled this minister to adopt the main substance of what Mazzini had been preaching.[83] Some people, then and later, considered Mazzini's contribution more important than that of Cavour.[84] Among French politicians, Quinet, Émile Ollivier and Guizot agreed that this outcast had succeeded in forcing a conservative government to follow in his footsteps,[85] and in England the Liberal Catholic Lord Acton sorrowfully admitted that Mazzini had 'seen the best part of his purpose accomplished for him by those who denounce him as a criminal and a fanatic'.[86] The same admission was sometimes half-conceded by Cavour himself,[87] as well as by opponents of both men and observers outside politics who were partisans of neither.[88]

Not only Mazzini's main objective but also his revolutionary methods had been adopted by the same ministers who continued to condemn his use of them as inept and intolerable. Cavour, the dedicated enemy of revolution, had attempted to start 'Mazzinian' insurrections in Lombardy and Central Italy in 1859, but without much success; and similarly the following year with equal lack of success in Sicily, Naples and the Papal States. At the end of 1860, Cavour once again put the authority of the state behind another attempt to create a series of revolutions throughout Eastern Europe 'from the Dalmatian coast to the Baltic'. He explained that his long-term purpose was to restore the 'Latin races' to their once dominant position in the Mediterranean.[89] In the short term he saw these revolutions as part of another war against Austria, a war that he said was needed 'for reasons of internal policy' to consolidate patriotic sentiment.[90] In words that might have been taken from Mazzini, the prime minister explained his intention of creating autonomous nationalities throughout Eastern Europe, helping the Greeks to take Constantinople and setting up an independent Hungary.[91]

Towards the end of 1860, in support of this extraordinary project, a flotilla of ships loaded with weapons, including heavy artillery, secretly set out from Genoa with manifests listing a cargo of coffee, but was shadowed from the moment of departure by the Austrian navy and then confiscated by the Turks. Cavour registered a formal protest at this confiscation and not only denied any personal involvement but insisted that such arms smuggling would invariably meet his firm opposition. Unfortunately the confiscated crates of weapons were very obviously labelled as having come from the Royal Arsenal in Turin, and though the embassy staff at Constantinople hurriedly boarded the ships in order to paint out the labels, this was too late. 'Never had there been such an infantile and ingenuous conspiracy', was the comment of one Piedmontese diplomat.[92] But Cavour found a convenient scapegoat and attempted to persuade the British that the weapons must have been sent by Garibaldi. He also tried to divert suspicion onto Mazzini and even invented another fantastic story about how the latter was sending assassins disguised as peasants to overturn the pope's government in Rome;[93] but few people can have believed him.

In January 1861, at a celebration organised in London by Herzen for the emancipation of Russian serfs, Mazzini explained that he was expecting another war against Austria in the course of the year – a celebrated diarist who was present noted that he was looking depressed and very old.[94] Other republicans were again urged by him to continue working with the monarchy for the acquisition of Venice and Rome. Whatever their private preferences, in his opinion they would be foolish to be irritated if the country supported Garibaldi's alternative monarchist programme. If the king ever reneged on this final move towards unification, which was far from impossible, they could again oppose him. Otherwise they should merely hope that he would accept his new status and respect the wishes of ordinary citizens who had voted to make him a national sovereign.[95] Mazzini believed that the king could easily treble the size of the Italian army if only he followed the example of Switzerland by abandoning his distrust of volunteer forces;[96] in which case there would be no need for further reliance on French military assistance. French help was largely an illusion because even the liberal opposition in France agreed with Napoleon in wanting to keep Italy divided and weak.[97] Another danger derived from the fact that Cavour had bargained for French help by endorsing encroachment by Napoleon on German and Belgian territory so as to re-establish the French frontier of 1814; and that not only antagonised Britain but was a blatant denial of the principle of nationality which alone justified Italian unification. 'Better remain enslaved and dismembered', wrote Mazzini, than participate in Bonapartist imperialism.[98]

In January 1861 he was hoping that Garibaldi would visit England where his presence would surely produce a flood of money from sympathisers. This secret proposal was made known to Napoleon by an informer among the exiles in London, and Cavour when told about it appealed to the British government to prevent any such visit.[99] Garibaldi was in any case not ready to commit himself to any political initiative. He confirmed his support for a movement in Venice but insisted that he alone should decide how and when. Past experience led him to mistrust Mazzini's judgement in military matters, and in particular he believed that Victor Emanuel with all his defects was necessary to the success of such an operation if only he could be persuaded to act independently of his ministers.[100]

While agreeing that Victor Emanuel was patriotic, Mazzini had doubts about the reliability of a monarch who in 1859 had accepted Lombardy as a gift from the French, and who in 1860 had then signed the cession of Nice and Savoy to Napoleon, apart from the fact that the king still kept the francophile Cavour as his chief adviser. In private Mazzini spoke much more favourably of Garibaldi as the person on whom future success would chiefly depend and whose decisions on policy would have to be accepted.[101] But there was increasing exasperation as letters to Caprera went unanswered, and once again Mazzini spoke of Garibaldi as lacking the political sense to understand that, after giving ten millions of southern Italians to the king, he could and should speak out publicly with authority;[102] he was a potentially great leader who unfortunately, in Venice as in Sicily, would never act until someone else had already started a revolt and demonstrated that it might succeed.[103]

The parliamentary elections in February gave no joy to the Party of Action, whose members mostly lacked a vote under the existing restricted suffrage. Despite what some people have alleged, Mazzini was not on principle hostile to parliamentary institutions, only to the fact that they were entirely unrepresentative so long as barely one per cent of the population voted. He would not stand himself for election because he could not take an oath of allegiance to the sovereign, but advised other friends to do so if their conscience allowed, and he knew it was important for the voice of opposition to be heard in the legislature.[104] Some of his former followers were elected among deputies on the left; perhaps as many, surprisingly, on the right.[105] Visconti Venosta, later a distinguished foreign minister, was not the only conservative who was anxious to eradicate evidence of his own earlier republicanism.[106] But another view among some conservatives was grudging admiration that the man who had taught all of them about patriotism should remain true to his convictions and refuse to compromise his integrity by bowing to the rising sun.[107] There was another move, supported by Garibaldi as well as Giuseppe Verdi and half-heartedly by the king,[108] to grant this exile an amnesty. But Cavour refused, arguing that he could never pardon anyone involved in Orsini's attempt to assassinate Napoleon:[109] and, fortunately for Cavour, no one knew that Orsini had been secretly subsidised by the Piedmontese authorities for the very reason that he was one of Mazzini's enemies. James Stansfeld commented that 'it was as if the Israelites had condemned to death their deliverer Moses when in sight of the promised land'.[110]

Official policy-makers in Turin had good reasons for hoping to make this dangerous man irrelevant and if possible forgotten. They recognised by now the wisdom of laying claim to many of his objectives. They proclaimed their ambition to acquire Rome and Venice at some time in the future, but never acknowledged any debt to the man who had made this the central mission of his life. His name was almost never mentioned in public without being coupled with some scornful adjective or as a byword for obtuseness and implacability; and on some occasions when an opposition deputy contrived to mention him there was a noisy reaction to what was considered unseemly or even indecent.[111] Nor even was there a whole-hearted commitment to making Rome into the national capital. Though this objective met with much public acclaim, Cavour and the king said in private that personally they had no intention of leaving Turin. According to Azeglio and other well-informed observers the unmention-able motive in announcing the desirability of annexing Rome was to capture from the radical patriots something of their intellectual and popular appeal.[112] Once again, Mazzini was forcing the Moderates to go further and faster than they intended, though in his view still not far enough.

CHAPTER SEVEN

Thought and Action: 1861–4

Political thought

WHILE CAVOUR'S TRAGIC death in June 1861, depriving the government of its only strong and experienced minister, created a hiatus in
official policy, Mazzini back in London returned to thinking and writing
as he waited for a new revolutionary situation to develop. He still intended to produce a book on his personal philosophy and perhaps another on Italian history, but was interrupted when an invitation arrived
from Milan to publish a collected edition of his earlier political and
literary essays. There was talk of twelve volumes, and Garibaldi accepted
with pleasure their dedication to himself. For each volume, with some
reluctance, Mazzini agreed to write an introduction on the public part of
his career, and this was the nearest he ever came to an autobiography. He
was reluctant because he thought his life insufficiently interesting for
readers.[1] But the offer of £60 a volume was untold riches and the proposal
provided a chance to inform a new Italian generation about earlier events
that the monarchists were trying to forget.[2]

Such an edition was not easy to produce. He had been so little concerned with his future reputation that he rarely kept articles he had
written. Though he was already known as 'the most prolific of extant
letter-writers',[3] some of his correspondence had been in by now forgotten
codes, much had been lost or confiscated by the police, and most had at
his request been destroyed by recipients for reasons of security. Since he
was not writing to make a name for himself in history he kept no copies
of letters and nearly always destroyed replies so as not to risk compromising his network of correspondents. This posed problems for biographers
and also for himself when he tried to remember the sequence and
motivation of past events. Another difficulty was that he rarely dated
correspondence and, as a security measure, often wrote on perishable
tissue paper in microscopic, almost illegible handwriting. Fortunately
Emilie Ashurst and Piero Cironi of Prato had been collecting all they
could. But he had not been able to give them much help. He even warned
Emilie that she would be a bad authority on his life because too friendly
to be aware of what he enigmatically called his 'shadowy side'. Never-

theless he let himself be persuaded that a collected edition of his writing might be a 'good illustration of the real condition of Italy, to show how a man whose aspirations and tendencies and dreams were all literary, artistical and philosophical has been driven to spend the whole life in organizing secret associations, raising money for muskets, and scribbling his soul away in some thousands of letters, notes and instructions a year'.[4]

Since he never had time, inclination or probably the ability to write a systematic treatise on politics or religion, Mazzini's ideas must often be pieced together from hastily written articles or letters intended for readers more interested in exhortation and action than logical argument. By his own admission he was in any case a man of heart rather than head, someone whose enthusiasm and sympathies mattered more than his intelligence[5] and who was interested much less in political theorising than in transforming society. Such a person can be misunderstood as a thinker because he never had occasion to link up adventitious remarks and reconcile apparent inconsistencies. Moreover someone so combative and forthright could create further confusion by provoking exaggerated criticism or exaggerated praise.

Some contemporary critics disparaged him for being unoriginal (which was often true enough) and even for deriving his opinions from Rousseau and Voltaire[6] whose ideas he in fact treated with some disrespect. Other contemporaries went to the opposite extreme by exaggerating his originality as 'one of the loftiest intellects which the world has known'; and Crispi subsequently looked back on him as 'the most eminent thinker of the century'.[7] Fifty years after his death, in a two-volume academic *History of Political Philosophy*, his ideas were given pride of place by Professor Charles Vaughan in a final chapter more substantial than those devoted to all other nineteenth-century thinkers. Vaughan admired Hegel but thought that Mazzini, whose ideas he had first studied as an Oxford undergraduate, wrote 'in a more concrete form, with a surer grasp of historical fact, and with at least equal rigour and consistency', leaving to posterity 'an example of speculative genius devoted to the active service of man such as Europe had not seen since the age of Luther and Calvin'.[8]

The object of this encomium never had the least concern with whether or how far his views were original. His wish was rather to find readers whom he could stimulate to political thought and action. The most simple expression of his ideas was in articles collected later into what became his best-known publication, the *Duties of Man*. The first of these articles appeared originally in England during the 1840s, some of them being immediately reproduced in a Chartist periodical because of their relevance to 'the proletarian class' in England.[9] In book form there were Swiss and English editions in 1860, since when over a hundred editions have appeared, including translations in over twenty languages, even one in Esperanto. Addressed to the working classes of Italy, this booklet was at first suppressed by the Piedmontese government because of its authorship and because in simple language it aimed at reaching the masses with opinions that sometimes challenged conventional orthodoxy.

Its principal and by now almost unexceptionable message was that Europe must come to terms with the fact of nationality. Another theme was that only a common market inside a united Italy would bring economic prosperity and so permit an urgently needed improvement in social conditions. Another central thesis was that citizens had not only rights but duties towards society, the former dependent on and conditioned by the latter. He endorsed Hegel's view that people's moral life was inseparably bound up with membership of their community, though he criticised the German philosopher for exaggerating the claims of the state. Two particular dangers in Italian history had been Caesarism and excessive individualism, the latter often leading directly to the former. Individual liberty was sacrosanct but in a healthy society should be balanced by a greater civic consciousness than was observable in contemporary Italy. He hoped at least that Italians would reject Hegel's 'adoration of force' and undervaluation of morality in politics.[10]

So strongly did Mazzini advocate duty, association and corporate feeling that he continued to be criticised as a collectivist who rejected the essentials of liberalism and overestimated the need for authority. By some of Cavour's propagandists he was even depicted as being potentially 'the most violent and savage of despots'.[11] Yet by others he has been called a more sincere liberal than either Cavour or the other Italian Moderates.[12] Admittedly he had an ingenuous overconfidence in the beneficent influence of popular sovereignty, and his ideal state was too far away in the unknowable future for him to investigate many of the obvious difficulties. Some Italian liberals were even alarmed by what seemed his excessive belief in liberty of conscience, freedom of the press and of assembly, free elections and the right to criticise and overturn a government. An extended franchise, as he agreed, was no guarantee of good government, but he thought it better than current practice, and 'the right to vote was a necessary part of political education'. He believed that governments could expect general obedience if they represented the will of the electorate, but he insistently rejected their authority to override the claims of individual conscience. Majorities had no right to oppress minorities. He used to say that most of the great ideas in history had come from persecuted individuals or minorities, and hence censorship was inexpedient as well as morally always wrong. Human rights were inviolable. 'Liberty is a gift of God; without liberty there can be no responsibility, no ability to choose between good and evil.'[13]

This led him to see local self-government as an essential check on the state. His demand for a united Italy still led some commentators to assume that he equated national unification with a centralised administration,[14] but in fact he was adamantly opposed to the highly centralised prefectorial system that the Italian liberals hurriedly imposed on the country in 1861. Since the bureaucracy of Turin was too remote to understand backward southern provinces that were at an altogether different level of culture and prosperity, the imposition by Cavour and successive governments of a single unified legislation was in Mazzini's view not only illiberal but by restricting local self-government would impede the country's political education. He had carefully studied British practice and hoped that Italian townships would retain sufficient powers to check any over-centralised authority. Education, local taxation and public works, agricultural policy and even the judicial and police system, all these might be better administered locally by people elected on a wide franchise who knew local problems at first hand. This would also reduce the expense of a grossly inflated civil service which he already saw as a major danger for Italy.[15] At an intermediate level he suggested the possibility of dividing the country into a dozen regions with some administrative powers devolved to elected regional assemblies[16] – an idea not accepted by the Italian government until after 1946.

Education, especially for the masses, should be given an absolute priority because in 1861 only one in twenty children attended school and this was a denial of individual freedom. As soon as enough school buildings could be built he wanted education to be obligatory for everyone and without payment. A national system of education should ensure that children learnt the basic values of a free society, values which included human rights as well as duties to fellow-citizens and to the international community. Here, too, some of the liberals criticised his advocacy of state supervision over education as potentially authoritarian, though it was no more so than the centralised system imposed by the Piedmontese educational reform of 1859. Whereas Cavour banned him and took away Cattaneo's academic position on the grounds that they were both dangerous heretics who undermined the basic preconceptions of existing society, Mazzini's personal preference was rather to ban the teaching of what he called unpatriotic, atheistic and immoral ideas. This could perhaps be called equally illiberal, but such restrictions should in his view be merely a temporary measure during the initial emergency of nation-building.

Italy in 1861 had the severe handicap of possessing a population of which official figures showed three-quarters as illiterate, and Mazzini blamed this fact on previous clerical and autocratic regimes which feared education as a potential challenge to their authority. Existing practice needed radical changes that could be effected only by a comprehensive national structure of education; but, once changed, private schools should be not only permitted but encouraged.[17] Nor was he as narrowly restrictive in his opinions as some other contemporary educationists. He wanted the curriculum to include more science, history, geography and foreign languages, though elected local authorities should decide such matters. History was particularly important: the past was not to be rejected but 'venerated' and built upon. Another hope was that private benefactors would endow evening classes and technical schools. He advised an English friend to teach his son the necessity of religion but not 'any positive religion. . . . At a later period he will choose.' Instead of the existing practice in Italy there ought to be 'a perfect liberty of religious instruction'.[18]

Although Mazzini's Italian critics occasionally challenged the sincerity of his patriotism,[19] abroad even his critics recognised him as the foremost champion of nationality in Europe.[20] In notes that he wrote in 1860 to help Stansfeld with a speech in the British parliament he wrote:

> the principle of nationality is sacred to me. I believe it to be the ruling principle of the future. I feel ready to welcome, without any fear, any change in the European map which will arise from the spontaneous general manifestation of a whole people's mind as to the group to which it feels naturally, not only by language, but by traditions, by geography, by tendencies, to belong.[21]

But he went much further and this was perhaps clearer to foreigners who had the advantage of talking to him. His idea of patriotism was always subordinated to the far wider claims of general humanity.[22] He even continued to hope, as did Garibaldi, that one day the concept of *patria* might altogether disappear in a United States of Europe that would remove some of the dangerous causes of international tension.[23] Like that other great patriot Garibaldi he hoped that a European congress might in the perhaps distant future draw up some kind of International Constitution to reduce some of the conflicts in international relations, and a European Court of Arbitration might have power to sanction intervention across frontiers in cases of flagrant injustice.[24]

For a long time to come, as he well knew, international rivalries could not be wished out of existence and politicians could only do what little was possible to moderate them with a minimum of defiance to popular wishes. Nations were subject to a moral law and ultimately to a painful expiation if they sought grandeur at the expense of their neighbours.[25] He was not unaware that patriotism was in some countries threatening to become an aggressive nationalism.[26] Such nationalism, as a perversion and parody of patriotism, threatened to prevent the development of a healthy international community.[27] Italy should here be able to set an example because it was his hope that her fairly well-defined frontiers would provide her with little temptation to encroach on the rights of others.[28]

One immediate problem was that many Germans strongly supported the Austrian presence in Venice and Trieste, and even the liberals in Germany refused to recognise Italian claims to Bolzano and Trent. Mazzini remonstrated against German 'aggrandisement' south of the Alps. Compelled to rely on second-hand information from interested parties, he greatly underestimated the size of the German-speaking minority in what they called Süd-Tirol. This is hardly surprising since senior Italian politicians, with better sources of information, made the same mistake; but where linguistic and strategic frontiers did not coincide, it is interesting that he gave Italy the benefit of any doubt and sometimes favoured the latter. Equally interesting is that he simultaneously denied strategic arguments advanced by France for Nice and by Austria for Trieste unless these should ever be sanctioned by a genuinely democratic vote.[29] From brief but direct personal experience, he took for granted that Nice and Corsica would be generally acknowledged as Italian; so would Malta, and so possibly would the Swiss canton of Ticino.[30] He was not sure whether Italian or Slav elements predominated in the Istrian peninsula beyond Trieste, but hoped that its inhabitants would one day agree to join Italy, leaving Fiume and Dalmatia to what he thought would become a confederation of southern Slavs.[31] Three-quarters of a century would elapse before an Italian government, after much grief and suffering, more or less accepted this Solomonic determination of an intractable conflict of interest.

Mazzini's over-simplified propaganda referred sometimes to 'the providential hand of God' marking out the frontiers between nations, but over much of Europe he knew that a confusion of peoples and loyalties meant that frontiers were impossible to define to everyone's satisfaction. Apart from Britain he had personal knowledge of only two countries, both in western Europe and seen only fleetingly as a fugitive. When asked what changes he would like in the political map of Europe his replies were tentative and changeable. He made clear that the main determinant would be popular wishes, which meant that forecasting could only be speculative until autocratic governments had been removed and some degree of self-determination was possible.[32]

In 1852 he had for instance suggested that the fifty or more recognisable national units in Europe might be reduced to thirteen or fourteen larger groups or federations, all allowing local autonomy to their component regions. Subsequently he continued to believe that many genuine but smaller nationalities might not be viable as separate states, at least not in the short term.[33] In 1857, replying to a request from an understandably confused Jessie White, he wrote a hurried, almost teasing, letter that reflects the impossibility of guessing what 'the people' would eventually decide.

> As I do never conceal my own ideas, if you persist, here they are. Spain and Portugal united – the Iberian peninsula. Sweden, Denmark and Norway united – the Scandinavian peninsula. England, Scotland and Ireland – *idem*. Italy, from the extreme Sicily to the Alps, including the Italian Tyrol, the Ticino, Corsica etc. – one. Switzerland, with the addition of Savoy, the German Tyrol, Carinthia and Carniola, transformed into a 'Confederation of the Alps'. Hellenia (Greece) having Epirus, Thessalia, Albania, Macedonia, Rumelia, reaching the Balkan mountains, including Constantinople. Constantinople to be the central town under Greek presidency of a confederation of the races (European and Christian) now constituting the 'Turkish Empire' – that is, Eastern Austria, Bosnia, Serbia, Bulgaria. (All this will set your Britishers in a frantic mood.) Austria to disappear. A great Danubian confederation – Hungary, the Roumain race (Wallachia, Moldavia, Transylvania, Herzegovina etc.), Bohemia etc., Germany comprising Holland and a portion of Belgium. France comprising the French part of Belgium, Brussels etc. Russia and Poland dividing the rest between themselves – two distinct associated nationalities. All this, dear, would be a volume which posterity will write, but I, busy about details concerning Italy, cannot.[34]

These were no more than hypotheses, and on other occasions he repeatedly made clear that they were not hard and fast categories. Obviously he did not believe that nationality coincided necessarily with statehood. He had strong doubts about federal constitutions for individual nations because that spelt weakness, but confederations between nations were desirable as one stage towards a federal Europe. He saw his thirteen or fourteen large groups as artificial geopolitical creations designed to balance each other and obstruct the emergence of a single dominant power.[35] He was never completely sure about their number or extent, but to the end of his life tended to believe not only in a union between Spain and Portugal but sometimes in a union between Belgium and Holland as counterweight to an emergent German empire.[36] Any multiplication of small political units would only increase potential conflict and postpone the integration of Europe.

For example he also believed, as did Garibaldi and Cavour, that the Irish should not aim to become a separate nation state. Britain was greatly at fault in her treatment of Ireland, but he suspected reactionary motives in some Irish patriots who wanted to end the union, and when the Fenians asked for his support he gave a discouraging answer. He believed unconvincingly that nations could sometimes be identified by their possession of a distinctive 'mission' for the progress of humanity, and failed to find such a mission in Ireland, Denmark or Portugal.[37] He never visited these countries and such ideas were put up by him as matter for discussion rather than out of settled conviction. Despite being personally inclined to favour Danish claims to Schleswig, he accepted contrary articles in *Pensiero ed Azione*, something he never did unless he was in some doubt.[38] One reason for the dogmatic tone of his pamphleteering was that public propaganda needed to be simple and categorical, yet he knew that his sources of information were defective and insisted that constructive disagreement on both theory and tactics was far from unwelcome.[39]

The confusion of peoples and languages in central and southeastern Europe posed a particularly baffling problem to everyone. In this area Mazzini had great expectations of Hungary and hoped that insurrections in Italy might coincide with a concerted revolt by Hungarians and Slavs against the Austrian emperor. The Austrian army in Italy contained many Hungarian as well as Italian soldiers and Kossuth repeatedly promised him that they would mutiny when the time came. But Kossuth wanted a greater Hungary that included other peoples who claimed their own national identity: he even accused Mazzini of having 'invented' a Romanian nation to deprive Hungarians of any claim to Transylvania, and insisted that without recognition of such a claim there could be no reliance on Hungarian help.[40] Mazzini had a different opinion but knew it would be impolitic to push this disagreement too far, thereby showing once again that he could sometimes subordinate the desirable to the expedient.[41] As well as an independent Hungary, he thought an enlarged Greece would be indispensable as a strategic barrier against the advance of tsarist Russia into Europe. He estimated that four million Greeks were still living outside the existing Greek frontier, and just possibly a confederation of Slavs and Greeks might replace Turkish rule in Constantinople.[42]

His information on such speculative and controversial matters was grossly insufficient, coming in part from much reading but largely from friendly exiles in London who all had strong and partisan opinions. Apart from Kossuth and Blind, there was the slightly unbalanced Harro Harring from Denmark. There were two remarkable Poles, Lelewel and Worcell; and, most intelligent of all, Herzen from Russia. Russia was a country which Mazzini saw as particularly ripe for revolution, and after talking to Herzen in 1857 he wrote that an event similar in scale to that of 1789 in France could not be long delayed in the tsarist empire. A few years later the emancipation of the Russian serfs was a welcome sign of change, but it seemed to him insufficiently radical to avert a major conflagration in the future.[43]

In 1863 his hopes were aroused by a rebellion in Poland against the tsar. One of its leaders was his friend Mieroslawski, once a member of Young Poland, and the fact that the rebellion lasted over six months confirmed his overconfident belief (which he shared with Cavour) that there would shortly be 'a general uproar from the Baltic to the Black Sea and the Adriatic'. He sent what help he could in money and arms and wished he were young enough to join the rebels in person, but Mieroslawski's son warned that he was being unrealistic.[44] The failure of other 'suppressed nationalities' to help Polish liberation was one of the greatest disappointments of his life, though he continued to believe that Poland and the Baltic states would eventually succeed in their 'providential mission' to act as a buffer between Russia and Germany.[45]

Mazzini was unusual among contemporaries for his interest in Slav literature and for his belief that Slavs might at some point become the 'dominant power in Europe'.[46] They would also be the natural allies of Italy in changing the political geography of Europe. He carefully studied maps and books to investigate population distribution in the Balkans and sent 'travellers' on fact-finding expeditions.[47] One danger was that the Russians, instead of pursuing their 'mission' in Asia, might prefer to create a western pan-Slav movement in the service of tsarist autocracy.[48] Fortunately four main Slav groups had individual patriotic aspirations of their own. As well as Poles and Russians, a third group located inside the Austrian empire comprised Bohemia and Moravia, what he called the Czech nationality, possibly grouped together with the Slovaks inside the frontiers of Hungary. A fourth group was composed of southern Slavs that he called the Illyrian nation.[49] He did not ignore the existence of differences between Serbs and Croats, but hoped that a federation of 'Greater Illyria' would one day include Serbs, Croats, Slovenes, Bosnians, Macedonians, even possibly Bulgarians.[50]

His published letters suggest that he had surprisingly few contacts with Germany, but he tried hard to believe in a 'solidarity of principles and interests' between their two countries, and in part ascribed the failure of the 1848–9 revolution to the 'narrow nationalism' of the elected deputies in Frankfurt and Turin.[51] He was sure that the Germans ought to follow the Italian example and unify their excessively divided country, though possibly eastern Germany and the southern area round Bavaria would need some degree of autonomy.[52] He again caused offence to Karl Marx and other German nationalists who accused him of trying to 'invent' a separate Czech nationality.[53] Sometimes such critics went further and accused him of aiming at a rival Italian policy of world domination; in reply to which he deplored 'the triumph of brutal force' in the continued German claims on Trent, Trieste and Schleswig[54] – even briefly wondering if the British would perhaps see the need to intervene forcibly against this potential maritime rival.[55] Nevertheless he hoped that the Germany of Luther, Lessing and Schiller would eventually triumph over the aberrations of Bismarck and the Hohenzollern monarchy. A new era of self-determination demanded that Germans should renounce their alliance with Viennese imperialism and recognise a common interest with Italy against the expansionist ambitions of Napoleon III.[56]

United Italy: 1861–2

In June 1861, two weeks after Cavour's untimely death at the age of fifty, Mazzini spent his fifty-sixth birthday in London. Most of Italy was by now unified, though not in the way he had hoped. In retrospect he continued to regret Cavour's 'Machiavellian calculations of expediency' and servility towards a foreign autocrat in Paris.[57] Too much in the Risorgimento had been brought about by diplomatic bargaining, too little by the popular initiative and enthusiasm that would properly justify nationhood. Cavour had admittedly been a remarkable statesman,[58] but his insistence on 'annexing' other regions rather than creating an altogether new Italian nation showed a calculated dislike of self-determination and suggested that one motive was the party–political ambition to defeat Garibaldi, Mazzini, and the radical opposition. Too many politicians in Turin identified Italian nationality with merely the enlargement of Piedmont, as shown by imposition of their own laws and institutions on regions with different traditions about which they knew little or nothing; and the fact that they did this hurriedly during a parliamentary recess revealed an element of cynicism in their much-publicised enthusiasm for representative government. Some observers in 1861 were surprised to find that, even now, many Piedmontese hardly regarded themselves as Italians and were seen by many southerners as yet another in a long succession of foreign, even barbarian, invaders.[59]

For the rest of this year Mazzini was unwell. He mentioned persistent dizziness and stomach pains that prevented work for more than an hour at a time; also 'a weakening of the spine with which I am threatened since a long while' that left him fearing he could not live much longer.[60] Bertani and Crispi, now members of parliament who had sworn allegiance to the crown, presented a petition with thousands of signatures to allow him back into Italy, and the new prime minister, Ricasoli, agreed that it would be shameful if the only Italian excluded from a royal amnesty might die in exile, whereas his return would help to reconcile and pacify the country at a very difficult moment.[61] Garibaldi supported this demand in a private talk with the king, but Napoleon again made objections and

Victor Emanuel, maladroitly presuming on his royal prerogative dismissed Ricasoli before anything could be done.[62] A German visitor to Italy noted as anomalous that the famous conspirator who 'invented' the idea of Italian unification and made it acceptable to foreigners should still be branded by the officially subsidised Italian press as a national enemy: the anomaly was all the greater in that Cavour and his successors claimed credit in retrospect for their own incessant conspiratorial activity during the previous decade.[63]

Victor Emanuel contributed to this black legend by exaggerating the not very serious prospect of a republican revolution in order to win sympathy and support from foreign governments.[64] In September 1861 he nevertheless agreed to meet in secret an envoy from Mazzini who brought the suggestion that the authorities might covertly connive at a revolutionary movement inside Austrian Venice, the idea once again being that an insurrection would give the government an excuse to intervene and carry unification one step further. If such a movement failed, the king would lose nothing; if it succeeded he could inherit any success as he had done in Sicily and Naples; and Mazzini again promised to maintain complete secrecy about any collusion.[65] The suggestion was listened to but rejected. Victor Emanuel had been publicly pledged by Cavour to win Rome, though only by peaceful means and only if or when France gave permission. As regards Venice, the king was ready to buy this region from Austria or else barter it against territorial compensation for the Austrians in Romania. But to the radical *italianissimi* both these proposals were anathema because they repudiated nationality and national rights. To win territory by another underhand deal with Napoleon or with the Austrian emperor Franz-Josef would be a scandal that deprived the monarchy of its claim on people's allegiance. Mazzini was prepared to continue supporting 'the monarchist experiment', but only on condition that king and people could together complete the process of unification by their own effort.[66]

Without doubt he was overoptimistic when he imagined that a petition with half a million signatures might force the rest of Europe to let Italy occupy Rome in the next few months. In this expectation he relied on support from London, and it is well worth recording that pragmatic politicians in Britain and France agreed with him in assuming that national unification could be completed within the year if Victor Emanuel truly wanted it.[67] Ricasoli and Garibaldi also hoped that an insurrection in Rome might soon force France to permit its annexation.[68] But the prime minister was here less realistic than Mazzini, who calculated that an internal insurrection would fail until the ground had been better prepared.[69] A more serious difficulty was that some Piedmontese politicians were against annexing Rome whether by force or negotiation. Azeglio was hoping that the French would continue to block such a move, mainly because possession of the Holy City might in his view introduce into Italy the corrupt practices of clerical government, but also because winning Rome was Mazzini's policy and would give too much credit to the radical opposition.[70]

The republican leader had discovered that ministers were again reading some of his private correspondence. But he fought back in kind by persuading a friendly official to show him a secret circular ordering the prefects to confiscate copies of his petition for Rome, and he publicly taunted ministers with this proof that they feared any open discussion of their policy.[71] They undoubtedly feared that his supporters were growing in numbers and strength. Once again he was therefore attacked as an outlaw and a socialist. More serious was their fear that he was undermining the subservience towards Napoleon which remained a premise of official policy.[72] Here too his attitude was hardly less sensible than that of successive prime ministers, because whereas they banked on French help out of habit, he in England could see that Napoleonic ambitions left France increasingly isolated in Europe, less able to help, and on balance a positive hindrance to Italian patriotic aspirations.

Garibaldi signed Mazzini's petition but was unhappy about any attempt to prescribe the details of policy in remote London. These two revolutionaries continued to see events differently, the one as a soldier, the other as a visionary intellectual, and their continued inability to work together was a piece of good fortune for the government. It can have been no accident that misinformation and forged documents were again put into circulation to turn them more against each other.[73] Both men agreed that the Risorgimento had taken a wrong turn. Both put much of the blame on Cavour. But Garibaldi did not share Mazzini's religious and anti-socialist enthusiasms, and rather criticised his former companion as an egoist who always wanted his own way, even as a coward who chose to stay out of danger. Jessie White, a loyal friend and biographer of both, wrote that Garibaldi's criticisms were mostly irrelevant or unfounded.[74] Her sympathies lay rather with Mazzini who, while greatly admiring the other as a man of action, was privately as critical as ever of Garibaldi for lacking political sense and for being too easily influenced by personal resentments or dubious advisers.

In March 1862, after Garibaldi had twice met the king, Mazzini's mysterious sources of information correctly reported that Victor Emanuel was working behind the back of his own ministers on another project to start a war in the Balkans. At first there was some hope that this might be part of a plan to attack Austria, but it soon became clear that the king was more interested in a private dynastic intrigue to place one of his sons on the throne of Greece. Such an intention would hardly appeal to Garibaldi who at the end of June, when he discovered that the government would thwart his plan to encourage a revolt in the Austrian Trentino, surprised almost everyone by suddenly leaving for Sicily. The intention was to raise another volunteer army and attempt a march on Rome, but Garibaldi did not tell Mazzini[75] who was known to believe that any move against Rome would be premature. When the latter offered to come to Italy for discussions the offer was again declined.[76]

Mazzini had intended to be in Lombardy if Garibaldi was planning to invade Venice, and again made clear that so long as there was some hope of joint action he would not work for a republic.[77] But in July he realised that the intention might be to use Sicily as the base for a move against Rome. Though he thought this a mistake he nevertheless promised support and asked Garibaldi to let him take part as a common soldier among the other volunteers; to which he was surprised to receive an enthusiastic and friendly reply.[78] But unfortunately the government at Turin, now in the incapable hands of Urbano Rattazzi, was already considering civil war as a method of last resort to defeat Garibaldi and preserve Napoleon's good will. Rattazzi sent money to persuade patriotic Italians in Rome to prevent any revolution in the Papal States[79] because he knew that such a movement could only favour the democrats and antagonise France. Many documents refer to the fear in Turin that Mazzini was once again a real danger, and inaccurately it was thought that he might be already in Sicily making preparations to strike.[80]

Rattazzi nevertheless stopped short of halting the recruitment of a volunteer army in Sicily because of his suspicion that Garibaldi might be acting on secret orders from the king. The prime minister therefore left Garibaldi unmolested for eight weeks while volunteers continued to assemble in Sicily, and rumours continued to circulate that this illegal activity had the secret backing of an eminent but unnamed personage in Turin.[81] Only at the end of August did Mazzini leave secretly for Switzerland after telling Herzen that, though he and Garibaldi might both be killed, their death would not be useless because the whole of Italy would rally to revenge it.[82] He intended to join Garibaldi in Naples and summoned a number of his followers to Lugano in preparation for simultaneous insurrections in the Trentino and Tuscany. But he was forestalled when, after Garibaldi and his volunteers landed in Calabria, the government ordered the regular army to halt their advance on Rome and the rebel commander was badly wounded in a one-sided engagement at Aspromonte during which he ordered his men not to fire. Mazzini was with Cattaneo when Jessie White arrived with the news, and was quite devastated. She had not realised until now his 'intense affection' for the person he called 'the living symbol of the whole nation' whose life was far more important for Italy than his own.[83]

A further sad disillusionment was that public opinion did not react strongly enough against Rattazzi for this tragic disaster. Garibaldi had evidently made a mysterious compact with the monarchy, only to be crippled by the royalist forces. He was not even given hospital treatment in Calabria but forced to submit to the atrocious torment of being taken to Genoa with a bullet still lodged in his ankle. Some of his volunteers, without even the pretence of a trial, were summarily executed on the not always accurate supposition of being deserters from the regular army.[84] The army commanders at first wanted to execute Mordini and two other members of parliament. Yet the authorities never dared to prosecute Garibaldi because they feared that in self-justification he might produce a private letter from the king encouraging his act of apparent rebellion; whereas Mazzini, who was known to have been only a reluctant and distant accessory, remained branded as an outlaw, lamenting 'the degrading immorality which monarchy and the Moderates are spreading to the heart of the country'.[85]

The government did its best to implicate Mazzini in the disaster of Aspromonte, producing further fabricated documents to suggest that he intended to 'drown the monarchy in blood', even possibly to snatch the revolutionary initiative from the hands of Garibaldi.[86] Ministers had an effective spokesman in Antonio Gallenga who, as well as being a member of the Italian parliament, was now a leader-writer on *The Times* of London who was encouraged by Italian politicians to use this position to influence pubic opinion in Britain against his former mentor.[87] In a diatribe against Mazzini, Gallenga condemned the 'pernicious influence' and 'tawdry declamations' of 'this Mephistopheles of democracy' and 'gifted evildoer', even accusing him of sending Garibaldi on a nearly fatal mission.

> Where any mischief is going forward in Europe we are pretty sure soon to hear of Joseph Mazzini. That storm-bird has been screaming in the midst of revolutionary turmoil so long. . . . He would not be true to his nature if he did not appear in this hour of his country's trial to scatter venom around, to alienate the friends of Italy, to embitter her foes. . . . No one could doubt that Mazzini was at the bottom of the matter. . . . His force of character and his unwearied activity have been exerted only for the ill of his country. During the struggle which liberated Italy he was but an obstacle to the cause.[88]

The object of this tirade always refused to answer such personal attacks. He himself put the blame for the tragedy at Aspromonte on an arbitrary and repressive system of government. Apart from the king's personal duplicity, chiefly at fault was the corrupting practice of what Mazzini called 'parliamentarism' and a lack of accountability to public opinion. Only two per cent of the population was enfranchised, only one per cent actually voted in parliamentary elections, and in any case over half the seats in the legislature were occupied by individuals appointed directly by the king or financially dependent on government patronage. The deputies were not only unrepresentative but gave automatic and servile obedience to each successive government of whatever political colour, since the practice of clientelism offered jobs and favours in return for their vote.[89]

One serious weakness in this system was the power it accorded to a king who had little aptitude for politics yet repeatedly acted to undermine the authority of his ministers and endanger the peace of his realm. Such a monarchy, in Mazzini's opinion, was incompatible with good government or true freedom. Italy's reputation was being damaged by the systematic violation of individual liberty, by denying freedom of the press and freedom of association, which were both guaranteed by the written constitution. He himself hoped that such violations would become impossible if Italy became a republic responsive to public opinion. In a meeting of friends at Lugano on 16 September he therefore advocated abandoning cooperation and starting a new republican campaign. This should continue so long as the government was slow in proceeding towards the completion of national unity, and of course only until the nation had the opportunity to express its wishes about possible changes in the constitution. But more than propaganda was now required. Aspromonte had taught him not the folly of rebellion but its necessity. The monarchy would mend its ways only under threat.[90]

In October he returned to London to collect money and prepare for further action in the spring. There he had to submit once again to a 'horrid, dreary, monotonous life which identifies me with a chair, a table and an inkstand, and which wears out the weak remnants of vigour, makes me useless, silent, invisible, and apparently unfeeling with those I love'. One hope sustained him. 'I must see before I *am removed* a second enlarged edition of 1848 in Europe: then I shall die in peace.'[91] His friends in Rome were told that he could provide experts to help with the manufacture of 'Orsini bombs', the cheapest and most effective weapon for revolutionary action. He appointed a commission to help with finance, and another under Baron Nicotera to make contact with sympathisers inside the national army, especially sergeants and corporals.[92] Little hope could be placed in politicians at Turin and none at all in the new prime minister chosen by the king in December. This was Luigi Carlo Farini, a one-time associate who many years earlier had changed into an enemy of Young Italy and the Party of Action. Mazzini somehow discovered what very few people were ever allowed to know, that Farini at the time of his appointment as head of government was almost completely incapacitated by serious mental illness.[93]

Victor Emanuel and Garibaldi: 1863–4

One reason for the choice of a severely disabled prime minister was Victor Emanuel's insistence on conducting a separate foreign policy of his own which he liked to organise through private and not very reputable agents in the capital cities of Europe. Among such agents was Diamilla Muller, a minor international arms dealer and ex-convict who early in 1863 arrived in London to act as an unofficial go-between with Mazzini. One purpose behind this bizarre mission was to discover what was being planned by the exiles and stop it. But as an earnest of good intentions the king sent a photograph of himself to the revolutionary leader and even hinted at wanting a personal meeting to discuss how they could conquer Venice. In reply to a direct question the monarch further tried to allay suspicion by pretending that he looked on France as an unfriendly power with whom he could never have serious dealings.[94]

Mazzini was disbelieving, and rightly so because ministers in Turin were in fact secretly negotiating with the French for a military alliance against Britain and other countries in Europe.[95] But for eighteen months he thought it worth while keeping up a desultory and inconclusive discussion with the royal palace through this strange interlocutor. In April he returned to Lugano, secretly crossing more than once into Italy and even visiting Turin.[96] The fact that he was paying for many 'travellers' and 'running dreadfully into debts' confirms his intention of starting an insurrection inside Venetian territory. Guns and munitions were being brought from Milan under bales of hay and smuggled across Lake Garda past the Austrian frontier guards.[97] He explained to Muller that, if only he could start something serious, the royal forces would then have an excuse to intervene and 'restore order' by occupying Venice.[98] He himself would make no formal compact with a king who continued to treat him as a public enemy; nevertheless he again admitted that by popular wish the new Italy would 'necessarily' be a monarchy,[99] and he would loyally collaborate in a royalist war so long as it was free from any association with French imperial ambitions. If no action took place by the spring of 1864 he would reclaim his freedom of action.[100]

Napoleon discovered about these not very serious secret negotiations and demanded of the king that they should stop.[101] The French government had recently tried to discredit Mazzini by reviving accusations of attempted regicide,[102] and in March 1864, after Pasquale Greco was arrested for an attempt on the emperor's life, the courts in Paris held Mazzini to be guilty by association because a year earlier he was said to have given this man money. Mazzini denied any involvement in Greco's plot; he admitted that Italian patriots were at war with Napoleon whose army was still occupying Rome, and repeated that he would not censure someone who believed in conscience that the death of a tyrant could sometimes be justified, but he himself never instigated assassination.[103] *The Times*, which under Gallenga's influence had become accustomed to write of 'Mazzinian cut-throats', had no hesitation in accepting his denial because 'he is well known to be a man of perfect truthfulness. . . . Whatever we may think of Mazzini, there can be no doubt that he has had the most extraordinary influence over the minds of the Italians and has received the confidence of some of their most distinguished leaders.'[104] In England, ironically, Mazzini had done something to correct the stereotype of Italians as a people characterised by the vendetta and the stiletto – two Italian words that already had been taken into the English language. In Italy, however, that he was a practised assassin was official dogma, though Garibaldi's much more enthusiastic support of tyrannicide was rarely if ever mentioned, nor of course was the assassination of Corrao and possibly other political opponents by the Italian police. Evidence was later produced indicating that Greco had been on the pay-roll of the police, and some people even wondered if ministers had been using him to manufacture a public scandal that would force the king to renounce Muller's unofficial diplomacy.[105]

At Westminster there was a long parliamentary debate over this incident because the French protested that Stansfeld, a minister in Palmerston's government, allowed his house to be used by Mazzini as a postal address for plotting murder. The debate ran along party–political lines. Irish members, despite their admiration for Catholic rebels in Poland, were bitterly hostile to the antipapal Italian patriots and described Mazzini as the most detested man in Europe. Disraeli and Robert Cecil repeated the conventional denunciation that he was 'the great promoter of assassination'. On the other side John Bright, who sometimes met Mazzini at dinner, spoke with 'the highest esteem and admiration' of a man who possessed 'a powerful and fascinating character'; and Bright caused a sensation when he informed the House that Disraeli was disingenuously concealing that he himself had once defended tyrannicide.[106] Another junior minister, W. E. Forster, argued from personal acquaintance in defence of Mazzini, and Gladstone called him someone of great talent, integrity and force of character.[107]

After being delayed in Lugano by painful spinal and digestive afflictions, Mazzini unknown to the Swiss authorities had returned to London in October 1863 where he remained for the next three years. He found it harder to ask his British friends for money now that Italy was a free country where Italians could be expected to pay for any enterprise thought necessary. Apart from his personal income, smaller after the authorities in Turin succeeded in stopping some payments from his mother's legacy, his political organisation nevertheless continued to depend on gifts and loans from sympathisers in England and Scotland. Some contributions arrived anonymously with no inconvenient questions about how they were used.[108] None was employed for his own personal needs. Often his party existed on what he could borrow, and he was notoriously precise in scrupulously accounting for loans made by a few rich friends.[109]

Much more money from the British public was forthcoming to help Garibaldi who was the hero of the hour: for example, a quarter of the population of Brighton seems to have contributed in 1861 for a testimonial to this celebrated rebel. Nevertheless, since these other contributions were administered much less scrupulously, it was Mazzini's committee that had to meet much of the debt incurred by the Aspromonte expedition and to help those among Garibaldi's volunteers who then fled to take refuge in England.[110] From inside Italy this committee continued to receive desperate appeals for financial help, and yet Mazzini had to lament the almost complete lack of subscribers in that country: a modest appeal for £200 in 1864 produced only £8.[111] Some financial support arrived from the United States, if not as much as he hoped. He had earlier paid for Jessie White to visit New York on a fundraising lecture tour with her new husband Alberto Mario, but this had not been a financial success and much more money from America seems to have been sent to help Garibaldi and Cavour.[112]

Mazzini greatly admired the United States. In particular he admired John Brown as a martyr in the cause of liberty.[113] Another of his American heroes was Abraham Lincoln, to whom in 1864 he addressed a memorandum against French imperial ambitions in the New World.[114] The United States, he wrote, stood 'higher and nearer to the Ideal than any nation actually existing', and he praised Americans for 'the almost fabulous amount of energies unknown to our old rotten monarchies'. Theirs was a leading nation 'in the onward march of mankind . . . in the great battle which is being fought throughout the world between right and wrong, justice and arbitrary rule, equality and privilege, duty and egotism, republic and monarchy, truth and lies'.[115] Though he strongly supported the northern states in the American Civil War, he assumed that the South would eventually secede from the Union because the country was too large for effective government.[116] But his radical opinions and strong support for the anti-slavery movement led to him becoming a cult figure in the eyes of some American progressives.[117]

In 1864 he at last helped to persuade Garibaldi to visit England and use his popularity to raise money for the cause. Such a visit would certainly be profitable because no one else in the whole world was so widely admired. Already for some years there had been coffee houses in London called after Garibaldi and the same magical name was appropriated by enterprising manufacturers in advertisements for biscuits, sweetmeats and clothing.[118] Sixteen different ceramic figurines of this celebrated patriot were soon being sold by the Staffordshire potteries, but not a single figure of Mazzini, and none even of Dickens, Palmerston or Tennyson. Garibaldi was someone whom a British prime minister and his senior colleagues were proud to invite home for lunch or dinner, something that no Italian premier could ever have done without scandal.

This international hero, changeful as ever, by the end of 1863 was again paying enthusiastic tribute to Mazzini as 'the great apostle of our sacred patriotic cause' who towered above the pygmies of Cavour's party.[119] When Garibaldi visited England in April 1864 he was given a tumultuous reception the like of which no other foreign visitor had ever received, and it caused the greatest anger in Turin where Victor Emanuel saw it as a slight upon himself and a dangerous encouragement to the Mazzinian party.[120] Queen Victoria agreed, indignant that her government 'lavished honours usually reserved for royalty' on someone who had rebelled against a brother sovereign. Already before disembarking in Southampton, this distinguished visitor was met on board by a deputation of well-established Italians from London to warn him against meeting the other revolutionary exiles.[121] Palmerston too, after receiving angry protests from the governments of Italy and France, asked Garibaldi to avoid provocation by not meeting Mazzini.[122] But Garibaldi insisted on three such meetings. In Herzen's house at Teddington he proposed a famous toast to the man he called his great friend and master, someone who for many years had stood alone keeping alight the sacred flame of Italian patriotism.[123] Hints were hurriedly dropped by Italian and British officials that Garibaldi after his recent wound was perhaps too frail for a protracted visit, and certainly the novelty of being obliged each day to fulfil dozens of public engagements left him exhausted. Mazzini delighted Lady Amberley by describing a comic episode like that from Rossini's *Barber of Seville* where everyone was trying to persuade the intrusive but unbelieving Don Basilio that he was too unwell to remain longer on the scene.[124]

Victor Emanuel was not dissuaded by this triumphal reception or by the Greco incident from continuing his secret negotiations with Mazzini – a fact suggesting that he knew the latter's involvement with Greco to be a fabrication. The king's ministers denied the very existence of such negotiations,[125] but quite possibly advised the king to continue them so as to sow dissension among the revolutionary leaders and weaken any attempt at invading Venice. The king sent a warning to Mazzini through Muller that the Venetians lacked any enthusiasm for rebellion against their Austrian masters.[126] Mazzini disagreed, yet also disagreed with republican friends who criticised his clandestine relations with the palace, and twice during May sent a personal envoy to discover from the king if there was still any chance of joint action.[127] Meanwhile he negotiated to charter a ship in England that Garibaldi could use for landing three hundred volunteers behind Austrian lines in the northern Adriatic when the time came to act against the national enemy.[128]

Confronted with this danger, Victor Emanuel gave up his private collusion with the revolutionaries. In a typical piece of boasting he tried to convince his entourage that he had always controlled the Party of Action by bullying or bribery and could easily prevent them by force from doing anything not sanctioned by Napoleon.[129] Eighteen months of sporadic secret discussions thus came to an end. Mazzini still thought the king to be a more sincere patriot than his ministers, but the subservient attitude of the monarchists towards France and their distrust of popular involvement made them an unreliable ally when the time came to do more than talk.[130] In July he was horrified to learn from his mysterious informers that the Italian government was secretly negotiating for another treaty in Paris that would formally renounce the objective of complete national unification. The main clauses of this 'Convention of September' were in fact known to him three weeks before the rest of the world knew anything. By this Convention the king guaranteed the existing frontiers of the Papal States, if necessary promising to use his army to halt any movement by the Party of Action.[131] The Italian capital would be moved from Turin to Florence as an indication that Rome was no longer on the agenda.

Victor Emanuel, not a very subtle politician, was surprised when the news of this Convention caused indignation among conservatives and radicals alike. As a clear repudiation of Cavour's promise to unify the whole peninsula it invited civil disobedience by violating the democratic plebiscites upon which Italian public law was grounded. Mazzini had a further objection because he correctly suspected that the Convention had been signed without any intention of observing its provisions; in other words it was a piece of hypocrisy and bad faith that would deprive Italians of international credibility.[132] So strong was his reaction and indictment of royal policy that in 1939 the editor of his correspondence (who was now responsible to a committee appointed by Mussolini) had difficulty in publishing some of his fiercer criticisms.[133]

CHAPTER EIGHT

The Later 1860s

Venice acquired

DURING THE FINAL decade of his life Mazzini was frequently unwell, sometimes in great pain. His usual and hitherto effective cure for sickness was 'make an effort of will and be well',[1] but increasingly he needed medication that he could with difficulty afford. Emily Winkworth wrote that 'he likes to hide away from everybody till he is better, and not be noticed'. She used to cheer him up with the gift of violets, his favourite flower, knowing he disliked roses as 'gaudy and sensuous'. She also dared to give him an easy chair but 'with fear and trembling lest he should be fierce about it instead of finding it a comfort'.[2] In September 1864, not far short of his sixtieth birthday, he wrote to the French writer Daniel Stern that he felt like a hollow tree which might tumble in the next violent wind. But despite moments of sadness he never lost hope. Italian official policy was admittedly in the hands of politicians he could not trust, yet there was an advantage in knowing himself and his conspiracies to be still an object of fear in Paris, Turin and at the papal court in Rome.[3] He still had a useful task, to act as a gadfly, to challenge the Establishment, to refuse absorption into the system, 'to provoke the anger of Austria against "official Italy"' and so lay the groundwork for another war of liberation.[4]

In October and November 1864, several minor risings took place in the northeastern province of Friuli, their aim being to invade the Trentino so as to force the hand of the Italian government and give it a pretext for intervention against Austria. Though they were started by members of his own party, Mazzini at first tried to prevent these risings because he needed time for coordination with other movements elsewhere; and yet, once they began, he as usual gave what help he could and was upset when others did not follow suit.[5] Assistance was also promised by a separate 'Garibaldi committee' at Genoa headed by Benedetto Cairoli, another future prime minister. The king himself boasted, or perhaps pretended, that he secretly contributed money.[6] But once again informers betrayed this conspiracy to the Austrians, and after Cairoli backed down at the last moment the Italian government arrested some of those involved. This was a repetition of past disappointments, to which Mazzini gave his usual rejoinder: 'we *know* that the only infallible method for our conquering is to persist in attempting', and one day an attempt would succeed 'either with or against the monarchy'.[7]

Ministers could not afford to let conspiracies succeed when they themselves were so conspicuously failing to devise an alternative strategy. They were sufficiently worried to copy the French by posting a police official in London to keep track of what was afoot,[8] and although this kind of surveillance left little trace in the official documentation, some reports sent back to Italy described details of Mazzini's journeys to the continent when he had never left England.[9] The British government, when asked for information about his movements, politely demurred and almost certainly knew nothing,[10] though the French assisted by sending copies of his intercepted correspondence.[11] Inside Italy, reports by police informers in January 1865 mentioned that his influence was advancing more dangerously than Garibaldi's. They described how many people, after comparing his programme with others, saw it as 'the most logical, the most courageous and most clearly based on principle'.[12] These police reports, if they can be believed, justify his own confidence that once again his network of supporters was strong all over Italy and soon might again be ready for action.[13]

Later this year the government received further information that, though he had little impact on prominent citizens, Mazzini's propaganda was reaching university students and 'the masses' to an extent not seen since 1859. Especially dangerous was that his writings found an eager readership among junior officers in the army.[14] 'His ability to persuade and fascinate by the written word is prodigious' and was making inroads even among moderate liberals.[15] One police agent warned that this dangerous exile had needed six years of planning in Sicily before finally succeeding in 1860, and the same could already be happening in Venice; indeed he might already have been successful had Garibaldi been less irresolute and less jealous of him.[16] In August the government received further alarming news that these two dangerous radicals were once more working closely with each other in joint opposition to the increasingly authoritarian tendencies of the royal court.[17]

Such reports may well have been overstatements by informers anxious to be paid for a not very exacting occupation. Undoubtedly the republicans were a nuisance, but Victor Emanuel may have wanted to exaggerate the threat so as to frighten the French into helping him win Venice without resort to revolution: hoping for further help from France he again promised Napoleon to crush the Party of Action, by civil war if need be.[18] The king must have known that he himself was widely unpopular among many patriotic Italians after signing the Convention of 1864 with

France, yet his throne was in no serious danger and the army commanders were solidly behind him. Even critics on the political left, including Garibaldi, Crispi, Depretis and others who in theory had moderate or strong theoretical affinities with republicanism, believed in practice that kingship, however defective, was now needed as a symbol of Italian unity, whereas agitation for a republic would be a divisive and dangerous leap in the dark.[19]

Garibaldi was the best-known of these defectors from the true republican faith, and though he now spoke of the king almost with contempt and of republicanism as his ideal preference, he wrote to Mazzini to confirm his opinion that the Italian people would never win freedom on their own without government help.[20] Garibaldi, however, was known as someone who frequently changed his mind on impulse: he was, in Mazzini's words, 'lazy, wavering and Hamlet-like; the initiating energy has abandoned him'.[21] Crispi's defection was almost more worrying because this future prime minister was an astute and ambitious politician with a keen sense of political realities. On occasion Crispi admitted that he accepted the monarchist alternative only 'for want of something better', and as recently as 1862 publicly drank a toast to the downfall of all kings,[22] despite having sworn allegiance as an elected deputy. But he told parliament that this oath of loyalty was conditional: it was, like the affirmative vote in the plebiscites of 1860, contingent on the acquisition of Rome and Venice. Crispi pointed out that Mazzini himself had been ready to accept monarchy on precisely the same condition, and ironically, if Italy was now united as a kingdom, that was largely Mazzini's handiwork.[23]

The latter, however, had once again lost his occasional illusions about help from the monarchists. Successive governments had spurned his offers of collaboration and clearly wanted merely to keep him quiet while they created something very different from the Italy of his dreams. When replying to Crispi in December 1864, he again admitted that a republic might be divisive if it fell into bad hands, but Victor Emanuel's concept of kingship was deeply corrupting and far more divisive, as could be seen from the government's harsh treatment of southern Italy and the democratic opposition. This was no time for that opposition to throw in its hand. Italy might well revert to its former territorial divisions if the democrats gave up the irredentist struggle before the nation was complete. Only under pressure would the king abandon his repeated violations of the constitution; only an outright challenge would force the government to liberate Venice and Rome by a patriotic *levée en masse* instead of by a humiliating reliance on diplomatic bargaining and foreign armies.[24]

Mazzini continued to think poorly of the kind of parliament that

Azeglio and Cavour had brought into existence, and this left him exposed once again to the charge of being anti-liberal, even dictatorial. Yet precisely the same charge of preferring to act dictatorially was made against a succession of prime ministers, including Cavour himself who had praised parliament as an instrument of personal government but regularly ignored or flouted it in practice.[25] Mazzini knew that a good cause could easily be vitiated by Cavour's resort to arguments of expediency: 'I abhor what people call politics, just as I abhor "art for art's sake".'[26] Nearly always, he used to say, compromises are immoral and useless – a remark that attested to his limitations as a politician. He was in fact less politician than moralist, much stricter than Cavour over issues of principle, though more tolerant towards individual opponents and far more hostile to censorship of ideas. He was no less fierce against Caesarism of any kind, and indeed criticised Cavour for praising in theory the ideal of personal freedoms while 'mutilating' them in practice.[27]

As to the Italian parliament, unlike his own Roman assembly of 1849 it represented only the rich and powerful who, often with scant respect for liberal theory, used it to further their own selfish interests. In any case elections were easily and regularly manipulated by that same elite and by the authorities. Not only members of parliament but in some constituencies half of the small voting electorate continued to be in receipt of salaries or pensions from the state, and ministers freely used financial grants and lucrative contracts in order to buy votes in selected areas where official candidates were at risk. Mazzini learnt from such facts that only in countries with a long parliamentary tradition did public opinion obtain fair representation in an elected legislature.[28] Though he encouraged republicans to vote in elections as part of their political education, and even to stand for election so as to make their voice heard, they should not take their seats in parliament unless they could in conscience swear an oath of allegiance. They should rather concentrate on what he hoped were the more genuine elections in local government where it was easier to call elected representatives to account.

Cavour sometimes used to boast that, on grounds of liberal principle, he would welcome the election to parliament of Mazzini's collaborators as useful critics of government, but in practice strove to win Napoleon's favour by using all the recognised methods of patronage and coercion to exclude from parliament those who held out against his various 'inducements'.[29] The same practice continued in subsequent years. In October 1865, Mazzini was put up for election by friends in Genoa and despite official pressure failed by only fifteen votes. The following January, in defiance of a protest from Napoleon, his name was entered by other friends at Naples and he lost by only five votes even though he made it clear that he would never agree to take the oath as a deputy. One month later the electors of Messina, encouraged by a strong letter of support from Garibaldi, gave him a handsome majority and the news caused a sensation. But the government reacted by demanding and receiving parliamentary approval to veto his election. Once again, in May, Messina gave him a clear majority, and a second time parliament annulled the election 'after a tempestuous and almost scandalous debate' during which opposition deputies left the chamber in protest against partisan rulings by the Speaker.[30]

Nothing could show more clearly that he was still an object of fear to the political class who held the levers of power. Their technical argument for this repeated veto was that a convicted criminal was barred from election, even though his conviction had been by the state of Piedmont which no longer existed. Giuseppe Zanardelli, another future prime minister, pointed out that most ministers and members of parliament were equally criminal by the very fact of having taken arms against legitimate governments in order to unify Italy. If Garibaldi and other rebels had recently been allowed to go free after actually clashing with the royal army at Aspromonte, the fact that Mazzini was treated more harshly was anomalous and could only testify to the extraordinary panic he inspired. Yet this single remaining outlaw, as parliament was told by one of Garibaldi's generals, would one day be hailed as 'the greatest European of his time', the one man from whom every member of the Italian parliament had learnt to be a patriot.[31] Public opinion was evidently not unsympathetic to this argument because he was elected a third time at Messina with a large majority over another national hero, General Medici. Medici received only thirty-seven votes, which infuriated the government because the two hundred state employees on the electoral roll were obviously failing in their 'duty', a disgraceful fact that should not be allowed to happen again.[32] To avoid further embarrassment, parliament accepted this third vote as valid, leaving Mazzini to say that he could not in conscience accept election. Thirteen deputies nevertheless voted to make him Speaker of the House.[33]

This last fact gave him some wry amusement. But illness was now compounded by financial problems to reduce his expectations of further political involvement. Though he received the £60 due by contract for the sixth volume of his collected works, his Italian publisher was also in financial difficulties and only £20 was forthcoming for the seventh volume in 1864, with little likelihood of completing the edition. He was again overspending his income, in part because of medical expenses. He had been hoping that by mid-1865 he could initiate another uprising that would force the government into fighting for Venice, until lack of money made this impossible. He was persuaded to send a thousand signed photographs of himself to be sold in Italy, but this earned nothing because by mistake they were routed through France and confiscated at Calais. Fancifully he imagined that if only four hundred thousand Italians contributed one *lira* each, that would produce about £16,000 in English money, enough to start another insurrection.[34]

Although this was a fairly modest expectation, subscriptions would have required an organisation inside Italy that would never have been permitted by the authorities. In May 1865 a less provocative collection was announced by enthusiastic supporters at Faenza as a personal tribute to 'the apostle and precursor of our national life', to which Garibaldi was one of the first to contribute in acknowledgement of 'the man who has taught us all'.[35] In England there were nearly four hundred subscribers to this fund to honour 'the friend of liberty throughout the world' who was 'not for an age, but for all time': they included Meredith, Swinburne, Morley, Holyoake, Linton, Seeley, Henry Fawcett and Mill.[36] George Eliot and her husband would have liked to contribute because of their 'real reverence for Mazzini', but while not opposed to financing conspiracy were deterred by the fear of abetting another 'hopeless' enterprise.[37] Inside Italy, where publicity was not easy, the proceeds were discouraging and mostly swallowed up in saving a few radical newspapers from closure. Another disappointment over finance was that the patriots in Venice, instead of helping to pay for their own deliverance, were appealing for help to the small group of impoverished exiles in London.

During the 1860s, three Italian newspapers were regarded as broadly representative of Mazzini's opinions. The *Popolo d'Italia* in Naples began in 1860 under the editorship of Nicotera. In Milan the *Unità Italiana* was edited by Quadrio, in Genoa the *Dovere* by Federico Campanella and Alberto Mario. They reached a respectable circulation of two thousand copies more or less, but like all newspapers in Italy needed subventions to survive, and such subventions had to come from the committee in London and Mazzini himself, who did not always agree with their editorial policy. He thought for instance that Quadrio should be less fierce in attacking the government so long as there was some chance of winning a broader consensus.[38] All three papers, though trying to keep within the law, were regularly at odds with the authorities who were especially sensitive about any public reference to acquiring Venice and Rome. There was occasional boasting by government supporters that freedom of the press was greater in Italy than in England, yet when legal prosecution failed, scores of issues of these newspapers were arbitrarily confiscated so as to drive these opposition newspapers into bankruptcy.[39]

In its convention with France the government had formally renounced the intention of acquiring Rome. Ministers were certainly anxious to acquire Venice but only by diplomatic negotiation or subterfuge, certainly not by a collaboration with the democrats that would upset the domestic balance of power. More than once in the greatest secrecy the government offered to purchase Venice with hard cash; and once again the suggestion was made for the Austrians to surrender this region in return for territorial compensation in Moldavia and the Balkans.[40] When such suggestions met a blank refusal, early in 1866 an alternative decision was taken by the king to ally with Bismarck, who was planning to make Prussia the dominant power in central Europe by fighting against Austria. Mazzini was appalled by both these examples of what he called egotism and moral cowardice. To admit that Italians could not win Venice by their own courage and sacrifice was a confession of weakness that invited the contempt of the outside world.[41] To win it by barter or by betraying other Balkan nationalities was an unworthy immorality. To win it by relying on the aggressive struggle for European domination by Prussia, 'an unjust, invading, illiberal Power', would be even more dishonourable, all the more so for being motivated by the wish to avoid cooperation with 'the popular element' in Italy.[42]

He nevertheless could not bring himself to oppose a war for Venice and had always consistently maintained that ideally such a war should be fought in collaboration with the royalist forces. He would dearly have liked to come in person to supervise the organisation of a volunteer movement to assist the government, because it was vital for ordinary Italian citizens to show by voluntary action 'whether they deserved to be a nation or remain enslaved'. But he was in bed with severe rheumatic cramps that kept him almost motionless, hardly able to write or even speak. He too easily assumed that, if only the government provided money and weapons, an army of volunteers could have been raised that, independently of the regular army, would greatly outnumber the Austrian forces in Italy. He was in touch with leaders of a Young Serbia and a Balkan Emancipation Society, once again hoping for simultaneous uprisings in Bosnia, Hungary and Poland that would convert a purely royalist war into a general war of nationalities. The thirty-seven million people who made up the Austrian empire included about ten million Magyars and eighteen million Slavs, from whom Garibaldi could attract many recruits if he took the enemy in the rear and marched on Vienna.[43]

Towards the end of April, at a meeting of democratic associations in Parma, a majority disagreed with Mazzini's decision to support such a royalist war. Most delegates felt that the king was an untrustworthy ally who feared democratic initiatives and would do his best to thwart them. Articles in the *Unità Italiana* made this disagreement public. Quadrio explained that his paper had been founded by Mazzini, who was still a trusted friend and leader, but past experience suggested that a royalist war would lead only to dishonour and disillusionment. Mazzini in reply begged the editors to think again and at least admit further discussion. He accepted that collaboration with the monarchy carried some risk, but insisted that democrats and republicans could not stand aside from a patriotic war which was bound to command support in the country.[44]

His initial enthusiasm was dampened by this controversy. Additionally discouraging was his discovery that the king was determined to command the army in person like his father in 1848–9, and it was soon obvious that neither the monarch nor his chosen generals had more than rudimentary knowledge about military strategy.[45] Nor had this royalist *camarilla* any intention of enlisting a large volunteer force or making full use of Garibaldi's talent for guerrilla warfare, or even of coordinating joint action with the Prussian army.[46] So confident in a quick victory was Victor Emanuel that he refused to encourage 'dishonourable' insurrections in Venice behind the enemy lines, and perhaps was as frightened of such insurrections as of the Austrian enemy. Mazzini wrote a desperate letter of protest to the prime minister, to which he received no reply.[47] When war broke out, the advantage of greatly superior numbers was thrown away by unbelievably inept leadership and failed to prevent two disastrous defeats, one of them at Custoza within a few hours of the war commencing, and then a naval battle off the island of Lissa in the Adriatic. Palmerston had earlier suggested the appointment of Garibaldi to command the Italian fleet in view of his remarkable successes as a naval commander in South America, but the king preferred a politically reliable and incompetent placeman. The result, to everyone's astonishment, left Italy in serious danger of being invaded, until fortuitously saved by a Prussian victory far away in the north. Venice was surrendered by Austria, but (like Lombardy in 1859) not to the Italians, only to neutral France, and by Napoleon was then 'tossed to Italy as a penny might be thrown to a beggar' – so wrote an indignant Mazzini.[48]

Final breach with the monarchy

In August 1866, desolated by such inglorious events, Mazzini was sufficiently recovered in health to leave England for Switzerland. At Lugano, close to the Italian frontier, he hoped to reorganise his party and galvanise ordinary citizens to rebel against a humiliating peace. He could admit his mistake in thinking that the government would ever accept his republican friends as an ally in war.[49] Another miscalculation had been to assume that the Venetians would take advantage of the fighting and rise *en masse* against Austria instead of waiting (as the king preferred) for deliverance by the Italian army,[50] and this fact brought into further question his assumptions about the strength of patriotism. More than once he crossed secretly into Italy, but Garibaldi, when a meeting was suggested, pleaded illness.[51] Garibaldi, who with limited resources had fought successfully in the war, blamed the king for what had happened and still thought that a republic was ideally preferable as a form of government, but continued to fear that Italy was not ready for such a fundamental change, and instead hoped to persuade Victor Emanuel to give up his autocratic pretensions by behaving more responsibly, more like Queen Victoria he said.[52]

The king refused to admit that as commander-in-chief he personally had any responsibility for military defeat. Like his father in 1848–9 he found it more convenient to blame his generals for incompetence. In private conversation with the victorious Austrians he even blamed Garibaldi and the volunteers for being a 'revolutionary rabble' who did not know how to fight.[53] When the Austrian emperor confessed to fearing the Party of Action as a force still to be reckoned with, this judgement was quickly rejected by the Italian royalists.[54] Yet defiant bluster could not conceal a deep sense of unease in the country at large. According to the American diplomatic representative, the 'monarchy has little moral strength in Italy' and a republican revolution would have a good chance of success.[55]

Such an opinion could not have been voiced in the Italian press without incurring severe punishment, but the distinguished historian Pasquale Villari gave indirect support to Mazzini's analysis of what had gone wrong. Villari's explanation was that Italy had been unified by fortunate circumstances and without a genuinely national revolution. An understandable fear of non-governmental initiative had led Cavour to rely on a mixture of luck, skilful diplomacy and foreign help, one result of which was that the political structure of the country had been allowed to emerge from the Risorgimento substantially unchanged. Ordinary people had been excluded from it and indeed had sometimes been actively hostile. A liberated Italy was still governed by a pre-1860 generation of politicians, bureaucrats and army generals who had learnt their trade as the servants of a more authoritarian and much less 'Italian' political regime.[56]

Mazzini's denunciation of the monarchy in September 1866 coincided with a major revolutionary outbreak in Sicily where the policy of imposing 'annexation' had sometimes forced the army to emulate the former Bourbon regime with occasional brutality and summary executions without trial. Mazzini had been warned that such a counter-revolution was possible and some of his own party were involved in it, but so were many clerical and reactionary opponents of the government, and he himself knew it was partially motivated by Sicilian separatist ambitions that he utterly rejected. Sicily was an unruly and disaffected region which he still hoped would at some point, as in 1848 and 1860, trigger off another patriotic rebellion, but this particular outbreak was a deplorable symptom of confused allegiances and regional disunity. Here was clear warning that some areas and sections of Italy were not reconciled to being simply 'annexed'. Discontent in the South might easily lead to the dissolution not the unification of the country.

His illness did not improve during two months spent in Switzerland. Once more he found himself an object of devoted admiration by other Italian exiles who met him for the first time,[57] but this was no relief for his sense of defeat and shame. In October he returned to London, reconciled to dying in exile unless the irresponsible power of the crown could be curtailed.[58] He had the chance of being included in another general amnesty, but he decided that, while he would welcome outright cancellation of the sentence of death imposed in 1858, he could not in conscience accept a royal pardon for acting as a patriot.[59]

On the contrary, if his kind of patriotism was still a crime, further extralegal action was required. After the inertia shown by Lombardy in 1859 and Venetia in 1866, it was vital for a general insurrection to take place in Rome that would show the Risorgimento to be something more than a mere cover for dynastic aggrandisement.[60] Such a rising might, he hoped, be possible after December, the month when Napoleon had agreed to withdraw the French garrison that had been in Rome for the past twenty years. A revolutionary committee in that city was in touch with Mazzini and he calculated that £6,000 might provide the necessary finance.[61] If it succeeded and the Romans then voted to join a monarchist Italy, their decision would of course be respected; but at least they should have the chance to express their wishes.[62] Unfortunately a second committee in Rome was being financed by the Italian government to prevent any insurrection happening; and, even more unfortunately, Garibaldi encouraged both the quasi-legal and the extra-legal committees without making up his mind between them.[63]

Mazzini's plan was to send a thousand men from Genoa to repeat the enterprise of May 1860, this time landing near the mouth of the Tiber to coincide with a rising inside Rome. Two ships were procured by friends in Genoa, but some of his weapons were sequestered by the government and its navy kept close watch at sea.[64] Moreover he knew by now that London was too remote a base for organising such an operation. Letters to and from Rome could take three weeks in transit, if indeed they ever arrived. At long last he discovered that his personal correspondence with Garibaldi had often failed to reach Caprera because this island was guarded by an Italian naval patrol: such letters are known to us only because, after confiscation, they were preserved in the royal archives, to which the official historian Luzio was briefly given privileged access.[65]

Finance, as ever, was another problem. Towards the £6,000 he required, a generous offer of £500 came from Peter Taylor and £75 from Gerrit Smith in America; contributions in this year from his home province of Liguria amounted to £80, another £80 arrived from France, and Mazzini added £20 he earned from the *Atlantic Monthly* for an article on the 'Moral Question'. Another £25 came from Harriet King, the wife of his English publisher. He issued tickets for 75,000 subscriptions in Italy of one shilling each, but distribution was immensely difficult and found only 350 takers. No doubt there were other contributions of which record never survived, but donations in England were fewer now that Italy was independent and in any case were directed rather towards Garibaldi. Italians, according to Mazzini, were more ready to give their lives than their money to the cause.[66]

By the end of July 1867 he realised he would be powerless unless or until Garibaldi decided to act. Two weeks later he returned to Switzerland where, in Lugano south of the Alps, he would be nearer any possible action, a fact that caused consternation in government circles at Florence.[67] Early in September, Garibaldi also arrived in Switzerland to address a pacifist congress at Geneva. Mazzini refused an invitation to attend this gathering, arguing in a written communication that, however admirable the motive, pacifism would merely encourage resignation and abstention from the immediate necessity of fighting for freedom and justice. At some point in the future, he explained, a United States of Europe or a League of Nations might make disarmament possible; but pacifism at the moment would leave tyrants in power and many submerged nationalities in bondage.[68]

Garibaldi kept any intentions to himself, partly because he had secretly been given money and arms by the Italian government for agitation inside the papal state in the hope that this might possibly provide another excuse for the national army to intervene.[69] Many of Garibaldi's friends, including Bertani and Crispi, feared he was being treated as a cat's-paw and might be led into repeating the tragedy of Aspromonte and civil war. Mazzini saw civil war as likely, especially as he correctly assumed that the government would turn against Garibaldi at the very first sign of disapproval from France. The one serious chance of success was for the citizens of Rome to precipitate matters by an insurrection, and he thought briefly of going personally to Rome to encourage them.[70] But the reality was worse than he can have guessed, because Victor Emanuel was secretly proposing to Napoleon that French and Italian troops should jointly enter Rome on the pretence of preventing the 'Mazzinian party' from dethroning the pope.[71] The king boasted to a number of people that, as an extra bonus, he deserved being given an opportunity to 'massacre' Garibaldi and every member of his volunteer force.[72] This word 'massacre', like Cavour's talk of 'extermination' in 1860, came oddly from those who claimed to despise Mazzini as a would-be assassin, and the fact that both words referred to the killing of other patriotic Italians made them doubly unfortunate.

As so often in moments of exceptional stress, Mazzini in Lugano was incapacitated by sickness. He knew things were going badly wrong when, towards the end of October, Garibaldi's volunteers crossed into papal territory, because a French expedition set out from Toulon to stop them. Without hesitation Mazzini urged his followers to support a national war against this French invasion. He also issued an appeal for organised opposition against Victor Emanuel when the king ordered the Italian army to support Napoleon in defeating the Italian volunteers; and although this appeal was suppressed by the censorship, it became generally known and aroused much enthusiasm. Garibaldi succeeded in fighting his way to within four miles of Rome, but according to the American consul found very little support inside the city where the two rival committees left people thoroughly confused.[73] After being defeated soon afterwards by the French at Mentana the revolutionary general blamed king and government for having deceived him, but also explained his defeat by inventing a story that Mazzini incited the volunteers to desert and diverted money to other purposes.[74] Mazzini denied both accusations and in fact many of his own supporters died at Mentana. Not until some years later was Garibaldi persuaded that this ungenerous criticism was unfounded, and until then this new breach between the two revolutionary leaders was irreparable.[75]

The return of French troops to Rome and the king's imprisonment of Garibaldi – again without daring to prosecute him – dealt a paralysing blow to the revolutionary patriots, but also to the reputation of the crown. The royal army was further humiliated when a threat from Paris forced it into a hurried withdrawal from papal territory. Public demonstrations in Turin, Milan and Florence called for a republic. Cabinet ministers privately spoke of the king's abdication as possible, even desirable.[76]

Mazzini at first hoped that public opinion would force the government to resign. He even sent a request to the Prussian government for money and arms to be used in a possible revolution.[77] But when nothing happened he returned disheartened to a former hideout in the Swiss Alps. In weeks of enforced isolation he was lucky to find a volume of Schiller and another by Byron that he had left behind on a previous escape. 'I have, throughout life, scattered Byrons of mine wherever I have been sojourning'; unlike Shakespeare, who 'may console by creating indifference to everything, Byron does not console but may awaken pride and push to action'. He also wished that on his earlier escape into these mountains he had left warm clothing for use in such an emergency.

When the immediate alarm subsided he moved down to the less severe climate of Lugano. There he could meet old comrades at La Tanzina, the house recently bought by his great friend Sara Nathan. She was an Italian from Livorno who for twenty years had lived in London where she knew him through her husband and her close relatives the Rosselli family. Now a rich widow, she provided him with another surrogate family during his last years of life, which led the Jesuit fathers of the *Civiltà Cattolica* to spread salacious rumours about his being the father of some of her children.[78] Other exiles long remembered the enchantment of his conversation during the long evenings at La Tanzina, 'especially on the religious and philosophical topics that he preferred'. But their memory was also of a very sick man. For a few days, to Bertani and Cattaneo who visited him, his life seemed in danger.[79] Napoleon learnt of his illness and 'did not express any wish for his recovery' – contrasting with Mazzini's less uncharitable reaction when he heard that the emperor was also seriously unwell.[80]

In January 1868, as soon as he was less in pain, he returned to England to see friends whom he had imagined he might never see again. Nor was his health improved by having to travel partly on foot through mountain passes in midwinter. On arrival in London he was depressed, talking of loneliness and 'a sense of disenchantment which grows on me more and more'. He felt 'old and shattered, and the crisis approaches which I shall not survive'.[81] His party was disorganised. 'Italy is falling apart, her finances in ruin, and corruption increasing at every level of society, with a universal discontent that sooner or later will lead to anarchy.'[82] Some of his strictures on the king were no stronger than those expressed in private by cabinet ministers, yet were too severe for inclusion in a published edition of his writing.[83] Believing that the monarchy remained the chief barrier to Italy's progress, he did not sufficiently appreciate that many Italians saw his republican alternative as too radical a challenge to the established order and to their own social position. The main republican newspapers in Italy, the *Dovere* and the *Popolo d'Italia*, lacked enough subscribers and continued to plague him with demands for money that he could no longer supply. When these papers were arraigned for printing criticism of the king, juries regularly acquitted them, but litigation cost money and he wondered if it was worth the expense.

What restored his sense of purpose was secret information from Paris that Victor Emanuel privately promised to join Napoleon in preparing for war against Prussia. Ever since the defeats of Custoza and Lissa the king had nourished the ambition to start another European war – any war, provided it would restore his self-respect and his prestige on the field of battle. Without consulting his cabinet the monarch secretly offered a military alliance to Austria for war against either Prussia or France; and then offered a quite different alliance to Prussia for a war against Austria.[84] When neither Austrians nor Prussians took him seriously he decided instead that his best hope of fighting was to cooperate with Napoleon in what eventually became the Franco-Prussian war of 1870.[85] Mazzini mysteriously received warning of this quixotic decision as early as the spring of 1867, and such was his horror of a French 'war for the Rhine' that he informed Berlin.[86] He had once discussed international politics with Bismarck's secretary whom he met in London. Though he strongly disliked Prussian *Realpolitik*, it still seemed to him a lesser evil than Bonapartism, and Germany possessed the same right as Italy to national unification, apart from the fact that both countries had a common interest against Austria. If Victor Emanuel seriously intended to send Italian troops to help France conquer the Rhineland, the Party of Action would assist Bismarck by starting another rebellion against the French garrison that once again was now defending the pope in Rome.[87] It should nevertheless be remembered that Mazzini often denounced the Italian government's reliance on foreign help, and in 1866 had actually criticised as 'shameful' the king's alliance with Bismarck.

Much depended on whether Garibaldi would support such a plan, and this victim of Mentana, though he continued to criticise the monarchy as dishonourable and financially corrupt,[88] was prudently determined to avoid another military engagement against the Italian army. The government was aware that Mazzini and Garibaldi in collaboration would pose a dangerous challenge to the crown and to the conservative ordering of society, but ministers took comfort in the likelihood that Garibaldi's resentment and jealousy of Mazzini, together with the latter's fear of Garibaldi's deviousness and inconsistency, would make such collaboration impossible.[89] Mazzini made one more attempt to persuade Garibaldi in July 1868 that they should meet to settle their differences before the outbreak of war gave them a chance to act; but no reply was forthcoming, and perhaps the government never allowed letters to penetrate its blockade of the lonely island of Caprera.[90]

Life in England

Mazzini's followers in Italy were devoted and immensely courageous, but not even a rough guess as to their numbers is possible and perhaps many of them supported his general ideas rather than his revolutionary

practice. After a brief period of fame in 1849 he became for most politically conscious Italians a remote figure in exile, feared or admired but
sometimes forgotten. Officialdom claimed to despise someone whom it
either tried to ignore or else depicted as a mere stage-conspirator. As he
was always dressed lugubriously in black from collar to toe, it was fairly
easy for official propaganda to turn him into a caricature of the *guastafeste*
who merely made trouble, or the *menagramo* who brought bad luck and
disaster to everything he touched, or at least the *tenebroso*, always sinister
and gloomy; and this same impersonation has endured in folk memory
ever since.

Much the same image, created out of fright and dislike, was nurtured
by a small group of Italians in London who made a successful and
sometimes distinguished career as naturalised British citizens. These men
were reluctant to contribute money to his school and for the most part
disdained close association with other exiles.[91] They included Sir Anthony
Panizzi at the British Museum, who had the added inconvenience of
being a friend of Louis Napoleon. Others were Leone Serena the
financier, Enrico Negretti a celebrated maker of scientific instruments, Sir
James Lacaita the close friend of Gladstone, and Gallenga on the staff of
The Times. Writing for English readers, Gallenga referred scornfully to the
incompetence of Italians in either war or politics; in particular Mazzini
was criticised for an 'overweening conceit' and narrow bigotry of views
that left him devoid of common sense and incapable of friendship; although this stormy petrel had once given an impulse to Italian nationality, the nation was said to have been created without his help. In one
leading article *The Times* accused him of aiming at 'rather the disunion
than the unity of Italy', and further stated that 'of twenty-five millions of
Italians there is hardly one who has not been of more practical use to the
cause of Italy than he'.[92]

No Englishman well acquainted with Mazzini would have recognised
this picture. But his name was far less familiar to public opinion than that
of Garibaldi. Moreover by temperament, and because of poverty and
single-minded dedication to Italian affairs, he still did nothing to seek new
acquaintances and avoided involvement in local politics. Only a literate
and politically conscious public knew of his presence. Yet Britain was
where he continued to find most of his money and many of his friends.[93]
Although the leaders of opinion in London discouraged revolution as an
instrument of politics except in the last resort, he benefited from support
given to the Risorgimento by liberals who saw it as not a series of
annexations by an aggressive Piedmont but a movement of national self-
determination. Such people admired him for his personality, his ideas,
and for what were recognised as genuine political achievements. Even
people he never met could regard him as a seer, almost a saint. Despite a

hermit-like existence, his presence in England over so many years, coupled with the absence of censorship, made his character better understood than it was in Italy. Some of the comments made about him in the British press or in personal memoirs are worth recording because they show how with little positive effort he won a quite unusual position in society.

Not everyone was favourable. Apart from *The Times*, the Brownings had been led to believe him responsible for the Orsini outrage against their hero Napoleon and had therefore transferred their enthusiasm to the more pragmatic Cavour. At Buckingham Palace, Queen Victoria occasionally mentioned his name, but always disparagingly. Cardinal Wiseman refused an invitation by Lord Houghton to meet him, and the future Cardinal Manning preached in Westminster Cathedral against 'the prophet of the Italian revolution' and his false 'doctrine of nationalities'.[94] 'Tolerance for Mazzini', wrote the great historian Lord Acton, 'is a criminal matter'.[95] Some Tories lacked any enthusiasm for the Risorgimento and for the man they persisted in calling 'the cold-hearted apostle of assassination',[96] but some conservatives were less censorious.[97] Among radicals there were those who compared him favourably to Garibaldi and thought his achievement of greater significance.[98] Some liberals agreed with admirers in other countries who thought Cavour to be a less effective figure.[99] Mazzini could be referred to as 'the greatest man in this nineteenth century',[100] 'one of the noblest Italians that have ever lived',[101] 'the greatest of living Italians'.[102] In the eyes of some admirers he was 'the master-mind of the century', 'the greatest man of his age', 'supreme among the ethical teachers of his time', and 'the only light in the sick chamber of Europe'.[103] Instead of being seen as the unpractical dreamer of conventional legend, he could even be praised for his 'foresight for the future and adaptation of means to ends'.[104] 'In European politics hardly any personality has counted for so much. . . . Mazzini represented a great idea, and represented it with an absoluteness and a sincerity almost unique in this faulty and imperfect world. . . . Excepting his idea and his genius, there was nothing to give him position and power.' Yet he was someone who aroused such hostile feelings that he was hunted like a wild beast throughout the rest of Europe.[105]

Apart from his political significance, certain positive aspects of his personality were more easily observed in London. Not the slightest hint, for instance, can be found to suggest that he was the extravagant and self-indulgent figure portrayed by some hostile propaganda in Italy. On the contrary, in his barely furnished and minute bed-sitting-room, 'austere in his private life and of the simplest habits, Mazzini led an existence of self-denial verging on asceticism'. Far from being narrow-minded in his interests, one friend thought that no one else had ever read so much over the whole field of human knowledge.[106] He was also said to have a singular 'power of seeing from the point of view of others' and, far from being a would-be assassin, what struck those who knew him was the essential nobility of someone who was 'a man of perfect honour'.[107] People spoke of his 'lovableness',[108] 'cordiality'[109] and 'intensely affectionate nature'.[110] 'Among intimate friends he was amiability personified.'[111] According to Sir John Robinson, a newspaper editor in London, 'not the least honourable fact in his history was that a life of exile had not imparted to his nature the least tinge of misanthropy'.[112] Despite plenty of reason for sadness, he was far from lugubrious by nature, and until his last illness the laughter and good humour of his company was singled out for comment.[113]

Such judgements, coming from many different people who wrote from personal knowledge, are a corrective to the caricature of Mazzini as the doleful, friendless conspirator, as depicted by those who knew him little or not at all. Another corrective is the statement by one of his translators that among his most notable characteristics was an unfeigned humility. 'He was the gentlest of human creatures, and the kindest. . . . His indignation itself, though fiery, had never anything violent or cruel. He *could* not be other than gentle in every action, word and tone. . . . Anguish, care and labour could not dim the essential simplicity, innocence, gaiety and charm of nature that made his the radiant presence of a child.'[114] The affection he inspired among the children of his friends must have helped to give him this reputation, and so did the uncommon fascination he exerted over animals, whether stray cats and dogs or the canaries and goldfinches that lived uncaged in his room.[115]

One relevant observation by Mathilde Blind was that 'pity and tenderness for all things weak, suffering and oppressed were the mainspring of Mazzini's political action'. She was another of those who above all remembered his personal magnetism. Never did she see him show anger except against Louis Napoleon, and then only in silent reprobation, while other political opponents were criticised only as a product rather than a cause of what was out of joint in society. He taught her to value the Christian injunction to love one's enemies, to do good for its own sake and not for reward or to make oneself happy. Happiness if sought deliberately 'will always evade your grasp', but would come unexpectedly if you set yourself a goal for the improvement of society and worked for it in patience and dedication.[116]

Another quality remarked upon was his lack of pretentiousness. 'Simple, unaffected and direct' was the comment of the socialist Henry Hyndman who, despite being a political opponent, often felt impelled to visit the humble lodging-house in Fulham Road where lived 'one of the really great figures of the nineteenth century'. Hyndman reported that 'a less self-seeking or personally proud man I have never met, yet he had an abiding consciousness of his own dignity'.[117] Emilio Castelar, future president of the Spanish Cortes who also remembered Mazzini's friendship as one of the great privileges of his life, was surprised at a first meeting to find him 'entirely without pretension or affectation'.[118] William Malleson, who once received from Mazzini a fascinating letter of advice about children's education, wrote that 'his manner was simple, entirely free from self-consciousness, gracious, full of charm, quiet, always courteous'.[119] According to one anonymous journalist he was 'singularly unobtrusive and averse to anything like show or notoriety'; indeed 'in private life Mazzini is the perfect gentleman, accomplished, gracious, and with a ready courtesy and genial warmth of expression that wins regard upon the instant'.[120]

The charm and fascination of his conversation were better appreciated in these later years when he felt more at home in London and in speaking English. 'Those who have heard Mazzini will never forget the eloquence, originality and range of his talk. . . . It had a prophetic grandeur, the urgency of a trumpet call'; and he was said to be far more impressive in conversation than in writing or public speaking.[121] He had 'a voice that thrilled like the voice of Kean or Kemble and made one ready to start for Milan at once should he desire it'.[122] Mendelssohn's godson, Felix Moscheles, knew him at this period and recalled no one whose conversation was more memorable.

> He held you magnetically. He would penetrate into some innermost recess of your conscience and kindle a spark where all had been darkness. Whilst under the influence of that eye, that voice, you felt as if you could leave father and mother and follow him, the elect of Providence who had come to overthrow the whole wretched fabric of falsehood holding mankind in bondage. He gave you eyes to see and ears to hear, and you too were stirred to rise and go forth to propagate the new Gospel.[123]

A later notice in the *Daily News*, while criticising his tactical mistakes as a politician, remembered qualities of leadership that aroused the admiration of all who met him. 'There was about him a suppressed fervour, a depth and dignity of assured conviction which at once revealed the secret of his great personal power. . . . He had that pent-up force of character which is a fuel to the fire of genius. There was an entire absence of self from his conversation and a complete absorption in his mission.'[124]

These testimonials are the more noteworthy coming from outside that group in the 'clan' who knew him most intimately. Mazzini tried to keep his address secret from strangers but almost every evening continued to meet close friends at the hospitable homes of either Stansfeld or Taylor, both of them members of parliament. This group included Emilie and

Caroline Ashurst who together with Harriet King were busy translating six volumes of his writings into English. Caroline's husband James Stansfeld, one of the most eloquent speakers in the House of Commons, had by now the benefit of twenty years' friendship with Mazzini and admitted the dominating influence on his own life exerted by this close friend.[125] Emilie after the death in 1866 of her husband, Carlo Venturi, kept a salon to which her intelligence and character attracted many celebrities of the time. She was said by Mrs King to be the most faithful and devoted of Mazzini's English followers, 'more witty and delightful in conversation than anyone I ever knew',[126] and as a translator who often had to consult him on the meaning of difficult passages she studied his written works as closely as anyone. Nor was Emilie alone in making the arresting observation that, while he regarded revolution as a necessary if regrettable means, he was basically a man of order and 'the severe supporter of every legitimate authority'. Though he was an opponent of Catholic orthodoxy, she also saw him as 'the most enlightened and devout religious thinker of the present day'.[127]

Among other prominent citizens who knew him and contributed to his funds, the American painter Whistler held him in high regard.[128] The lawyer William Shaen called him 'the greatest, the wisest, and the best man I have known, and to him I owe more than to any other teacher', adding that many Englishmen would say the same.[129] Other Americans, notably Gerrit Smith and William Lloyd Garrison who knew him through the anti-slavery movement, continued among his active supporters. Garrison, meeting him in 1867 after a long gap, found 'the same grand intellect, the same lofty and indomitable spirit, the same combination of true modesty and heroic assertion, of exceeding benignity and inspirational power',[130] while the American Unitarian minister Moncure Conway, whom he saw often in London, called him 'the bravest and the purest man that walked in Europe', the greatest Italian since Dante.[131] Sir Charles Dilke, subsequently a cabinet minister, kept in his study a portrait of Mazzini 'whose conversation and close friendship I deeply valued';[132] yet neither Dilke nor Conway was an unqualified enthusiast for Italian unification. William Lecky the Irish historian was another who, while sharing doubts about the Risorgimento, recalled how almost all young men of his generation were inspired by Mazzini's teaching about the rights of nationalities.[133]

Though greatly enjoying the relaxation of meeting old friends, Mazzini disliked attending large parties of strangers and even hesitated over an invitation to meet Ruskin, Frederick Harrison and F. D. Maurice.[134] Harrison and Maurice were fellows of Oxford and Cambridge colleges, and both of them, despite reservations about his practicality, expressed great interest in his ideas on nationality and religion.[135] Eventually he also met Ruskin, who wrote of loving someone so 'wholly upright, pure and noble, and of subtlest intellectual power'.[136] Mazzini responded by referring to Ruskin as 'the highest critic in the best philosophical and artistical sense', and once wrote to him that

> I shall always remember yesterday's evening as one of the dearest to me. Everything you have been writing had appeared to me as coming from one of the most powerful minds and deeply conscientious souls in this troubled period of ours. I have often felt comforted and strengthened by pages of yours. For God's sake do not forsake our camp. Do not believe that because a form of religion is perishing before our eyes, religion is going to vanish. . . . We need such voices as yours to urge us on in hope and faith.[137]

Late in life he again repaired his friendship with Thomas Carlyle, who was sorry to think how little he had made of the chances for serious talk 'with such a thinker as he now saw Mazzini to be'. Carlyle recommended his writings as 'well worth reading' and thought their author to be a far more significant figure than Garibaldi.[138] Anthony Trollope was fascinated by him after a single meeting, and George Eliot called him 'a true hero' whom 'it was riches to have known'.[139] George Meredith not only helped with proof-correcting of Mazzini's collected works but put him into a novel, as also did both Disraeli and Swinburne. According to Meredith 'the Risorgimento is the greatest historical fact of the nineteenth century' and Mazzini 'one of the chiefs of our age'.[140] John Stuart Mill, by now an acquaintance for over twenty years, presented him in 1859 with a copy of On Liberty, and not only complained at his unjust treatment in Italy but regarded him as among the few people always welcome as a visitor. 'I have the highest admiration for Mazzini, and although I do not sympathise with his mode of working I do not take upon myself to criticise it, because I do not doubt that to him is mainly owing the unity and freedom of Italy.'[141] The object of this praise was not always so appreciative in his estimate of Mill's writing, but the two men shared many ideas about liberty, patriotism and equality between the sexes.[142]

Among politicians his appeal was chiefly to radicals and Whigs. Lord Bryce as a young man knew Mazzini and came under the spell of someone he likened to St Francis, St Ignatius of Loyola and Calvin.[143] Walter Bagehot, the great constitutional lawyer, at first accepted the conventional opinion that he was wrong-headed and mischievous, but on closer knowledge came to admire his disinterestedness as well as the sagacity, moderation and magnanimity of someone who 'undoubtedly had revivified the political life of Italy and furnished the war materials of which the great political strategy of Count Cavour was able to make such wonderful use. Cavour without Mazzini would have been an engineer without a supply of force.'[144] Lord Morley, ministerial colleague and biographer of

Gladstone, when in Mazzini's presence 'could not resist this feeling of greatness', and remembered 'nobody in London who was more impressive or more seductive'. United Italy according to Morley was an

> idea that he invented and brought to life. . . . His was the moral genius that spiritualised politics and gave a new soul to public duty in citizens and nations. . . . Those of us who could see only too clearly Mazzini's deficiency in affairs, still felt good reason for honour and gratitude to him as evangelist and prophet. . . . It was Mazzini who went nearest to the heart and true significance of democracy: he had a moral glow and the light of large historical and literary comprehension that stretched it into the foremost place in the minds of men with social imagination. . . . He did more: though figuring as restorer of a single nation, he was as earnest as Kant himself in urging the moral relations between different states, and the supremacy and overlordship of cosmopolitan humanity.

Gladstone, who never met Mazzini, demurred at this eulogy, but Morley in reply stood up for 'one of the most morally impressive men I had ever known or that his age knew'.[145]

Though he had no academic pretensions to philosophy and never sought an audience in the universities, Mazzini's ideas were valued by many prominent intellectuals of the time. At Cambridge university, as well as Sir John Seeley and Professor Maurice, a group which used to read and discuss the *Duties of Man* included the sociologist Edward Carpenter and the future professor of political economy, Henry Fawcett. Frederick Myers of Trinity College was another who wrote a long and admiring essay about him. Henry Sidgwick, the professor of philosophy, sought his views on questions of crowd psychology and mass hysteria: when Sidgwick once tried to defend Spiritualism, Mazzini 'bore down on me with such a current of clear, eager argument I was quite overwhelmed'.[146] At London university he was befriended by David Masson and the Latinist Francis Newman. At Oxford, in addition to James Bryce and Goldwin Smith, he knew Benjamin Jowett who became Master of Balliol in 1870. Jowett enjoyed their discussions on religion, concluding that 'he was a very noble character and had a genius far beyond that of ordinary statesmen. Though not a statesman, I think that his reputation will increase as time goes on when that of most statesmen disappears.' Jowett was told by friends that this shy and withdrawn exile was the most fascinating person they knew.[147]

This group at Balliol included other well-known academics. One was the young jurist A. V. Dicey. Another was the philosopher T. H. Green, who acknowledged Mazzini's influence, publicly vindicating his views against those of Cavour, in particular arguing that sometimes rebellion was a positive duty even if success was impossible. Another Balliol admirer was the Shakespearean critic A. C. Bradley, who kept several portraits of Mazzini in his college rooms.[148] Among their pupils were Charles Vaughan and Bolton King, whose enthusiasm eventually produced the two best studies on Mazzini in English. Yet another fellow of Balliol, the economist Arnold Toynbee, ended his famous lectures on the Industrial Revolution with an encomium of the *Duties of Man*: 'for not Adam Smith, not Carlyle great as he was, but Mazzini is the true teacher of our age'.[149] Toynbee Hall, the adult education centre in east London which Bolton King and others in this group helped to establish, had part of its ancestry in the night-school for Italian workers that Toynbee's father and uncle had helped Mazzini to organise in Hatton Garden.

Jowett it was who, at a meeting in the house of the Earl of Carlisle, asked Mazzini 'to take intellectual charge' of another Balliol alumnus, the poet Algernon Swinburne. Not only did the theme of Italian liberty inspire some of Swinburne's finest writing, but he too owned a portrait of Mazzini and wrote an ode to him long before they met. At their meeting, ten years after Swinburne sent his first subscription to Mazzini's National Fund, the poet dramatically fell on his knees to kiss the hand of 'the man whom I most loved and honoured of all men on earth . . . the most wonderfully and divinely unselfish man I ever knew', 'a born king and chief and leader' who was 'clearly the man to create a nation'. Swinburne later described their friendship as 'the highest honour of my life and one of its greatest and purest pleasures': only after listening to Mazzini had he understood the message of the New Testament and the teaching of Christ.[150]

CHAPTER NINE

Final Polemics

Religion

RELIGION REMAINED CENTRAL to Mazzini's personality and thinking, as Swinburne was far from alone in realising. Serious historians have challenged orthodoxy by calling him the most eminent religious thinker in the Risorgimento, or even Italy's one great religious reformer since Savonarola; and a distinguished historian of literature wrote that an article he published in English on the Vatican Council of 1870 'crowns the public eloquence of our time'.[1] In the later 1860s, Mazzini was still hoping that despite political preoccupations and failing health he could put his creed into a book, and this was the project that seems to have occupied what little time he had for reading. But he lacked the physical strength and perhaps the clarity of mind required to bring his ideas into communicable shape, and sometimes could understand why some of his opinions might be hard for others to comprehend, though he thought them less unintelligible than those of Hegel.[2] Ultimately, as he admitted, religious belief depended on faith, since the active presence in history of a benevolent and intelligent God was an axiom upon which logical scrutiny would be almost blasphemous.[3]

The book he might have written would have described the main enemy as materialism in its various guises, whether in Marx or Comte, or at a more practical level in the nice calculations of tactical expediency used by politicians to confuse issues of principle. He never abandoned his unfashionable criticism of politicians who put pragmatic success above principle or material force above morality; nor, despite his early scientific interests, could he in any way sympathise with the new generation of positivists who believed that 'science is now the only religion'.[4] For three centuries Italy had been corrupted by Machiavelli, or more precisely by Machiavellism which he described as 'an ignoble travesty of the doctrine of a great but unhappy man'.[5] People were deluded if they thought Italy would ever be regenerated by the compromisers and tacticians, or by people seeking rights while denying duties, or by those who would sacrifice ideals in the opportunistic search for selfish and material gain.[6]

The papacy was no less an enemy, all the more so because its ostenta-tious wealth and claims to temporal authority led to a confusion between the spiritual and the material, a confusion which contributed to giving Italian society the deserved reputation of being irreligious and materialis-tic.[7] To defend the minuscule papal state against Italian patriotism, Pius IX continued to employ a mercenary force recruited in Switzerland, Ireland and elsewhere, while only the additional presence of French soldiers in Rome and Austrian troops in Bologna protected him from the resentment and disloyalty of a disaffected subject population. To Mazzini and others there was a repugnant incongruity in the fact that many years witnessed dozens of people guillotined by the official papal executioners. The per-haps less final weapon of excommunication was also employed against Victor Emanuel and his ministers. There was a desperate attempt to proscribe what Pius derisively called 'modern civilisation' by criminalising liberal ideas, especially the heresy of religious toleration. Mazzini contin-ued all his life to venerate the teaching of Christ as an immense step forward for humanity. Sometimes, as he confessed, 'a touch of old Chris-tianity came over me when I was *feeling* more than *thinking*'. If the official state religion was insufficient, that was not because its central message was wrong, but because western civilisation had already accepted and incorporated the more positive aspects of its teaching. Regrettably the Church was now governed by a narrow clique caught up in power politics and failing to adjust to irreversible changes in society.[8]

Although Mazzini saw no need for priests as intermediaries between God and man, he hated the positive anticlericalism of Garibaldi and other Risorgimento leaders: one source of his differences with Garibaldi was that the latter proclaimed himself an atheist and nurtured a fierce enmity towards the priesthood.[9] Mazzini was also less friendly than Garibaldi to the anticlerical freemasons. When invited to become a mason he refused and was sometimes overtly critical.[10] Many of his followers nonetheless became active freemasons, and he himself welcomed political support from individual lodges that sympathised with republicanism.[11]

Despite any superficial resemblance he remained some way removed from Protestantism. One welcome result of the sixteenth-century Re-formation was that it had redressed defects in Catholicism by challenging hierarchy and championing liberty of conscience. But regrettably the Reformation had broken the unity of Christendom, and some kind of unity he hoped would one day be partially restored in a new dispensation that emphasised values held in common.[12] He admired Jan Huss and often spoke well of Luther, though never of Calvin. He attracted Unitar-ians in particular, and many devout nonconformists were delighted to discover that in Italy, unlike France or Germany, 'the party of progress is not the party of scepticism but of religious belief'.[13] Though he was

essentially undenominational in his views and averse to formal religion
and dogma, an edition of his religious writing was published in London
'on a distinctly Christian basis' by an Anglican bishop who enormously
admired him, and it sold well enough to be given a second edition.[14]
Freethinkers and secularists on the other hand were surprised when he
refused on principle to write for their journals.[15] Yet he remained on good
personal terms with Hyndman and an atheist such as Holyoake, while the
notorious Bradlaugh not only supported his causes but kept a framed
portrait of him prominently displayed. The secularist Karl Blind long
remembered their verbal battles about religion, after which 'a treaty of
peace was tacitly agreed upon'; and Mazzini's kindliness and good humour made reconciliation not too difficult.[16]

One rabbi thought his beliefs were close to Judaism.[17] Some essential
truths, Mazzini used to say, could be found in all the great religions,
which should be studied with an open mind to discover what each
contributed to a progressive revelation of the divine will.[18] 'Nothing
would have more distressed and shocked Mazzini than to be regarded as
the founder of a religious sect', wrote Harriet King, who remained his
devoted disciple despite being an equally devoted and practising Catholic.
In many conversations with Mrs King he always showed complete respect
for her beliefs. Though he thought outward forms of religious practice to
be relatively unimportant, he agreed with her that belief itself was fundamental, like the chief message of the Gospel which was love for God and
one's neighbour. In a letter to her he wrote: 'I fear, dear friend, that you
are bent too much on self-analysing, on thinking too much of your
salvation. Let God think of it: your task is to act for the fulfilment of his
law whenever and as much as you can. . . . Love him in a simple,
unexacting, unscrutinising way, as a child his mother, and remember that
self-torturing has in itself an unconscious hidden taint of egotism.'[19]

Unfortunately these basic teachings had in course of the centuries
become obscured. Catholic Christianity had once been a great repository
of religious truth. It had also been a force for liberty and equality as well
as for scholarship and art and great works of charity, but had now lost its
way. The great humanitarian achievements of the nineteenth century
had a different provenance, such as the abolition of slavery, or popular
education, the achievements of science, the liberation of Italy and other
nationalities from cruel political oppression. Too often the Church had
come to stand for persecution and not freedom, for worldly success rather
than charity, for absolutism not self-government; and something in its
teaching must therefore be badly awry.[20]

What worried many of his party and friends was that he did not share
the liberal belief in a lay and secular state. On some points he appeared as
impervious to argument as his opponents, for example in his almost

mystical idea that sovereignty resided in 'God and the people'; and he never properly explained how this particular juxtaposition could be reconciled. Other apparent contradictions were equally left unexplained. Believing that any healthy society must have some shared values, he often continued to speak of his hope for a moral consensus of mankind in which the state might once again become almost identified with the Church. Individual conscience was sacred, but equally sacred was the common consent of humanity and the working of a divine providence which individuals could delay or accelerate but not ignore.[21]

Alberto Mario and Cattaneo were among many republicans who could make no sense of such a metaphysical and illiberal idea. Pisacane called it theocratic and historians have occasionally used the same word.[22] When tackled in private about his talk of a common religion for humanity, Mazzini sometimes showed a sense of unease by changing the subject, but on one occasion casually admitted to being 'authoritarian in principle' on this issue. Though he usually preferred to be vague and imprecise, one perhaps chance remark was remembered many years after his death when 'he fervently spoke of the desirability of proclaiming a kind of State creed through a National Constituent Assembly. It was to be a religious system "not bound to special Church tenets", but still a profession of faith acknowledged and proclaimed by the representatives of the people in parliament.'[23]

Never did he spell out what he hoped such a parliament would decide. On the contrary, in practice he confirmed his earlier opinion that 'progressive revelation' was bound in time to modify his own as well as other current beliefs.[24] On one point, however, he was adamant, because although he could accept a democratic vote in favour of monarchy, he could never have approved of a constitution based on atheism. To that extent he was undoubtedly theocratic, but hardly more so than the existing constitution of Italy which he condemned precisely because it declared Catholicism to be the official state religion.[25] Liberty of conscience for everyone remained one of his fundamental beliefs and there should never be any imposition of dogmas by a priesthood. Bigotry was as misguided as indifferentism. Heresy was to be tolerated, even welcomed as a means of arriving at a higher truth, and individuals must be entirely free to choose their beliefs or else there could be no responsibility for personal action.[26] Intolerance, he used to say, merely betrayed a fear of being wrong, and hence there should be 'freedom for all religious ideas to manifest themselves'. Tolerance need not mean indifference. Though he could not understand disbelief in God, his faith was characterised by repeated injunctions for tolerance, respect for other points of view, and by what his friends saw as a remarkable lack of dogmatism.[27] Lord Bryce thought that of all the Europeans of their generation, Mazzini and

Gladstone were the two who had the greatest faith in liberty and 'an almost excessive faith in its power for good'.[28]

Socialism

Some of Mazzini's critics questioned whether he was a genuine democrat.[29] Others, more plausibly, have regarded his Party of Action as being the first truly democratic movement in Italian history.[30] He himself was not unaware that democracy had many meanings, some of which could be manipulated and exploited by a tyrant such as Napoleon III or even by an authoritarian Church. He also knew that universal suffrage required a far more politically conscious electorate than existed in Italy and in any case would be no guarantee of good government.[31] Yet an extension of the existing franchise would be an essential prelude to the diffusion of social consciousness and a sense of individual political responsibility. The experience of a lifetime had not changed his mind on such an issue. He always maintained that government must be accountable to the people and depend for survival on a popular vote.[32] Admittedly human imperfections made popular sovereignty fallible, but it was far better than current practice in Italy after 1860 where a narrow and irresponsible political class governed in its own interests after selfishly assuming that such interests were identical with those of the whole community. Despite his belief in popular sovereignty, he knew the Risorgimento was a minority movement, inevitably so, yet was also sure that its ultimate success would depend on winning support from the masses, which could only be done by giving them a more obvious share in its duties and benefits.

He was accused by the Marxists of being a 'bourgeois reactionary' who, perhaps inadvertently, was helping the privileged classes to set up a corrupt and tyrannical regime in a united Italy.[33] This accusation was a rejoinder to Mazzini's fierce attack on the French socialists when he accused them of helping Napoleon III into power by antagonising the middle classes with gratuitous talk about confiscating private property. He had good reason to fear that a class war in Italy might produce a similar reaction and would certainly delay the achievement of nationhood as well as retard economic development. Though by experience he had learnt that the bourgeoisie was fickle and only 'the working-class element keeps faithful', he also had no doubt that many of the most patriotic, hard-working and socially aware Italians were in the middle class;[34] their contribution and indeed their leadership were vital for success. This was one reason why he continued to denounce the divisive effects of communism, a political system which in his view was not only based on false economic theory but represented an illiberal and oppressive means by which a small group of cynical intellectuals sought absolute power over the whole community.[35] Though communism was a false Utopia, he was nonetheless sure that the working classes would one day obtain fuller recognition in society and this should be welcomed, though he hoped 'that they would not themselves become a new bourgeoisie by an excessive pursuit of their own material interests'.[36] Nor could such a social revolution be acceptable or durable if effected by force without consent. As he now repeated to a friend, any new order established through violence, even though superior to the old, would still be a tyranny.[37]

To the end of his life he continued to believe that the political Risorgimento would be incomplete and might even go into reverse if it did not change what he called the scandal of existing social relations.[38] Once again he stated that the French Revolution of 1789 had done much to win individual liberties, but its achievement was insufficient because, although some people had thereby become prosperous, society was no more equitable and standards of living for perhaps most people had improved little if at all.[39] Support for law and order could hardly be expected from the majority for whom justice and the courts of law were almost completely inaccessible.[40] The unlimited competition of *laissez-faire*, which was often said to result almost automatically in increased production, sometimes did the very opposite by lowering wages and the purchasing power of ordinary citizens. Excessive individualism was for that reason, perhaps unexpectedly, one factor that kept Italy backward. Only with more cooperation and a greater sense of community and social obligation would a truly liberal and prosperous Italy emerge. Only if economists studied distribution as much as they studied production would necessary political changes take place with general consent.[41]

Among desirable social reforms, Mazzini in the mid-1860s was ahead of most politicians in demanding compulsory insurance for sickness and old age.[42] He also wanted to end military conscription:[43] Garibaldi's volunteer armies had been more effective than the regular army, and there was an appalling unfairness in the Italian practice that permitted rich people to buy themselves a reduction in or exclusion from 'compulsory' military service, leaving the poor to fight for a country that denied them a right to vote. Similarly the tax system was heavily weighted in favour of the landed interest and required radical alteration for reasons of good budgeting as well as equity. He wanted to abolish indirect taxes on essential food: direct taxation was far less expensive to collect and fell less heavily on those citizens who could barely afford the basic necessities of life.[44] There ought to be an income tax proportionate to wealth and an inheritance tax on large landed properties. According to his English friend Myers, this proposal to raise most revenue from income and property taxes was the only point in his economic policy that could not have been subscribed to by a liberal politician at Westminster.[45]

Twenty years earlier, Mazzini had begun to create an organisation for self-help among the Italian workers in London, and in the 1860s was still preaching this same message in his Sunday lectures 'to my working men' in Hatton Garden. He was also encouraging the formation of cooperatives in a dozen of the principal Italian towns, and proudly wrote to inform Palmerston that his Genoese Working Men's Association had nearly five thousand members.[46] To them he stressed not only the economic advantages of shared property and profits, but the need to set up free schools, circulating libraries, reading rooms, and health insurance for their membership.[47] *The Times* referred to this as creeping socialism, and blamed Mazzini as much as Marx for 'insisting on the rights of labour, on high wages and short hours, and laying upon the government the duty of finding work for those who are unwilling to work for themselves'.[48]

His opinions were nevertheless far removed from the socialist doctrine of mobilising the masses to seize power by violence. And yet the cooperative movement and the union of capital and labour in the same hands would, he hoped, be 'the beginning of an immense social revolution which will do more for the brotherhood of man to man than all the eighteen centuries of Christianity have done': he was proud to point out that he had been advocating this since 1832, long before 'all the French socialistic hubbub'.[49] A preliminary financial endowment could be provided from the extensive properties of the Church – which, incidentally, the Italian government was already nationalising and selling cheaply to existing landowners. This vast wealth could in his opinion be far more productively and equitably used to finance smallholdings and cooperatives.[50] He was also intending to form trade unions and a nationwide Trade Union Congress in the hope that his own party rather than the socialists would dominate the burgeoning working-class movement.[51]

Mazzini perforce addressed himself to urban workers, among whom he could find readers for the written propaganda that was the only resource for an exile. This fact continued to leave him exposed to criticism by socialists for neglecting rural society and not recognising its great potential as a revolutionary force.[52] And yet the important problem of how to reach agricultural workers was something he often continued to discuss. He saw them as the chief wealth producers in the community despite their unspeakable poverty which was one of the most debilitating plagues affecting Italy.[53] From what he had observed, particularly in Sicily and Russia, he had no doubt that they were a potentially revolutionary force,[54] but inevitably their interest was far more in social and economic change than in a patriotism they imperfectly understood. One of his own arguments for a unified Italy was that by removing trade barriers it would bring greater prosperity, which in turn would permit this terrible plague to be cured. *Jacqueries* and hunger riots would never make a successful revolution. The threat of class war in the countryside spelt probable disaster because time after time it alienated poorer people from patriotism at the same time as forcing middle-class liberals to fall back on throne and altar in self-defence.[55]

He had personally encountered this problem at Rome in 1849 where he found the peasants 'indifferent but not antagonistic': one positive sign in those dramatic months was that the rural population had not risen to defend papal sovereignty and on the contrary hoped to gain from the agrarian reforms he tried to introduce.[56] But he was sure that any socialist attempt to make such people the chief actors in revolution would end in grief and almost certainly leave everyone poorer than before. Their political unreliability was such that many of them actively backed Austria in the war of 1848; they had supported the king of Naples in the slaughter of Pisacane and the Bandiera brothers; and Garibaldi confessed, to his shame and dismay, that not a single *contadino* joined his volunteer armies.[57]

Yet the repeated criticism that Mazzini ignored this largest of all classes was wide of the mark. Since they were illiterate he could not influence them directly by written propaganda from England, but repeatedly he urged his party to make personal contact by word of mouth, to make their welfare a primary concern and do everything to convince them that representative government in a united nation would give them some chance of a better life.[58] By abolishing local taxes on flour and salt, by restoring to them the twelve million acres of communal land that had been arbitrarily confiscated by neighbouring landlords and often left uncultivated, above all by creating a new class of smallholders,[59] a major and necessary revolution would be effected in Italian society.

Karl Marx was living a few streets away from him in London and at least once they attended the same meeting.[60] Marx, too, was stimulated by the dramatic social changes in England to develop his own very different analysis of society and a desire for wholesale social revolution. The communist leader despised Garibaldi and refused an opportunity to meet him, but his attitude to Mazzini was one of alarm and anxiety as well as contempt. Marx's rejection of transcendental religion and suspicion of 'bourgeois patriotism' made their views unreconcilable. So, quite as much, did the Marxist doubts about private property and belief in a class war leading to dictatorship by the proletariat. Marx acknowledged that Mazzini had for thirty years led the Italian revolution and was 'the ablest exponent of the national aspirations of his countrymen', but the Marxists had derisive scorn for the 'false sublimity, puffy grandeur, verbosity and prophetic mysticism' which in their view made the older man a dangerous irrelevancy in the new socialist era. Some socialists could admit that the republican leader still had a truly important function in leading the one radical group in Italy that refused to be corrupted and absorbed by the ruling class, but others accused him of condemning the peasants to a slavery worse than that of ancient Rome.[61] Already in December 1858 a socialist manifesto in London had warned the working classes of Europe against an alliance with this representative of 'bourgeois republicanism' and the 'so-called democrats'.[62]

Among other English socialists who were more friendly to Mazzini, some in 1864 joined a group of European exiles to create what became the Socialist International. He himself was unwell and did not attend their inaugural meeting, but some of his companions were present and the first manifesto of the International was condemned by Marx as 'a concoction of Mazzini's'.[63] Marx, too, missed some of the early meetings but was elected to its general council and almost immediately steered it in a quite different direction. Mazzini was too ill to put up much of a fight against a younger, more politically astute and ruthless rival, though two years later was still offering in vain to discuss their differences. When a false rumour circulated that he had died, the executive council of the International proposed putting on record their condolences at 'the great loss we have sustained', but this pacificatory gesture was vetoed by Marx.[64] A cruel surprise and disappointment was that, after many of Mazzini's less radical associates had deserted to support the victorious Italian monarchy, some of the more radical deserted to join either Marx or Bakunin, and this was a clear sign that he was no longer abreast of current thinking among Italian youth. He could do little more than prophesy that class war would lead to disillusionment and almost certainly in the long run to despotism. Marx, he wrote, was someone of penetrating intelligence but with more hatred than love in his heart, someone who could only aggravate a division in society that should have been avoided or at least mitigated.[65]

Mikhail Bakunin, on the other hand, had been a friend and admirer of Mazzini,[66] even though anarchist and federalist leanings made him of little use as a political ally. The two men saw each other often in London during 1862 when Mazzini defended Bakunin against Marx. But by 1866 they were openly at odds. After making a thorough study of Mazzini's writings Bakunin levelled fundamental criticisms against them. His chief and plausible objection was that cooperation between labour and capital was an unrealistic ideal because the bourgeoisie would merely pretend and never give way on points of substance. Moreover belief in God was an unpardonable eccentricity; and the 'detestable theory of patriotism', by playing into the hands of the Italian monarchy, threatened to make Italy an over-centralised and militaristic state in which resources were switched from social reform to the pursuit of national grandeur. With equal plausibility Mazzini was said by Bakunin to have worked all his life on the false premise that national unification would solve Italy's problems, and unfortunately the newly created state was hardly setting the outside world an example of liberty, morality, or greater social equality.[67]

Bakunin and not Marx was the dominant influence on Italian socialism during the next ten years, and though the Russian was no less critical of Mazzini, he remained grateful and even affectionate towards his former friend. He argued that Mazzini was open to criticism for being too preoccupied with conspiracy to read enough about recent intellectual developments leading away from idealism towards positivist philosophy and socialist theory, and yet no one in Europe was more respected for nobility of character. Bakunin recognised his fine intelligence, kindness, good nature, love for humankind, and entire lack of thought for himself. These qualities were said to be hard to square with the undoubted fact that the republican leader 'had given sleepless nights to most rulers in contemporary Europe'.

At the end of such a long and magnificent career, he has at last found us to be his irreconcilable enemies, though we fight with sadness and no pleasure against this implacable enemy of the revolution. . . . He is the noblest and purest human being I have met in my life . . . whose existence is enough by itself to show how Italy in a decadent Europe remains a great and vigorous nation. . . . All his insurrections failed. Yet . . . their results as an educative force on Italian youth have been incalculable. He is the person who awoke and inspired the young patriots at the heart of Italy's Risorgimento. This is his great immortal handiwork. . . . But by remaining aloof from the real life of the masses, his gigantic enterprise, undertaken by the greatest man of our century and two generations of martyr-heroes, has produced something more dead than alive.

One final criticism was that religious convictions had finally triumphed over Mazzini's revolutionary temperament. Tragically this elder statesman of the revolution refused to change his mind and had to watch events slipping from his control along a different path that many young Italians were eager to follow.[68]

Other former critics showed the same or a slightly different mixture of admiration and regret as Mazzini's influence seemed on the wane in the late 1860s. Pallavicino, once a bitter enemy, could now admit that, whereas Cavour to the end of his life 'preferred Piedmont to Italy', Mazzini had been the one genuine representative of Italian patriotism.[69] Herzen agreed that he had worked a miracle in awakening a sense of nationality, though unfortunately his achievements had been purloined by a military-minded royal court that rejected his democratic ideals and mainly sought to cut a *bella figura* among the great powers.[70] Other socialists still retained an almost religious veneration for the man who alone and for thirty years had kept alive a belief in liberty, but who in exile was inevitably out of touch with a quite different society that he had done much to bring into existence.[71] Some of his ideas had proved exaggerated, others were false, but in an almost magical way, and despite what Bakunin believed, the essential elements in his writing were said to have succeeded in reaching the 'popular masses', giving them a degree of political awareness that marked a fundamental change from the Italy of the 1830s.[72]

Alberto Mario, a former disciple married to Jessie White, was one of those who moved away in a different direction to join Cattaneo in thinking that Italy should be not only a republic but a federal state in which the development of internal liberties took precedence over national unification. Mario and Cattaneo never lost their affection and admiration for Mazzini.[73] Cattaneo lived just outside Lugano, effectively banished by Cavour, and the two leading republican intellectuals met frequently on the half-dozen occasions that Mazzini visited Switzerland in the 1860s. Cattaneo went even further than Mazzini in disappointment at the way that Cavour's party created anarchy and counter-revolution by trying to impose a 'military hegemony' on southern Italy.[74] But ever since 1850 he had recognised Mazzini as the real 'precursor' who more than anyone had imposed ideas of Italian patriotism on a reluctant ruling class.[75] The differences between these two men were less discordant than some people imagined, because Cattaneo accepted Italian nationality and Mazzini wanted regional devolution. Their personal esteem and friendship were mutual. Both raised serious objection to the political system imposed on Italy in 1861 and feared its effect on the future development of their country. Mazzini was the last person Cattaneo recognised as he lay dying in 1869.

More conspiracy: 1868–70

To win Rome and make it the Italian capital was Mazzini's principal remaining ambition. This would be very far from easy, and indeed some people in Italy as elsewhere thought it more likely that the partially unified state might before long split up again into its separate kingdoms and duchies. Lord Clarendon on a visit early in 1868 discovered 'a great expectation in Rome that Italy will break up and that the Holy Father will recover his provinces'. In Florence this leading British politician found 'universal agreement' among senior Italian politicians that Victor

Emanuel's dynasty would not last much longer unless he learnt to behave more like a parliamentary sovereign.[76] The king was held partly responsible for the military defeats of 1866, and also for the fact that in 1867 his French ally, after defeating Garibaldi, sent French troops back to Rome as guardians of papal sovereignty. Mazzini by now knew that the royal court furthermore intended to join the French in a war of aggression against Prussia, and to prevent this he hoped there might be some support in Italy for another popular insurrection. Italians should acquire Rome as they had won Sicily and Naples, by their own effort, not by relying upon foreigners as in Lombardy and Venice.

To be near the scene of action he returned to Switzerland in August 1868, secretly crossing at least once into Italy over the next weeks. Though the loss of an address book interfered with recreating his former network of agents, before long he was again in touch with local revolutionary committees over most of the country.[77] A number of people in Switzerland must have known his whereabouts but never was he betrayed. The Italian government was alarmed at continued indications of his 'great influence' in Italy. Ministers discovered from intercepted letters that he must be somewhere near the southern Swiss frontier, and they also learnt that he was in touch with Bismarck to frustrate any royalist war against Prussia.[78] Another official demand was therefore sent to Berne for his expulsion; and ironically this demand had to be delivered by Melegari, now the Italian ambassador, the same person who in 1833–4 had conspired as a refugee in Switzerland to help Mazzini rebel against the Piedmont of Charles Albert.[79]

To confuse the authorities and obtain money, Mazzini returned to London in December, but after ten days was back in Lugano. These two journeys in midwinter further damaged his health, and newspapers all over Europe printed another false announcement of his death.[80] What aggravated his illness was distress at seeing the political class in Italy content to wait in hope of receiving Rome as a gift from the French emperor. Americans had won independence by their own efforts, Frenchmen had stormed the Bastille and Spanish guerrillas defeated the Grand Army of the first Napoleon,[81] but Italians remained inert and were now suffering the consequences. 'Nobody can understand how wretched I feel at seeing corruption, scepticism about the advantages of Unity, financiary ruin, shame of subalternity, and moral anarchy increasing from year to year and under a materialist immoral government, all the future of Italy disappearing, all the ideal Italy, the inspiring dream of my whole life and the soul of all my belief.'[82]

He nonetheless set to work in another frenzy of activity, spreading disaffection inside the Italian army, preparing concealed deposits of weapons, recruiting friendly officials in the railway and telegraph systems, agitating among peasants and students, finding printers who in their spare time would secretly publish republican propaganda. He had to make one perhaps final effort to start another chain reaction of insurrections like that of 1848, with simultaneous outbreaks in Turin, Genoa, Naples, Palermo and throughout Emilia. Admittedly there was a by now familiar risk that this might begin prematurely before preparations were complete, yet it was important to act before plans leaked out and if possible before the royalists had time to carry out their alternative plan to join a Franco-Prussian war.[83] He was not without expectations. The prestige of the Italian monarchy, according to *The Times*, was very low. Corruption in high places was seriously weakening the nation's attachment to their king and there was republican agitation in the universities and in some provincial towns.[84]

Because of poor health and of lessons learnt from experience, he decided to seek another collective decision among other republicans, and twenty delegates from different Italian regions were summoned in February 1869 to a meeting in Lugano. Though in great pain, he addressed them at length to explain his intentions and hopes. But after long discussion he gave way with regret to the majority who preferred to delay action. One army officer present, who later was thought to have been an *agent provocateur*, argued at this meeting for an immediate uprising, and perhaps it was through his agency that some participants were imprisoned on their return to Italy. Ministers in Florence knew almost at once about what took place at Lugano and renewed their demand that Switzerland should expel someone they called not a political conspirator but a vulgar criminal, assassin and anarchist.[85] Whether truthfully or not, Victor Emanuel admitted to bribing four or five republicans to learn about their intentions and about their relations with Bismarck.[86] Mazzini soon discovered that his plans were no longer secret and he knew that some republican groups were determined to disregard the collective decision for delay. In April, against his wishes, an ill-considered attempt to seize arms from a military barracks in Milan led to further arrests.[87]

This was enough for the Swiss to decree his expulsion, though they still took some time to locate him. Once again a town council in Switzerland tried to protect him by the grant of honorary citizenship and for another month he was able to hide in Zürich, existing 'as if in a whirlwind, something like Paolo without Francesca'.[88] Concealing his frustration and disappointment he spoke as if the year would not end without one more insurrection, even though privately he was doubtful about its chances of success.[89] But first, since he 'could not plunge into the abyss without seeing the few I love in England', he returned to London for the month of July. Then the rest of 1869 was spent hiding and housebound in Switzerland with occasional clandestine excursions into northern Italy.

Since he was now more careful about sending letters through the post, his day-to-day activity is harder to trace. Further evidence of caution was his urgent advice to abstain from any premature and isolated action like that at Milan.[90] In the course of time he hoped it would be possible to exploit widespread opposition against the increasingly obvious attempts by the king to revert to a system of personal government. Newspapers in Italy reported frequent urban riots as well as protest movements by students and there was local agitation in the countryside against new taxes on food. Tension was also increased after several exposures of corruption in public life in which the king himself was thought to be involved. But although people all over Italy sent him word of their readiness to support a revolution against misgovernment, Mazzini had learnt that to organise many simultaneous movements was beyond his capacity as a sick and exiled refugee in hiding. Most of the more prudent republicans had in any case learnt from previous experience to be wary and were waiting for others to act before joining a concerted rebellion.[91] He told friends that once again he was tempted to give up action and return to his perhaps more useful life of thinking and writing.[92]

Particularly disheartening was Garibaldi's silence despite repeated letters asking for a meeting to discuss objectives and tactics.[93] These two strong characters might once more have been a major force had they cooperated as in 1860. Both of them believed that only a popular insurrection would compel the king to act over Rome. But in other matters they were more in disagreement than ever, especially as Garibaldi now supported Marx's Socialist International and again spoke of despising Mazzini as 'a man of theory, not practice, who incessantly talks of "the people" but without knowing them'. Nor was Garibaldi's former mentor forgiven for having shown greater wisdom in doubting the king's good faith and foretelling the disasters of Aspromonte and Mentana. As well as disliking Garibaldi's religious unbelief and 'anticlerical monomania', Mazzini was frustrated by the other's understandable prudence and reluctance (just as in 1860) to join any rebellion until it had already begun and showed at least some possibility of succeeding.[94]

What prompted Mazzini to attempt a final revolutionary gamble was further confirmation from his informants in Paris about the imminent Franco-Prussian war that might force French troops to withdraw from Rome. On 7 January 1870 he therefore moved secretly to Genoa where he remained in hiding for six months while he waited for this war to begin. At first he changed his lodgings every two or three days, moving only by night and keeping well away from any window where he might be seen. But despite this concealment, English friends managed to remain in touch, among them Lord and Lady Amberley who passed through Genoa. He was also able to send greetings to Carlyle and Swinburne, and his thanks to Whistler for a contribution of £5. An almost complete lack of books was a cruel but familiar deprivation during these months of solitude until he fortunately found a volume by Emerson. One letter to England asked for details of a book he might like to read, Mrs Beecher Stowe's *Uncle Tom's Cabin*.[95]

The new Italian prime minister was Giovanni Lanza, a more serious politician, more honest and liberal than the three army generals whom the king had recently preferred as heads of government. The foreign minister was Visconti Venosta who, like his later replacement Melegari, had once been a close associate of Mazzini's but had long since changed sides. Lanza, despite rumours to the contrary, continued to hope that their elusive republican enemy was still in England. In March, and as late as June, ministers believed he had moved to Switzerland though he was still hiding in Genoa.[96] What chiefly disturbed them was that he was continuing to find adherents in the middle and lower ranks of the Italian armed forces. There was also continuing support for him in universities where students rioted when denied a holiday to celebrate the saint's day of San Giuseppe in his honour.[97] According to Lanza as well as Saffi a nucleus of supporters could still be found in every Italian town, and dozens of provincial newspapers, despite frequent sequestration, were fairly open in showing disloyalty to the monarchy.[98]

During months of hiding in Genoa, Mazzini was poorly placed to exploit this potential support or even to judge the chances of success and give clear directions. Unwilling to issue orders in correspondence that might be intercepted, he took the risk of letting his lieutenants know that they might have to act on their own initiative.[99] Occasionally he advised restraint, but at other times felt he had to raise morale by incautiously saying that any spontaneous insurrection might succeed,[100] and this was a recipe for disaster. Fearful of another premature outbreak, he once confessed to feeling like the sorcerer's apprentice who had forgotten the formula to stop a movement he had started. Nevertheless he had so often spoken of the time being ripe for action that he could not without embarrassment insist on others remaining passive. On the one hand he was determined not to repeat earlier mistakes by imposing his own views or taking personal responsibility for something that had to reflect popular wishes if it was to succeed;[101] on the other hand, fearing he had not long to live, he was instinctively ready to magnify every circumstance in favour of action.[102]

With such an abdication of leadership, confusion was inevitable. In fact it led in March, without his prior knowledge, to an abortive attack on another barracks at Pavia. At Piacenza another similar movement was easily put down and one of its participants, Corporal Barsanti, was subsequently executed. Over the next few weeks there took place other minor and uncoordinated insurrections in Reggio, Carrara, Lucca and Porlezza, all without his authorisation and rather inspired by friends of Garibaldi. In May a few hundred rebels in Calabria boldly attempted to set up an independent republic in the village of Maida. Such episodes at least reassured him that the materials for combustion were once again ready in place and the imminent war in northern Europe might provide the necessary spark of ignition.

He decided to concentrate his own attention on Sicily, mindful that this was where the two great revolutions of 1848 and 1860 commenced and where he had found enough personal support for election to parliament. Another favourable circumstance was Sicilian disaffection with the authoritarian and sometimes cruel methods of the prefect General Medici, another early associate of Young Italy who had defected to support the monarchy. When a deputation of Sicilians came to ask for Mazzini's assistance, he at first demurred out of fear that any protest movement in Sicily might be captured by autonomists wanting secession from the mainland, but eventually promised he would come in person to assist in averting such a disaster. Medici learnt about this promise from an informer and, quite as alarming, discovered a sizeable secret arms factory in Palermo. A request by this prefect persuaded Lanza to send naval vessels and four additional battalions of troops to repel any Sicilian insurrection,[103] an important fact that Mazzini would not have known.

France declared war against Prussia on 19 July and may well have hesitated to do so without the enthusiastic but totally irresponsible promise of active military support from Victor Emanuel – support which in fact was never forthcoming. Mazzini, who expected as well as hoped for a Prussian victory,[104] called on his followers to seize this opportunity to rebel and again appealed to Berlin for financial help. This caused panic in government circles at Florence where private and certainly false information arrived to say that Bismarck sent the large sum of eight hundred thousand francs to assist a republican rising. It is true that the Prussian premier was quite ready to enlist help from any quarter, from Karl Marx as well as Mazzini, but though some promise of money seems to have been made it is hardly likely that their help was thought to be worth so much.[105] The French were nevertheless worried because a republican uprising in Italy would weaken their chances of military victory. The Austrian government, no friend to the Prussians, similarly feared that Mazzini and Garibaldi acting together might take the opportunity to seize Rome and proclaim a republic. The same possibility was foreseen by the American ambassador in Florence, and the Italian foreign office had to agree that it was a serious threat.[106]

As French troops began to leave Rome the Italian government became ever more anxious. So long as there was danger of a republican rebellion,

Lanza knew that he had to try his hardest to stop the king from exercising the royal prerogative of declaring war and sending armed forces to assist Napoleon. A further embarrassment was that some politicians wanted the government to act quite otherwise and forestall the republicans by defying Napoleon and winning prestige for the monarchy by a march on Rome. As for Victor Emanuel, though he had set his heart on leading his troops to victory in France, he at last was persuaded that the army might be needed at home against domestic opposition. Never since 1860 had Mazzini been able to exert such influence on major decisions of government policy. The police, who by now suspected he was hiding in or near Genoa, were ordered on 8 August to arrest him without waiting for a warrant, but they failed to find him; and although ministers punished the prefect for disobedience (he, too, had once been an associate of Mazzini's) it is clear that the government's intelligence services were at fault in failing to keep track of their intended victim, who was in fact living immediately opposite the prefecture.[107]

What Mazzini did not know was that Garibaldi had turned against him to the extent of secretly offering thirty thousand of his volunteers to support Lanza in preventing any republican revolution.[108] Nor did Mazzini know that another of his close collaborators was a spy paid by the French and perhaps also in the service of the Italian police. He even sent this man, Major Wolff, to prepare for an insurrection in Sicily that was timed to break out on 15 August. By that date he himself intended to be in Sicily in fulfilment of his earlier promise, despite the advice of many friends and despite knowing that he might be arrested en route.[109] He even thought once again that his own arrest or death, especially if it coincided with a Prussian military success, might be beneficial in galvanising the republicans into action.[110] When news came on 6 August that the French had suffered two serious defeats, he emerged from concealment and hurried by train to Naples. There he was recognised at his hotel, and Medici at Palermo also learnt of his arrival, probably from Wolff; but the Neapolitan authorities failed or possibly feared to arrest him, and after waiting two days to discover how they would react, he embarked very publicly for Sicily. It almost seems as though he was deliberately courting capture or death in the hope that this would precipitate a general rebellion.

Arriving at Palermo on 13 August, he was arrested by Medici while still on board ship. This was his first arrest since 1830 apart from a few hours' detention in Switzerland. Lanza thought of deporting him to England as a means of avoiding any popular outcry at such a delicate moment, but a hurriedly convened cabinet meeting decided to transfer him 'with full regard for his age and quality' to a fortress at Gaeta near Naples. For three days of this journey on a naval frigate he was treated with friendliness and even cordiality by a sympathetic, almost admiring crew. What he never understood was why the news of his capture did not immediately provoke an insurrection throughout Sicily using the money and arms he had already provided. Others agreed with him that such a rising would at once have been imitated elsewhere, and in fact there were minor outbreaks at Lecce, Ancona and Pavia. But the republican revolutionaries in the two main Sicilian towns of Palermo and Messina waited for each other to begin, and after the shock of losing their leader, neither would take any initiative.[111]

CHAPTER TEN

Failure and Achievement

The capture of Rome

MAZZINI IN AUGUST 1870 might have found comfort from knowing that even as a prisoner he could influence government policy. Victor Emanuel's dominant ambition over the past three years had been to make war against Prussia but, after pledging his word to fight, he was humiliated by having to confess that he was held back by the fear of civil war; and some politicians agreed that, had he not broken his word to Napoleon, he would have been compelled to abdicate.[1] Rattazzi, Minghetti and Crispi, all of them premiers at some time and well-equipped to judge, feared that the republicans might stage an attack on Rome unless the king arrived there first,[2] and a very quick decision had to be taken at the beginning of September when Napoleon's empire collapsed. This victory of republicanism in France destroyed the alliance that for fifteen years had been the basic premise of Italy's foreign policy.

After weeks of paralysing indecision, ministers finally made up their minds and later in September, by threatening resignation, forced the king to invade the last remnant of the Papal States. To exclude any move by the republicans, security at Mazzini's prison was redoubled and a cordon of naval ships prevented Garibaldi leaving the island of Caprera.[3] A letter from Victor Emanuel was then sent to the Vatican explaining that military action was unfortunately forced upon him in order to save Italy and the pope from a republican revolution.[4] Pius made an indignant protest, but without the support of a French garrison was defenceless.

The pope was not alone in accusing the king of saving his throne by adopting the programme of the Party of Action. In Vienna, too, this final triumph of the Risorgimento was described as a victory for Mazzini who even in apparent defeat was compelling the monarchists to realise the most enduring ambition of his life.[5] The same conclusion was regretfully reached by some Italian Moderates who would have preferred to leave Rome outside the new kingdom. Azeglio had already warned that to annex this city would be a humiliating and dangerous concession to the *italianissimi*, and the same admonition was repeated by other leading politicians.[6]

Indignation would have been greater had it been known that the government also adopted Mazzini's revolutionary tactics, organising an insurrection inside Rome to give the impression that the last-minute decision to attack this city was in response to an irresistible popular demand.[7] Still more unfortunate was that the local population was unenthusiastic and this popular rising failed to materialise.[8] Worst of all was that the king then concocted the excuse that he hoped not so much to defeat the pope as to defend him by slaughtering thirty thousand of the 'verminous rabble' of Garibaldi's and Mazzini's supporters who were hoping for a genuine revolution.[9]

The military conquest of Rome took place on 20 September while Mazzini was in prison. For almost two months this solitary rebel was held captive in a fourteenth-century castle jutting into the sea at Gaeta, protected by no less than five naval vessels guarding the port. Though allowed neither visitors nor writing materials, he otherwise received every consideration, and a suite of three rooms with carpets and easy chairs was much more commodious than his lodgings in London. The government offered to supply him with cigars and ice cream, though he refused to burden the State with payment for such luxuries. Under interrogation, while confirming his republican convictions, he refused to implicate anyone else and explained that, if brought to trial, he would not defend himself but merely make a public statement of his political creed.[10] To avoid such publicity, ministers, though they had recently executed Mazzini's humble follower Barsanti, decided not to risk a prosecution and may have feared that no jury would dare to convict. Nor, after the occupation of Rome, did their prisoner represent a serious danger. Surveillance was therefore partially relaxed and he was allowed to write letters which were read and copied before despatch. Although forbidden to see members of the parliamentary opposition, he was now permitted visits by Emilie Ashurst and Carlotta Benettini, a devoted friend from Genoa, but only in the presence of the colonel commanding his guards. Emilie thoughtfully brought him an appliance for making coffee.

After several weeks he was allowed newspapers and a copy of Dante's *Divine Comedy*, though the small print troubled his eyesight. He was also lent an Italian translation of *Hamlet*, his favourite Shakespeare play, and meditated pertinently on how the Prince of Denmark let too much analysis cloud any instinct for action. Chiefly he studied Byron, on whom he began to compose a long article until the effort aggravated his stomach pains. To his English friends he thoughtfully sent appreciation of their work for the Women's Emancipation Movement.[11] Early in October, in a letter that shows an excellent command of English, he wrote to Lady Amberley:

> I am tolerably well in health; rather sad but not on account of my imprisonment. Life has ever been with me a thing drawn from within and very little influenced by outward circumstances. Here I have the wide sea before me and the Italian sky above me. It is quite enough; and I am sorry more for a few of my friends who are thinking sadly about me than for myself. I know nothing as yet about the government's intention concerning me and I dare say they know very little themselves.[12]

Mazzini's good nature and affability were appreciated by his guards with whom he discussed such varied subjects as compulsory education, social reform and astronomy. He admitted to them his sadness at the casualties suffered in so many insurrections, but not remorse, because martyrs had been necessary for their country's rebirth.[13] From these conversations he received the unlikely impression that many soldiers might still support a republican revolution, and reports of their possible disloyalty caused alarm to ministers in Rome.[14] Among his friends in Genoa and London there was loose talk about organising an expedition to liberate him, but he refused to hear of such an absurdity.[15]

Eventually he was released under a general amnesty decreed on 9 October, but again refused an act of royal clemency for the 'crime' of having acted as a patriot, and insisted on returning into exile instead of recognising a regime he thought would one day be seen as a disaster for the country. His intention was to withdraw from politics and write a book in England – he had recently told the French writer Daniel Stern that he would give half of his remaining life to write a history of the French Revolution.[16] Travelling north from Gaeta he was excited but upset when at each station people broke into the railway carriage to greet him. Most painful of all, he had to wait for a connecting train in Rome and could not bear to leave his hotel to visit the scenes of his triumph in 1849. He then briefly joined the Rosselli family in Livorno where once again he had to escape a noisy public demonstration in his honour. The same happened in Genoa where he saw his surviving sister and at long last visited his mother's tomb. Because of illness he then broke his journey and spent two months in the hospitable care of Sara Nathan at Lugano.

Waiting in Switzerland to recover his health he reflected with melancholy on recent events. 'I had hoped to evoke the soul of Italy and instead find merely her inanimate corpse.'[17] He had wanted a Risorgimento characterised by the popularly based action so successful in 1848 and 1860, but victory had instead gone to professional politicians who feared and resented any initiatives from below. Italian unity had finally been imposed from above, partly by the same Moderates who for decades had denounced his ideas of democratic patriotism, partly by foreigners fighting from disreputable motives of power politics and dynastic egoism. Rome, like Venice and Lombardy, had in fact been won as a by-product of victories by a Prussian army that had little interest in self-determination or Italian unification.

Additionally humiliating was that Italians, despite a formal promise by King Charles Albert and the Piedmontese parliament, had never been allowed to express their wishes in a constituent assembly and were still governed by a not very progressive constitution conceded unwillingly in 1848 as an act of royal grace.[18] Far from deploring this fact, Victor Emanuel, whose government ten years earlier confirmed his own father's promise to summon a constituent assembly, was instead supported by a court *camarilla* in planning to make the constitution still less liberal and more authoritarian.[19] Mazzini admitted that much of the blame should fall on weakness and miscalculations by himself.[20] He had overestimated both the capability of 'the people' and the possibility of reaching them with his patriotic message. Forty years earlier he had mistakenly assumed that, since political unification would be relatively easy, he could spend most of his life trying to solve the more difficult problems of Italy's moral and spiritual regeneration; but he had been deceiving himself. Unfortunately 'the Italian question, which I believed might ere this have become a question of action and realisation, is still a question of education'.[21]

He therefore once more resigned himself to the slow and frustrating task of trying to educate public opinion, in the belief that some unforeseen event in European politics might at some point permit further political action. As he told Emilie, the more distant the goal the greater the need for constant struggle – quoting Goethe, 'without haste but without rest'.[22] Italians would eventually understand how noble ideals had been perverted to their disadvantage. Unlike its counterpart in England, the Italian monarchy was shallowly based and acted as a brake on modernisation, economic development and greater morality in politics. It stood for privilege and inequality, for corruption and financial extravagance, for a cumbersome and inefficient administrative centralisation, for divisiveness between one class and another, for restriction of individual liberty except to a favoured few; and worst of all it stood for an immoral chauvinism and a chimerical search for glory on some future field of battle.[23]

To propagate his republican alternative he proposed to start another weekly periodical, but first was eager to renew his regular custom of celebrating New Year's Day with his London friends. Crossing the Alps in midwinter was slow and hazardous for an old and sick man, and he arrived much too late. Nor was his health then improved when he was knocked down by a carriage in a London street. He was nevertheless inundated with invitations, among them one from the Master of Balliol, and many people visited his lodgings in Fulham.[24] So pleased was the *Fortnightly Review* with the article he wrote on the Vatican Council that Morley offered nearly two pounds sterling a page for another on the Franco-Prussian War. But all Mazzini could manage was a sad valedictory message.

> On the eve of quitting, it may be for the last time, the land I have learned to love as a second country, in order more effectually to continue the Italian republican apostolate to which I intend to devote the remainder of my life, I desire to recapitulate, for those English friends whose affection had afforded me my best consolation for the loss of the home denied me in my native Italy, the reasons of the unshaken republican faith which is in me; the duty which impels me now to renounce the consolations of age, as I formerly renounced the joys of youth, in the service of the republican unity of Italy which was the prophetic dream of my boyhood and the religious faith of my manhood.[25]

In February 1871, as he prepared to leave England for the last time, Carlyle came to see him and they talked for an hour.[26] Mazzini had spent some twenty-five years in London. By now, according to Holyoake, he knew the country better than any other foreigner.[27] Unlike Panizzi and Gallenga he would never have let it cross his mind to apply for British nationality, but was immensely grateful for what he had learnt and received during these long years of exile. He had won the friendship of what he called 'some of the best minds of the island', friendships that were not made easily in England, but once made were more sincere and lasting than elsewhere and which, much more than elsewhere, could exist between people of radically differing opinions. 'Nothing of what I have felt, loved, sympathised with in England is lost to me: it is treasured up in my soul and there it will remain for ever.'[28]

At first in 1837 he had been strongly critical of the political and intellectual isolationism in Britain and her inequalities in class structure, yet he had seen these change, surely if still too slowly. Civil disturbances could take place in England but were rare, and that was because the humblest citizen identified himself with the nation and felt sure that majority wishes would in course of time prevail. When the country was in danger from Napoleon, hundreds of thousands volunteered immediately for its defence. Mass meetings in Hyde Park could take place against unpopular laws, meetings at which speakers were protected by the police even if they advocated socialism or atheism. Much was still wrong in this society and he wondered if the monarchy and the House of Lords could survive much longer. But when compared to Italy he had to admire the respect for individual rights and the inestimable benefit of a free press through which even republicanism and religious dissent could be defended. Politicians were not so much masters as servants of the people. Prisoners in England were not kept without trial as so many republicans had been in Italy. Centuries of resistance to royal autocracy had resulted in a cult of individual freedom and a healthy refusal to adopt any political system that even remotely resembled the over-centralised administration that Italians were importing from France.[29]

A final year of journalism

In February 1871, returning to Switzerland, Mazzini made the perilous winter crossing of the St Gotthard Pass in a horse-drawn sledge. Some of his travelling companions were lucky to survive when they slipped on the ice and plunged two hundred feet into a ravine. By chance sharing the journey and the same hotel was Friedrich Nietzsche, who never thereafter forgot his conversations with a person he described as one of the most heroic and noble characters of the age.[30]

After a short stay with the Nathans in Lugano, Mazzini moved to Italy to supervise the launch of his newspaper. His arrival was greeted by popular demonstrations in his honour[31] but he was not deceived. Italy was unified; the temporal power of the papacy had been destroyed and this was another major turning-point in European history; but the education of public opinion in national consciousness and social responsibility had barely begun. What strength remained in his last year of life would be spent as a journalist campaigning for republicanism and internationalism, and resisting the mounting socialist tide. *La Roma del Popolo*, the last of his twenty newspapers, was published in the new capital, a city he was too upset to visit in person. Optimistically it aimed at a circulation of ten thousand copies. Friends had been collecting money to launch it while he was in prison but half the proceeds disappeared before reaching him.[32] A useful £80 was now contributed by Adriano Lemmi. Another £25 was received from Joseph Cowen in Newcastle, £100 from Peter Taylor, and John McAdam hoped to raise £250 from his friends in Glasgow. Emilie Ashurst painstakingly wrote out many copies of the newspaper's prospectus to be sent all over Italy.

Mazzini himself wrote fifty articles for the paper. Its editor was Giuseppe Petroni, released after nearly two decades in a papal prison. Its administrative director was Sara's son Ernesto Nathan, still English by nationality and according to Mazzini two-thirds an Englishman, who later became a celebrated mayor of Rome. The first issue on 1 March was automatically sequestered by the police, but this was at once seen to have been a mistake and the persecution suffered by his earlier newspapers was not repeated. After a few weeks it had two thousand subscribers.

Its first target was the Socialist International and the increasingly frequent invocation of class war. Ever since the 1840s, Mazzini had called socialism 'a symptom of a tremendous crisis that hovers over all the nations of Europe' and for which a remedy was imperatively required if society were not to be devastated by fratricidal strife. The most urgent remedy was to eliminate extreme poverty, for which his proposed remedies had always included liberalisation of trade, an increase in production and consumption through a greater diffusion of purchasing power, which in turn would involve putting the relations between capital and labour on a less unequal footing. As many as seven hundred and fifty workers' associations and cooperatives had already come into existence under his influence, and his newspaper campaigned for legal recognition so that their voice could be effectively heard.[33] To arbitrate in industrial controversies he proposed setting up councils with equal representation of employers and workers presided over by a neutral judge.[34] The middle and upper classes had to be persuaded that a better deal for labour was the most important problem of the day and every class had far more to gain than lose from its solution.[35]

What shattered this dream was the victory of French insurgents who in March rebelled against the republican government of Thiers and briefly turned Paris into an independent socialist Commune. Mazzini had no love for Thiers who, though a critic of Napoleon III, was a declared enemy of Italian unification. But nor did he share the very different views of Garibaldi, who positively welcomed the Commune. After a few weeks he was appalled by its excesses and cruelties, finding himself allied with the conservatives in condemning a blatant example of class war that as well as being immoral in itself would antagonise the middle classes and damage any chances of peaceful social reform.[36] Unlike some of his democratic supporters, and completely contradicting the ritual abuse from his conservative enemies, he confirmed an aspect of his nature that only close friends had known. He was opposed to violent revolt except as a very last resort. As a general rule 'I declare myself a man of authority and government' opposed to the 'large portion of the democratic camp' which failed to realise that an antagonism between government and governed would be 'productive of constant strife and hostile to all progress'.[37]

Mazzini had been a rebel for patriotism. But further rebellion might now threaten national unity and make cooperation less easy between classes in society. Though at first he had shared some of the motives and ideals of the Socialist International, this organisation had been captured by the Marxists who were the greatest enemy of inter-class cooperation. Before passing judgement he carefully studied what writings he could find by Marx, Engels and Bakunin. Apart from their atheism and materialism, he condemned the socialist objective of 'war against capital, abolition of private property, hostility to the bourgeoisie, and their crusade against the Catholic clergy'. Any dictatorship by the proletariat would deny the freedom of the human spirit, and so would speculation about a depersonalising dialectical process. He himself was hoping for social progress by evolution as in England, not by the kind of self-destructive revolution that would alienate potential allies among intellectuals and the propertied classes.[38]

Such views were heresy in the eyes of Bakunin and Marx. Bakunin had sympathised with the struggle for Italian liberation but retrospectively recognised that the Italian republicans, as they themselves now agreed, had inadvertently contributed to the victory of an authoritarian monarchy and a small political elite who had minimal sympathy with the poor. Worse still, Mazzini in the process was said to have become a 'bourgeois reactionary' who presumably would prefer Austrian domination in Italy rather than instigate a class war by peasants and workers against their oppressors.[39] Marx too, apart from disliking Bakunin's libertarian anarchism, agreed in criticising the 'authoritarian Mazzini' who 'with his old-fashioned republicanism knew nothing and accomplished nothing. In Italy he had created a military despotism by his cry for nationality. With him the state, which was an imaginary thing, was everything, and society, which was a reality, was nothing. The sooner the people repudiated such men the better.'[40]

Against such extravagant criticism the ailing Mazzini used the *Roma del Popolo* to develop the arguments he had employed twenty years earlier in a criticism of communism which, according to some people, had never been bettered. But he lacked the physical strength and elasticity of mind to recapture the high ground of this debate. In the years before 1870 he had helped to delay the diffusion of socialism because he feared it would cut across the patriotic movement and weaken national solidarity. Now in 1871, the civil war in Paris was a terrible threat to his hopes of peaceful collaboration between social classes. More of his followers now rallied to the monarchy in reaction against the new forces of social revolution released by the Commune, while other younger disciples who could share neither his idiosyncratic religious beliefs nor his elevation of social duties above agitation for material betterment deserted in the other direction to join the Socialist International. In November 1871 he made one last effort to stop defections by organising a national congress of workers' cooperatives and unions, but it was only a partial success. He could not attend in person because 'I *cannot* go to Rome except under a republican flag; besides, I hate meetings, applause, having to talk, mean-ingless *vivas* – everything.'[41]

Another recurrent theme in his journalism was that the principle of nationality was gradually and inevitably redrawing the map of Europe. For forty years he had argued that until national self-determination was accepted as rightful and irresistible, wars of liberation would continue to take place, whereas triumph of this principle would remove at least one cause of war and, so he imagined, produce a more peaceful Europe.[42] Until now, according to Bryce, Mazzini had been right to concentrate on the struggle for liberty and nationality which was the central theme of the century, and he could not be expected to realise that the faults he denounced would subsequently emerge in other forms.[43] But already he had to admit that the nascent nationalities could be as hostile to each other as to their former oppressors, indeed regarding their own national-ity as almost an end in itself.[44] His own contrary opinion was that nations had a higher mission and purpose, to create an international community in which they would be a necessary but subordinate constituent. Having won their own freedom, enlightened self-interest if not altruism would in time teach them the need to respect the freedom of other countries. Idealising 'the people', he had always hoped that ordinary citizens, as they gradually became of more political consequence, would counteract the aggressive and imperialist urges of ambitious dynasties with their professional armies.[45]

Such over-sanguine expectations had recently been put to a further test in the Franco-Prussian war of 1870–1. He was at first strongly pro-German in this war, praising Bismarck for understanding nationality better than Cavour and for resisting French imperialist ambitions in Belgium and the Rhineland,[46] but he nevertheless recognised the other danger to Europe of a militarist and authoritarian monarchy in Berlin.[47] Nations, he always maintained, were subject like ordinary individuals to a moral law and would eventually suffer if they defied it. Bonapartist France, which once championed liberty, fraternity and equality, had latterly sent armies to crush freedom in Rome and Mexico, so forfeiting respect, alienating potential allies, and condemning herself to defeat.[48] France, however, had been punished enough by military defeat and he hoped Britain would help to save her from a punitive peace. The German annexation of Alsace and Lorraine was wrong and would some day lead almost inevitably to another war of revenge.[49]

Mazzini's influence in Italian history cannot be fully comprehended without noting that some historians have discerned in his writing at this period the germs of an idea that would lead to a desire for 'national self-glorification' and 'depreciation of other peoples'.[50] But this indictment is properly directed against a minority of his one-time disciples, some of whom developed into supporters of Crispi, Medici and the Italian Nation-alist Party. Other self-styled Mazzinians were subsequently still more extreme and even praised him as a precursor of fascist imperialism and totalitarianism; and a similar opinion, without any praise, was held by the communist leader Togliatti.[51] The fascist philosopher Giovanni Gentile initially affected to despise Mazzini as 'an absolutely inept politician' who in some paradoxical way hindered Italian unification,[52] but later swung to the opposite extreme and heaped extravagant admiration on a 'fascist Mazzini' of his own invention.[53] Mussolini, too, made a similar *volte-face* as later in life he sought intellectual respectability by linking fascism with the great names in Italian history; the Duce even tried to convince people of his enthusiasm by telling them he was one of the few people who had found time to read all the hundred volumes of Mazzini's writing.[54]

The legend of this 'fascist Mazzini' arose from a single article he wrote in 1871 which mentioned cultural imperialism and the fact that the Mediterranean had once been *mare nostrum*. It was true, as Mazzini told Stansfeld, that 'he had an immense ambition for his country, a pride in her as he would have her, an affection for her at all times and even as she was that knew no bounds'.[55] He also believed that European political ideas were imposing themselves in Africa, as Spain was extending her culture into Morocco and France into Algeria. Italy's 'mission' was first of all to take the lead in producing a community of nations in Europe, and thereafter to help in extending European civilisation into Tunisia and Libya, as well as joining Russia and Britain in the 'civilising' of the Far East.[56] But he never amplified this latter idea. The nationalists and fascists of a later generation found it convenient to ignore that he was always sharply critical of the 'brutal conquest' that regularly characterised colo-nialism. He believed that nations who sought to increase the extent of their territory were betraying the 'European mission' and would invite retribution, as the ancient Romans and now the British had learnt to their cost. The 'expansion of Europe' was inevitable, but would be justifiable only insofar as it fostered emancipation, education, democratic rights and abolition of slavery; and only if it aimed at establishing new self-govern-ing nations.[57] Many years earlier he had welcomed the gradual if grudging emancipation of colonies in the British empire.[58] Nor is it surprising that he became a hero to Gandhi, Nehru, Sun Yat Sen and the early Zionists. His *Duties of Man* was translated into six Indian languages.[59] He was admired not only by Gentile the intellectual fascist, but also by the pacifist Tolstoy and the anti-colonialists in North America.[60]

In Italy the anti-fascists had a much easier task claiming to inherit from this very different Mazzini: a man who believed in democracy and liberty, in international morality, who condemned militarism and authoritarian-ism, who championed international cooperation and respect for the rights of other peoples.[61] Mazzini certainly exalted nationality and patriotism as a necessary factor or phase in human development, but 'nationalism' he continued to denounce as an unpleasant and dangerous perversion of patriotism, and for him the Mediterranean was not *mare nostrum* but a *lago Europeo*.[62] The nation, like republicanism, was no more than a means to an end. Nations would even lose much of their *raison d'être* when a 'United States of Europe' was seen to be in the general interest. On this point he agreed with his friend Sir John Seeley who, as well as writing a celebrated book on *The Expansion of England*, wrote about the need for a United States of Europe with its own constitution and legislation, possessing 'an executive force greater than that of its component states'.[63]

Mazzini was equally insistent that nations must never override the basic liberties of the individual citizen which were a guarantee against intolerance. In the words of one of his more subtle and knowledgeable commentators, Charles Vaughan,

> he does not exalt the individual at the expense of the nation, like the disciples of Rousseau; nor the nation at the expense of the individual, as was the tendency of Hegel; nor humanity at the expense of both, as was the incurable aberration of Comte. Recognising that each of these has its peculiar function, he recognises no less fully that no one of them can put forth its energies without the others; that each of them is conditioned absolutely by the others; and that only to the most limited extent is it possible to mark off the sphere in which each operates. . . . At the same time he marks out the limits beyond which the instinct of nationality becomes dangerous, or even harmful. He denies that it is a final and absolute principle. He persistently subordinates it to the larger claims of humanity. . . . He declares the free development of the national spirit to be essential to the true life of humanity. So far as it serves that end, it is nothing but good. As soon as it throws itself athwart that end, it becomes an enormous evil.[64]

After 1870, Mazzini's 'Europe of peoples' was scorned as utopian nonsense by successive Italian governments dedicated to conventional power politics, and Graham Wallas correctly wrote that 'Bismarck's conception of an artificial uniformity created by "blood and iron" corresponded more closely than did Mazzini's to the facts of the nineteenth century.' Yet Benedetto Croce was not the only commentator who insisted that the Mazzinian dream of a European union among free and autonomous states remained perfectly valid and was certainly more realistic than the Marxist international Utopia,[65] a judgement that events in the twentieth century have tended to confirm. On the one hand were those Italian ministers in government who did not look kindly on the challenge posed by the appearance of new nations on the far shore of the Adriatic. On the other hand were Salvemini and Giolitti (and for very brief moments even Mussolini himself) who agreed with Mazzini in accepting a Slavophile policy as in Italy's national interest. As well as being a committed Slavophile, Mazzini was described by a contemporary as 'the one statesman in Europe who had a European mind'.[66] His own modified version of power politics was that smaller nations, many yet to be born, might join each other and Britain in resisting any future aggression by Germany, Russia or France. Collective security would at some point have to replace the 'absurd and immoral' precept of 'every nation for itself'.[67]

In 1870–1 this may have seemed an impossible or at best distant goal, but it should be remembered that Mazzini's argument was later invoked by another generation of hard-headed Italian politicians who recognised its utility when they joined Serbia in the Great War of 1914–18. It was also the inspiration of President Wilson and Lloyd George. In January 1919, travelling from the United States to attend the peace conference in Paris, Woodrow Wilson visited Genoa to pay a moving tribute in front of Mazzini's monument, and claimed not only to have made a close study of his ideas during his career as a university professor, but to be intentionally aiming in 1919 to realise the ideals of this lonely thinker who had 'by some gift of God been lifted above the common level'; and Wilson added in private that perhaps only Lincoln or Gladstone had such clarity of insight into the essence of liberalism.[68] Lloyd George, a more pragmatic politician than Wilson and a fellow architect of the Versailles settlement, also claimed to have studied Mazzini and learnt from him not only the value of patriotism but the equally imperative need to curb national pride:

> I doubt whether any man of his generation exercised so profound an influence on the destinies of Europe as did Mazzini. The map of Europe as we see it today is the map of Joseph Mazzini. He was the prophet of free nationality. . . . The glittering imperial fabric reared by Bismarck is humbled in the dust, but the dream of this young man, who came over as an exile to England and lived in poverty here for years, dependent on the charity of friends and armed only with a pen, have now become startling realities through the whole continent. . . . He taught us not merely the rights of a nation; he taught the rights of other nations. . . . He is the father of the idea of the League of Nations.[69]

The end

In March 1871, Mazzini secretly took up residence in Pisa, and apart from two short visits to Livorno and Florence (to lay a wreath on the monument to Foscolo) he remained there for six months. Not having accepted the royal amnesty he lived in almost complete isolation because he was liable to arrest if caught. Once again his everyday life was entirely taken up writing letters and articles. Hearing that Giuditta Sidoli was gravely ill in Turin, he sent an affectionate letter that she probably received the day before her death at the end of March.

In an article published this same month in London he wrote once again of his despondency about the new Italy. This was a pessimism shared in differing degrees by many other Italians across the political spectrum.[70] The article repeated his regret that national unification, far from being a spontaneous achievement dictated by public opinion, had been imposed by a narrow and privileged elite governing in their own sectional interest. Evidently not even now was there any chance of the promised constituent assembly being summoned, and a conscript army was being used as 'an instrument of internal repression' rather than of national liberation. Taxation still spared the rich and penalised the poor. He himself would have liked to see

> suppression of all offices created for the purpose of exercising governmental influence in local districts; . . . abolition of the political oath; universal suffrage as a first step towards the political education of the people; legislation directed towards the assistance and encouragement of economic and intellectual progress in the more needy classes; national encouragement given to all voluntary, industrial and agricultural associations among working men, . . . reclaiming unhealthy or uncultivated tracts of land; restitution of neglected communal rights and consequent creation of a new class of small proprietors; . . . abolition of all restraints upon the circulation of internal and foreign produce; . . . abolition of all monopolies.

Instead, so this article continued, he found in practice a 'dread of popular progress' and a determination by ministers 'never to yield to public opinion until it threatens to burst forth in open and overpowering conflict'. Instead of encouraging local self-government, an inflated bureaucracy was being created largely to fuel the practice of clientelism, but also for the purpose of controlling local authorities and by that means packing parliament with obedient deputies. The legislature itself was treated as a rubber stamp in the hands of a powerful executive that governed with 'a policy of expedients, opportunism, concealment, intrigue, reticence, and parliamentary compromise characteristic of the languid life of nations in decay'. Instead of setting an example of international cooperation, Italy was acting as 'a useless member of the European community, abdicating every duty, ministry or mission towards the rest, and concentrating its whole activity upon paltry, individual interest'.[71]

Mazzini nevertheless had no intention of encouraging further insurrections, because Italians had been numbed by centuries of subjection and lacked a sense of their strength. They would have to wait until a new system of education could produce its results, and he himself was too frail to do more than exhort. 'My day is therefore spent in writing, only getting up every quarter of an hour and walking up and down the rooms during three minutes. I smoke perennially, I am sorry to say, but what can I do? I write unwillingly, through a sense of mere duty, without a spark of enthusiasm, and smoking is a mere diversion to the soul's fog which is coming heavy on my head like a leaden cap.'[72] In the perhaps not very distant future a spontaneous movement of rebellion might bring down the government 'like a paper castle', but this would be after his death. Popular action in such an eventuality would do far more to transform the country than ten years of mere preaching, and if it was truly spontaneous, 'without anger, intolerance or hatred', it would be welcome.[73] Equally welcome would be a war that sooner or later was needed to redraw the map of Europe and liberate the Slavs from Austrian and Turkish imperialism. Violent action should nevertheless be avoided wherever possible and always kept to a minimum; nor was war or revolution ever justifiable except to force an entrenched minority to let popular wishes be expressed. In his opinion, as he now repeated, no regime should ever be imposed on any country by force.[74]

Once his newspaper was successfully launched, he returned to live from September 1871 until February 1872 with the Nathans in Lugano. He offered to visit Genoa to console his devoutly Catholic sister Antonietta after her husband's death, and was upset when she refused 'on account of her principles and of what she owes to the memory and presumed wish of the dead husband'.[75] Another bitter disappointment was when he again suggested to Garibaldi that they should meet on the island of Caprera, and the reply came that it was too late for reconciliation. Garibaldi now made the offensive and quite gratuitous accusation that Mazzini had opposed the conquest of Sicily in 1860.[76] This unkind and incredible indictment was said to have hastened Mazzini's death. According to mutual friends, Garibaldi's 'almost invariably unfounded criticisms' were always influenced by malicious gossip from interested parties.[77] Though the two men had often disagreed, Mazzini in private was far more generous, and despite confidence in the rightness of his own political beliefs, continued to recognise that Garibaldi had far greater capacity than himself to translate beliefs into effective action.[78]

Already before leaving England, Mazzini was physically 'only the shadow of his former self', of 'an almost spectral thinness, kept together by spiritual energy'.[79] He wrote of passing from one illness to another with permanent coughs and colds and a 'general atony in all organic functions'. Doctors recorded asthma and bronchitis in both lungs that left him breathless and almost unable to climb stairs. But since his newspaper was losing money he had to continue writing because he could pay almost nothing for articles and some contributors submitted unfair attacks on other countries, attacks that on principle he felt obliged to reject.[80] Once more he wrote of the need to transform society and also of the legitimacy of revolutions aiming at human betterment. Nor could a nation be regenerated by mere adjustment to preexistent circumstances, but only by actively creating the necessary circumstances for change and refusing to compromise once people clearly saw what was right. Mere contemplation of the world's problems was insufficient; so was detached criticism; only embattled commitment would help to make a just society. His final injunction to Petroni was to use the *Roma del Popolo* to fight against the 'official economists' who championed the selfishness of free enterprise based on individual rights and not social obligation.[81]

On 4 February 1872 he left Switzerland for the warmer climate of Pisa to stay with Pellegrino Rosselli whose wife Janet, daughter of Sara Nathan, was his particular favourite among the younger generation. After the exhausting journey he felt so ill that for three days he was unable to swallow food. Almost no one knew he was in Italy, and though an informer warned the authorities, they failed to identify him correctly and only on the 24th did the local police suspect that he might be a man travelling as Dr Georg Brünn.[82] To a local physician he identified himself as an Englishman, George Brown. Some of his letters were still partly written in code because he suspected they were being opened, and his true identity was finally discovered only on 8 March when a telegram was intercepted from the Rossellis summoning his old friend Dr Bertani for an urgent medical consultation. A last letter to England told Emilie nothing at all about his own troubles but, characteristically, asked her help in finding a teaching job for Cesare Barbieri, another companion in exile.

Two days later, not long before his sixty-eighth birthday and before Bertani arrived, he died. The end came suddenly and he had no time to voice any wishes or send messages to absent friends. Janet had vainly tried to calm him as he spoke in great agitation and distress of his differences with Garibaldi. His last words, so she reported, were 'I do believe in God.'[83]

The news caused consternation among the citizens of Pisa who until this moment were unaware of his presence. Students demanded a brief closure of the university as a sign of respect, and when the prefect intervened to prevent this they refused to attend lectures.[84] As a final indignity the doctors tried to embalm his body 'by a new process which resulted in absolute petrifaction', and either they or the process went badly wrong. Garibaldi joined English friends in voicing his abhorrence at a procedure that Mazzini had once denounced as a Benthamite 'profana-tion'.[85] The body had to be hurriedly taken to Genoa for burial in the spectacular cemetery of Staglieno. Shops in this city were shut, ships in the bay lowered their flags, thousands of people accompanied the fune-ral procession. In Rome another mile-long demonstration stopped traffic for an hour as a bust of Mazzini was carried through the main streets to be erected on the Capitol between the figures of Michelangelo and Columbus;[86] but official Italy was represented on neither occasion. Though a formal vote of condolence was carried in parliament, the Speaker prohibited any speeches of tribute and the prime minister re-mained ostentatiously mute.[87] Conservatives as well as radicals protested against such uncharitable behaviour, and one Catholic paper in Turin commented that Lanza and his colleagues were pygmies in comparison with the deceased.[88] In death as in his life, ministers refused reconciliation with a lone rebel who had caused them a great deal of trouble, but who more than anyone had taught them to be patriots.

Epilogue

TIME NEEDED TO elapse before Mazzini could be judged without animus or prejudice, and first reactions to the news of his death varied from one extreme to the other. Some people were able to call him the chief architect of united Italy, while others claimed that the nation was made in his despite. When town councils proposed to erect monuments or rename streets in his honour they were forbidden by royal decree, though such a veto was hard to enforce.[1] His portrait by Mendelssohn's godson, offered by the painter as a gift to the government, was refused[2] and fifty years later had to be purchased by a less ungrateful nation. The general public had been told repeatedly that he was a villain and assassin who disgraced the name of Italy and was best forgotten. One obituary even ridiculed his defence of Rome in 1849 and invented a new legend that this 'dangerous enemy of free and united Italy' had made 'frantic efforts' to keep the country divided.[3] Agricultural labourers near Mantua were actually imprisoned for nothing more serious than to be found reading his *Duties of Man*. Demonstrations on the anniversary of his death were forbidden. On one occasion, the police broke into the house where he died and confiscated wreaths of remembrance.[4]

Some immediate judgements in Italy were nevertheless generous. Others were favourable but grudging. In Turin the conservative *Opinione* and in Milan the *Perseveranza*, both of them newspapers that had consistently criticised him, now recognised the great qualities of mind and heart that had helped to create a new nation.[5] Another former opponent astonished parliament by quoting a very private remark of Cavour's that, when the dust of political controversy had settled, Mazzini might safely be allowed into the pantheon of national heroes.[6] Already his friends and disciples placed him on a level with Dante and Galileo as the greatest man of his century.[7] Garibaldi's son, while greatly admiring his own father, thought that Mazzini made a more essential contribution to their country's history. Crispi called him a greater man than either Garibaldi or Cavour, and added that future historians would refer to the nineteenth century as 'the century of Mazzini'.[8] The Swiss journalist Marc-Monnier, who had lived in Italy as a first-hand witness of events but had hitherto been afraid to flout the authorities by defending such a dangerous outlaw, could now admit admiration for someone who, almost alone, 'turned the world upside down'.

This great agitator was often more pragmatic and opportunistic than he admitted in his writing. While dreaming of a republic he repeatedly offered to help the monarchy, so sacrificing ideals to the search for what was possible. . . . Even though his enterprises seemed to fail, he always re-emerged without being discouraged by disillusionment or defeat, giving us a marvellous example of audacity and consistency, reaffirming his beliefs more strongly than ever, conjuring up combatants with a word and throwing them into mad escapades in which they knew they would die. This man had no title or position, no home to live in, expelled from one country after another until he found refuge in a distant island. Isolated and alone he stood up against the whole of Europe and made the whole continent afraid of him.[9]

Favourable notices were more frequent outside Italy where he was personally better known and newspapers could sometimes refer to his death as a great European calamity. 'The unity of Italy is of all political revolutions the grandest achieved in modern times', and Mazzini, 'the most misrepresented man of our day', was 'the great constructive genius' who made that unification possible, 'one of the founders of the future whose work is not understood in his time'. This lone exile could be described as 'the most eminent publicist which Europe has seen for centuries', a 'born leader of men', 'the inspirer of nations' and 'foremost teacher of our time', 'the greatest, bravest, most heroic and persistent of the long roll of Italian worthies'. 'In him, democratic Europe possessed a revolutionary force, than which a more indefatigable one has never been concentrated at any time, in any country, in a single man'.[10] Such remarks would have sounded eccentric to the Italian political establishment but elsewhere did not seem excessive. William Roscoe Thayer, the American biographer and great admirer of Cavour, called Mazzini 'the greatest moral force in Europe during the nineteenth century', and 'as Dante speaks for the medieval world, so Mazzini is thus far Europe's most authentic spokesman of the ideals and hopes of our new epoch'.[11]

The Times of London made amends for previous criticism by giving him a more substantial obituary than it accorded Dickens, Manzoni or King Victor Emanuel. Though admitting his impracticality in worldly affairs, this newspaper particularly praised him as a writer, and it was noted with some surprise that books by and about him already filled nearly ten pages of the catalogue in the British Museum library. Especially singled out for praise by *The Times* was his so far unsurpassed analysis of the internal contradictions and disastrous consequences of communism. The European revolution of 1848 was said to have owed as much to him as anyone, and it could now be admitted that the conquest of southern Italy in 1860 was as much his handiwork as Garibaldi's. He was

> a man who in his time has played a most singular part upon the theatre of European politics; one whose name has for years been regarded as a symbol of revolution or rather republicanism, one in whose personal character there were many fine and noble qualities; but still a man who was feared even more widely than he was loved, and one whose departure from the scene of action, to say the least, will be no unwelcome news to several crowned and discrowned members of the family of European sovereigns. . . .
>
> In private life Giuseppe Mazzini was accomplished and courteous and gifted with a genial manner which won regard almost instantly, at least unconsciously. In London he lived in the humblest manner, occupying often only a single room and generously bestowing the earnings of his pen on the cause which lay nearest to his heart. His tall, gaunt form, long face, and high, narrow forehead must be familiar to many of our readers; and whatever we may think of his political opinions, few will be disposed to question the sincerity even to fanaticism of his devotion to one idea – the cause of Italian unity. . . . His depth of thought, his earnest, impassioned manner, his emphatic and almost mystical language, and his warm, expansive sympathy with all that was great and good, took the hearts of his young contemporaries by storm and made of him one of the leading lights of the age.

This tribute is at first sight hard to square with the fact that the same paper had spoken very differently about Mazzini when alive. The ambivalence was exemplified by an editorial article in the same issue which reflected the very different views of the acrimonious renegade, Gallenga. Here Italy was said to have been made 'without him', even 'in spite of him'.

> No man won so many admirers as Mazzini and yet secured so few friends. If we except a few devoted Englishwomen, there is hardly a human being whom long familiarity had not estranged from Mazzini. With manners consummately affable and courteous he combined an overweening conceit and a narrowness and bigotry of view which hardly tolerated independent minds. He was a lonely genius, all apart from the common ways of other mortals, spurning the suggestions of the plainest common sense, professing to do all for his fellow-beings, yet nothing with them or by their aid.[12]

Professor Masson knew him far better than Gallenga and published a much less jaundiced valedictory notice. He found some of Mazzini's writings disappointing, mainly because they aimed at stimulating action rather than nourishing logical thought. In them could be found 'the recurrence continually of one or other of a certain limited number of fixed ideas in impressive but nebulous phrases such as "God and Humanity", "Progress", "the unity which is the soul of the universe"', all presented as 'maxims which there was a baseness in not accepting'. This did not prevent Masson from calling Mazzini one of the most memorable Europeans of his time. As a respected professor of literature and a successful magazine editor, Masson was a fair judge of intelligence. He called Mazzini 'the most *tenacious* man I ever met', a philosopher with 'a very powerful, original and various mind, . . . a thinker on all subjects, a universal critic of art and literature', who 'knew something about everything', whether the poets of ancient Greece and Rome or present-day Spanish and Slav writing, while his knowledge of French literature was extensive and minute. He it was who first awakened public opinion in Britain to an interest in current Italian politics. He could also talk knowledgeably about Kant and Hegel and 'had no objection to the last novelty in physical science'. His conversation was utterly unpedantic and entertaining, yet when serious he surprised you by 'a rigour and an acuteness of analysis which you were hardly prepared to expect from your ordinary experience of him'. After one long argument, though unconvinced, Masson 'had never before been engaged in such an exercise of give and take, or had my mind so raked and refreshed by the encounter'.[13]

Another eulogy in the *Spectator* described 'a character which hardly belonged to our time'. He was a truly great person whose extraordinary influence was owing

> partly no doubt to his intellectual force which was very great, partly to his perfect disinterestedness, but mainly to his lovability, an instinctive quality in which he surpassed almost all living men. . . . For forty-five years his name had been a watchword. When he began his course, Italy was a geographical expression, when he finished his course it was the sixth great power. . . . He was that rare character a practical ideologue, who swayed men by the force of his ideas, the holiness of his life and the unique loftiness of his character. . . . This influence, rising in some cases to an ascendancy such as has hardly been given to the greatest religious teachers, was employed unswervingly for a single end and it was employed successfully. Cavour made Italy, but it was due to Mazzini, not Cavour, that such making was possible. . . . In modern history no man armed only with spiritual weapons, strong only in his cause, his genius and his character, has ever performed such a feat and made so deep a personal impression on the history of mankind. . . . It is among the greater popes that we must seek for the analogue of Joseph Mazzini . . . whose gentleness was as inflexible as other men's obstinacy. . . . Unstirred by the ordinary ambitions of men and unaffected by their ordinary passions, an ascetic by habit rather than

conviction, incapable of envy as of doubt ... yet averse to life in
public ... Joseph Mazzini was what in the Roman Catholic ideal every
pope should be. ... He was as incapable of compromise as the Church
whose greater chiefs he in mind so closely resembled. Compromises were
as sinful as bribes, truces as unworthy as concessions, and to every argument and every offer, whether pressed by statesmen, or urged by followers,
or suggested by hearty friends, this sweet-natured, gentle-mannered, immovable old man answered as the Church.[14]

Mazzini used to say that he hoped his name would be forgotten after
his death. Notoriously he disliked what he called the Italian mania for
building extravagant monuments to the dead instead of using the money
for schools, hospitals and works of public utility that over large areas of
the country were entirely lacking.[15] Parliament automatically voted
money for grandiose memorials to Cavour, Garibaldi and a miscellany of
army generals, but fifteen years after Mazzini's death it rejected a proposal for erecting at public expense a monument to him in Rome. Three
years later a more friendly prime minister agreed to grant 150,000 lire
(about £6,000 sterling) for this purpose, a larger sum than Mazzini earned
in his lifetime though only an insignificant fraction of one per cent of
what was allocated to commemorate King Victor Emanuel. The monument was eventually built but only fifty years later, after the monarchy
had been voted out of existence. Long after Italy became a republic in
1946 the conventional wisdom of liberal historians sometimes continued
to depreciate Mazzini as a not very admirable or likeable person who had
been 'above all a terrorist'.[16]

One early sign of change was in 1903 when, after decades of hostile
criticism, a liberal administration tentatively sanctioned the *Duties of Man*
as an approved text for middle schools, though only in a bowdlerised
edition from which all anti-monarchist passages and its dedication to the
working class had been decently purged. Even so, there was furious
opposition from socialists and Catholics to the inclusion of this booklet in
the curriculum, and other textbooks continued to manipulate the record
by depicting both Garibaldi and Mazzini as little better than vulgar brig-
ands.[17] More serious was a decision two years later, marking the centen-
ary of Mazzini's birth, for the state to subsidise an edition of his collected
writing. This publication, as must have been realised from the first, was
on too grand a scale to have any impact on the general public and was
received with what Gentile called general indifference. Thirty years later,
after its seventieth volume appeared, the number of subscribers (including libraries) had dwindled from four thousand to only two hundred and
fifty.[18] But as a work of scholarship it has become a fundamental source
for one of the more interesting periods of Italian history. Not the least

remarkable fact was that its editor Mario Menghini, for whom it represented a lifetime's work, modestly refused to let his own name appear on
the title-page of this majestic tribute to one of the great men of modern
Italian history.

Bibliographical Note

DURING THE HUNDRED years after Mazzini's death, occasional complaints were heard that in spite of superabundant documentation, and despite excellent studies on individual moments or aspects of his life, there has been a strange reluctance to write a full study of his career. Some distinguished historians, notably Adolfo Omodeo and Nello Rosselli, never carried out their declared intention of repairing this omission. The republican philosopher Giovanni Bovio finished a few chapters but then gave up. And Gaetano Salvemini, who wrote a serious critical essay in 1905 (later expanded and in 1956 translated into English with further additions and corrections), became increasingly fascinated by the remaining fifty years of his life, often saying that he hoped to produce a large-scale biography. Why these books never appeared must be a matter for speculation. One reason was political, and Rosselli might have filled this gap had he not been assassinated by Mussolini at the age of thirty-seven. So might Salvemini had he not been driven by the fascists into exile. Another reason may be the inhibiting size of Mazzini's output. Yet another explanation was that a secluded conspirator lived much less in the public eye than Cavour or Garibaldi and his practical influence was harder to establish. No doubt, too, his ideas posed an awkward challenge to the main schools of Italian historiography, whether to the liberal-conservative tradition represented by Benedetto Croce, or the subsequently fashionable communist school of Antonio Gramsci, or to the anticlericals and positivists whom Mazzini fought so fiercely during his lifetime, or to the numerous Catholic and fascist historians who for various reasons found most of his ideas unpalatable.

In other countries there has been much less research into Mazzini's life and achievement, but London and Edinburgh had one advantage in that he was known personally to a number of contemporaries who were eager to record their impressions. Someone who for long periods saw him almost every day was Emilie Ashurst, who wrote a short memoir, *Joseph Mazzini*, in 1875. She also collected his letters written to her family in London, many of them later published by her friend Elinor Richards in three volumes as *Mazzini's Letters to an English Family*, which is among the most attractive literary products of the Italian Risorgimento. Another close friend was Harriet King, the wife of his English publisher, and her *Letters and Recollections of Mazzini* was edited by George Trevelyan in 1912. An even closer English friend, Jessie White Mario, used a great deal of personal information when she wrote a fairly substantial biography in 1886, though the official archives were closed to her by what she called a conspiracy of silence. Her biography was published only in Italian, as indeed were her other books on Cattaneo, Bertani, Nicotera and Alberto Mario; but her posthumous *Birth of Modern Italy*, edited in 1909 by Duke Litta-Visconti-Arese, was a fine tribute in English to Mazzini. Her transcription of documents was not always accurate, but she did as much as anyone to ensure that much first-hand evidence was preserved for posterity. She had the good fortune to possess the archives of Saffi, Cattaneo and Bertani, and also used the private papers of her other friends James and Caroline Stansfeld. Since she checked her facts in frequent conversations with both Mazzini and Garibaldi, what she had to say was authentic if partisan and is always interesting. Her patience in deciphering Mazzini's handwriting and coded letters was extraordinary.

As we approach the end of the twentieth century it is surprising to find that the best biography of Mazzini in any language is probably that written in English as long ago as 1902 by an inspector of schools from Warwickshire, Bolton King. This has of course been in part superseded by later research, but the author had the privilege of being able to see evidence not available to subsequent writers and his book is still frequently quoted in Italy. Two other biographies in English and well worth reading are over fifty years old: Gwilym Griffith's *Mazzini: Prophet of Modern Europe*, which appeared in 1932, and three years later Stringfellow Barr's *Mazzini: Portrait of an Exile*, published in New York. Neither is uncritical but both, in particular that by Griffith, were written by enthusiasts and helped to rescue the subject from neglect. Other short general studies have since appeared in Italy and elsewhere but none of them with the same quality, range and readability.

One essential primary source is the introduction written by Mazzini for each of the first eight volumes of *Scritti Editi e Inediti di Giuseppe Mazzini* produced in the years immediately after 1861. Another dozen volumes were edited posthumously by Aurelio Saffi and Ernesto Nathan, and Saffi's highly informative introductions were also included in the *Ricordi e Scritti di Aurelio Saffi* published with some modifications after 1892. A shorter version of the *Scritti* in English was edited in six volumes by Emilie Ashurst during the 1860s as *The Life and Writings of Joseph Mazzini*, a second edition following in 1891. A number of single-volume collections have since been published, one of them in English edited in 1939 by another persecuted exile, Ignazio Silone, as *The Living Thoughts of Mazzini*.

Mazzini's correspondence, pamphlets and occasional journalism were gradually put together by Mario Menghini to be used in the national edition of his collected work under the imprint of Galleati of Imola. A nucleus of his letters had first been collected by Emilie Ashurst to whom Mazzini's mother gave all she possessed. Piero Cironi later worked with Emilie to collect as many of Mazzini's writings as possible, and by the time of his own death in 1862 had amassed about three thousand letters but without producing the biography he had intended. Sara Nathan in 1872 purchased everything that Mazzini's sister inherited as Mazzini's legatee. All this material was later assembled by Sara's son Ernesto and given to Menghini. Jessie White contributed her own collection of documents; so did Elinor Richards; and Trevelyan succeeded in locating Mazzini's letters to Peter and Clementia Taylor and William Shaen. Between 1906 and 1943, Menghini was able to produce sixty-four volumes of letters, thirty volumes of Mazzini's political writing and five volumes of his essays in literary criticism. Mazzini almost never dated letters, a fact that gives them the authenticity of not having been written with publication in mind, but posing enormous problems to an editor. Although some of Menghini's dating was clearly wrong, his inspired conjectures have been an indispensable starting-point for subsequent studies, and have recently been made even more useful by an index in four volumes compiled by Guglielmo Macchia and Enrico Golfieri.

A detailed bibliography of other contemporary sources and secondary books can be found in the references that follow, and a short list is available for English readers in Harry Rudman's *Italian Nationalism and English Letters* (London, 1940). Among important books by Italian historians, special mention should be made of those by Alessandro Luzio and Gaetano Salvemini, and more recently others by Emilia Morelli, Franco Della Peruta, Salvo Mastellone and Alessandro Galante Garrone. For help in locating much relevant material I am grateful to innumerable antiquarian bookshops all over Italy; and to individual scholars, especially Terenzio Grandi; also to Luigi Donato, Giacomo Adami and Angelo Ciampi of the Domus Mazziniano in Pisa; and to Leo Morabito of the Istituto Mazziniano in Genoa; to the Associazione Mazziniana of Milan; the Centro di Studi Mazziniani at Naples; and Emilia Morelli of the Istituto per la Storia del Risorgimento in Rome; also to Marco Paolino, Luigi Polo Friz and Luigi Majno. In England I particularly acknowledge generous assistance from James Stansfeld, the descendant of Mazzini's great champion, and from the family of Bolton King; also from Gwilym Griffith, Noel and Georgiana Blakiston, E. E. Y. Hales, Miles Taylor, Derek Beales, Mrs J. Berkeley, Lucio Sponza and I. G. Doolittle of Ashurst, Morris and Crisp. At Oxford the Taylor Institution has three of Mazzini's newspapers presented to it by Mrs Richards, and the Bodleian Library owns a few of Mazzini's letters. Among other important manuscript collections in Britain are the McAdam papers in Glasgow University, the Cowen papers in the Tyne and Wear archives, and others in the British Library, the National Library of Scotland and the City Library of Liverpool. For help and permission to consult these I am indebted to their respective curators, and also to archivists in the national archives of London, Berne, Paris, Rome, Vienna and Merseburg. Miscellaneous pamphlets by Mazzini's English supporters can be found in the Bishopsgate Institute in East London, the library of the Victoria and Albert Museum, and among Garrison's papers in the Boston library. I am also grateful for being allowed to see documents at Windsor by gracious permission of Her Majesty the Queen.

Finally I should add that when quoting from Mazzini, while retaining his sometimes idiosyncratic use of English, I have occasionally made minor changes in punctuation.

Abbreviations

Ed. Naz.	*Scritti Editi ed Inediti di Giuseppe Mazzini*, the national edition edited by Mario Menghini, published by Paolo Galeati, Imola, 1906–43, with supplements to 1986
Daelli	*Scritti Editi ed Inediti di Giuseppe Mazzini*, edited by Mazzini and Aurelio Saffi, published in Milan, Florence and Rome, 1861–91, the initial volumes by G. Daelli
DDI	*I Documenti Diplomatici Italiani*, published by Ministero degli Affari Esteri, Rome, 1952
Domus	*Bollettino della Domus Mazziniana*, Pisa, 1955–93
FO	Foreign Office documents in the Public Records Office, London
Hansard	Proceedings of the British Parliament
PRO	Public Records Office, Kew, London
Rassegna	*Rassegna Storica del Risorgimento*, published by the Istituto per la Storia del Risorgimento, Vittoriano, Rome, 1914
Richards	*Mazzini's Letters to an English Family, 1844–1872*, edited by E. F. Richards, London, 1920–2
Saffi	*Ricordi e Scritti di Aurelio Saffi*, published by the Municipio of Forlì and Barbèra of Florence, 1892–1905

In the 'Notes' which follow on p. 237 *et seq.*, volume numbers are given in italicised form, *I, II, III* etc.

Notes

CHAPTER ONE. *Beginnings*

Apprenticeship

1 *Ed. Naz. 1*, 180, 192, 215–16.
2 R. Ciampini, *Gian Pietro Vieusseux*, Turin, 1953, 93.
3 *Il Ponte*, Florence, May 1951, 469–71, Galante Garrone; *ibid.* May 1961, 716–27; Émile Ollivier, *L'Empire Libérale*, Paris, 1896, *1*, 256–8; Salvo Mastellone, *Mazzini e la 'Giovine Italia' (1831–1834)*, Pisa, 1960, *2*, 124–7.
4 L. Mariotti (Gallenga), *Italy Past and Present*, London, 1848, 19; *The Birth of Modern Italy: Posthumous Papers of Jessie White Mario*, ed. Duke Litta-Visconti-Arese, London, 1909, 11; Giovanni Ruffini, *Lorenzo Benoni*, Edinburgh, 1853, 224.
5 Alessandro Luzio, *Giuseppe Mazzini Carbonaro*, Turin, 1920, 106.
6 *Ed. Naz. 2*, 203; Jessie White Mario, *Della Vita di Giuseppe Mazzini*, Milan, 1886, 487.
7 Cristina Trivulzio di Belgiojoso, *Osservazioni sullo Stato Attuale dell'Italia*, Milan, 1868, 59; C. Cattaneo, *Scritti Politici ed Epistolario*, ed. J. W. Mario, Florence, 1892, *1*, 250, 262–3; G. Montanelli, *Memorie sull'Italia e specialmente sulla Toscana dal 1814 al 1850*, Turin, 1853, *2*, 131.
8 *Ed. Naz. 2*, 194, 219–20; *ibid. 3*, 231–4, 239; Franco Della Peruta, *Mazzini e i Rivoluzionari Italiani*, Milan, 1974, 74–5.
9 Narciso Nada, *Metternich e le Riforme nello Stato Pontificio*, Turin, 1957, 142; Domus, 1974, *1*, 215, Nevler; *FO Confidential Print*, London, no. 35, 22 Nov. 1832, 4–6.
10 *Il Risorgimento Italiano*, Turin, July 1924, 479–82, Rinieri; *ibid.* Jan. 1927, 242–4, Rinieri; *Rassegna*, May 1941, 360, 364, Morelli; *Le Relazioni Diplomatiche fra Lo Stato Pontificio e La Francia*, ed. G. Procacci, Rome, 1963, *ser. 2, 2*, 315.
11 Francesco Salata, *Carlo Alberto Inedito: dal diario autografo del re*, Milan, 1931, 120, 219–21.
12 *Carte Segrete e Atti Ufficiali della Polizia Austriaca in Italia dal 4 Giugno 1814 al 22 Marzo 1848*, Capolago, 1851, *2*, 343, 379; F. A. Gualterio, *Gli Ultimi Rivolgimenti Italiani: Memorie storiche*, Florence, 1850, *4*, 393; *Le Relazioni Diplomatiche fra la Francia e il Regno di Sardegna*, ed. A. Saitta, Rome, 1976, *ser. 2, 2*, 470–80; Richard Blaas, in *Atti del Convegno sul tema 'Mazzini e l'Europa'*, Rome, 1974, 59–60; Mastellone, *Mazzini, 2*, 82–3.
13 A. Sandonà, *Il Regno Lombardo-Veneto 1814–1859*, Milan, 1912, 172.
14 C. Benso di Cavour, *Discorsi Parlamentari*, ed. A. Omodeo and A. Saitta, Florence, 1969, *14*, 190; Francesco Ruffini, *La Giovinezza di Cavour*, Turin, 1937, *1*, 223–4; A. Brofferio, *Storia del Piemonte dal 1814 ai Giorni Nostri*,

Turin, 1849, *3*, 38; *Revue des Deux Mondes*, Paris, 1 Jan. 1845, 176; E. Michel, *F. D. Guerrazzi e le Cospirazioni Politiche in Toscana dall'Anno 1830 all'Anno 1835*, Rome, 1904, 35; P. Anichini, *Strictures on the Publication of Count Dal Pozzo*, London, 1834, 68, 75; C. Rusconi, *Memorie Aneddotiche per servire alla Storia del Rinnovamento Italiano*, Rome, 1886, 15; *Foreign Quarterly Review*, London, May 1834, 342; Mastellone, *Mazzini*, 2, 212, Panizzi.

Switzerland

15 Paolo Harro Harring, *Memorie sulla Giovine Italia*, ed. M. Menghini, Milan, 1913, 43–4, 60, 101.

16 *Ed. Naz. Appendice, 1*, 166, 376.

17 *Rassegna*, Sept. 1938, 1285, Ferraris; Alessandro Luzio, *Carlo Alberto e Giuseppe Mazzini*, Turin, 1923, 233, 352–3; P. Silva, *Figure e Momenti di Storia Italiana*, Milan, 1939, 154.

18 *Ed. Naz. 5*, 37–8; *ibid. 9*. 107; *ibid. 20*, 88; *ibid. 26*, 23.

19 Richards, *1*, 288; *Ed. Naz. 9*, 347; *ibid. 55*, 156–7; *ibid. 59*, 45; *ibid. Zibaldone Giovanile*, Imola, 1981, *3*, 161; Marco Minghetti, *Miei Ricordi*, Turin, 1889, *1*, 163.

20 *Ed. Naz. 9*, 102–5, 114, 347; *ibid. 57*, 142; *ibid. 77*, 167–8.

21 *Ed. Naz. 9*, 5–6, 366; Louis Blanc, *Histoire de Dix Ans 1830–1840*, Paris, 1844, *4*, 192.

22 Hans Keller, *Das 'Junge Europa'*, Zürich, 1938, 72–4; Prince Clemens Metternich, *Mémoires, Documents et Écrits Divers*, Paris, 1908, 2nd ed., *5*, 617; *ibid. 6*, 46–9; Blaas, *Atti del Convegno*, 65, 72–3.

23 Keller, *Das 'Junge Europa'*, 56; *Il Risorgimento Italiano*, Turin, July 1924, 506, Rinieri.

24 M. Battistini, *Esuli Italiani in Belgio (1815–1861)*, Florence, 1968, 348, 381.

25 *Ed. Naz. 4*, 338; *ibid. 7*, 237.

Politics and religion

26 Benedetto Croce, *Pagine Sparse*, Bari, 1942, *1*, 100.

27 *Ed. Naz. 7*, 346; *ibid. 15*, 323; *ibid. 26*, 42; *ibid. 34*, 115; *ibid. 36*, 43; *ibid. 43*, 276; *ibid. 69*, 150; *ibid. 77*, 197; *ibid. 93*, 85.

28 *Ed. Naz. 3*, 73; *ibid. 5*, 106; *ibid. 94*, 280; *ibid. Appendice, 1*, 147.

29 *Ed. Naz. Zibaldone Giovanile, 3*, 181; *Ed. Naz. 2*, 104, 276; *ibid. 6*, 125–6; *ibid. 92*, 203; *ibid. 93*, 92–3.

30 *Ed. Naz. 2*, 50; *ibid. 3*, 18, 269; *ibid. 22*, 35–8; *ibid. 31*, 418.

31 *Ed. Naz. 3*, 64, 66; *ibid. 4*, 35.

32 *Ed. Naz. 3*, 90, 269; *ibid. 5*, 202, 385.

33 *Ed. Naz. 10*, 116–17; *ibid. 11*, 177.

34 *Ed. Naz. 2*, 301; *ibid. 3*, 211–12; *ibid. 5*, 276.

35 Giovanni La Cecilia, *Memorie Storico-Politiche*, ed. R. Moscati, Varese, 1946, 153–4.

36 *Ed. Naz. 2*, 68–9, 155, 181, 191; *ibid. 3*, 18, 67; *ibid. 4*, 10–11; *ibid. 5*, 16, 56–7; *ibid. 9*, 98; *ibid. 17*, 256; *ibid. 25*, 110.

37 *Ed. Naz. 10*, 258; *ibid. 11*, 226; *ibid. 14*, 300.

38 *Ed. Naz. 2*, 195, 210; *ibid. 10*, 298–9; *ibid. 17*, 250–9.

39 *Ed. Naz. 36*, 88–9; *ibid. 93*, 79.

40 *Ed. Naz. 7*, 285; *ibid. 34*, 206–7, 211; *ibid. 46*, 258; Alessandro Galante Garrone, *L'Albero della Libertà: dai Giacobini a Garibaldi*, Florence, 1987, 245; Gaetano Salvemini, *Mazzini*, Rome, 1920, 22.

41 *Ed. Naz. 5*, 239; Alessandro Galante Garrone, *Filippo Buonarroti e i Rivoluzionari dell'Ottocento (1828–1837)*, Turin, 1951, 323–7; Arthur Lehning, *From Buonarroti to Bakunin*, Leiden, 1970, 61–2; Salvo Mastellone, *Giuseppe*

Mazzini e l'Associazione dei Veri Italiani, Naples, 1962, 6.

42 Mountstuart Grant Duff, *Notes from a Diary 1851–1872*, London, 1897, *1*, 283.

43 *Ed. Naz. 14*, 223–5; *ibid. 79*, 325; Jessie White Mario, in *The Nation*, New York, 2 July 1903, 8.

44 *Ed. Naz. 6*, 182; *ibid. 7*, 283; *ibid. 18*, 20; *ibid. 34*, 290–1; *ibid. 36*, 6.

45 *Ed. Naz. 5*, 216; *ibid. 64*, 162.

46 G. Mazzini, *Zibaldone Pisano*, Pisa, 1955, ed. R. Carmignani, 31, 46–55, 74–7; *Ed. Naz. 19*, 248, 357–8; *ibid. 52*, 150; *ibid. 77*, 95; *ibid. Appendice, 1*, 159.

47 *Ed. Naz. 5*, 29; *ibid. 19*, 244–6; *ibid. 31*, 5; *ibid. 32*, 302; *ibid. 56*, 61–2.

48 *Ed. Naz. 21*, 163; *ibid. 26*, 91.

49 *Ed. Naz. 8*, 187.

50 *Ed. Naz. 2*, 243; *ibid. 3*, 144–9; *ibid. 16*, 239; *ibid. 23*, 234; *ibid. 26*, 70.

51 Ernesto Buonaiuti, *Storia del Cristianesimo*, Milan, 1951, *3*, 435.

52 *Ed. Naz. 18*, 197; *ibid. 20*, 119; *ibid. 54*, 190–1; *ibid. 83*, 204; *ibid. 92*, 152.

53 Richards, *3*, 161–4; *Rivista di Storia della Chiesa in Italia*, Rome, 1962, *16*, 318, 320, E. Morelli; *Ed. Naz. 10*, 143; *ibid. 12*, 369; *ibid. 15*, 91–2.

CHAPTER TWO. *England: 1837–45*

First years in England

1 Marguerite Mauerhofer, in *Zeitschrift für Schweizerische Geschichte*, Zürich, 1932, *12*, 84, 87, 94.

2 P. Anichini, *Strictures on the Publication of Count Dal Pozzo*, London, 1834, i.

3 Carlo Cagnacci, *Giuseppe Mazzini e i Fratelli Ruffini*, Porto Maurizio, 1893, 157–8, 163, 183, 245.

4 *Ed. Naz. 11*, 130.

5 *Lettere a Mazzini di Familiari ed Amici 1834–1839*, ed. S. Gallo and E. Melossi, Imola, 1986, *2*, 504, 509, 531.

6 Eliza Fletcher, *Autobiography of Mrs Fletcher of Edinburgh*, Carlisle, 1874, 200.

7 *Ed. Naz. 14*, 213, 245; *ibid. 15*, 199.

8 *Ed. Naz. 14*, 384; *ibid. 20*, 390; *ibid. 32*, 263; Giacinto Fassio, *Mazzini a Gaeta*, Poggio Mirteto, 1912, 75.

9 *Ed. Naz. 8*, 107–9, 371–2; *ibid. 18*, 10; *ibid. 22*, 303; Leona Ravenna, *Il Giornalismo Mazziniano*, Florence, 1939, 57–8.

10 *Ed. Naz. 1*, 5–7, 271–3, 329; *ibid. 3*, 69–70; *ibid. 8*, 379; *ibid. 22*, 292.

11 William Malleson to Bolton King, in Bolton King Papers (private collection).

12 *Ed. Naz. 17*, 3–164.

13 *Ed. Naz. 12*, 398–9; *ibid. 14*, 216; *ibid. 15*, 4; *ibid. 21*, 253; *ibid. 23*, 14.

14 *The Earlier Letters of John Stuart Mill 1812–1848*, ed. F. E. Mineka, Toronto, 1963, *2*, 378, 548; *The Later Letters of John Stuart Mill, 1849–1873*, ed. F. E. Mineka and D. N. Lindley, Toronto, 1972, *4*, 1978.

15 Jessie White Mario, *The Birth of Modern Italy*, London, 1909, 30.

16 *Ed. Naz. 14*, 192.

17 *Ed. Naz. 16*, 139–40, 217–18.

18 *Ed. Naz. 16*, 20, 66.

19 *Ed. Naz. 15*, 467–70.

20 *Ed. Naz. 22*, 4–5, 17, 20–1, 70.

21 *Ed. Naz. 8*, 301; *ibid. 23*, 93; *ibid. 29*, 160; *Opere di Francesco De Sanctis*, ed. C. Muscetta and G. Candeloro, Turin, 1951, *12*, 57.

22 *Ed. Naz. 32*, 148.

23 *Ed. Naz. 8*, 185–9; *ibid. 54*, 107; *Fortnightly Review*, London, May 1891, 702, Mathilde Blind; Benedetto Croce, *Ariosto, Shakespeare e Corneille*, Bari, 1944, 181.

24 *Ed. Naz. 20*, 335; *La Commedia di*

Dante Alighieri Illustrata da Ugo Foscolo, edited by 'An Italian', London, 1842.

25 *Ed. Naz. 58*, 346; *ibid. 32*, 112; *ibid. 77*, 91–2.

26 *Ed. Naz. 8*, 165.

27 *Ed. Naz. 1*, 378; *ibid. 8*, 149; *ibid. 10*, 186; *ibid. 19*, 149; *ibid. 23*, 29, 218; *ibid. 28*, 80.

28 *Ed. Naz. 23*, 212; *ibid. 80*, 270; *ibid. 85*, 45–6; M. de Angelis, *Giuseppe Mazzini: Filosofia della musica*, Florence, 1977, 21; Library of Scotland MS 3218, f 54, Mazzini, letter to Miss Hill.

29 *Ed. Naz. 14*, 6, 207; *ibid. 15*, 386; *ibid. 18*, 118–20; *ibid. 22*, 375, 380–4.

30 *Ed. Naz. 18*, 119, 173; *ibid. 22*, xxv–xxvi; *ibid. 66*, 402–3.

31 *Ed. Naz. 14*, 350; *ibid. 15*, 245–6; *ibid. 20*, 63, 356–8; Jessie White Mario, *Della Vita di Giuseppe Mazzini*, Milan, 1886, 472.

32 *Ed. Naz. 14*, 26–7; *ibid. 17*, 44–5, 144, 210–17.

33 *Ed. Naz. Zibaldone Giovanile, 1*, 199; *ibid. 3*, 10, 15, 67, 139, 143.

34 *Ed. Naz. 17*, 117; *ibid. 34*, 107, 118–24, 133, 150.

35 *Ed. Naz. 22*, 388; *ibid. 29*, 70; *ibid. 92*, 242.

36 *Ed. Naz. 7*, 159–60; *ibid. 15*, 14–15; *ibid. 18*, 118; *ibid. 34*, 111–12, 125–6, 131.

37 *The Collected Letters of Thomas and Jane Welsh Carlyle*, ed. C. R. Sanders and C. de L. Ryals, Durham, North Carolina, 1985, *12*, 37–8, 117–18; *ibid. 13*, 31.

38 *Ed. Naz. Appendice, 2*, 181; *Fortnightly Review*, May 1891, 706.

39 *Ibid*, 707; H. E. Litchfield, *Emma Darwin Wife of Charles Darwin*, Cambridge, 1904, *2*, 79; Charles Gavan Duffy, *Conversations with Carlyle*, London, 1892, 109; *The Collected Letters of Thomas and Jane Carlyle, 12*, 43, 82; Gwilym Griffith, *Mazzini Yesterday and Tomorrow*, Turin, 1954, 10.

40 *Ed. Naz. 21*, 145–7, 169–75; *ibid.*

22, 292; *ibid. 29*, 92–4; A. Galante Garone, in *Saggi Mazziniani Dedicati a Emilia Morelli*, Genoa, 1990, 45–6.

41 Thomas Carlyle, *Reminiscences*, ed. C. E. Norton, London, 1932, 75; Moncure Conway, *Autobiography*, London, 1904, *2*, 59–60; J. A. Froude, *Thomas Carlyle*, London, 1882, *1*, 454.

42 *Harpers New Monthly Magazine*, New York, July 1872, 282.

43 *Ed. Naz. 14*, 10–11, 332; *ibid. 18*, 76–8, 109; *ibid. 19*, 154, 161–2, 340.

44 Cesare Abba, *Cose Garibaldine*, Turin, 1907, 314.

45 *Lettere a Mazzini di Familiari, 2*, 394–5, 402, 518, 557.

46 *Ibid. 2*, 527; E. A. V. (Emilie Ashurst), *Joseph Mazzini: A Memoir*, London, 1875, 60–2; J. W. Mario, *Mazzini*, 315.

Politics: 1838–43

47 *Ed. Naz. 15*, 54, 152, 157; *ibid. 18*, 158–62, 189.

48 *Revue des Deux Mondes*, Paris, 1 Jan. 1845, 177.

49 *Carte Segrete e Atti Ufficiali della Polizia Austriaca in Italia dal 4 Giugno 1814 al 22 Marzo 1848*, Capolago, 1851, *2*, 447; Alessandro Luzio, *Garibaldi, Cavour, Verdi*, Turin, 1924, *5*, 17, 24; Gustavo Sacerdote, *La Vita di Giuseppe Garibaldi*, Milan, 1933, 119–24; *Domus*, 1972, *2*, 125–30, Candido.

50 *Ed. Naz. 14*, 166–7; *ibid. 15*, 254, 414; *ibid. 18*, 161; *ibid. 20*, 164–5, 231–2; *ibid. 25*, 304; E. A. V., *Joseph Mazzini*, 47.

51 *Ed. Naz. 22*, 44, 199.

52 *Ed. Naz. 20*, 69.

53 F. Della Peruta, *Mazzini e i Rivoluzionari Italiani: il 'Partito d'Azione' 1830–1845*, Milan, 1974, 269, 366; *Ed. Naz. 20*, 101; *ibid. 23*, 310–11.

54 *Il Risorgimento Italiano*, Turin, Oct.

1927, 347–8, 361, Lemmi.

55 *Ed. Naz. 17*, 285; *ibid. 19*, 120; *ibid. 22*, 75–6.

56 *Ed. Naz. 25*, 229–30, 280–1; *ibid. 30*, 143; *ibid. Appendice, 2*, 279–80.

57 *Ed. Naz. Protocollo della Giovine Italia (congrega centrale di Francia)*, Imola, 1916, *2*, 148; *Ed. Naz. 15*, 71; *ibid. 20*, 119; *ibid. 23*, 303; *ibid. Appendice, 2*, 267–8.

58 *Lettere a Mazzini di Familiari, 2*, 689.

59 *Ed. Naz. 39*, 9.

60 Antonio Manno, *Aneddoti Documentati sulla Censura in Piemonte dalla Restaurazione alla Costituzione*, Turin, 1906, 57–8, 69; Francesco Predari, *I Primi Vagiti della Libertà Italiana in Piemonte*, Milan, 1861, 66–7; Camillo Cavour, *Epistolario*, Bologna, 1962, *1*, 142; *Il Risorgimento Italiano*, Turin, June 1909, 507–8, Malamani; *Ed. Naz. 18*, 171; *ibid. 19*, 129.

61 *Ed. Naz. 15*, 113; *ibid. 20*, 313; *ibid. 25*, 186; *ibid. 29*, 123–4; *ibid. 31*, 366.

62 *Ed. Naz. 22*, 310–14.

63 *Ed. Naz. 11*, 43, 269; *ibid. 20*, 88, 124, 174–5, 311–12; *ibid. 26*, 23; *ibid. 77*, 122, 240; Marco Minghetti, *Miei Ricordi*, Turin, 1889, *1*, 163.

64 *Ricordi di Michelangelo Castelli (1847–1875)*, ed. Luigi Chiala, Turin, 1888, 36–7.

65 Vincenzo Gioberti, *Epistolario*, ed. Giovanni Gentile, Florence, 1928, *4*, 343.

66 Vincenzo Gioberti, *Il Rinnovamento Civile d'Italia*, Paris, 1851, *2*, 626–8; E. Solmi, *Mazzini e Gioberti*, Rome, 1913, 180, 278–80; Antonio Anzilotti, *Gioberti*, Florence, 1922, 87, 142; Alessandro Luzio, *Profili Biografici e Bozzetti Storici*, Milan, 1928, *1*, 280; *Ed. Naz. 8*, 35.

67 *Gioberti-Massari Carteggio (1838–1852)*, ed. G. Balsamo-Crivelli,

Turin, 1920, 267, 273; V. Gioberti, *Della Nazionalità*, Livorno, 1847, 42–4; V. Gioberti, *Del Primato Morale e Civile degli Italiani*, Brussels, 1843, *1*, 92–3.

68 Cesare Balbo, *Delle Speranze d'Italia*, Capolago, 1844, 18–21; C. Balbo, *Sommario della Storia d'Italia*, ed. A. Solmi, Milan, 1927, 527, 530.

69 Balbo, *Delle Speranze*, 239; *Foreign Quarterly Review*, London, April 1845, 260.

70 *Ed. Naz. 24*, 220; *ibid. 26*, 193; *ibid. 38*, 270; *ibid. 39*, 10–14.

71 Balbo, *Delle Speranze*, 123–4.

72 *Ed. Naz. 20*, 312–13, 340; *ibid. 25*, 53.

73 *Ed. Naz. 1*, 33. *ibid. 3*, 228; *ibid. 4*, 350; *ibid. 6*, 24; *ibid. 7*, 401; *ibid. 17*, 210; *ibid. 22*, 62; *ibid. 23*, 28; *ibid. 29*, 125–6.

74 *Ed. Naz. 25*, 119–20.

75 *Ed. Naz. 20*, 327; *ibid. 23*, 89; *ibid. 27*, 197; Ersilio Michel, *Esuli Italiani in Tunisia (1815–1861)*, Milan, 1941, 269; Ersilio Michel, *Esuli Italiani in Egitto*, Pisa, 1958, 85; Mario Degli Alberti, *La Politica Estera del Piemonte sotto Carlo Alberto*, Turin, 1909, *2*, 484.

76 Charles Babbage, *A Chapter on Street Nuisances*, London, 1864, 5–8; *Ed. Naz. 27*, 101; *ibid. 77*, 267–9.

77 Antonio Gallenga, *Episodes of My Second Life*, London, 1884, *2*, 26; *Ed. Naz. 18*, 331.

78 *The Collected Letters of Thomas and Jane Carlyle, 17*, 201–2.

79 *Ed. Naz. 27*, 84, 110–11; Mario, *The Birth of Modern Italy*, 89; R. Paulucci di Calboli, *I Girovaghi Italiani in Inghilterra ed i Suonatori Ambulanti*, Città di Castello, 1893, 38, 141–2.

80 *The Letters of Charles Dickens*, ed. M. House and G. Storey, Oxford, 1980, *4*, 418–19; *ibid. 5*, 258; *Harpers Magazine*, New York, July 1872, 274–5; *Ed. Naz. 23*, 38; *ibid. 32*, 255; Richards, *2*, 42–3.

Conspiracies in Italy

81 F. A. Gualterio, *Gli Ultimi Rivolgimenti Italiani*, Florence, 1850, *4*, 532–3; *Revue Des Deux Mondes*, 1845, *9*, 179.

82 *Ed. Naz. Protocollo della Giovine Italia*, *1*, 241; *ibid.* *3*, 25, 40, 93, 160; Maria Bornate, *La Giovinezza e l'Esilio di Agostino Ruffini*, Aquila, 1922, 134.

83 *Ed. Naz. 23*, 31, 284; *ibid. 24*, 35, 273, 282; *ibid. 31*, 366.

84 *Ed. Naz. 24*, 194, 198–9, 229–30, 233, 256, 262–3; *ibid. 57*, 195; *Collected Letters of Carlyle*, 17, 92–3; C. Spellanzon, *Storia del Risorgimento e dell'Unità d'Italia*, Milan, 1934, *2*, 831; P. E. Santangelo, *Massimo d'Azeglio Politico e Moralista*, Turin, 1937, 36.

85 *Ed. Naz. 31*, 365; F. Della Peruta, *I Democratici e la Rivoluzione Italiana: Dibattiti ideali e contrasti politici*, Milan, 1958, 307–8; Jessie White Mario, *Birth of Modern Italy*, 75; A. M. Ghisalberti, *Cospirazioni del Risorgimento*, Palermo, 1938, 77–80; L. Salvatorelli, *Spiriti e Figure del Risorgimento*, Florence, 1961, 378.

86 *Ed. Naz. 25*, 298, 301–4; *ibid. 26*, 162; *ibid. 31*, 98; *ibid. Appendice*, 2, 287–9; Carlyle, *Collected Letters*, 17, 253–4.

87 *Ed. Naz. 31*, 9; *ibid. Appendice, 3*, 304.

88 *Ed. Naz. 26*, 228; *ibid. 27*, 135; *ibid. 31*, 50, 53–4; *ibid. Appendice, 3*, 32; F. Della Peruta, *Mazzini e i Rivoluzionari Italiani*, Milan, 1974, 416.

89 *Protocollo, 1*, 280, 338, 343; Luzio, *Profili, 1*, 309; *ibid. 2*, 51; R. Pierantoni, *Storia dei Fratelli Bandiera*, Milan, 1909, 133–4; *Rassegna*, May 1941, 371, 375, Morelli.

90 *The Times*, 13 Mar. 1845; *Gioberti-Massari Carteggio*, 325; *Miscellanea di Storia del Risorgimento in Onore di Arturo Codignola*, Genoa, 1967,

29, Morelli; *La Critica*, Bari, Nov. 1903, 462, Gentile.

91 *PRO*, FO 7/319, Aberdeen to Neumann, 22 Jan. 1844; *Rassegna*, April 1930, 369, 362–4, Ricci; A. Monti, *Vittorio Emanuele II*, Milan, 1941, 104.

92 *Ed. Naz. 26*, 201; *ibid. Appendice*, 2, 320–1; *ibid. 3*, 17.

93 *Ed. Naz. 27*, 177, 218–19.

94 Nello Rosselli, *Inghilterra e Regno di Sardegna dal 1815 al 1847*, ed. P. Treves, Turin, 1954, 804.

95 *Hansard, 78*, 1343–6, 1 April 1845; *ibid. 80*, 238, 7 May 1845.

96 *Ibid. 78*, 1332, 1 April 1845; F. B. Smith, 'British Post-Office Espionage 1844', in *Historical Studies*, April 1970, Melbourne, 192; *Report from the Select Committee on the Post Office*, London, 1844, 14; E. Morelli, *L'Inghilterra di Mazzini*, Rome, 1965, 47–9, 71; *Carte Segrete e Atti Ufficiali della Polizia Austriaca in Italia*, Capolago, 1851, *2*, 431.

97 *Hansard, 76*, 303, 2 July 1844.

98 *Hansard, 77*, 967, 21 Feb. 1845.

99 *Hansard, 75*, 1274–5, 24 June 1844; *The Times*, 22 Aug. 1907 (letter of 20 Mar. 1845).

100 *Hansard, 77*, 988, 995, 21 Feb. 1845; *Ed. Naz. 30*, 90; *English Songs of Italian Freedom*, ed. G. M. Trevelyan, London, 1911, 50; *Letters of Dickens, 4*, 151.

101 *The Pictorial Times*, London, 7 Sept. 1844, 148–9.

102 *Hansard, 89*, 206–7, 4 April 1845.

103 *Westminster Review*, London, Sept. 1844, 237.

104 *The Times*, 15 June 1844; *Collected Letters of Carlyle, 20*, 253.

105 *Ed. Naz. 31*, 356, 363–8.

106 Leigh Hunt, *Stories from the Italian Poets with Lives of the Writers*, London, 1846, *1*, xiv.

107 *Collected Letters of Carlyle, 20*, 8.

108 *Ed. Naz. 11*, 317; *ibid. 20*, 299; *ibid. 23*, 221; *ibid. 24*, 361; *ibid. 45*, 13, 81; *ibid. 54*, 251.

109 W. J. Linton, *Memoirs*, London,

1895, 152–3; W. J. Linton, *European Republicans: Recollections of Mazzini and his Friends*, London, 1893, 163; Domus, 1975, *2*, 297, Shaw; *Rassegna*, April 1970, 349, Ricci.

110   David Masson, *Memories of London in the 'Forties'*, London, 1908, 160, 206; J. A. Froude, *Thomas Carlyle: A History of His Life in London 1834–81*, London, 1884, *1*, 344.

111   *Ed. Naz. 19*, 230, 348–9.

112   *Ed. Naz. 14*, 35; *ibid. 69*, 73.

113   *Once a Week*, London, 1 Nov. 1862, 509; *Ed. Naz. 23*, 11.

114   *Ed. Naz. 12*, 371; *ibid. 33*, 340; *ibid. 42*, 265.

115   *Letters and Memorials of Jane Welsh Carlyle*, ed. Thomas Carlyle and James Anthony Froude, London, 1883, *1*, 337–8, 354; *Ed. Naz. 27*, 26, 82, 108; *ibid. 30*, 9, 70–3; note by William Malleson in Bolton King Papers.

116   *Ed. Naz. 31*, 245, 338–40; *North British Review*, Edinburgh, Nov. 1846, 173; *Bentley's Quarterly Review*, London, Mar. 1859, 333.

117   *Rivista di Storia della Chiesa in Italia*, Roma, 1962, *16*, 330, Morelli; *Ed. Naz. 27*, 281.

118   *Ed. Naz. 26*, 245, 249–50; *ibid. 27*, 226, 259; *ibid. 28*, 139; *ibid. Appendice*, *2*, 326–7.

119   Gualterio, *Gli Ultimi Rivolgimenti*, *2*, 355; F. Della Peruta, *Mazzini e i Rivoluzionari*, 406–7, 428; *Ed. Naz. 28*, 157; *ibid. 57*, 195; *Memorie Politiche di Felice Orsini*, ed. A. M. Ghisalberti, Rome, 1946, 95.

120   *Ed. Naz. 27*, 105; *ibid. 28*, 163; *ibid. 30*, 101, 155, 317.

121   *Apostolato Popolare*, London, 25 Nov. 1842, 72; *The Times*, 30 June 1846; Mario, *Birth of Modern Italy*, 100–1; *Ed. Naz. 23*, 290, 335; *ibid. 24*, 316; *ibid. 25*, 390; *ibid. 30*, 61, 235.

122   Alessandro Luzio, *Garibaldi, Cavour, Verdi*, Turin, 1924, 12;

Filiberto Sardagna, *Garibaldi in Lombardia 1848*, Milan, 1927, 47–50; *Ed. Naz. 32*, 105.

123   *Tutti gli Scritti di Camillo Cavour*, ed. C. Pischedda and G. Talamo, Turin, 1976, *2*, 952.

124   *The Harney Papers*, ed. F. G. and R. M. Black, Assen, 1969, 49; *Ed. Naz. 28*, 112–13, 156, 353–5; *ibid. 30*, 141–2, 149–50, 250.

CHAPTER THREE. *The Revolution: 1846–9*

Prelude to Revolution

1   *Ed. Naz. 23*, 281; *ibid. 25*, 270.

2   William W. Story, *Roba di Roma*, London, 1863, *1*, 201; *Memoirs and Artistic Studies of Adelaide Ristori*, ed. G. Mantellini, London, 1907, 17–18; J. T. Headley, *Letters from Italy*, London, 1845, 224; *Journal of Central European Affairs*, Boulder, Colorado, July 1946, 175, Monaro.

3   *Ed. Naz. 30*, 143, 193–4, 226; *ibid. 32*, 222; *ibid. 34*, 289.

4   *Ricordi di Michelangelo Castelli*, ed. L. Chiala, Turin, 1888, 49.

5   Nicomede Bianchi, *Scritti e Lettere di Carlo Alberto: Indicazioni documentate*, Turin, 1879, 52–3; *Rassegna*, 1924, 897, Colombo.

6   *Il Risorgimento Italiano*, July 1913, 784, Passamonti; *Ed. Naz. 30*, 9, 16, 26; *ibid. 32*, 221–3; *ibid. 33*, 62, 218; L. Mariotti, *Latest News from Italy*, London, 1847, 24.

7   *Ed. Naz. 34*, 92–3.

8   Antonio Casati, *Milano e i Principi di Savoia: Cenni storici*, Turin, 1853, 145; Carlo Cattaneo, *Scritti Politici ed Epistolario*, ed. G. Rosa and J. W. Mario, Florence, 1892, *1*, 250; *Foreign Quarterly Review*, London, Jan. 1845, *34*, 523; *ibid.* Oct. 1845, *36*, 195; Mary Wollstonecraft Shelley, *Rambles in Germany and Italy in 1840, 1842, and 1843*, London, 1844, *2*, 178.

9   A. Gallenga, *Italy Past and Present*, London, 1848, *2*, 24.

10 *Gioberti-Massari Carteggio (1838–1852)*, ed. G. Balsamo–Crivelli, Turin, 1920, 371; *Ed. Naz. 30*, 183.

11 Prince Clemens Metternich, *Mémoires, Documents et Écrits Divers*, Paris, 1883, *7*, 299, 303, 407, 437.

12 *Ed. Naz. 24*, 220, 393; *ibid. 32*, 78–9; *ibid. 34*, 315, 323–4; *ibid. 36*, 9–10, 117, 132.

13 *Correspondence Respecting the Affairs of Italy Presented to Parliament*, July 1849, *1*, 74, 78, 220, 223.

14 *Ed. Naz. 30*, 42; *ibid. 32*, 8, 51.

15 *Ed. Naz. 32*, 223; Alessandro Luzio, *Profili Biografici e Bozzetti Storici*, Milan, 1928, *1*, 267–8.

16 *Ed. Naz. 30*, 328; *ibid. 32*, 236–8; *ibid. Appendice, 3*, 331–3.

17 *Ed. Naz. 28*, 35–6, 223; *ibid. 32*, 31–2; *ibid. 33*, 103–4; *ibid. 36*, 240.

18 *Ed. Naz. 36*, 227–32.

19 *Ed. Naz, 32*, 318–19; Domus, 1961, *1*, 10, Candido; E. Morelli, *Giuseppe Mazzini: Saggi e Ricerche*, Rome, 1950, 31; Gaetano Salvemini, *Scritti sul Risorgimento*, ed. P. Pieri and C. Pischedda, Milan, 1961, 267; Alessandro Levi, *La Filosofia Politica di Giuseppe Mazzini*, ed. S. Mastellone, Naples, 1967, 68; *Dublin Review*, Jan. 1913, 56–7, Mrs King.

20 *Ed. Naz. 28*, 264; *ibid. 36*, 5.

21 E. Morelli, *L'Inghilterra di Mazzini*, Rome, 1965, 92–3; Thomas Frost, *Forty Years' Recollections*, London, 1880, 127; *The Times*, 7 June 1847; F. B. Smith, *Radical Artisan: William James Linton 1812–1897*, Manchester, 1973, 62.

22 *The Life of Thomas Cooper written by himself*, London, 1872, 299.

23 *The Life and Writings of Joseph Mazzini*, London, 1870, ed. E. Ashurst, *6*, 293–8; *Ed. Naz. 36*, 8–10.

24 *Memoirs of Margaret Fuller Ossoli*, London, 1852, *2*, 100–1; *The Letters of Margaret Fuller*, ed. R. N. Hudspeth, Ithaca, 1983, *4*, 240; *ibid. 5*, 152, 154.

25 William Lloyd Garrison, introduction to *Joseph Mazzini: His Life, Writings and Political Principles*, New York, 1872, xii, xii–xxii, xxx.

26 *Protocollo della Giovine Italia*, Imola, 1922, *6*, 44, 236; *Ed. Naz. 35*, 213, 247; *ibid. 37*, 290, 321; *ibid. Appendice, 6*, 322–3.

27 Richards, *1*, 41.

28 *The Letters of Charles Dickens*, ed. M. House and G. Storey, Oxford, 1980, *4*, 485–6.

29 *Ed. Naz. 33*, 252.

30 *Ed. Naz. 30*, 263, 293; *ibid. 32*, 200; *ibid. 33*, 35, 106.

31 Library of Scotland MS 2883 f 60, appeal of Jan. 1848 signed by Mazzini and Gallenga; A. Gallenga, *Episodes of My Second Life*, London, 1884, *2*, 163; *Carte Segrete e Atti Ufficiali della Polizia Austriaca in Italia*, Capolago, 1852, *3*, 310.

32 C. Cagnacci, *Giuseppe Mazzini e i Fratelli Ruffini*, Porto Maurizio, 1893, 299; *Epistolario di Nino Bixio*, ed. E. Morelli, Rome, 1939, *1*, 10; *Ed. Naz. 33*, 74–5.

33 Louis Des Ambrois, *Notes et Souvenirs Inédits*, Bologna, 1901, 13; Agostino Gori, *Storia della Rivoluzione Italiana durante il Periodo delle Riforme 1846–1848*, Florence, 1897, 316; *Ed. Naz. 33*, 24; *ibid. 36*, 249; Mariotti, *Latest News*, 23.

34 *Archivio Triennale delle Cose d'Italia*, Capolago, 1850, new edition of 1974 by L. Ambrosoli, Milan, 1974, *1*, 566.

35 *The Spectator*, London, 18 Sept. 1847, 899.

36 *Ed. Naz. 33*, 76, 85; Giuseppe Gadda, *Ricordi e Impressioni della nostra Storia Politica*, Turin, 1899, 3–4, 9; C. Cavour, *Epistolario*, ed.

N. Nada, Florence, 1978, *4*, 394; *Studi Carlo-Albertini*, Turin, 1933, 378, Colombo.

37 *Ed. Naz. 33*, 268; *ibid. 36*, 254–5.

38 *Ed. Naz. 32*, 126; *ibid. 33*, 62, 113, 118, 202–3, 218.

The Revolution of 1848

39 *Dalle Riforme allo Statuto di Carlo Alberto*, ed. Adolfo Colombo, Casale, 1924, 2; Arturo Codignola, *Dagli Albori della Libertà al Proclama di Moncalieri*, Turin, 1931, 382; Niccolò Rodolico, *Carlo Alberto negli Anni 1843–1849*, Florence, 1943, 239; *Carte Segrete della Polizia Austriaca*, *3*, 369; *Ed. Naz. 33*, 241–2.

40 Vito Riccobono MS, *Deputazione di Storia Patria*, Palermo; *Epistolario di Giuseppe La Farina*, ed. A Franchi, Milan, 1869, *1*, 422–3.

41 *Ed. Naz. 33*, 218; Evelyn Ashley, *The Life of Henry John Temple Viscount Palmerston 1846–1865*, London, 1876, *1*, 63–5; P. Silva, *La Monarchia di Luglio e l'Italia*, Turin, 1917, 437.

42 *Correspondence Presented to Parliament*, London, July 1849, *2*, 69; *Ed. Naz. 33*, 250; *ibid. 35*, 9, 14; *Rivista di Storia della Chiesa in Italia*, Rome, 1962, *16*, 337, E. Morelli.

43 *Epistolario di Quintino Sella*, ed. G. and M. Quazza, Rome, 1980, *1*, 84; Cagnacci, *Mazzini e i Fratelli Ruffini*, 319, 321; *Ed. Naz. 35*, 30; *ibid. 39*, 53, 60.

44 Carlo Cattaneo, *Considerazioni sulle Cose d'Italia nel 1848*, ed. C. Spellanzon, Turin, 1946, 34; *Archivio Triennale*, *1*, 565–6, 641.

45 Ralph Abercromby, despatch of 20 Mar. 1848 from Turin, in Royal Archives, Windsor, J. 2/83.

46 *Correspondence presented to Parliament July 1849*, *2*, 325.

47 *Ibid.* 184–5, 206–7, 292; Nassau

William Senior, *Journals kept in France and Italy from 1848 to 1852*, London, 1871, *1*, 294–7 (quoting Balbo); *Le Relazioni Diplomatiche fra la Gran Bretagna e il Regno di Sardegna*, ed. F. Curato, Rome, 1961, *ser. 3, 1*, 171; *I Rapporti fra Governo Sardo e Governo Provvisorio di Lombardia durante la Guerra del 1848*, ed. M. Avetta, Rome, 1938, 95, 384.

48 *Le Relazioni Diplomatiche fra L'Austria e il Regno di Sardegna e la Guerra del 1848–1849*, ed. A. Filipuzzi, Rome, 1961, *ser. 3, 1*, 417; Carlo Casati, *Nuove Rivelazioni su i Fatti di Milano nel 1847–1848*, Milan, 1885, *2*, 217; *Ed. Naz. 36*, 301.

49 *Carteggio Casati-Castagnetto (19 Marzo–14 Ottobre 1848)*, ed. V. Ferrari, Milan, 1909, 18, 25.

50 A. Brofferio, *Storia del Parlamento Subalpino: per mandato di Sua Maestà il Re d'Italia*, Milan, 1866, *1*, 447.

51 *Le Relazioni Diplomatiche*, ed. Curato, *1*, 142, 145, 157; *Carteggio Casati-Castagnetto*, 56.

52 *Correspondence, 2*, 294–5, 319.

53 Carlo Cattaneo, *Scritti Politici ed Epistolario*, ed. G. Rosa and Jessie White Mario, Florence, 1892, *1*, 262–3.

54 *Revue des Deux Mondes*, Paris, 1 Jan. 1845, 179.

55 *Ed. Naz. 38*, 277; *ibid. 77*, 318–19; Luigi Stefanoni, *Giuseppe Mazzini: Notizie storiche*, Milan, 1863, 97.

56 *Contemporary Review*, London, Oct. 1870, 393; Pietro Silva, *Il 1848*, Rome, 1948, 124–5.

57 *Ed. Naz. 35*, 111–16; *ibid. 39*, 304; C. A. Costa de Beauregard, *Épilogue d'un Règne: les dernières années du Roi Charles-Albert*, Paris, 1895, 212; *Il Veltro*, Rome, August 1973, *17*, 527, Ghisalberti.

58 James Stansfeld, *The Italian Movement and Italian Parties*, London, 1862, 39.

59 Domus, 1965, *1*, 40, Montale; *Ed.*

Naz. 36, 273, 288.

60 Brofferio, *Storia del Parlamento 1*, 469, 472.

61 *Ed. Naz. 55*, 346–7.

62 G. Ferrari, *La Federazione Repubblicana*, London (but in fact Capolago), 1851, 102, 107; *Rassegna*, Oct. 1925, 760, Saffiotti.

63 Giovanni Visconti Venosta, *Ricordi di Gioventù 1847–1860*, Milan, 1904, 112, Revue des Deux Mondes, 15 Sept. 1848, 811.

64 Antonio Monti, *Un Dramma fra gli Esuli*, Milan, 1921, 80–5.

65 *Carteggio Casati-Castagnetto*, 56.

66 *Ibid.* 59; *Rapporti fra Governo Sardo*, ed. Avetta, 139, 141; Federico Patetta, 'Lettere di Carlo Alberto', in *Atti della Reale Accademia delle Scienze di Torino*, Turin, 1921, 269–70.

67 Nassau William Senior, *Conversations with M. Thiers*, London, 1878, *1*, 406; *Revue des Deux Mondes*, 15 Sept. 1848, 794; Giuseppe Montanelli, *Memorie sull'Italia e specialmente sulla Toscana dal 1814 al 1850*, Turin, 1853, *2*, 308–12, 357, 432; *Documenti e Scritti Autentici Lasciati da Daniele Manin*, ed. F. Planet de la Faye, Venice, 1877, *1*, 295.

68 *Ed. Naz. 35*, 190, 218, 221; *Epistolario di Luigi Carlo Farini*, ed. L. Rava, Bologna, 1911, *3*, 295; Ludmilla Assing, *Vita di Piero Cironi*, Prato, 1865, 47.

69 *Ed. Naz. 38*, 18, 146; Ferdinand Boyer, *La Seconde République et Charles Albert en 1848*, Paris, 1967, 136; Montanelli, *Memorie 2*, 349.

70 *Ed. Naz. 38*, 22.

71 *Ed. Naz. 38*, 74–6.

72 *Ed. Naz. 38*, 25, 154–7, 184.

73 *Ed. Naz. 38*, 165; *ibid. 94*, 254–5.

74 Rodolico, *Carlo Alberto, 3*, 322; Charles MacFarlane, *A Glance at Revolutionized Italy*, London, 1849, *2*, 243; Patetta, 'Lettere', 279; Constance d'Azeglio, *Souvenirs Historiques*, Turin, 1884, 331.

75 *Ed. Naz. 38*, 34; Piero Pieri, *Storia Militare del Risorgimento*, Turin, 1962, 328; G. F.-H. and J. Berkeley, *Italy in the Making: January 1st 1848 to November 16th 1848*, Cambridge, 1940, 325, 391–2.

76 Generale Bava, *Relazione delle Operazioni Militari*, Turin, 1848, 21; *Correspondence, 3*, 121; Casati, *Nuove Rivelazioni, 2*, 336; F. della Peruta, *Democrazia e Socialismo nel Risorgimento*, Rome, 1965, 94–9; *Dublin University Magazine*, Feb. 1849, 207, Charles Lever.

77 Bava, *Relazione*, 116, 132–3; *Lettere di Massimo D'Azeglio a sua Moglie Luisa Blondel*, ed. G. Carcano, Milan, 1870, 375–6; Alfonso La Marmora, *Un Episodio del Risorgimento Italiano*, Florence, 1874, 66.

78 M.B. Honan, *The Personal Adventures of 'Our Correspondent' in Italy*, London, 1852, *1*, 98–9, 267; *ibid. 2*, 6; A. Monti, *Carteggio del Governo Provvisorio di Lombardia con i suoi Rappresentanti al Quartier Generale di Carlo Alberto*, Milan, 1923, 191; Montanelli, *Memorie, 2*, 368; *Revue des Deux Mondes*, 15 Sept. 1848, 801; A. Malvezzi, *Il Risorgimento Italiano in un Carteggio di Patrioti Lombardi*, Milan, 1924, 300; Costa de Beauregard, *Épilogue*, 364–5.

79 Luigi Chiala, *La Vita e i Tempi del Generale Giuseppe Dabormida 1848–9*, Turin, 1896, 434–5; *Ricordi di Michelangelo Castelli 1847–1875*, ed. L. Chiala, 52; *Carteggi di Bettino Ricasoli*, ed. M. Nobili and S. Camerani, Rome, 1945, *3*, 183–4; *Lettere di Carlo Alberto a Ottavio Thaon di Revel*, ed. G. Gentile, Milan, 1931, 130, 150; Patetta, 'Lettere', 279–80.

80 *Lettere di Carlo Alberto a Revel*, 78; Camillo Cavour, *Epistolario*, ed. C. Pischedda, Florence, 1980, *5*, 268; C. Benso di Cavour, *Discorsi Parlamentari*, ed. A. Saitta, Florence, 1969, *14*, 191; V. Gioberti,

Il Saggiatore: Discorso proemiale, Florence, 1849, 8; Luigi Cibrario, Origine e Progressi delle Istituzioni della Monarchia di Savoia, 2nd ed., Florence, 1869, 1, 210.

81 The Spectator, London, 3 Mar. 1849, 198; Ed. Naz. 6, xi; Richards, 1, 92; F. Sardagna, La Battaglia di Milano, 4 Agosto 1848, Modena, 1932, 81.

82 Domus, 1965, 2, 96, Martinola; Ed. Naz. 38, 280–1; Il Risorgimento, Turin, 15 Dec. 1847, 30 July 1848 and 1 Jan. 1849.

83 Nicomede Bianchi, Scritti e Lettere di Carlo Alberto, Turin, 1879, 64–5; L. Marchetti, Il Secondo Ministero Costituzionale di Carlo Alberto, Milan, 1948; 124; Rassegna, Jan. 1924, 143–50, Neri; Marco Minghetti, Miei Ricordi, Turin, 1889, 2, 426; Costa de Beauregard, Les Dernières Années du Roi Charles-Albert, Paris, 1895, 364–5.

84 Giovanni Arrivabene, Memorie della mia Vita, Florence, 1880, 1, 253–4.

85 Giovanni Pasini, Vita del Generale Giacomo Medici, Florence, 1882, 37–8; Visconti Venosta, Ricordi, 143; A. Gori, Milano fra il Cadere del Luglio e l'Entrare dell'Agosto 1848, Rome, 1901, 144–5; Harper's New Monthly Magazine, New York, July 1872, 284.

86 Jessie White Mario, Della Vita di Giuseppe Mazzini, Milan, 1886, 451; Memorie Politiche di Felice Orsini, ed. A. M. Ghisalberti, Rome, 1946, 124; Jasper Ridley, Garibaldi, London, 1974, 252; Giuseppe Garibaldi, Scritti e Discorsi Politici e Militari, Bologna, 1937, 3, 483.

87 A. Bianchi-Giovini, Mazzini e le sue Utopie, Turin, 1849, 23, 45, 61, 67, 74.

88 Ed. Naz. 37, 57, 107; ibid. 38, 276, 284, 290–1.

89 Ed. Naz. 37, 227–8, 238.

90 Ed. Naz. 38, 292.

91 The Spectator, London, 2 Dec. 1848, 1155; Ed. Naz. 17, 299, 309, 338; ibid. 37, 215–16.

92 Luigi Cibrario, Notizie sulla Vita di Carlo Alberto, Turin, 1861, 96; Jules de Bréval, Mazzini Judged by Himself and by his Countrymen, London, 1853, 123–5; Hansard, 104, 969, 30 April 1849, Brougham.

93 J. Crétineau-Joly, L'Église Romaine en Face de la Révolution, Paris, 1859, 2, 445, 449; Father Bresciani, The Jew of Verona: An Historical Tale of the Italian Revolutions of 1848–9, London, 1851, 250.

The Roman Republic

94 The Spectator, 3 Mar. 1849, 200.

95 Rivista Storica del Risorgimento, Turin, 1899, 8, 789, Sforza; F. D. Guerrazzi, Lo Assedio di Roma, Livorno, 1864, 661.

96 Ferdinando Ranalli, Le Istorie Italiane dal 1846 al 1853, Florence, 1855, 3, 194; Niccola Nisco, Storia Civile del Regno D'Italia Scritta per Mandato di Sua Maestà, Naples, 1883, 1, 545.

97 Apologia della Vita Politica di F. D. Guerrazzi, Florence, 1851, 241; Giovanni La Cecilia, Memorie Storico-Politiche, ed. R. Moscati, Varese, 1946, 640; Giuseppe Beghelli, La Repubblica Romana del 1849, Lodi, 1874, 180–6; A. Savelli, Leonardo Romanelli e la Toscana del suo Tempo, Florence, 1941, 71–7.

98 Le Assemblee del Risorgimento: Roma, Rome, 1911, 3, 611, 784; Ed. Naz. 41, 4, 24; Saffi, 13, 55.

99 R. Moscati, La Diplomazia Europea e il Problema Italiano nel 1848, Florence, 1947, 141–2; Le Relazioni Diplomatiche fra la Francia e il Granducato di Toscana, ed. A. Saitta, Rome, 1959, ser. 3 (1848–1860), 1, 170.

100 V. Gioberti, Il Saggiatore, Flor-

ence, 1849, 5; V. Gioberti, *Del Rinnovamento Civile d'Italia*, Paris, 1851, *1*, 482.

101 G. Massari, *Il Conte di Cavour: Ricordi biografici*, Turin, 1873, 43–4; Cavour's newspaper *Il Risorgimento*, Turin, 13 Jan., 16 Jan., 17 Feb. 1849; *FO Confidential Print*, no. 113, pp. 173–6, 18 Feb. 1849, Abercromby; Library of Scotland, MS 3109/189, 15 Aug. 1851, Mazzini; *The Roman Advertiser*, Rome, 17 Feb. 1849, 341.

102 Cavour, *Epistolario*, 5, 296, 386, 388; *ibid.* 6, 44, 72–3; Cavour, *Discorsi Parlamentari*, *1*, xxxvii, Omodeo.

103 *Le Relazioni Diplomatiche fra l'Austria e il Regno di Sardegna e la Guerra del 1848–1849*, ed. A. Filipuzzi, Rome, 1961, *ser. 3, 1*, 417.

104 Bianchi, *Scritti di Carlo Alberto*, 69.

105 *Carteggi di Ricasoli*, 3, 372.

106 Gioberti, *Del Rinnovamento*, *1*, 611.

107 *Le Relazioni Diplomatiche fra la Gran Bretagna e il Regno di Sardegna*, ed. F. Curato, Rome, 1961, *2*, 244, 312; Massimo d'Azeglio, *I Miei Ricordi*, ed. A.M. Ghisalberti, Turin, 1949, 490; Codignola, *Dagli Albori della Libertà*, 632, 652, 665.

108 *Ed. Naz. 38*, 83–5; *ibid. 61*, 236; Rodolico, *Carlo Alberto*, 3, 566.

109 Nassau Senior, *Journals*, 1, 157, 256; Nassau Senior, *Conversations*, 236; *Studi Carlo-Albertini*, 370.

110 Gino Capponi, *Scritti Editi e Inediti*, ed. M. Tabarrini, Florence, 1877, *2*, 73–4; Constance d'Azeglio, *Souvenirs Historiques*, Turin, 1884, 331.

111 *Ed. Naz. 37*, 320; *ibid. 40*, 8; *La Repubblica Veneta nel 1848–49*, Padua, 1949, *2*, 638.

112 Giacomo Adami, *Atto Vannucci: Maestro di umanità e storico moralista*, Prato, 1968, 273.

113 *Le Assemblee: Roma*, 4, 1013; *Ed. Naz. 37*, 309.

114 *Opere di Francesco de Sanctis*, ed. C. Muscetta and G. Candelero, Turin, 1951, *12*, 35, 51–4; G. Gabussi, *Memorie per Servire alla Storia della Rivoluzione degli Stati Romani*, Genoa, 1854, *3*, 523; R. Bonafadini, *Mezzo Secolo di Patriotismo: Saggi storici*, Milan, 1886, 207; Castelli, *Ricordi*, 38; Theodore Dwight, *The Roman Republic of 1849*, New York, 1851, 92–3; Luigi Carlo Farini, *Lo Stato Romano dall'Anno 1815 al 1850*, Florence, 1851, *3*, 313.

115 Daelli, *9*, xiii; Carlo Rusconi, *La Repubblica Romana*, Capolago, 1852, 307; *La Civiltà Cattolica*, Rome, Aug. 1851, 6, 490.

116 Arthur Hugh Clough, *Letters and Remains*, London, 1865, 144–5, 152; Joseph Rossi, *The Image of America in Mazzini's Writings*, Madison, 1954, 71; *The Letters of Margaret Fuller*, ed. Robert Hudspeth, Ithaca, 1983, *5*, 198, 201, 210; *The Writings of Margaret Fuller*, ed. M. Wade, New York, 1941, 539; Horace Greeley, *Recollections of a Busy Life*, New York, 1868, 186.

117 FO 43/45, Freeborn's reports dated 23 Mar. and 6 April 1849; Leo F. Stock, *United States' Ministers to the Papal States 1848–1868*, Washington, 1933, 30, 52; Leo F. Stock, *Consular Relations between the United States and the Papal States*, Washington, 1945, 172–4; Nassau Senior, *Journal*, 1, 145; *ibid.* 2, 137; 181; Clough, *Letters*, 147, 157; *The Spectator*, 14 July 1849, 649; *The Edinburgh Review*, April 1851, 424; *Daily News*, 12 Mar. 1872; Farini, *Lo Stato Romano*, 3, 245; *Illustrated London News*, 14 July 1849, 26; *Quarterly Review*, June 1849, 232; *ibid.* Sept. 1850, 553.

118 Giacomo Martina, *Pio IX (1846–1850)*, Rome, 1974, 333; Farini, *Lo Stato Romano*, 3, 323.

119 *The Times*, 11 June 1849;

Rassegna, April 1970, 226, Laureano.

120 *Gli Ultimi Sessantanove Giorni della Repubblica Romana: Narrazione*, Rome, 1849, 112.

121 *Il Risorgimento*, Turin, 28 Feb. 1849.

122 Clough, *Letters*, 125; Stock, *Consular Relations*, 173; the Consul of Würtemberg, cit. by R. Moscati, *La Diplomazia Europea*, 158–9.

123 P. Pietro Pirri, *Pio IX e Vittorio Emanuele dal loro Carteggio Privato*, Rome, 1944, *1*, 24*; *Il Risorgimento*, Turin, 23 April 1849; Antonio Anzilotti, *Gioberti*, Florence, 1922, 373.

124 Ferdinand de Lesseps, *Recollections of Forty Years*, London, 1887, 27; André Lebey, *Louis-Napoléon Bonaparte et le Ministère Odillon Barrot 1849*, Paris, 1912, 229.

125 Giuseppe Mazzatinti, *Diario Epistolare di Giovita Lazzarini, Ministro di Grazia e Giustizia nella Repubblica Romana*, Rome, 1899, 111; *Saffi*, 3, 288; *Correspondence Respecting the Affairs of Rome: Presented to parliament on 14 April 1851*, 16–17.

126 Jan Philip Koelman, *Memorie Romane*, ed. M. L. Trebiliani, Rome, 1963, *1*, 269–70.

127 Nassau Senior, *Journal*, *1*, 122–4; FO 27/844/231, 8 May 1849, Normanby.

128 Carlo Pisacane, *Guerra Combattuta in Italia negli Anni 1848–49*, ed. Luigi Maino, Rome, 1906, 184–6; Carlo Pisacane, *Scritti Vari Inediti o Rari*, ed. A. Romano, Milan, 1964, 22–3; Jessie White Mario, *Mazzini*, 336; Emilio Dandolo, *The Italian Volunteers and Lombard Rifle Brigade*, London, 1851, 235; E. Morelli, *Giuseppe Mazzini: Saggi e ricerche*, Rome, 1950, 67–8.

129 Cavour, *Epistolario*, 6, 114; *Il Risorgimento*, Turin, 14 May 1849; *Carteggio Politico di Michelangelo Castelli*, ed. L. Chiala, Turin, 1891, *1*, 35, 40.

130 *Ed. Naz. 53*, 161–2; *ibid. 59*, 207; *ibid. 80*, 101; Pisacane, *Scritti*, 260–1; Carlo Pisacane, *Epistolario*, ed. A. Romano, Milan, 1937, 98; Nello Rosselli, *Carlo Pisacane nel Risorgimento Italiano*, Turin, 1932, 81, 86–7; Jack La Bolina, *Cronachette del Risorgimento Italiano*, Florence, 1920, 82; *Goffredo Mameli e i Suoi Tempi*, ed. E. Michel, Venice, 1946, 344–5.

131 Ferdinand de Lesseps, *Réponse de M. F. de Lesseps au Ministère et au Conseil d'État*, Paris, August 1849, 27; *Le Constitutionnel*, Paris, 9 May 1849; A. Balleydier, *Histoire de la Révolution de Rome*, Brussels, 1851, *2*, 108–9; Rusconi, *Memorie*, 146; Stock, *Consular Relations*, 176.

132 Moscati, *La Diplomazia Europea*, 166; Alexis de Tocqueville, *Oeuvres Complètes*, ed. A. Jardin, tome 3, vol. 3, 325–6.

133 De Tocqueville, *ibid.*; Ferdinand de Lesseps, *Ma Mission à Rome*, Paris, 1849, 32, 39; de Lesseps, *Réponse*, 3–4, 39; *The Times*, London, 11 June 1849.

134 De Lesseps, *Réponse*, 17–19; *Ed. Naz. 43*, 5–6; FO 43/45, 19 May 1849, Freeborn's report.

135 FO 43/45, 31 May 1849, Freeborn; *Rivista Storica del Risorgimento*, Turin, Sept. 1895, 168, Mazzatinti; Federico Torre, *Memorie Storiche sull'Intervento Francese in Roma nel 1849*, Turin, 1851, *2*, 111.

136 *Ed. Naz. 40*, 127, 137, 155; *Le Memorie di Garibaldi nella Redazione Definitiva del 1872*, Bologna, 1932, 287–94.

137 Cesare Balbo, *Della Monarchia Rappresentativa in Italia*, Florence, 1857, 93.

138 *Lettere Inedite di Massimo d'Azeglio e F. Gualterio a Tommaso Tommasoni*, Rome, 1885, 154; *Rassegna*, April 1920, 400–4; *Epistolario di*

Luigi Carlo Farini, ed. L. Rava, Bologna, 1911, *3*, 70, 80–2.

139 Cavour, *Epistolario*, *6*, 147–9, 161, 164; *Il Risorgimento*, Turin, issues dated 9 June, 14 June, 19 June 1849.

140 Martina, *Pio IX*, 347.

141 De Tocqueville, *Oeuvres, tome 15, vol. 1*, 292–7; De Courcelles, quoted by Nassau Senior, *Conversations*, *1*, 33.

142 *Ed. Naz. 40*, 182, 245; *ibid. 43*, 171, 177; *ibid. Appendice, 5*, 181–3.

143 *Correspondence and Conversations of Alexis de Tocqueville with Nassau William Senior from 1834 to 1859*, London, 1872, *1*, 236.

144 *The Gladstone Diaries*, ed. R. M. D. Foot and H. C. G. Matthew, Oxford, 1974, *4*, 138.

145 De Tocqueville, *Oeuvres, tome 3, vol. 3*, 323, 328, 335.

146 *Ibid.* 328–9; Moscati, *La Diplomazia*, 179; Clough, *Letters*, 162; C. Augusto Vecchi, *Storia di Due Anni 1848–1849*, Turin, 1856, *2*, 301; Stock, *Consular Relations*, 369; *Edinburgh Review*, April 1851, 552–3; *The Spectator*, London, 14 July 1849, 659.

147 Farini, *Lo Stato Romano*, *4*, 233; Moscati, *La Diplomazia*, 181–2; *Gli Ultimi Giorni*, 112.

148 De Tocqueville, *Oeuvres, tome 15, vol. 1*, 305–17; *Epistolario di Farini*, ed. L. Rava, *3*, 63; *FO Confidential Print*, no. 277, 18 Jan. 1853, Henry Bulwer; *Edinburgh Review*, April 1851, 525–6; *The Democratic Review*, London, Nov. 1849, 226.

149 *La Politica di Massimo d'Azeglio dal 1848 al 1859*, ed. Nicomede Bianchi, Turin, 1884, 195.

150 Farini, *Lo Stato Romano*, *4*, 260, 281–2, 301–2; Story, *Roba di Roma 2*, 64, 201; Vecchi, *Storia di Due Anni*, *2*, 262–3; *Ed. Naz. 39*, 109, 146–50; *Rivista Contemporanea*, Turin, Jan. 1857, 8.

151 Nassau Senior, *Journal*, *1*, 145;

Correspondence of De Tocqueville with Senior, *1*, 239; Royal Archives, Windsor, J.9/108, despatch of 11 July 1849; *Il Risorgimento Italiano*, Turin, June 1909, 578, Casati; *Edinburgh Review*, April 1851, 515, 524; *Fortnightly Review*, Oct. 1877, 554–5; *Bentley's Miscellany*, London, Sept. 1850, 304.

152 James Stansfeld, *The Italian Movement and Italian Parties*, London, 1862, 24; Jules Michelet, *Journal*, Paris, 1862, *2*, 76; General Schönhals, *Erinnerungen eines Oesterreichischen Veteranen*, Stuttgart, 1952, *1*, 25.

153 J.A. Froude, *Thomas Carlyle: A History of his Life in London*, London, 1885, *1*, 454, 488; F.P. Perrens, *Deux Ans de Révolution en Italie (1848–49)*, Paris, 1857, 116, 124–5; *Westminster Review*, April 1850, 82–4; *Edinburgh Review*, April 1852, 384; *Letters and Memorials of Catherine Winkworth*, Clifton, 1883, *1*, 177–8 (quoting Mrs Gaskell); *The Letters of Dickens*, *5*, 579; *The Life of Edward Bulwer Lytton*, by his grandson, London, 1913, *2*, 127; *The Economist*, 16 Mar. 1872, 323–4; Moritz Hartmann, *Gesammelte Werke*, Stuttgart, 1874, *10*, 167–70.

154 Franco Della Peruta, *I Democratici e la Rivoluzione Italiana*, Milan, 1958, 12; *Il Carteggio Cavour-Nigra*, Bologna, 1926, *2*, 265; Andrea Giannelli, *Aneddoti Ignorati ed Importanti: brevi ricordi Mazziniani dal 1848 al 1872*, Florence, 1905, 17–18.

155 C. de Cavour, *Lettere Edite ed Inedite*, ed. Luigi Chiala, Turin, 1884, *1*, 419.

156 Gioberti, *Del Rinnovamento*, 1851, *1*, 478–9, 506.

157 C. Antonelli d'Oulx, *Al Servizio di Quattro Re, 1808–1894*, Turin, 1951, 118–19; Camillo di Cavour, *Scritti Inediti e Rari, 1828–1850*, ed. R. Romeo, Santena,

1971, 174–5; N. Bianchi, *Vicende del Mazzinianismo Politico e Religioso dal 1832 al 1854*, Savona, 1854, 201; *Memorie di Giorgio Pallavicino*, ed. by his wife, Turin, 1886, *2*, 113–14; *Lettere di d'Azeglio a Tommasoni*, 165; Capponi, *Scritti*, *2*, 208; De Bréval, *Mazzini Judged by Himself*, 115.

158 Massimo d'Azeglio, *Scritti e Discorsi Politici*, ed. M. de Rubris, Florence, 1936, *2*, 58–60; 167; Massimo d'Azeglio, *Timori e Speranze*, Turin, 1848, 8, 13–17; N. Bianchi, *La Politica di Massimo d'Azeglio dal 1848 al 1859: Documenti*, Turin, 1884, 39.

159 *Camera dei Deputati, Discussioni*, 10 Sept. 1849, 375–80; *Rassegna*, April 1920, 400–4; Francesco Poggi, *L'Emigrazione Politica in Genoa ed in Liguria dal 1848 al 1857*, Modena, 1957, 259–64; C. Cavour, *Nouvelles Lettres Inédites*, ed. A. Bert, Turin, 1889, 335.

160 Lamarmora, *Un Episodio*, 116.

161 Pirri, *Pio IX e Vittorio Emanuele*, *1*, 4; *Journal of Modern History*, Chicago, June 1935, 163–8, Smyth; *Carteggi di Ricasoli*, *3*, 371; *Rassegna*, 1950, *4*, 530, Vidal; Antonio Monti, *La Giovinezza di Vittorio Emanuele II (1829–1849)*, Milan, 1939, 508.

162 *Le Relazioni Diplomatiche fra l'Austria e il Regno di Sardegna, 1848–1860*, ed. F. Valsecchi, *ser. 3, 3*, 60, 79–82; *Le Relazioni Diplomatiche fra lo Stato Pontificio e la Francia*, ed. M. Bettoni, Rome, 1976, *Ser. 3, 3*, 146; *Politica d'Azeglio*, ed. Bianchi, 89–90; *Archivio Veneto*, Venice, 1959, *65*, 94, Gambarin.

CHAPTER FOUR. *Further Conspiracies after 1850*

Back to the drawing board

1 *Ed. Naz. 39*, 191; *ibid. 42*, 52; *ibid. 46*, 15 (the original, before translation and longer, is in privately owned Stansfeld Papers).

2 Daelli, *9*. xviii.

3 *Revue Roumaine d'Histoire*, Bucharest, Oct. 1972, 972, Netea.

4 Alexander Herzen, *My Past and Thoughts*, ed. C. Garnet and H. Higgens, London, 1968, *2*, 694–5; *Italia e Inghilterra nella Prima Fase del Risorgimento*, ed. E. Morelli and F. Venturi, Rome, 1952, 34; F. Della Peruta, *I Democratici e la Rivoluzione Italiana all'Indomani del 1848*, Milan, 1958, 455; *Autour d'Alexandre Herzen: Documents inédits*, ed. M. Vuilleumier, Geneva, 1973, 33.

5 *Ed. Naz. 39*, 221; *ibid. 42*, 213; *ibid. 44*, 79.

6 Camillo Cavour, *Epistolario*, ed. R. Roccia, Bologna, 1982, 7, 315; Schweizerisches Bundesarchiv E. 21/139–41.

7 Massimo d'Azeglio, *Scritti e Discorsi Politici*, ed. M. de Rubris, Florence, 1936, *2*, 55–7, 108–9; *La Politica di Massimo d'Azeglio dal 1848 al 1859: documenti*, ed. N. Bianchi, Turin, 1884, 198.

8 *Rassegna*, July 1930, 781, 792–5, Pirano; Giorgio Asproni, *Diario Politico*, ed. B. Josto Anedda, C. Sole and T. Orrù, Milan, 1982, *5*, 401; *The Democratic Review*, London, June 1850, 55; *Ed. Naz. 42*, 69–72, 100–3.

9 *Le Relazioni Diplomatiche fra l'Austria e il Regno di Sardegna 1848–1860*, ed. F. Valsecchi, *ser. 3, 3*, 82; H. Bessler, *La France e la Suisse de 1848 à 1852*, Neuchâtel, 1930, 293; *Diplomatische Dokumente Der Schweiz*, Berne, 1990, *I*, 137, 140; Schweizer-isches Bundesarchiv, E. 21/139, 30 Jan. 1850.

10 *Ed. Naz. 44*, 217–18.

11 *Ed. Naz. 44*, 315; *ibid. 45*, 59; *ibid. 47*, 145; *Le Relazioni Diplomatiche fra la Francia e il Granducato di Toscana*, ed. A. Saitta, Rome, 1959, *ser. 3, 1*, 365; *ibid. 2*, 70; *Le*

Relazioni Diplomatiche fra l'Austria e il Granducato di Toscana, ed. A. Filipuzzi, *ser. 3, 2,* 373, 424; *Le Relazioni Diplomatiche fra lo Stato Pontificio e la Francia*, ed. M. Bettoni, *ser. 3, 3,* Rome 1976, 147.

12 Giovanni Visconti Venosta, *Ricordi di Gioventù*, Milan, 1904, 197; Rinaldo Caddeo, *La Tipografia Elvetica di Capolago 1830–1853*, Milan, 1931, 481; *Il Risorgimento Italiano*, Turin, 1913, 368.

13 *Epistolario di Carlo Cattaneo*, ed. R. Caddeo, Florence, 1954, *2,* 44–5; F. Spatafora, *Il Comitato d'Azione di Roma dal 1862 al 1867*, ed. A. Isastia, Pisa, 1982, *1,* 81; *Ed. Naz. 51,* 23.

14 *Ed. Naz. 42,* 166; *ibid. 44,* 351; F. Brancato, in *Democrazia e Mazzinianesimo nel Mezzogiorno d'Italia 1831–1872*, Geneva, 1975, 257–9.

15 M. Cassetti, *Le Carte di Alfonso Ferrero Della Marmora*, Turin, 1979, 482.

16 *Rassegna*, July 1941, 488–94, Morelli.

17 *Rassegna*, Oct. 1924, 841–3, Casanova; *Rassegna*, Jan. 1926, 93, 103, Casanova; *Lettere di Rosalino Pilo*, ed. G. Falzone, Rome, 1972, 76; *Ed. Naz. 47,* 87–8.

18 *Ed. Naz. 42,* 246–7, 256; *ibid. 43,* 223.

19 Luigi Carlo Farini, *Lo Stato Romano dall'Anno 1815 al 1850*, Florence, 1851, *3,* 322; Vincenzo Gioberti, *Epistolario*, ed. G. Gentile, Florence, 1937, *10,* 155.

20 Nassau Senior, *Journals kept in France and Italy from 1848 to 1852*, London, 1871, *1,* 309, 341; *Carteggi e Documenti Diplomatici Inediti di Emanuele d'Azeglio*, ed. A. Colombo, Turin, 1920, *1,* 51; *Quarterly Review*, London, June 1848, 236.

21 FO 79/187, 23 Aug. 1856.

22 *The Letters of Robert Browning 1845–1846*, ed. E. Kinter, Cambridge, 1969, 278; *Letters of*

Charles Eliot Norton, ed. S. Norton and M. A. De Wolfe Howe, London, 1913, 75–6; Charles Eliot Norton, *Considerations on some Recent Social Theories*, Boston, 1853, 10.

23 *Ed. Naz. 39,* 304; *ibid. 42,* 154; *ibid. 45,* 167–9.

24 *Ed. Naz. 46,* 117.

25 *Ed. Naz. 43,* 245; *Life of Frances Cobbe as told by herself*, London, 1904, 367–8.

26 *Ed. Naz. 38,* 133; *ibid. 43,* 248, 254–8.

27 *Relazioni Diplomatiche*, ed. Valsecchi, *ser. 3, 4,* 26.

28 *Ed. Naz. 45,* 119.

29 Constance d'Azeglio, *Souvenirs Historiques*, Turin, 1884, 425; Della Peruta, *I Democratici*, 350–2.

30 *Relazioni Diplomatiche*, ed. Filipuzzi, *2,* 452–3; *Relazioni Diplomatiche*, ed. Saitta, *1,* 370; *ibid. 2,* 84, 224; A. Giannelli, *Aneddoti Ignorati ed Importanti*, Florence, 1905, 14–18; *The Spectator*, London, 2 July 1851, 657.

31 Eugenio Kastner, *Mazzini e Kossuth: Lettere e documenti inediti*, Florence, 1929, 143–5.

32 C. Cagnacci, *Giuseppe Mazzini e i Fratelli Ruffini*, Porto Maurizio, 1893, 369; Nicomede Bianchi, *Vicende del Mazzinianismo Politico e Religioso dal 1832 al 1854*, Savona, 1854, 210; *The Times*, 15 May 1851; *Memorie Politiche di Felice Orsini*, ed. A. Franchi, Lugano, 1860, 288; *Memorie di Giorgio Pallavicino*, Turin, 1886, *2,* 382.

33 *Ed. Naz. 47,* 52–3; *ibid. 48,* 29; *ibid. Appendice, 4,* 140–1.

34 *Ed. Naz. 39,* 343; *ibid. 46,* 103, 131–2; *ibid. 49,* 256; Domus, 1968, *1,* 192, Terenzio Grandi.

35 *Ed. Naz. 46,* 104.

36 Karl Marx and Frederick Engels, *Collected Works*, London, 1982, *38,* 459; *Le Relazioni Diplomatiche*, ed. Bettoni, *ser. 3, 3,* 190.

37 V. Gioberti, *Il Piemonte nel 1850–2: Lettere di Vincenzo Gioberti e*

Giorgio Pallavicino, ed. B.E. Maineri, Milan, 1875, 157; Giacomo Adami, *Atto Vannucci*, Prato, 1968, 269.

38 *Epistolario di Nino Bixio*, ed. E. Morelli, Rome, 1939, *1*, 53.

39 *Ed. Naz. 45*, 252; *ibid. 46*, 159; *ibid. 47*, 102–4; Spatafora, *Il Comitato d'Azione, 1*, 59; Nassau Senior, *Journal, 2*, 182; Ettore Montecchi, *Mattia Montecchi nel Risorgimento Italiano*, Rome, 1932, 107; Domus, 1968, *1*, 191, Terenzio Grandi; Howard Payne, *The Police State of Napoleon Bonaparte 1851–1860*, Seattle, 1966, 47.

40 Gioberti, *Il Piemonte*, 186; Cavour, *Lettere*, ed. Chiala, *1*, 542; *Carteggi di Emanuele d'Azeglio*, ed. A. Colombo, Turin, 1920, *1*, 257.

41 Ferdinand Lassalle, *Nachgelassene Briefe und Schriften*, ed. G. Mayer, Stuttgart, 1925, *5*, 101.

42 *The Reasoner*, London, 14 and 21 April, 12 and 19 May 1852.

43 *Ed. Naz. 44*, 162–3; *ibid. 47*, 109.

44 *La Civiltà Cattolica*, Rome, April 1850, 108; F. A. Gualterio, *Gli Ultimi Rivolgimenti Italiani*, Florence, 1850–1, *1*, 639; *Le Relazioni Diplomatiche fra la Gran Bretagna e il Regno di Sardegna*, ed. Federico Curato, Rome, 1966, *ser. 3, 3*, 42; *Le Relazioni Diplomatiche*, ed. Valsecchi, *3*, 60; R. Ciampini, *Gian Pietro Vieusseux*, Turin, 1953, 434; *Hansard, 120*, 522, 1 April 1852, Cochrane; R. Barbiera, *Passioni del Risorgimento: con documenti inediti*, Milan, 1929, 122.

45 Della Peruta, *I Democratici*, 283–5; *Correspondance de P.-J.P. Proudhon*, Paris, 1875, *4*, 262–5; Maurice Dommanget, *Auguste Blanqui à Belle-Ile (1850–1857)*, Paris, 1935, 179, 186.

46 Benedetto Musolino, *Giuseppe Mazzini e i Rivoluzionari Italiani*, ed. P. Alatri, Cosenza, 1982, *1*,

59–60, 491, 522–4, 657; *Studi Storici*, July 1960, 727, Berti.

47 Marx and Engels, *Collected Works*, *38*, 454–5; *ibid. 39*, 47, 73.

48 *Ed. Naz. 34*, 207–10, 217–20, 223, 240–1; *ibid. 36*, 102–3; *ibid. 46*, 210.

49 *Ed. Naz. 36*, 89; *ibid. 62*, 364.

50 *Ed. Naz. 34*, 203–6; *ibid. 36*, 99–100.

51 *Ed. Naz. 34*, 160, 165, 184, 206; *ibid. 46*, 255–6.

52 *Ed. Naz. 46*, 210, 253; *ibid. 47*, 228–9.

53 *Ed. Naz. 46*, 76–7, 141, 185; Rodolfo Mondolfo, *Sulle Orme di Marx*, Rocca S. Casciano, 1923, *2*, 129–30.

54 *Ed. Naz. 34*, 92–3, 104–5; *ibid. 46*, 129, 170, 247; *ibid. 51*, 41; *Westminster Review*, London, April 1850, 455.

55 Farini, *Lo Stato Romano, 3*, 275–6.

56 *Movimento Operaio*, Milan, July 1953, 573–5, Della Peruta.

57 Marx and Engels, *Collected Works*, *38*, 454–5.

58 R. Pierantoni, *Storia dei Fratelli Bandiera*, Milan, 1909, 96; *The Life and Letters of Benjamin Jowett*, ed. E. Abbott and L. Campbell, London, 1897, *2*, 11–12.

Friends in Britain

59 *British Quarterly Review*, London, Dec. 1851, 243, 253.

60 *Westminster Review*, April 1852, 466–7; *The George Eliot Letters*, ed. Gordon Haight, London, 1954, *2*, 5.

61 *Hansard, 111*, 739, 22 June 1849; *Hansard, 116*, 771–2, 9 May 1851; *Hansard, 122*, 667, 14 June 1852; E. Ashley, *The Life of Henry John Temple Viscount Palmerston*, London, 1876, *1*, 126–7; A. Luzio, *I Martiri di Belfiore e il loro Processo*, Milan, 1925, 257; W. E. Gladstone, *Gleanings of Past Years 1851–1877*, London, 1879, *4*, 176; FO Confidential Print, no. 193,

14 Jan. 1850, Abercromby; *The Autobiography of Leigh Hunt*, London, 1860, 389–90; William Arthur, *Italy in Transition*, London, 1860, 204.

62 *British Quarterly Review*, London, Feb. 1851, 192; *The Examiner*, London, 22 Sept. 1849, 597, Landor; *Daily News*, London, 9 Nov. 1850; *Edinburgh Review*, April. 1851, 515; *North British Review*, Edinburgh, May 1853, 208, Masson; *Illustrated London News*, 12 May 1849, 312; *The Spectator*, 29 Mar. 1851, 302; *Hansard, 120*, 491–2, 511–12, 1 April 1852; *Correspondence Respecting Foreign Refugees in London*, 1852, 1, 14, 17–18, 24–5; *Further Correspondence Respecting Foreign Refugees in London*, 29 Mar. 1852, 7; *The Letters of Elizabeth Barrett Browning*, ed. F. E. Kenyon, London, 1897, 109, 117; *Ed. Naz. 45*, 318–19.

63 Emilia Morelli, *L'Inghilterra di Mazzini*, Rome, 1965, 101–2; *The Letters of Charles Dickens*, ed. M. House and G. Storey, Oxford, 1981, *5*, 579, 598–600; *The Dickensian*, London, Dec. 1914, 319–20; *The Letters and Private Papers of William Makepeace Thackeray*, ed. Gordon Ray, London, 1945, *2*, 775.

64 *The Times*, 16 May and 20 June 1851; *Hansard*, House of Lords, *104*, 968–70, 30 April 1849; *Royal Archives Windsor*, J.5, 7 Oct. 1848, to Earl Russell; Lord Brougham, *Letters to the Marquess of Landsdowne on the late Revolution in France*, London, 1849, 129–31; Earl of Mount Edgecombe, *Extracts of a Journal kept during the Roman Revolution*, London, 1849, 50–1; *Ed. Naz. 45*, 265–6, 269; *New Monthly Magazine*, London, Dec. 1849, 385.

65 *The Autobiography of Mrs Fletcher of Edinburgh*, Carlisle, 1874, 256.

66 Margaret J. Shaen, *Memorials of Two Sisters: Susanna and Catherine Winkworth*, London, 1908, 59–60.

67 Herzen, *My Past*, 2, 697; *Autour d'Alexandre Herzen*, ed. M. Vuilleumier, 33.

68 Adolf Friedrich von Schack, *Joseph Mazzini und die Italienische Einheit*, Stuttgart, 1891, v–vi, 56–7; *British Quarterly Review*, Feb. 1851, 192; David Masson, *Memories of London*, Edinburgh, 1908, 205–6.

69 Richard Renton, *John Forster and His Friendships*, London, 1912, 41–2; Goldwin Smith, *Reminiscences*, ed. A. Haultain, New York, 1910, 96, 155.

70 Moritz Hartmann, *Gesammelte Werke*, Stuttgart, 1874, *10*, 167–9.

71 *The Reminiscences of Carl Schurz*, London, 1909, *1*, 380–2; S. Gwynn and C. M. Tuckwell, *The Life of the Rt Hon. Sir Charles Dilke*, London, 1917, 2, 542.

72 *Letters and Memorials of Jane Welsh Carlyle*, ed. Thomas Carlyle and J. A. Froude, London, 1883, *1*, 338, 354; *New Letters and Memorials of Jane Welsh Carlyle*, ed. Alexander Carlyle, London, 1943, 2, 39; *The Letters of Elizabeth Barrett Browning to Mary Russell-Mitford, 1836–1854*, ed. M. B. Raymond and M. R. Sullivan, Winfield, 1983, *3*, 330, 364.

73 *The Correspondence of Thomas Carlyle and Ralph Waldo Emerson, 1834–72*, ed. C. E. Norton, London, 1883, 2, 199; David Alex Wilson, *Carlyle at His Zenith (1845–53)*, London, 1927, 473.

74 Wilson, *Carlyle at His Zenith*, 92, 299; *Jane Welsh Carlyle: Letters to Her Family, 1839–1863*, ed. L. Huxley, London, 1924, 344–5; *New Letters of Jane Carlyle, 2*, 33; B. and H. Wedgwood, *The Wedgwood Circle 1739–1897*, London, 1980, 248; Sir Charles Gavan Duffy, *Conversations with Carlyle*, London, 1892, 109.

75 Carlo Pisacane, *Epistolario*, ed. A. Romano, Milan, 1937, 148;

Giuseppe Mazzini: Notizie tratte dalle carte di Pietro Cironi, ed. G. Baccini, Florence, 1901, 153–6; La Rivista d'Italia, Rome, 1905, 9; Jessie White Mario, Birth of Modern Italy, London, 1909, 238; Ed. Naz. 47, 372–3.

76 Stansfeld Papers, undated note; Malvida von Meysenbug, Der Lebensabend einer Idealistin, Berlin, 1922, 2, 83; Elizabeth Adams Daniels, Jessie White Mario: Risorgimento Revolutionary, Athens, Ohio, 1972, 35; Ed. Naz. 42, 178; ibid. 91, 206.

77 Ed. Naz. 45, 154–5; The Century Illustrated Monthly Magazine, New York, Nov. 1891, 67–8.

78 Bodleian Library, MS, Eng. Lett. d.486, 26 Feb. 1855, Emilie to Linda White; Richards, 2, 13.

79 Domenico Giuriati, Memorie d'Emigrazione a Torino (1848– 1866), Milan, 1897, 237; Ed. Naz. 50, 107; Enrico Montazio, Giuseppe Mazzini, Turin, 1862, 64.

80 The Cornhill Magazine, London, July 1903, 97; H. E. Litchfield, Emma Darwin: A Century of Family Letters, Cambridge, 1904, 2, 154.

81 Macmillan's Magazine, April 1872, 519.

82 The Reasoner, 14 Nov. 1849, 305; The Life of Peter Stuart, the Ditton Doctor, London, 1920, 33; J. M. Wheeler, A Biographical Dictionary of Freethinkers, London, 1889, 355.

83 The Reasoner, 29 Nov. 1848, 428; Giacomo Adami, Piero Cironi, Dibattiti e Contrasti per la Libertà Nazionale, Florence, 1962, 158.

84 Carteggi di Emanuele d'Azeglio, ed. A. Colombo, 1, 364; Le Relazioni Diplomatiche fra Sardegna e Gran Bretagna, ed. F. Curato, Rome, 1964, 4, 176.

85 Daelli, 9, lxxxviii; Ed. Naz. 56, 141; ibid. Appendice, 6, 129; Tyne and Wear archives (Newcastle), MS 634, A.659; Civiltà Cattolica, April 1851, 5, 242–3.

86 Luigi Carlo Farini, The Roman State from 1815 to 1850, London, 1851, 1, xi, introduction by Gladstone the translator.

87 English Historical Review, London, July 1970, 481, Schreuder; Gladstone, Gleanings, 4, 113.

88 Ibid. 119; Hansard, 161, 1576–7, 7 Mar. 1861; Hansard, 174, 279, 17 Mar. 1864.

89 Ed. Naz. 46, 189; ibid. 62, 344; ibid. 69, 216–17; Lord Vernon, Osservazioni intorno alle Carceri di Sardegna, Turin, 1851, 3–13; Camera dei Deputati Discussioni, 21 Sept. 1849, 516; Lettere ad Antonio Panizzi di Uomini illustri e di Amici Italiani, ed. L. Fagan, Florence, 1880, 461; C. Benso di Cavour, Discorsi Parlamentari, Florence, 1957–69, ed. A. Saitta, 11, 298; ibid. 14, 570–80.

90 Morelli, L'Inghilterra, 113–15; Atlantic Monthly, Boston, Spring 1969, 243, Gossman; Rassegna, Jan. 1961, 31–6, Rothney; Diary of the Late John Epps, London, 1875, 483; Litchfield, Darwin, 2, 154; Contemporary Review, London, Oct. 1916, 447–8, Flora Masson.

91 A. Dallolio, Cospirazioni e Cospiratori, 1852–1856, Bologna, 1913, 46–7.

92 Weekly Chronicle, London, 11 Feb. 1852; La Politica di Massimo d'Azeglio: Documenti, ed. N. Bianchi, 183; Horace Greeley, Glances at Europe during the Summer of 1851, New York, 1851, 212; Ed. Naz. 47, 199; other documents in Ed. Naz. 46, and fuller texts in the original English are in Stansfeld Papers.

93 Atlantic Monthly, Boston, Spring 1969, 244, Gossman.

94 Nello Rosselli, Carlo Pisacane nel Risorgimento Italiano, Turin, 1932, 369; The Reasoner, 10 Nov. 1852; Herzen, My Past, 3, 1143; Epps, Diary, 510; Rassegna, Jan. 1964, 12, Mackay; George Holyoake,

Bygones Worth Remembering, London, 1905, *1*, 209–11; Address book in Stansfeld Papers; *Ed. Naz. 48*, 21, 88; ibid. *Appendice*, 4, 109–10.

95 *Ed. Naz. 42*, 323; ibid. *47*, 396; ibid. *53*, 348; ibid. *Appendice*, 4, 240; *Montecchi nel Risorgimento* 185; Jessie White Mario, introduction to *Scritti Scelti di Giuseppe Mazzini*, Florence, 1901, xlvi; Moncure Daniel Conway, *Autobiography*, London, 1904, *2*, 59.

Insurrections: 1853

96 *Atti del Convegno sul Tema 'Mazzini e l'Europa'*, Rome (Accademia dei Lincei), 1972, R. Blaas, 72–3; Alessandro Luzio, *Felice Orsini*, Milan, 1914, 91.

97 Comte de Ficquelmont, *Lord Palmerston, L'Angleterre et le Continent*, Paris, 1852, *1*, 81.

98 Luzio, *I Martiri di Belfiore*, 50; *Rivista Storica del Risorgimento*, 1897, 7, 602–4, Bargoni; Daelli, *9*, xxii; E. Tivaroni, *Storia degli Italiani, 1849–1859*, Turin, 1895, *1*, 10.

99 *Ed. Naz. 51*, 142; Alexis de Tocqueville, *Nouvelle Correspondance*, Paris, 1866, 7, 256; FO Confidential Print no. 277, 5, 31 Jan. 1853, Bulwer; *Revue des Deux Mondes*, 15 Sept. 1852, 1210; *The Spectator*, 29 Mar. 1851, 302–3.

100 *Relazioni Diplomatiche*, ed. Saitta, 2, 224; *Rassegna*, July 1991, 313, Schiavo; Ludmilla Assing, *Vita di Piero Cironi*, Prato, 1865, 63.

101 *Ed. Naz. 46*, 298; Daelli, *9*, xxii; *Rivista Storica del Risorgimento*, Dec. 1896, 837–43, Pognisi; *Il Risorgimento Italiano*, June 1909, 584, Casati; *Dublin Review*, Spring 1959, 42, Randall; *The Spectator*, 30 Oct. 1852, 1041; *Hansard*, 10 Aug. 1855, 2114, Palmerston.

102 Silvio Spaventa, *Dal 1848 al 1861*, ed. B. Croce, Naples, 1898, 48; Cesare Cantù, *Alcuni Italiani Contemporanei*, Milan, 1870, *2*, 214; *Corriere della Sera*, 14 Sept. 1928, Luzio; Tullio Tazzoli, *Don Enrico Tazzoli e i Suoi Tempi*, Bergamo, 1960, 485, 501; *Ed. Naz. 48*, 82.

103 *Edinburgh Review*, Jan. 1861, 253; Asproni, *Diario Politico*, 5, 566; *Ed. Naz. 42*, 194; ibid. *44*, 106; ibid. *45*, 253.

104 *Rivista d'Italia*, June 1905, 958, 972–5; Giovanni Cadolini, *Memorie del Risorgimento dal 1848 al 1862*, Milan, 1911, 241–5; Herzen, *My Past*, 3, 1030–1; Alessandro Galante Garrone, *I Radicali in Italia (1849–1925)*, Milan, 1973, 30–1.

105 Leo Pollini, *Mazzini e la Rivoluzione Milanese del 6 Febbraio 1853*, Milan, 1930, 82–3; A. Luzio, *Profili Biografici e Bozzetti Storici*, Milan, 1906, *2*, 153; F. W. Newman, *Reminiscences of Two Exiles*, London, 1888, 39; I. G. Sieveking, *Memoir and Letters of Francis W. Newman*, London, 1909, 148–9.

106 Saffi, *13*, 79; J. W. Mario, *Birth of Modern Italy*, 241.

107 *Ed. Naz. 47*, 299; ibid. *48*, 292–7; ibid. *77*, 381; *Lettere di Rosalino Pilo*, ed. G. Falzone, Rome, 1972, 199–200; Gaspare Finali, *Memorie*, ed. G. Maioli, Faenza, 1955, 67–8.

108 *Ed. Naz. 48*, 60, 234–6; Daelli, *9*, xliv, xlix; F. Crispi, *I Doveri del Gabinetto del 25 Marzo*, Rome, 1876, 48; Domus, 1968, *1*, 195; *Rassegna*, Oct. 1952, 629, Librino; A. Dallolio, *Cospirazioni e Cospiratori*, Bologna, 1913, 25.

109 *The Harney Papers*, ed. F. G. Black and R. M. Black, Assen, 1969, 55–6.

110 *Ed. Naz. 47*, 360–1; ibid. *48*, 149–50.

111 *Rivista Storica del Risorgimento*, 1897, 7, 618–20, Bargoni.

112 *Ed. Naz. 48*, 129–30, 194–5; Saffi, 4, 37–8; Pollini, *Mazzini e la*

Rivoluzione Milanese, 39–40, 81, 187–8; *L'Emigrazione Politica in Genoa ed in Liguria dal 1848 al 1857,* Modena, 1957, *3,* 535, Barberis; F. Della Peruta, *I Democratici e la Rivoluzione Italiana,* Milan, 1958, 394–5.

113 Ferdinando Ranalli, *Le Istorie Italiane dal 1846 al 1853,* Florence, 1855, *3,* 252.

114 Visconti Venosta, *Ricordi,* 241.

115 Daelli, *9,* li–lii; *Ed. Naz. 48,* 207–8; Luigi Polo Friz, 'Ludovico Frapolli e Giuseppe Mazzini', in Domus, 1979, *2,* 154.

116 Domus, 1959, *2,* 47; Alessandro Luzio, *Studi e Bozzetti di Storia Letteraria e Politica,* Milan, 1910, *2,* 175.

117 N. Bianchi, *Storia Documentata della Diplomazia Europea in Italia dall'Anno 1814 all'Anno 1861,* Turin, 1872, *7,* 127–8; *Corriere della Sera,* 14 Sept. 1928, Luzio; Adolfo Omodeo, *L'Opera Politica del Conte di Cavour,* Florence, 1940, *1,* 249; *Le Relazioni Diplomatiche fra la Grande Bretagna e il Regno di Sardegna,* ed. F. Curato, *ser. 3, 4,* 152–3; *Le Relazioni Diplomatiche,* ed. Valsecchi, *ser. 3, 4,* 46, 65.

118 *Le Relazioni Diplomatiche,* ed. Valsecchi, *ser. 3,* 76; *Le Lettere di Vittorio Emanuele II,* ed. Francesco Cognasso, Turin, 1966, *1,* 407–8.

119 *Westminster Review,* Jan. 1857, 130.

120 *Ed. Naz. 48,* 256, 269.

121 Pollini, *Mazzini e la Rivoluzione Milanese,* 113, 119.

122 Cesare Cantù, *Della Indipendenza Italiana: Cronistoria,* Turin, 1876, *3,* 42; *Ed. Naz. 48,* 274–5.

123 *Il Regno di Sardegna nel 1848 nei Carteggi di Domenico Buffa,* ed. E. Costa, Rome, 1970, 9; *Carteggio Politico Inedito di Michelangelo Castelli con Domenico Buffa (1851–1858),* ed. E. Costa, Santena, 1968, 98, 118.

124 J. de Bréval, *Mazzini Judged by Himself and by his Countrymen,* London, 1853, 229–30.

125 *The Times,* 22 Feb. 1853; *The Friends of Italy: Monthly Record,* no. 23, June 1853, 3; *Blackwoods Edinburgh Magazine,* Mar. 1853, 366, 369.

126 Royal Archives, Windsor, Diary of Queen Victoria for 6, 11 and 18 March 1853; *The Letters of Queen Victoria (1837–1861),* ed. A. C. Benson and Viscount Esher, London, 1907, *2,* 535; *The Times,* 22 and 28 Feb. and 5 Mar. 1853; *Hansard, 126,* 1162, 5 May 1853, Russell.

127 *Ed. Naz. 39,* 240; *ibid. 49,* 100, 195.

128 Clarendon Papers, Bodleian Library, Oxford, Dep. c. 212, 27 Feb. 1853, Hudson; Luzio, *Profili, 1,* 292.

129 *Ed. Naz. 26,* 265; *Cosmopolis: An International Review,* London, June 1897, 662, Moscheles; M. J. Shaen, *Memorials of Two Sisters,* London, 1908, 104; Richards, *1,* 127; *Review of Reviews,* June 1895, 511; C. Bollea, *Una Silloge di Lettere del Risorgimento (1839–1873),* Turin, 1919, 102–3; *Giuseppe Mazzini: Notizie tratte dalle carte di Pietro Cironi,* Florence, 1901, 65.

130 *Carteggio Castelli-Buffa,* 149.

131 *Ed. Naz. 48,* 271, 276, 313; *ibid. 49,* 225.

132 *Ed. Naz. 48,* 314–15, 392; *ibid. 49,* 34.

133 Royal Archives, Windsor, J. 12/14, 22 Mar. 1853, Sir William Temple.

134 *Ed. Naz. 48,* 395–6; *ibid. 51,* 66–7; *ibid. 77,* 382–3; Domus, 1968, *1,* 196, Grandi; G. Spadolini, *Autunno del Risorgimento,* Florence, 1971, 154–5; *Corriere della Sera,* 14 Sept. 1928, Luzio.

135 Marx and Engels, *Collected Works, 11,* 536; *ibid. 23,* 162; Alessandro Luzio, *Carlo Alberto e Giuseppe Mazzini,* Turin, 1923, 234–5; A.

Omodeo, introduction to Giuseppe Mazzini, *Scritti Scelti*, Milan, 1934, 15; Alessandro Levi, *Mazzini*, Florence, 1955, 162–3; *The Letters of Thomas Babington Macaulay*, ed. T. Pinney, Cambridge, 1981, 5, 359.

136 F. Bunsen, *A Memoir of Baron Bunsen*, London, 1868, 296–7.

137 Giuseppe Berti, *I Democratici e l'Iniziativa Meridionale nel Risorgimento*, Milan, 1962, 590–2.

138 *Ed. Naz.* 49, 34, 62, 79; *The English Republic*, London, 2, 313; *Harney Papers*, 55–6.

139 *Ed. Naz.* 51, 94, 99, 321–2.

140 *FO Confidential Print*, no. 277, 31 Jan. 1953, 5; Luigi Carlo Farini, *Lo Stato Romano*, 2nd ed., Florence, 1853, 4, 307, 344; Horace Greeley, *Glances*, 212; *The Spectator*, 8 June 1850, 542–3; *La Rivista Contemporanea*, Turin, Jan. 1857, 5, Farini.

141 *Risorgimento*, Brussels, 1947, 1, 3, 24 Mar. 1853, ed. Van Nuffel.

142 *Rassegna*, July 1941, 493–4, Morelli; Spatafora, *Il Comitato d'Azione*, 1, 93; *Gli Inconciliabili Eroi: Lettere di Mazzini e Garibaldi a Petroni*, ed. Anna Maria Isastia, Rome, 1987, 26; *Scritti Scelti di Mazzini*, ed. Jessie White Mario, 294–5; *Ed. Naz.* 49, 327–30; *ibid.* 51. xxiii; *ibid.* 65, 228; *ibid.* 77, 393–5; Comandini, *Cospirazioni*, 510–11.

143 *Ed. Naz.* 49, 282; *ibid.* 50, 300; *ibid.* 51, 203–4.

144 *Ed. Naz.* 47, 88; *ibid.* 50, 273–4, 306–7, 313; *ibid.* 52, 6–7; *ibid.* 53, 64.

CHAPTER FIVE: *Marking Time: 1854–8*

Garibaldi and Cavour: 1854–5

1 Alexander Herzen, *My Past and Thoughts*, London, 1968, 2, 701; *ibid.* 3, 1033; *Epistolario di Giuseppe Garibaldi*, ed. G. Giordano, Castello, 1981, 3, 62–4; *Ed. Naz.* 50, 273–4.

2 *Ed. Naz.* 51, 203, 321–2; *ibid.* 52, 4; L.C. Farini, *Lo Stato Romano*, Florence, 1853, 4, 340; N. Bianchi, *I Ducati Estensi dall'Anno 1815 all'Anno 1850*, Turin, 1852, 2, 323.

3 *Illustrated London News*, 25 Feb. 1854, 158; *The Reasoner*, London, 26 Feb. 1854, 157; Saffi, *13*, 85; Charles Gavan Duffy, *Conversations with Carlyle*, London, 1892, 110; Herzen, *My Past*, 3, 1168.

4 *Ed. Naz.* 6, 413–16; *ibid.* 11, 121; *ibid.* 14, 257; *ibid.* 29, 285, 291; *ibid.* 46, 185; *ibid.* 49, 279–80, 316–17; *ibid.* 50, 73; *ibid. Appendice*, 5, 195; Henry D. Lloyd, *Mazzini and Other Essays*, New York, 1910, 8–10; *The Inquirer*, London, 3 Sept. 1853; *Westminster Review*, April 1852, 467.

5 *Ed. Naz.* 52, 318; *ibid.* 53, 13; *ibid. Appendice*, 5, 122.

6 Derek Beales, *England and Italy 1859–1860*, London, 1961, 30; *Quarterly Review*, June 1849, 237.

7 *Edinburgh Review*, April 1854, 565–72, Greg; *Quarterly Review*, June 1855, 46, Gladstone; *Westminster Review*, July 1855, 45–7, Newman; *North British Review*, Edinburgh, Feb. 1856, 553–4, 562–3, Greg; I. G. Sieveking, *Memoir and Letters of Francis W. Newman*, London, 1909, 155–6.

8 *Ed. Naz.* 50, 287; *ibid.* 52, 67–8.

9 *Ed. Naz.* 51, 313; *ibid.* 52, 153, 201; *ibid.* 53, 102; *ibid. Appendice*, 5, 11.

10 Giuseppe Garibaldi, *Scritti Politici e Militari*, ed. Domenico Ciàmpoli, Rome, 1907, 1, 71–2; *I Moti della Lunigiana nei Carteggi di Domenico Buffa (1853–1854)*, ed. E. Costa, Genoa, 1972, lxxiv, 192; *Le Relazioni Diplomatiche fra la Gran Bretagna e il Regno di Sardegna*, ed. F. Curato, Rome,

1968, *ser. 3, 4,* 288.

11 *Ed. Naz. 53,* 13; *ibid. 54,* 36; *ibid. 56,* 44; *ibid. Appendice, 5,* 111; Richards, *1,* 306.

12 Joseph Rossi, *The Image of America in Mazzini's Writings,* Madison, 1954, 98; Daelli, *9,* xcv.

13 *Dall'Archivio di un Diplomatico (il Barone Alessandro Jocteau),* ed. Maria Avetta, Casale, 1924, 123; Camillo Cavour, *Epistolario,* ed. C. Pischedda, Bologna, 1954, *11,* 13–14; Bundesarchiv Bern, E. 21/139, 30 Aug. 1854.

14 C. de Cavour, *Lettere Edite ed Inedite,* ed. L. Chiala, Turin, 1884, *1,* 397; *Tutti gli Scritti di Camillo Cavour,* ed. C. Pischedda and G. Talamo, Turin, 1976, *3,* 1166; C. Benso di Cavour, *Discorsi Parlamentari,* ed. A. Omodeo, Florence, 1932, *1,* 74.

15 *Cavour e l'Inghilterra,* Bologna, 1933, *1,* 463; *Il Carteggio Cavour-Nigra dal 1858 al 1861,* Bologna, 1926, *1,* 105, 214; *Lettere,* ed. Chiala, *2,* clxxxiv; Mme Rattazzi, *Rattazzi et son Temps,* Paris, 1881, *1,* 320; V. Gioberti, *Del Rinnovamento Civile d'Italia,* Paris, 1851, *2,* 313–14; N. Bianchi, *Storia Documentata della Diplomazia Europea in Italia,* Turin, 1872, *8,* 78.

16 I. Artom and A. Blanc, *Oeuvre Parlementaire du Comte de Cavour,* Paris, 1862, 32.

17 Cavour, *Epistolario, 9,* 96.

18 Cavour, *Discorsi Parlamentari, 14,* 190.

19 *Scritti di Cavour,* ed. Pischedda and Talamo, *3,* 1591.

20 Daelli, *9,* xc; *Rivista d'Italia,* Sept. 1902, 433; A. Dallolio, *Cospirazioni e Cospiratori 1852–1856,* Bologna, 1913, 95; *The Beacon,* London, 23 Nov. 1853; 71; *Risorgimento,* Brussels, 1972, 107; A. Omodeo, *L'Opera Politica del Conte di Cavour,* Florence, 1940, *2,* 141.

21 Giovanni La Cecilia, *Memorie Storico-Politiche,* ed. R. Moscati,

22 Varese 1946, 652–3. Alessandro Luzio, *Garibaldi, Cavour, Verdi,* Turin, 1924, 693–4; Walter Maturi, *Interpretazioni del Risorgimento,* Turin, 1962, 293–9; *Nuova Antologia,* 1 July 1970, 27; *Rassegna,* Mar. 1917, 238–40; *ibid.* Jan. 1948, 110, Giuntella; Nicomede Bianchi, *Vicende del Mazzinianismo Politico e Religioso dal 1832 al 1854,* Savona, 1854, 87.

23 *Ed. Naz. 60,* 57; Bianchi, *Vicende,* 144.

24 Cavour, *Epistolario, 7,* 249, 316.

25 Bianchi, *Vicende,* 46, 132–3, 197–201.

26 Bayle St John, *The Subalpine Kingdom,* London, 1856, *2,* 63, 68, 73, 200–1.

27 *The Times,* 28 Sept. 1854.

28 *Ed. Naz. 53,* 200.

29 Saffi, *13,* 82; *Bulletin of the International Institute of Social History Amsterdam,* Leiden, 1953, 24–7, Herzen.

30 Giorgio Asproni, *Diario Politico,* ed. B. Anedda, Milan, 1974, *1,* 247–8, 410, 436.

31 *Ed. Naz. 54,* 50–1, 173–6.

32 Richards, *2,* 20, 25; *Ed. Naz. 55,* 29; John A. Langford, *Kossuth, Mazzini, Urquhart and the Conferences,* London, 1855, 11.

33 *Ed. Naz. 54,* 316; *ibid. 55,* 24–30; *ibid. 59,* 22; Daelli, *9,* xciv.

34 *Ed. Naz. 54,* 81–2.

35 *Ed. Naz. 54,* 232.

36 Saffi, *13,* 85.

37 *Ed. Naz. 54,* 118; *ibid. 55,* 13–17.

38 *Ed. Naz. 54,* 276–7, 315; Langford, *Kossuth,* 5; *The Free Press,* Sheffield, 13 Oct. 1855; *The Reasoner,* 14 Oct. 1855, 227; Asproni, *Diario, 5,* 566.

39 *Ed. Naz. 54,* 194; *ibid. 56,* 187; Domus, 1968, *1,* 204, Grandi.

40 *Le Relazioni Diplomatiche fra la Francia e il Granducato di Toscana,* ed. A. Saitta, Rome, 1959, *ser. 3, 2,* 395, 435, 458; Alessandro Luzio, *Carlo Alberto e Giuseppe*

Mazzini, Turin, 1923, 235–6; *Le Relazioni Diplomatiche fra la Gran Bretagna e il Regno di Sardegna*, ed. F. Curato, Rome, 1969, *5*, 205; *Risorgimento*, Brussels, 1973, *1*, 6.

41 J. R. H. Myers, *Baron Ward and the Dukes of Parma*, London, 1938, 212; G. Ferrata and E. Vittorini, *La Tragica Vicenda di Carlo III, 1848–1859*, Milan, 1939, 154.

42 *Ed. Naz. 54*, 91, 131, 149, 152; *ibid. 55*, 45, 55; Piero Zama, *Giovanni Pianori contro Napoleone III*, Modena, 1933, 93–8; Harold Kurtz, *The Empress Eugénie*, London, 1964, 82; N. Blayau, *Billault Ministre de Napoléon III*, Paris, 1969, 291; *Rassegna: XXXVI Congresso del Risorgimento*, Rome, 1960, 98, Mazzotti.

43 *Ed. Naz. 44*, 17, 23; Goldwin Smith, *Reminiscences*, ed. A. Haultain, New York, 1910, 96.

44 Mazzini, in *The Reasoner*, 6 May 1855; F. W. Newman, *Reminiscences of Two Exiles*, London, 1888, 37, Panizzi.

45 G. B. Henderson, *Crimean War Diplomacy and Other Historical Essays*, Glasgow, 1947, 238–41; Constance Brooks, *Antonio Panizzi Scholar and Patriot*, Manchester, 1931, 107–10; Jessie White Mario, *Agostino Bertani e i Suoi Tempi*, Florence, 1888, *1*, 217–30; Richards, *2*, 38.

46 *Cavour e l'Inghilterra: Carteggio con V.E. d'Azeglio*, Bologna, 1933, *1*, 355, 442.

Further setbacks: 1856–7

47 Gaspare Finali, *Memorie*, ed. G. Maioli, Faenza, 1955, 490–1; *Revue des Deux Mondes*, 1856, *3*, 436–7; *Dall'Archivio di Jocteau*, ed. Avetta, Casale, 1924, 220.

48 *Scritti Politici di Giuseppe La Farina*, ed. A. Franchi, Milan, 1870, *2*, 494; Artom, *Oeuvre Parlementaire de Cavour*, 33; *Carteggio Cavour-*

Salmour, Bologna, 1936, 99; *Nuove Lettere Inedite del Conte Camillo di Cavour*, ed. Edmondo Mayor, Turin, 1895, 236; *Diario Politico di Margherita Provana di Collegno 1852–1856*, ed. A. Malvezzi, Milan, 1926, 497; A. Gallenga, *Italy Revisited*, London, 1875, *2*, 122.

49 Artom, *Oeuvre Parlementaire*, 7–8; Émile Ollivier, *L'Empire Libérale*, Paris, 1897, *4*, 596; *Cavour e l'Inghilterra*, *1*, 463.

50 *Memorie di Giorgio Pallavicino*, Turin, 1882, *2*, 380, 479, 488; *Daniele Manin e Giorgio Pallavicino: Epistolario politico (1855–1857)*, ed. B. E. Maineri, Milan, 1878, 25, 357; *Il Piemonte nel 1850–1852: Lettere di Vincenzo Gioberti e Giorgio Pallavicino*, ed. B. E. Maineri, Milan, 1875, 325.

51 Nassau William Senior, *Conversations with M. Thiers, M. Guizot, and other Distinguished Persons*, London, 1878, *2*, 86.

52 *Ministère des Affaires Étrangères* (French National Archives), Paris, Sardaigne, *332*, 16 Oct. 1852, to Butenval; D. Mack Smith, *Vittorio Emanuele II*, Bari, 1972, 361.

53 *Ibid. 53*, 359.

54 *Manin*, ed. Maineri, 120; *Cavour e l'Inghilterra*, *2*, 33.

55 *Nuove Lettere*, ed. Mayor, 356; *Le Relazioni Diplomatiche*, ed. Curato, *5*, 293.

56 Caroline Stansfeld, diary for 27 June 1856, Stansfeld Papers; Jessie White Mario, *The Birth of Modern Italy*, London, 1909, 263; Daelli, *9*, cxxxi; *Ed. Naz. 56*, 299–303.

57 Pietro Pirri, *Pio IX e Vittorio Emanuele II dal loro Carteggio Privato (1848–56)*, Rome, 1944, *1*, 237.

58 *Ed. Naz. 55*, 205; *ibid. 56*, 335; *ibid. 57*, 95; *ibid. 59*, 236–7.

59 Giorgio Asproni, *Diario Politico*, Milan, 1974, *1*, 451, 455; *ibid. 2*,

100–1; Ernesto Ravvitti, *Delle Recenti Avventure d'Italia*, Venice, 1864, 184; Omodeo, *L'Opera di Cavour*, 2, 140, 220–1; R. Romeo, *Cavour e il Suo Tempo (1854–1861)*, Bari, 1984, 281, 285; E. Di Nolfo, *Europa e Italia nel 1855–1856*, Rome, 1967, 434–6.

60 *Min. des Affaires Etrangères*, 340, 26 Aug. 1856, Gramont; *Carteggio Cavour-Salmour*, 110; *Risorgimento*, Brussels, 1973, 1, 12; Marco Minghetti, *Miei Ricordi*, Turin, 1889, 3, 126.

61 *Ed. Naz. 56*, 300; *ibid. 57*, 5–6.

62 *Ed. Naz. 57*, 18, 26, 108; *Le Relazioni Diplomatiche*, ed. Curato, 5, 306; *Le Relazioni Diplomatiche fra l'Austria e il Regno di Sardegna*, ed. F. Valsecchi, *ser. 3, 4*, 286–7; *Opere di Francesco de Sanctis*, ed. C. Muscetta, Turin, 1965, *19*, 420.

63 Cavour, *Discorsi Parlamentari*, 13, 19.

64 Some of its publications are in the Bishopsgate Institute, London.

65 *The Times*, 2 and 29 Aug. 1856.

66 *The Newcastle Chronicle*, 9 May 1857; *The National Review*, London, Oct. 1856, 3, 419–20.

67 *Ed. Naz. 57*, 25, 109, 135, 189; *ibid. 58*, 138; R. Villari, *Cospirazione e Rivolta*, Messina, 1881, 291; *Memorie di Pallavicino*, 3, 355; *Epistolario di Giuseppe La Farina*, ed. A. Franchi, Milan, 1869, 2, 25–6; *Emigrazione Politica in Genoa ed in Liguria dal 1848 al 1857*, Modena, 1957, 3, 621, Barberis; Nello Rosselli, *Carlo Pisacane nel Risorgimento Italiano*, Turin, 1932, 411.

68 Carlo Pisacane, *La Rivoluzione*, ed. A. Romano, Milan, 1957, 162–3, 193, 198; Carlo Pisacane, *Saggio su la Rivoluzione*, ed. G. Pintor, Turin, 1956, 160, 169; Carlo Pisacane, *Scritti Vari Inediti o Rari*, ed. A. Romano, Milan, 1964, 2, 16; Carlo Pisacane, *Epistolario*, ed. A. Romano, Milan, 1937, 396.

69 *Ed. Naz. 58*, 115, 123, 137, 169; Richards, 2, 80.

70 *Ed. Naz. 58*, 178; Luzio, *Carlo Alberto e Mazzini*, 423–5.

71 *Nuove Lettere*, ed. Mayor, 530–1; *Il Carteggio Cavour-Nigra dal 1858 al 1861*, Bologna, 1926, 1, 45.

72 *Lettere Edite ed Inedite di Camillo Cavour*, ed. L. Chiala, Turin, 1883, 2, ccxlv–ccxlvi; *Carteggio Cavour-Salmour*, 124; Mme Rattazzi, *Rattazzi et son Temps*, Paris, 1881, 1, 334; Minghetti, *Miei Ricordi*, 3, 457.

73 Cavour, *Discorsi Parlamentari*, 14, 157; Rosselli, *Pisacane*, 255, 409, 411, 414; Romeo, *Cavour e il suo Tempo*, 331–7; Attilio Bargoni, *Memorie di Angelo Bargoni*, Milan, 1911, 43.

74 *Lettere di Cavour*, ed. Chiala, 2, 266; *Nuove Lettere*, ed. Mayor, 538–40.

75 *Min. des Affaires Etrangères*, 342, 1 July 1857, Gramont; *Le Relazioni Diplomatiche fra la Gran Bretagna e il Regno di Sardegna*, ed. G. Giarrizzo, *ser. 3, 6*, 139.

76 *Carteggio Cavour-Salmour*, 129; *Min. des Affaires Étrangères*, 342, 7 July 1857; Gramont; *Relazioni Diplomatiche*, ed. Giarrizzo, 6, 131; *Nuove Lettere*, ed. Mayor, 536, 538; *Carteggio Cavour-Nigra*, 1, 54–5, 58.

77 *The Paris Embassy during the Second Empire*, ed. F. A. Wellesley, London, 1928, 117–18; *The Diplomatic Reminiscences of Lord Augustus Loftus 1837–1862*, London, 1892, 1, 308; Bernard Porter, *The Refugee Question in Mid-Victorian Politics*, Cambridge, 1979, 61; *Cavour e l'Inghilterra*, 2, 148; Royal Archives, Windsor, B16, 23 July 1857, Clarendon to the Queen; Comte Fleury, *Memoirs of the Empress Eugénie*, London, 1920, 1, 416; A. Luzio, *Felice Orsini*, Milan, 1914, 271–4; *The Times*, 23 July and 11 Sept. 1857.

78 *Ed. Naz. 58*, 291–2.

79   *Contemporary Review*, London, Nov. 1917, 568–9, Bice Pareto; Richards, *2*, 82–4; Jessie White Mario, *Della Vita di Giuseppe Mazzini*, Milan, 1886, 376.

80   Omodeo, *L'Opera di Cavour, 2*, 219; Giorgio Candeloro, *Storia dell'Italia Moderna*, Milan, 1964, *4*, 276–8; Antonio Gramsci, *Quaderni del Carcere*, ed. V. Gerratana, Turin, 1975, *3*, 2010, 2014.

81   Cesare Cantù, *Della Indipendenza Italiana: Cronistoria*, Turin, 1876, *3*, 713; *Nuove Lettere*, ed. Mayor, 544; *The Times*, 22 Jan. 1858.

82   *Ed. Naz. 59*, 121; *ibid. 60*, 18.

83   *Ed. Naz. 57*, 172.

84   *Ed. Naz. Appendice, 5*, 223.

85   *Epistolario di Gustavo Modena (1827–1861)*, ed. Terenzio Grandi, Roma, 1955, 269–70; Asproni, *Diario, 1*, 643; Finali, *Memorie*, 490–1; *Aspromonte e Mentana: Documenti inediti*, ed. A. Luzio, Florence, 1935, 333; A. Omodeo, *Difesa del Risorgimento*, Turin, 1951, 84; *Ricordi di Michelangelo Castelli 1847–1875*, ed. L. Chiala, Turin, 1888, 221.

86   *Ed. Naz. 58*, 31.

87   *Ed. Naz. 60*, 113.

88   *Ed. Naz. 46*, 219; *ibid. 59*, 121.

Orsini and Plombières

89   Felice Orsini, *Memorie Politiche*, ed. A. Franchi, Lugano, 1860, 371–3, 399, 423; *Lettere Edite ed Inedite di Felice Orsini*, Milan, 1861, 178, 238; Justin McCarthy, *Portraits of the Sixties*, London, 1903, 320; *Le Relazioni Diplomatiche*, ed. Giarrizzo, *6*, 194; *Le Figaro*, Paris, 17 Mar. 1894; *Cosmopolis*, London, June 1897, 650.

90   J. S. Mill, *On Liberty*, London, 1859, 32; Viscount Morley, *Recollections*, London, 1917, *1*, 55; G. J. Holyoake, *Bygones Worth Remembering*, London, 1905, *1*, 222–6; *Il*

Risorgimento Italiano, Milan, April 1909, 253, Astegiano; *Ricordi di Michelangelo Castelli*, ed. L. Chiala, Turin, 1888, 227.

91   *Aspromonte e Mentana*, ed. Luzio, 84.

92   *Carteggi e Documenti Diplomatici Inediti di Emanuele d'Azeglio*, ed. A. Colombo, Turin, 1920, *2*, 169; *Revue des Deux Mondes*, 1 Feb. 1899, 538.

93   Cavour, *Discorsi Parlamentari*, ed. A. Saitta, *14*, 180, 192–4; *Cavour e l'Inghilterra 2*, 177; *Carteggio Cavour-Nigra, 1*, 149.

94   *Ed. Naz. 59*, 236–9.

95   *The Morning Advertiser*, London, 23 Sept. 1858; *Lettere di Cavour*, ed. Chiala, *6*, 137, 148; *Rivista Storica Italiana*, Rome, 1931, *48*, 16, Luzio; *Saggi Mazziniani Dedicati a Emilia Morelli*, Genoa, 1990, 109–10, 121–3, Montale; *Saggi di Storia del Giornalismo in Memoria di Leonida Balestrieri*, Genoa, 1982, 101–2, Morabito.

96   Comte De Hübner, *Neuf Ans de Souvenirs d'un Ambassadeur d'Autriche à Paris 1851–1859*, Paris, 1908, *2*, 105; *L'Armonia*, Turin, 31 July 1858; *Carteggio Politico di Michelangelo Castelli*, ed. L. Chiala, Turin, 1891, *2*, 495; Omodeo, *L'Opera di Cavour, 2*, 178-81; M. Cassetti, *Le Carte di La Marmora*, Turin, 1979, 837.

97   *Ricordi di Castelli*, 37–8, 221; Luigi Pianciani, *Dell'Andamento delle Cose in Italia: Rivelazioni, memorie e riflessioni*, Milan, 1860, 18–19.

98   *Ed. Naz. 60*, 23, 115; *ibid. 62*, 99.

99   *Ed. Naz. 55*, 299–300; *ibid. 60*, 114; James Stansfeld, *The Italian Movement*, London, 1862, 18; Jessie White Mario, *Mazzini*, 485.

100 *Ed. Naz. 56*, 231; *ibid. 59*, 330; *ibid. 61*, 9; *ibid. Appendice, 5*, 279; Felix Moscheles, *Fragments of an Autobiography*, London, 1899, 252.

101 L. Kossuth, *Meine Schriften aus der*

Emigration, Leipzig, 1880, *1*, 221; *Correspondence and Conversations of Alexis de Tocqueville with Nassau William Senior from 1834 to 1859*, London, 1872, *2*, 225; Nassau Senior, *Conversations with Thiers*, London, 1878, *2*, 207–8; L. K. Laughton, *Memoirs of the Life and Correspondence of Henry Reeve*, London, 1898, *2*, 5; Theodore Martin, *The Life of H.R.H. The Prince Consort*, London, 1879, *4*, 358; Comte Fleury, *Memoirs of the Empress Eugénie*, London, 1920, *1*, 426.

102 *Ed. Naz. 67*, 254–5; *ibid. 84*, 134; Karl Blind, 'The Life and Labours of Mazzini', in *Dark Blue*, London, May 1872, 315; Saffi, *4*, 98.

103 Charles F. Vitzthum von Eckstädt, *St Petersburg and London in the Years 1852–1864*, London, 1887, *2*, 9; Karl Marx and Frederick Engels, *Collected Works*, London, 1982, *16*, 354; *ibid. 17*, 190–1; *Lettere di Cavour*, ed. Chiala, *2*, 332–3.

104 *Ed. Naz. 59*, 266, 318–20; *ibid. 61*, 30, 123; F. Della Peruta, *Democrazia e Socialismo nel Risorgimento*, Rome, 1965, 175–6.

105 *Ed. Naz. 15*, 71; *ibid. 62*, 96–100; J. W. Mario, *Mazzini*, 383.

106 Undated newspaper cutting in Nelson Gay Collection, Harvard Library, with a note by Mrs Osler; *Newcastle Chronicle*, 8 May 1857.

107 *Cavour e l'Inghilterra*, *2*, 147.

108 Charles Bradlaugh, *Five Dead Men whom I Knew when Living*, London, n.d., 13.

109 *Annali dell'Istituto Italiano per gli Studi Storici*, Naples, 1968, *1*, 342, Gustavo Costa; W. Knight, *Memoir of John Nichol*, Glasgow, 1896, 97; *Undergraduate Papers*, Oxford, 1858, 186; Richards, *3*, 241.

110 *Letters and Memorials of Catherine Winkworth*, edited by her sister, Clifton, 1886, *2*, 254; *Ed. Naz. 63*,
38.

111 *Pensiero ed Azione*, London, 15 Sept. 1858, 30–1; *ibid.*, 15 Oct. 1858, 326–30; *Ed. Naz. 94*, 290; J. W. Mario, *Mazzini*, 384.

112 *Harper's New Monthly Magazine*, New York, 1872, *45*, 283, Moncure Daniel Conway

113 Mathilde Blind, 'Personal Recollections of Mazzini', *Fortnightly Review*, London, May 1891, 702–3.

114 Malvida von Meysenbug, 'Erinnerungen an Joseph Mazzini', *Cosmopolis*, London, Sept. 1897, 821, 824–5.

115 Malvida von Meysenbug, *Der Lebensabend einer Idealistin*, Berlin, 1922, *2*, 82–4, 91–2, 136–7.

116 *Lettere di Cavour*, ed. Chiala, *6*, 322; *Ministère des Affaires Étrangères*, *344*, 31 Dec. 1858, La Tour d'Auvergne; *Il Problema Italiano nei Testi di una Battaglia Pubblicistica*, ed. A. Saitta, Rome, 1963, *3*, 82; C. de Bussy, *Les Conspirateurs en Angleterre 1848–1858*, Paris, 1858, 8, 24, 104.

117 *The Times*, 7 Apr. 1858.

118 *Daily Telegraph*, London, 18 Sept. 1858.

CHAPTER SIX. The Making of Italy: 1859–61

The war of 1859

1 *Ministère des Affaires Étrangères*, *Sardaigne*, *345*, 18 April 1859, Walewski; *Ed. Naz. 62*, 144, 182; *ibid. 63*, 110.

2 Tyne and Wear Archives (Newcastle), 634/A, 640, 18 Jan. 1859, Mazzini to Cowen; *Rivista d'Italia*, June 1905, 1003, Rosi; *Ed. Naz. 62*, 217–18; *ibid. 63*, 137–8.

3 *Ed. Naz. 64*, 231; J. W. Mario, *Agostino Bertani e i suoi Tempi*, Florence, 1888, *1*, 311.

4 *Ed. Naz. 62*, 214–18; *ibid. 63*, 205.

5   *Il Carteggio Cavour-Nigra*, Bologna, 1926, *2*, 135.

6   Giuseppe Massari, *Diario dalle Cento Voci*, ed. E. Morelli, Rocca S. Casciano, 1959, 153, 284.

7   *Die Auswärtige Politik Preussens 1858–71*, ed. C. Friese, Oldenburg, 1933, *1*, 366, Brassier; Geheimes Staats Archiv, Merseburg, 'Turin', *426*, 20 April 1859, Brassier; *Ministère des Affaires Étrangères*, *346*, 5 May 1859, La Tour d'Auvergne; L. Chiala, *Politica Segreta di Napoleone III e di Cavour in Italia e in Ungheria (1858–61)*, Turin, 1895, 37.

8   C. Bollea, *Una Silloge di Lettere del Risorgimento (1839–1873)*, Turin, 1919, 138; *Carteggio Cavour-Nigra*, *2*, 255; *Ministero Degli Affari Esteri*, Rome, *Pièces Chiffrées*, 116, 17 Oct. 1859, Benzi; A. Tamborra, *Cavour e i Balcani*, Turin, 1958, 117–20.

9   Massari, *Diario*, 57, 140, 142, 147, 206; *Epistolario di Giuseppe La Farina*, ed. A. Franchi, Milan, 1869, *2*, 129; *Lettere Edite e Inedite di Camillo Cavour*, ed. L. Chiala, Turin, 1884, *3*, 11; W. De La Rive, *Le Comte de Cavour: Récits et souvenirs*, Paris, 1862, 385; *Rassegna*, Jan. 1956, 49, Hearder; D. Mack Smith, *Cavour*, London, 1985, 146.

10 *Carteggio Cavour-Nigra*, *1*, 167; C. Benso di Cavour, *Discorsi Parlamentari*, Florence, 1969, *14*, 167; *Epistolario di La Farina*, *2*, 82; *Lettere di Cavour*, ed. Chiala, *2*, 441, 444.

11 *Ministère des Affaires Étrangères*, *346*, 5 May 1859, La Tour; Gaspare Finali, *Memorie*, ed. G. Maioli, Faenza, 1955, 120; *La Liguria nel Risorgimento: Notizie e documenti*, ed. F. L. Mannucci, Genoa, 1925, 205; R. Grew, *A Sterner Plan for Italian Unity: The Italian National Society in the Risorgimento*, Princeton, 1963, 212.

12 *Carteggio Cavour-Nigra*, *1*, 250; Geheimes Staats Archiv, Merseburg, 'Turin', *426*, 18 May 1859, Brassier.

13 Giorgio Asproni, *Diario Politico*, ed. B. Anedda, Milan, 1974, *2*, 208; *Carteggio Cavour-Nigra*, *2*, 219.

14 *Epistolario di La Farina*, *2*, 151; *Lettere di Cavour*, ed. Chiala, *3*, 88; *Ed. Naz. 63*, 256, 260; *ibid. 64*, 14, 36–7; *Il Politecnico*, Milan, 1860, *8*, 271; A. Bertani, *Ire Politiche d'Oltre Tomba*, Milan, 1869, 40; Karl Marx and Frederick Engels, *Collected Works*, London, 1982, *16*, 533; Staats Archiv, Merseburg, 'Turin', *426*, 26 May 1859, Brassier.

15 Lajos Kossuth, *Memories of My Exile*, London, 1880, 419; Saffi, *5*, 49; *Liguria nel Risorgimento*, 208.

16 *Ed. Naz. 64*, 102, 142, 152; *ibid. 70*, 260; *ibid. Appendice*, *6*, 56–7.

17 PRO Russell Papers, 30/22/27, 28 June 1859, Palmerston; FO 244/161, 7 July 1859, Russell; *Il Problema Veneto e l'Europa 1859–1866*, ed. Noel Blakiston, Venice, 1966, *2*, 13, 95; Lord Fitzmaurice, *The Life of the Second Earl Granville*, London, 1905, *1*, 325–6.

18 *Fraser's Magazine*, London, Dec. 1859, 771–2; *Saturday Review*, London, 13 Aug. 1859, 188–9; Matthew Arnold, *England and the Italian Question*, London, 1859, 42.

19 *Toscana e Austria: Cenni storico-politici*, Florence, 1859, 18–19; Ludmilla Assing, *Vita di Piero Cironi*, Prato, 1865, 149; *Carteggi di Bettino Ricasoli*, ed. G. Camerani and C. Rotondi, Rome, 1986, *29*, 11; Bolton King, *Mazzini*, London, 1902, 179–80; J. W. Mario, *Agostino Bertani e i Suoi Tempi*, Florence, 1888, *2*, 139; R. Ciampini, *Il '59 in Toscana*, Florence, 1958, 229.

20 Finali, *Memorie*, 147; D. Mack Smith, 'Cavour and the Tuscan

Revolution of 1859', in *Victor Emanuel, Cavour and the Risorgimento*, Oxford, 1971, 127, 142–3.

21 *Ed. Naz. 64*, 137–42; *ibid. 65*, 101, 161; *Carteggi di Ricasoli*, 9, 104–5, 167; Massari, *Diario*, 401.

22 *Newcastle Daily Journal*, 5 April 1861.

23 *Ed. Naz. 64*, xix, 263; *ibid. 65*, 267; *ibid. 66*, 230; *ibid. 67*, 146; Jessie White Mario's notes to her edition of *Scritti Scelti di Giuseppe Mazzini*, Florence, 1916, 246–7, 288; *Atti del xlii Congresso di Storia del Risorgimento Italiano*, Rome, 1966, 103–4, E. Morelli.

24 *Ministère des Affaires Étrangères, 350*, 167–8, 24 Aug. 1860, Talleyrand; I. Artom and A. Blanc, *Oeuvre Parlementaire du Comte de Cavour*, Paris 1862, 7–8; *Carteggio Cavour-Nigra*, 1, 214.

25 Charles de Rémusat, *Mémoires de ma Vie*, ed. Charles Pouthas, Paris, 1967, 5, 122.

26 *Ibid.*; Massari, *Diario*, 451, 466; *Lettere di Cavour*, ed. Chiala, 4, cxx–cxxi; Comte de Reiset, *Mes Souvenirs*, Paris, 1903, 3, 23.

27 *Epistolario di Carlo Cattaneo*, ed. R. Caddeo, Florence, 1954, 3, 209; Carlo Cattaneo, *Scritti Politici ed Epistolario*, ed. G. Rosa and J. W. Mario, Florence, 1892, 2, 244; Carlo Cattaneo, *Scritti Politici*, ed. M. Boneschi, Florence, 1965, 4, 49.

28 *The Saturday Review*, London, 22 Oct. 1859, 472.

Garibaldi and 'The Thousand'

29 McAdam Papers, Glasgow University, MS General 530, letter of 1 Feb. 1860.

30 *Tutti gli Scritti di Camillo Cavour*, ed. C. Pischedda and G. Talamo, Turin, 1976, 4, 2039.

31 *Ed. Naz. 67*, 118–19, 130, 167.

32 *Ed. Naz. 65*, 371–2; *ibid. 66*, 84–5; *ibid. 67*, 49, 129–30, 144–5; J.W.

Mario, *Agostino Bertani, 1*, 311.

33 Domus, 1961, 2, 53, Candido; *La Liguria*, ed. Mannucci, 202; *Le Relazioni Diplomatiche fra la Francia e il Granducato di Toscana*, ed. A. Saitta, Rome, 1859, ser. 3, 3, 484.

34 *Ed. Naz. 66*, 23; *ibid. 67*, 215.

35 *Ed. Naz. 66*, 19, 44–5; *ibid. 67*, 255.

36 *Lettere di Cavour*, ed. Chiala, 4, lxxxviii–lxxxix; Cesare Cantù, *Della Indipendenza Italiana*, Turin, 1876, 3, 425; Daelli, *11*, xxvi; *Ed. Naz. 64*, 258; *ibid. Appendice, 6*, 45.

37 *Ed. Naz. 67*, 146; Giovanni Cadolini, *Memorie del Risorgimento dal 1848 al 1862*, Milan, 1911, 372; J. W. Mario, *Bertani*, 2, 13; F. Della Peruta, *Democrazia e Socialismo nel Risorgimento*, Rome, 1965, 176.

38 *Dark Blue*, London, May 1872, 320; *The Nation*, New York, 29 Aug. 1872, 136; *Fraser's Magazine*, Aug. 1882, 239, 248; *The Contemporary Review*, Nov. 1888, 384; *Westminster Magazine*, Jan. 1904, 53, 58.

39 Alessandro Luzio, *La Massoneria e il Risorgimento Italiano*, Bologna, 1925, 2, 7; Alessandro Luzio, *Garibaldi, Cavour, Verdi*, Turin, 1924, 93; *Le Carte di Giovanni Lanza*, ed. De Vecchi di Val Cismon, Turin, 1935, 3, 24–5; Adolfo Omodeo, *Il Senso della Storia*, Turin, 1955, 417; Jessie White Mario's supplementary chapters to *Autobiography of Giuseppe Garibaldi*, London, 1889, 3, 225; Attilio Bargoni, *Memorie di Angelo Bargoni*, Milan, 1911, 97; A. Elia, *Ricordi di un Veterano*, Rome, 1910, 435.

40 *Lettere di Rosalino Pilo*, ed. G. Falzone, Rome, 1972, 509; Giuseppe Garibaldi, *Scritti Politici e Militari*, ed. D. Ciàmpoli, Rome, 1907, *1*, 130; *Le Memorie di Garibaldi*, Bologna, 1932, *1*, 288;

M. Quadrio, *Il Libro dei Mille del General Garibaldi*, Milan, 1879, 183.

41 *Discorsi Parlamentari di Francesco Crispi*, Rome, 1915, *1*, 145; *Ed. Naz. 70*, 44.

42 *Lettere di Pilo*, 525, *Archivio Storico Siciliano*, Palermo, 1948–9, 116, Librino.

43 *The Times*, 18 May 1860, letter from Saffi; *Ed. Naz. 68*, 67, 83–5.

44 McAdam Papers, Glasgow, Mazzini letter of 6 Sept. 1860; *Discorsi Parlamentari di Agostino Bertani*, Rome, 1913, 100; Saffi, *9*, 51; *Ed. Naz. 67*, 144–5, 325; *ibid. 68*, 70, 89.

45 *La Liberazione del Mezzogiorno e la Formazione del Regno d'Italia*, Bologna, 1949, *1*, 37; *Le Lettere di Vittorio Emanuele II*, ed. F. Cognasso, Turin, 1966, *1*, 600; *Lettere di Cavour*, ed. Chiala, *3*, 273–4.

46 D. Mack Smith, 'Cavour and the Thousand', in *Victor Emanuel, Cavour and the Risorgimento*, 176–89.

47 'The Peasants' Revolt in Sicily, 1860', *ibid.* 213; *Il Problema Veneto*, ed. Blakiston, *2*, 275.

48 *Carteggi di Ricasoli*, *13*, 212; *Carteggio Cavour-Nigra*, *3*, 297; Jessie White Mario, *Mazzini*, 405; C. Di Persano, *Nella Campagna Navale degli Anni 1860 e 1861*, Florence, 1869, *1*, 31, 44.

49 *Ed. Naz. 66*, 125, 177; *ibid. 67*, 342; *ibid. 68*, 22, 215, 222.

50 *Carteggi di Ricasoli*, *14*, 172–3.

51 McAdam Papers, Glasgow, 6 Sept. 1860; *Ed. Naz. 67*, 325; *ibid. 68*, 55, 338; *ibid. 70*, 26–8, 69, 99.

52 *Ministère des Affaires Étrangères*, 350, 31 Aug. 1860, Rayneval; *Die Auswärtige Politik*, 2, part 1, 683, Brassier; *Carteggio Cavour-Nigra*, 4, 202; *Epistolario di La Farina 2*, 417; A. Dallolio, *La Spedizione dei Mille nelle Memorie Bolognesi*, Bologna, 1910, 131.

53 FO. 519/10, 1 Sept. 1860, Cowley; *Carteggio Cavour-Nigra*, 4, 224, 235; *La Questione Romana negli Anni 1860–1861*, Bologna, 1929, *1*, 44.

54 *Carteggi di Ricasoli*, *14*, 335, 359, 363; *ibid. 15*, 14.

55 *Ed. Naz. 70*, 63.

56 *Ed. Naz. 70*, 79, 99; *Il Nazionale*, Naples, 18 Sept. 1860.

57 Francesco De Sanctis, *Scritti e Discorsi Politici*, ed. N. Cortese, Naples, 1939, 52.

58 *Ed. Naz. 66*, 238; *ibid. 70*, 123, 136, 141; *Epistolario di Gustavo Modena*, ed. Terenzio Grandi, Rome, 1955, 417; *Scritti Politici di Alberto Mario*, ed. Giosuè Carducci, Bologna, 1901, 74–5; Andrea Giannelli, *Cenni Autobiografici e Ricordi Politici*, Milan, 1926, 343.

59 Letter from Giorgio Asproni to Brofferio, 29 Sept. 1860, in *Raccolta Martini*, Museo del Risorgimento, Rome.

60 Maxime Du Camp, *Expédition des Deux-Siciles: Souvenirs personnels*, Paris, 1861, 248–9; *The Times*, 27 Mar. 1872; C. Grünn, *L'Italie en 1861*, Brussels, 1862, *2*, 345–8.

61 Giuseppe Bandi, *I Mille: da Genova a Capua*, ed. D. Mack Smith, Milan, 1981, 323.

62 Charles Stuart Forbes, *The Campaign of Garibaldi in the Two Sicilies: A Personal Narrative*, London, 1861, 242–3.

63 G. E. Curàtulo, *Garibaldi, Vittorio Emanuele, Cavour nei Fasti della Patria: Documenti inediti*, Bologna, 1911, 355.

64 N. Nisco, *Storia Civile del Regno d'Italia*, Naples, 1888, 4, 339.

65 De Rémusat, *Mémoires*, 5, 124; *Lettere di Vittorio Emanuele II*, ed. Francesco Cognasso, Turin, 1966, *1*, 652.

66 *Liberazione del Mezzogiorno*, 3, 9, 63–4, 326.

67 *Ed. Naz. 70*, 155–6; J. W. Mario, *Mazzini*, 413–14; Costanzo Maraldi, *Documenti Francesi sulla*

Caduta del Regno Meridionale, Naples, 1935, 198, 200; Annali Feltrinelli, Milan, 1960, 3, 103–4, Della Peruta.

68 D. Mack Smith, Cavour and Garibaldi 1860, Cambridge, 1954, 395; Scritti Politici di Giuseppe La Farina, ed. A. Franchi, Milan, 1870, 2, 345–6.

69 Camera dei Deputati: Discussioni, 8 Oct. 1860, 929; ibid. 10 Oct. 1860, 980; A. Colombo, La Missione di G.B. Gassinis nelle Provincie Meridionali 18 Nov.–27 Dec. 1860, Turin, 1911, 38; Raccolta delle Leggi, Regolamenti e Decreti, Milan, 1861, 2, 1245.

Cavour's final victory

70 Ed. Naz. 70, 184, 195, 216; Rear-Admiral Sir Rodney Mundy, 'H.M.S. Hannibal' at Palermo and Naples during the Italian revolution 1859–1861, London, 1863, 282; Rassegna, Oct. 1963, 549, Dethan.

71 Liberazione del Mezzogiorno, 3, 316, 326–7, 386.

72 Ibid. 4, 89, 98, 160, 198; La Missione di Cassinis, 47.

73 Liberazione del Mezzogiorno, 3, 56, 72, 76; Carteggio Cavour-Nigra, 4, 292.

74 Jack La Bolina, Cronachette del Risorgimento Italiano, Florence, 1920, 67–8; Andrea Giannelli, Cenni Autobiografici e Ricordi Politici, Milan, 1926, 375–6; Generale Enrico della Rocca, Autobiografia di un Veterano: Ricordi storici e aneddotici, Bologna, 1897, 2, 96; Ed. Naz. 72, 199.

75 The Times, 21 Nov., 27 Nov. and 11 Dec. 1860; Carteggio Cavour-Nigra, 4, 123; Further Correspondence Relating to the Affairs of Italy, London, 1861, 7, 142.

76 Massimo d'Azeglio, L'Italie de 1847 à 1865: Correspondance politique, ed. E. Rendu, Paris, 1867, 200, 209–10, 236–8; Massimo d'Azeglio e Diomede Pant-

aleoni: Carteggio inedito, ed. G. Faldella, Turin, 1888, 486; Carteggi e Documenti Diplomatici Inediti di Emanuele d'Azeglio, ed. A. Colombo, Turin, 1920, 2, 308; N. Bianchi, Carlo Matteucci e l'Italia del suo Tempo, Rome, 1874, 317–18; Liberazione del Mezzogiorno, 4, 507.

77 Federigo Sclopis, Diario Segreto (1859–1867), ed. P. Pietro Pirri, Turin, 1959, 368; R. Bonfadini, Vita di Francesco Arese, con Documenti Inediti, Turin, 1894, 300; Mme Rattazzi, Rattazzi et son Temps: Documents inédits, Paris, 1881, 2, 427–8; Prince von Bülow, Memoirs, London, 1932, 1, 654.

78 Ed. Naz. 70, 261–3.

79 Ed. Naz. 71, 26–7; D. F. Mackay, 'The Influence of the Italian Risorgimento on British Public Opinion', Oxford D.Phil. thesis 1959, 309.

80 George Buckle, The Life of Benjamin Disraeli, London, 1916, 4, 321; Hansard, 156, 104, 20 Jan. 1860; ibid. 164, 1235, 17 July 1861; Ed. Naz. 70, 250.

81 The Morning Star and Glasgow Examiner, quoted by Miriam B. Urban, 'British Opinion and Policy on the Unification of Italy 1856–1861', Columbia Ph.D. thesis, 1938, 551.

82 The London Review, 7 July and 1 Nov. 1860.

83 Carteggio Politico di Michelangelo Castelli, ed. L. Chiala, Turin, 1891, 2, 495; Federico Chabod, Storia della Politica Estera Italiana dal 1870 al 1896, Bari, 1931, 209; A. Omodeo, introduction to G. Mazzini, Scritti Scelti, Milan, 1934, 13–15; G. Salvemini, Scritti sul Risorgimento, ed. P. Pieri and C. Pischedda, Milan, 1961, 222–3.

84 Georges Sorel, Réflexions sur la Violence, Paris, 1972, 151; Rivista Popolare, Milan, 1903, 197; West-

minster Review, Jan. 1904, 53.

85 François Guizot, *The Christian Church and Society in 1861*, London, 1861, 122–4; Edgar Quinet, *Lettres d'Exil*, Paris, 1885, *1*, 303; *Carteggio di Castelli*, 2, 495.

86 Lord Acton, *History of Freedom and Other Essays*, London, 1907, 194.

87 U. Marcelli, *Marco Minghetti e Diomede Pantaleoni: Carteggio*, Bologna, 1978, 105; *L'Opera di Stefano Türr nel Risorgimento Italiano*, Florence, 1928, *1*, 197; Aldo Ferrari, *Giuseppe Ferrari: Saggio critico*, Genoa, 1914, 311.

88 *L'Armonia*, Turin, 7 Feb. 1862; G. Ferrari, *L'Annexion des Deux Siciles*, Paris, 1860, 18; *Camera dei Deputati, Discussioni*, 26 Mar. 1861, 304, Ferrari; Theodore Trollope, *Social Aspects of the Italian Revolution*, London, 1861, 283, 291.

89 *Liberazione del Mezzogiorno*, 5, 519–20.

90 Chiala, *Politica Segreta*, 158.

91 *Liberazione del Mezzogiorno*, 5, 519; *La Questione Romana*, *1*, 170; *ibid.* 2, 119; Schweizerisches Bundesarchiv, Berne, E.2300,1, Turin, 23 Aug. 1860, Tourte.

92 Giacomo Durando, *Episodi Diplomatici del Risorgimento dal 1856 al 1863*, ed. C. Durando, Turin, 1901, 102–3; *Le Relazioni Diplomatiche fra La Gran Bretagna e il Regno di Sardegna*, ed. G. Giarrizzo, *ser. 3*, 8, 253–4, 259, 262; La Marmora Papers, Biella, casetta ciii, 167, 6 Jan. 1861, Cavour; Ministero degli Esteri, Rome, *Affari Politici Vari 1815–61*, Turin, 2 Dec. 1860, Leardi; *ibid.* 9 Dec. 1860, Cerruti.

93 Giovanni Silengo, *L'Archivio Cavour: Inventario*, Santena, 1974, *1*, 228; *Il Problema Veneto e l'Europa*, *1859–1866*, ed. N. Blakiston, Venice, 1966, *2*, 454; *Le Relazioni Diplomatiche*, ed. Giarrizzo, 264; Edmond About, *The Roman Question*, London,

1859, 8–9.

94 Mountstuart Grant Duff, *Notes from a Diary 1851–1872*, London, 1897, *1*, 155–6.

95 *Ed. Naz.* 64, 280; *ibid.* 66, 245–7; *ibid.* 71, 298.

96 *Ed. Naz.* 69, 172; *ibid.* 71, 117.

97 Nassau Senior, *Conversations with Distinguished Persons during the Second Empire from 1860 to 1863*, London, 1880, *1*, 146.

98 J. W. Mario, Supplement to *Autobiography of Garibaldi*, London, 1889, *3*, 361; *Ed. Naz.* 64, 273; *ibid.* 70, 171–2, 372; *ibid. Appendice*, 6, 138; *Liberazione del Mezzogiorno*, 3, 402.

99 *Ed. Naz.* 70, 272; *DDI ser. 1*, *1*, 50; FO 45/3, 20 Jan. 1861, Hudson.

100 Saffi, 7, 45–6; *Edizione Nazionale degli Scritti di Giuseppe Garibaldi*, Bologna, 1933, *3*, 71; *ibid. 12*, 30.

101 Alexander Herzen, *My Past and Thoughts*, London, 1968, *3*, 1029–30; Saffi, 7, 57; *Ed. Naz.* 71, 133.

102 *Westminster Review*, Jan. 1904, 58, Karl Blind; Viscount Morley, *Recollections*, London, 1917, *1*, 80; *Ed. Naz.* 70, 350.

103 *Ed. Naz.* 70, 50, 103, 169–70.

104 *Ed. Naz.* 70, 282; *ibid. Appendice*, 6, 133.

105 F. Petruccelli della Gattina, *I Moribondi del Palazzo Carignano*, Milan, 1862, 157; Alberto Mario, *Teste e Figure*, Padua, 1877, 527.

106 G. Silengo, *Inventario dell'Archivio Visconti Venosta*, Santena, 1970, *2*, 3.

107 Castelli, *Ricordi*, 38.

108 *Ed. Naz.* 71, 28, 216; *Corriere della Sera*, 17 Sept. 1931, Luzio; Alfredo Comandini, *L'Italia nei Cento Anni del Secolo XIX*, Milan, 1900, 4, 75; *Edizione Nazionale degli Scritti di Garibaldi*, 12, 52.

109 *Liberazione del Mezzogiorno*, 3, 318.

110 *Tyne and Wear Archives* (Newcastle), 634, 14678, Stansfeld note of Feb. 1861.

111 *Il Parlamento dell'Unità d'Italia*

(1859–61): *Atti e documenti della Camera dei Deputati*, Rome, 1961, 2, 174, 524; Ferdinando Martini, *Confessioni e Ricordi (1859–1892)*, Milan, 1929, 71; *Le Relazioni Diplomatiche*, ed. Saitta, ser. 3, 3, 186.

112 Henry d'Ideville, *Journal d'un Diplomate en Italie 1859–1862*, Paris, 1872, 1, 18; Mme Rattazzi, *Rattazzi*, 1, 589; d'Azeglio, *L'Italie*, ed. Rendu, xx, 189; *Carteggi di Emanuele d'Azeglio*, 2, 469; *Lettere di Massimo d'Azeglio a Giuseppe Torelli*, ed. C. Paoli, Milan, 1870, 102–3; Sclopis, *Diario Segreto*, 368; De Reiset, *Mes Souvenirs*, 3, 11–12; B. Ferrari, *Eugène Rendu e Massimo d'Azeglio*, Santena, 1967, 152; E. Tavallini, *La Vita e i Tempi di Giovanni Lanza*, Turin, 1887, 1, 257.

CHAPTER SEVEN. *Thought and Action: 1861–4*

Political thought

1 *Ed. Naz. 17*, 221, 224; *ibid. 37*, 127; *ibid. 42*, 238; *ibid. 53*, 45; *ibid. 77*, 3–4; *Life and Writings of Joseph Mazzini*, London, 1864, 1, v–vi.

2 *Ed. Naz. 70*, 233; *ibid. 71*, 9, 165.

3 *The Saturday Review*, London, 3 April 1858, 339–40.

4 *Ed. Naz. 52*, 133; *ibid. 57*, 242.

5 *Ed. Naz. 63*, 314–15.

6 C. De Meis, *Il Sovrano*, ed. B. Croce, Bari, 1927 (written 1868), 85; A. del Vecchio-Veneziani, *La Vita e L'Opera di Angelo Camillo de Meis*, Bologna, 1921, 262; *Rivista Bolognese*, 1865, 205.

7 Giorgio Asproni, *Diario Politico*, ed. B. Anedda, C. Sole and T. Orrù, Milan, 1980, 4, 271; *Fortnightly Review*, London, April 1877, 561; A. Ghisleri, *Democrazia in Azione*, Rome, 1904, 193;

Bolton King, *Mazzini*, London, 1902, 333–6.

8 Charles Edward Vaughan, *Studies in the History of Political Philosophy before and after Rousseau*, ed. A. G. Little, Manchester, 1925, 2, 254, 289, 322–3.

9 *The English Republic*, ed. William Linton, London, 1851, 1, 195, 227, 259, 291.

10 *Macmillan's Magazine*, July 1865, 254; *Ed. Naz. 8*, 381; *ibid. 78*, 354; *ibid. 83*, 97; *ibid. 88*, 81; *ibid. 93*, 255.

11 B. Croce, *Storia d'Europa nel Secolo Decimonono*, Bari, 1932, 121–3, 146; Alessandro Levi, *La Filosofia Politica di Giuseppe Mazzini*, ed. S. Mastellone, Naples, 1967, 135; *Rivista Storica Italiana*, 1985, 53–5, Vivarelli; G. Salvemini, *Mazzini*, London, 1956, 93–4; L. Salvato-relli, *Pensiero e Azione del Risorgimento*, Turin, 1944, 203; G. Colamarino, *Il Fantasma Liberale*, Milan, 1946, 72; G. La Farina, *Scritti Politici*, ed. D. Mack Smith, Palermo, 1972, 292; *Harper's New Monthly Magazine*, New York, August 1872, 376, Castellar.

12 Lord Bryce, *Modern Democracies*, New York, 1921, 1, 66.

13 Giuseppe Mazzini, *Doveri dell'Uomo*, ed. Guglielmo Macchia and Giuliana Limiti for Camera dei Deputati, Rome, 1972, 38–40, 90–3; *Ed. Naz, 3*, 324–5, 330–1; *ibid. 46*, 255; *ibid. 59*, 41–2; *ibid. 69*, 190; *ibid. 83*, 163–4; *ibid. 92*, 110–12.

14 Norberto Bobbio, introduction to Carlo Cattaneo, *Stati Uniti d'Italia*, Turin, 1945, 32; B. Croce, *Storia d'Italia dal 1871 al 1915*, Bari, 1928, 39; Aldo Romano, *Storia del Movimento Socialista in Italia*, Bari, 1966, 1, 38.

15 *Ed. Naz. 3*, 329–32; *ibid. 92*, 114; Jessie White Mario, *Mazzini*, Milan, 1886, 472.

16 Ed. Naz. *3*, 333–4; *ibid. 39*, 341; *ibid. 43*, 185, 223; *ibid. 92*, 339.

17   Mazzini, *Doveri*, 102; *Ed. Naz. 3*, 327–9; *ibid. 92*, 301; *ibid. 93*, 3–4, 78, 164; Lamberto Borghi, *Educazione e Autorità nell'Italia Moderna*, Florence, 1951, 80–1.

18   *Ed. Naz. 2*, 96–7; *ibid. 81*, 220–1; *Fortnightly Review*, 1 Mar. 1871, 309.

19   *Le Memorie di Giorgio Pallavicino*, Turin, 1882, *2*, 371.

20   *Home and Foreign Review*, London, July 1862, 14, Lord Acton.

21   *Ed. Naz. 94*, 280.

22   Alexander Herzen, in July 1855, *Bulletin of the International Institute of Social History*, Amsterdam, Leiden, 1953, 23; *The Reasoner*, London, 10 June 1855, 86; *Fortnightly Review*, London, 1 April 1877, 559; *The Nation*, New York, 22 June 1905, 498.

23   *Ed. Naz. 62*, 62; *ibid. 64*, 163–4; *ibid. 69*, 166–7; Mazzini, *Doveri*, 72; G. Garibaldi, *Scritti e Discorsi Politici e Militari*, Bologna, 1934, *1*, 339.

24   *Ed. Naz. 43*, 202–3, 276–7; *ibid. 51*, 27–8; *The Life and Writings of Joseph Mazzini*, ed. Emilie Ashurst, London, 1870, 6, 302, 307–8; *Rassegna*, Oct. 1960, 598 (Garibaldi, cited by A. Campanella).

25   *Ed. Naz. 34*, 225; *ibid. 46*, 140; *ibid. 92*, 137.

26   British Library Add. MS 40123/ 29, 3 Feb. 1861, Mazzini to Karl Blind.

27   *La Voix du Proscrit*, Paris, 27 Oct. 1850, 1; *Ed. Naz. 45*, 157; *ibid. 46*, 219; *ibid. 69*, 150, 190; *ibid. 77*, 197–8.

28   Mazzini, *Doveri*, 62; *Ed. Naz. 92*, 29; *ibid. Appendice*, 6, 143.

29   *Ed. Naz. 18*, 228; *ibid. 70*, 286; *ibid. 86*, 19; *Il Veltro*, Rome, Aug. 1973, 690–1, Angelo Ara; *Lettere di Camillo Cavour*, ed. L. Chiala, Turin, 1887, 6, 686; Richards, *2*, 169.

30   *Ed. Naz. 62*, 55; *ibid. 66*, 6; *ibid. 84*, 24; *ibid. 92*, 165; Mazzini,

31   *Doveri*, 62.

     Ed. Naz. 56, 192; *ibid. 86*, 18, 256; *ibid. 92*, 158.

32   *Ed. Naz. 3*, 117–18; *ibid. 46*, 262; *ibid. 56*, 192.

33   *Ed. Naz. 46*, lxxii, 262–3; *ibid. 62*, 62.

34   *Ed. Naz. 58*, 43–4.

35   *Ed. Naz. 46*, 262–3; *ibid. 94*, 286–7.

36   *Ed. Naz. 92*, 158.

37   *Ed. Naz. 24*, 165, 320; *ibid. 32*, 65; *ibid. 89*, 51; *ibid. 91*, 219; *Annali Feltrinelli*, Milan, 1962, 4, 296, ed. Della Peruta; *Fraser's Magazine*, London, Aug. 1882, 244; John Vincent, *Disraeli, Derby and the Conservative Party, Journals and Memoirs of Edward Henry, Lord Stanley, 1849–1869*, London, 1978, 296–7.

38   McAdam Papers, Glasgow, 17 Feb. 1863, Mazzini to McAdam; *Pensiero ed Azione*, London, 15 Dec. 1858, 118; *ibid.*, 1 Jan. 1859, 150–1; *ibid.*, 15 Jan. 1859, 150–1, 184–6.

39   *Ed. Naz. 52*, 137; Mazzini, *Doveri*, 101.

40   E. Kastner, *Mazzini e Kossuth: Lettere e documenti inediti*, Florence, 1929, 124, 136–9; *Rassegna*, Jan. 1921, 23, 35–6, Menghini; *Revue Roumaine d'Histoire*, Bucharest, 1972, 974–6, Netea.

41   *Ed. Naz. 56*, 191–2; *ibid. 74*, 210.

42   *Ed. Naz. 85*, 101; *Ed. Naz. 86*, 9–10; *Annali Feltrinelli*, Milan, 1962, 145.

43   *Ed. Naz. 60*, 198; *ibid. 69*, 271–5, 325–6; Wolfgang Giusti, *Mazzini e gli Slavi*, Milan, 1940, 249.

44   Richards, *3*, 46–7; *Ed. Naz. 73*, 172, 366; *ibid. 74*, 58, 156, 245; *ibid. 75*, 230.

45   *Ed. Naz. 92*, 159.

46   *Ed. Naz. 36*, 136–9, 165, 198; *ibid. 59*, 28–9; Mrs Hamilton King, *Letters and Recollections of Mazzini*, London, 1912, 56.

47   *Ed. Naz. 74*, 32; *ibid. 78*, 5;

Andrea Giannelli, *Lettere di Giuseppe Mazzini ad Andrea Giannelli*, Prato, 1888–92, *3*, 414.

48 *Pensiero ed Azione*, 15 Dec. 1858, 118; *Ed. Naz. 59*, 24–5; *ibid. 62*, 62; *ibid. 71*, 74.

49 *Ed. Naz. 3*, 117; *ibid. 31*, 26; *ibid. 36*, 117, 154; *ibid. 59*, 19–21.

50 *Ed. Naz. 36*, 150; *ibid. 46*, 263; *ibid. 59*, 27; *ibid. 75*, 121; *ibid. 86*, 10.

51 *Ed. Naz. 45*, 158.

52 *Ed. Naz. 62*, 62.

53 Karl Marx and Frederick Engels, *Collected Works*, London, 1982, *38*, 363; E. J. Hobsbawm, *Nations and Nationalism since 1870*, Cambridge, 1990, 34–5.

54 *Ed. Naz. 15*, 323; *ibid. 78*, 25; Johann Karl Rodbertus, *Germany and Italy: Answer to Mazzini's 'Italy and Germany'*, London 1861, 13; Carl Rodbertus-Jagetzow, *Kleine Schriften*, Berlin, 1890, 290, 295.

55 *Ed. Naz. 78*, 262; F. Della Peruta, *Democrazia e Socialismo nel Risorgimento*, Rome, 1965, 244–5.

56 *Ed. Naz. 69*, 154, 188; *ibid. 71*, 238–9.

United Italy: 1861–2

57 *Ed. Naz. 64*, 174; *ibid. 71*, 48, 235; *ibid. 72*, 25.

58 *Ed. Naz. 92*, 95.

59 *Ed. Naz. 69*, 281; Schweizerisches Bundesarchiv, Berne, E.2300/2, 4 June 1861, Tourte report from Turin; Clara Lovett, *Giuseppe Ferrari and the Italian Revolution*, Chapel Hill, 1979, 168; *Quarterly Review*, London, Jan. 1861, 175–6.

60 *Ed. Naz. 71*, 341; *ibid. 72*, 125–7, 143, 178.

61 *Lettere e Documenti del Barone Bettino Ricasoli*, ed. M. Tabarrini and A. Gotti, Florence, 1891, *7*, 22–3; *Ricasoli e il suo Tempo: Atti del convegno*, Florence, 1981, 74, Aquarone.

62 *Discorsi Parlamentari di Agostino Bertani*, Rome, 1913, 19–20; *Ed. Naz. 71*, 199; *Edizione Nazionale degli Scritti di Giuseppe Garibaldi*, Bologna, 1935, *5*, 50.

63 Charles Grün, *L'Italie en 1861*, Brussels, 1862, *2*, 345–51; C. Benso di Cavour, *Discorsi Parlamentari*, ed. A. Saitta, Florence, 1973, *15*, 507.

64 *Die Auswärtige Politik Preussens*, ed. R. Ibbeken, Oldenberg, 1935, *2*, 2.

65 *Ed. Naz. 72*, 26–7, 37–8, 378–9; A. M. Ghisalberti, *Attorno e Accanto a Mazzini*, Milan, 1972, 106; J. La Bolina, *Cronachette del Risorgimento Italiano*, Florence, 1920, 50–1.

66 *Ed. Naz. 66*, 408; *ibid. 69*, 243; *ibid. 71*, 205, 378.

67 *Ed. Naz. 71*, 167, 222; *Cavour e l'Inghilterra*, Bologna, 1952, *3*, 188; *Hansard, 161*, 1622, 7 Mar. 1861; *Correspondence and Conversations of Alexis De Tocqueville with Nassau William Senior from 1834 to 1859*, London, 1872, *2*, 225; Gladstone, cited by A. Colombo, *L'Inghilterra nel Risorgimento Italiano*, Milan, 1918, 69.

68 *Lettere del Ricasoli*, ed. Tabarrini, *7*, 85.

69 *Ed. Naz. 71*, 344; *ibid. 72*, 39, 252, 295.

70 Massimo d'Azeglio, *L'Italie de 1847 à 1865: Correspondance politique*, ed. E. Rendu, Paris, 1867, 199–200, 232, 255; *Massimo d'Azeglio e Diomede Pantaleoni: Carteggio inedito*, ed. G. Faldella, Turin, 1888, 446–7; *Lettere Inedite di Massimo d'Azeglio al Marchese Emanuele d'Azeglio*, ed. N. Bianchi, Turin, 1883, 356.

71 *Ed. Naz. 69*, 259, 265.

72 *Carteggi di Bettino Ricasoli*, ed. G. Camerani and C. Rotondi, Rome, 1984, *17*, 157; *Lettere di Ricasoli*, ed. Tabarrini, *6*, 186, 189; Andrea Maurici, *L'Opera della Sicilia per la Cessazione del Potere Temporale e la Liberazione di Roma*

e di Venezia, 1861–2, Palermo, 1914, 142–3; A Luzio, *Aspromonte e Mentana: documenti inediti*, Florence, 1935, 117; *Études sur l'Italie*, Turin, 1862, *1*, 65.

73 *The Times*, 10 Oct., 21. Dec. and 31 Dec. 1861; Saffi, 7, 49, 284–5; Andrea Giannelli, *Due Clandestine a Roma negli Anni 1861 e 1862*, Pistoia, 1894, 139, 147; J. W. Mario, *Della Vita di Giuseppe Mazzini*, 427; *Giacomo Dina e l'Opera sua nelle Vicende del Risorgimento Italiano*, Turin, 1899, *2*, 711–13, 724; F. E. Morando, *Mazziniani e Garibaldini nell' Ultimo Periodo del Risorgimento*, Genoa, 1920, 122.

74 Jessie White Mario, *Agostino Bertani e i suoi Tempi*, Florence, 1881, *2*, 232.

75 *Contemporary Review*, London, Mar. 1888, 379; *Murray's Magazine*, London, June 1891, 761; Saffi, 7, 86.

76 DDI ser. *1*, *2*, 368; *Ed. Naz. Appendice*, *6*, 210.

77 *Episodi Diplomatici del Risorgimento Italiano dal 1856 al 1863 estratti dalle carte del Generale Giacomo Durando*, ed. C. Durando, Turin, 1901, 249–50; *Ed. Naz.* 72, 326.

78 McAdam Papers, Glasgow, no. 64, Mazzini's letter of 28 July 1862; *Ed. Naz.* 72, 348, 369; *ibid.* 73, 21, 29; Felix Moscheles, *Fragments of an Autobiography*, London, 1899, 259.

79 *Carteggio e Bibliografia di Costantino Nigra*, Turin, 1930, 228, 244; *Episodi Diplomatici dalle Carte di Durando*, 262–3.

80 *Ibid.* 232; DDI ser. *1*, *3*, 11, 27, 103, 171; *Lettere del Ricasoli*, 7, 110–13; Luzio, *Aspromonte*, 189–90, 250; *Memorie per la Storia de' nostri Tempi dal Congresso di Parigi nel 1856 ai Giorni Nostri*, Turin, 1865, ser. *3*, *2*, 33–7.

81 *Lettere ad Antonio Panizzi di Uomini Illustri*, ed. L. Fagan, Florence, 1880, 480; Saffi, 7, 88–92; Jessie White Mario, supplementary volume to *Autobiography of Giuseppe Garibaldi*, London, 1889, *3*, 369; *Journal of Central European Affairs*, Boulder, July 1947, 157, Marraro.

82 Alexander Herzen, *My Past and Thoughts*, ed. C. Garnet and H. Higgens, London, 1968, *4*, 1717–18.

83 *Ed. Naz.* 73, 89–90; J. W. Mario, *Mazzini*, 422–4; J. W. Mario, *Agostino Bertani*, *2*, 296.

84 FO PRO, ser 30/22/70, 22 May 1864, Minghetti.

85 *Ed. Naz.* 73, 185, 213–14.

86 *Le Carte di Agostino Bertani*, ed. L. Marchetti, Milan, 1962, 996; *Discorsi Parlamentari di Urbano Rattazzi*, ed. G. Scovazzi, Rome, 1880, *6*, 158; Cesare Cantù, *Della Indipendenza Italiana*, Turin, 1876, *3*, 591; A. Spallici, *Alberto Mario*, Milan, 1955, 316–17; *Ed. Naz.* 73, 237.

87 *Le Relazioni Diplomatiche fra il Regno di Sardegna e la Gran Bretagna*, ed. F. Curato, Rome, 1964, ser. *3*, *4*, 177–8; L. Mariotti, *Italy in 1848*, London, 1851, 18.

88 *The Times*, 7 Oct. 1862.

89 *Ed. Naz.* 69, 311; *ibid.* 76, 339; M. Rosi, *Il Risorgimento Italiano e l'Azione d'un Patriota*, Rome, 1906, 439–40.

90 *Ed. Naz.* 73, 100, 126–7, 362; *ibid.* 75, 11, 19, 64.

91 *Ed. Naz.* 73, 161, 163.

92 *Ed. Naz.* 73, 129, 387–8; *ibid.* 74, 22.

93 *Ed. Naz.* 73, 259–60.

Victor Emanuel and Garibaldi: 1863–4

94 Diamilla Muller, *Politica Segreta Italiana (1863–1870)*, 2nd ed., Turin, 1891, 28.

95 *Il Problema Veneto e l'Europa*, ed. Georges Dethan, Venice, 1967, *3*, 409.

96 Asproni, *Diario Politico*, *3*, 409–

10; *Ed. Naz. 74*, 240.

97 Livio Marchetti, *Il Trentino nel Risorgimento*, Milan, 1913, *2*, 119–23.

98 *Ed. Naz. 74*, 218; *ibid. 78*, 290; Saffi, *7*, 130–1.

99 *Ed. Naz. 76*, 189, 231; James Stansfeld, *The Italian Movement and Italian Parties*, London, 1862, 38–9.

100 *Ed. Naz. 76*, 318–20, 337; *ibid. 78*, 14, 18.

101 *DDI ser. 1 3*, 379; *ibid. 4*, 478.

102 *Carteggio di Nigra*, 75; Maurizio Cassetti, *Le Carte di Alfonso Ferrero Della Marmora*, Turin, 1979, 151; Elpis Melena, *Garibaldi: Recollections of his Public and Private Life*, London, 1887, 172–3; G. E. Curatulo, *Soliloqui, Colloqui*, Rome, 1942, 254.

103 *Ed. Naz. 59*, 295; *ibid. 73*, 164; *ibid. 76*, 22–3; *ibid. 82*, 266; *ibid. 85*, 99; *The Economist*, 26 Mar. 1864, 382–3; Wilfrid Ward, *The Life and Times of Cardinal Wiseman*, London, 1897, *1*, 407; *Il Risorgimento*, Milan, Feb. 1965, 9, Gasparini; M. D. Conway, *Autobiography*, Boston, 1904, *2*, 58.

104 *The Times*, 6 Sept. 1862; *ibid.* 15 Jan. 1864; Muller, *Politica Segreta*, 25.

105 *Roma e Venezia: Ricordi storici d'un Romano*, Turin, 1895, 208, 240–2; Asproni, *Diario Politico*, *4*, 8, 15; *Ed. Naz. 74*, 170–1, 204–5; Francesco Crispi, *Carteggi Politici Inediti 1860–1900*, ed. T. Palamenghi-Crispi, Rome, 1912, 195; Cassetti, *Le Carte Della Marmora*, 153, 722–3; *The National Review*, London, Jan. 1864, 23, Cobbe; R. Romeo, *Il Giudizio Storico sul Risorgimento*, Catania, 1966, 39; *Dizionario Biografico degli Italiani*, Rome, 1983, *29*, 419, Agnello.

106 *Hansard, 173*, 1937–8, 14 Mar. 1864; *ibid. 174*, 261–3, 275, 17 Mar. 1864; E. Morelli, *L'Inghilterra di Mazzini*, Rome,

1965, 191–201; Justin McCarthy, *Reminiscences*, London, 1899, *2*, 189–90; W. F. Monypenny, *The Life of Benjamin Disraeli*, London, 1910, *1*, 241; *The Diaries of John Bright*, ed. R. A. J. Walling, London, 1930, 282; *Ed. Naz. 78*, 258.

107 Hansard, *174*, 277–9, 326, 17–18 Mar. 1864.

108 Janet Fyfe, *Autobiography of John McAdam (1806–1883)*, Edinburgh, 1980, 42; Richards, *2*, 128.

109 *Ed. Naz. 80*, 174–5; William Malleson letter to Bolton King, 25 June 1902, in Bolton King Papers.

110 *Ed. Naz. 73*, 50, 59, 195, 208–9, 322; *Rassegna*, July 1949, 165, Conti.

111 *Ed. Naz. 74*, 123; *ibid. 76*, 197; *ibid. 78*, 4, 317; *ibid. 80*, 106, 238, 275; *ibid. 81*, 289, 343–4; *ibid. 85*, 13.

112 Joseph Rossi, *The Image of America in Mazzini's Writings*, Madison, 1954, 113, 122; *Ed. Naz. 61*, 194–5; *ibid. 63*, 105; *Le Carte di Giovanni Lanza*, ed. De Vecchi di Val Cismon, Turin, 1935, *2*, 125.

113 *Ed. Naz. 76*, 34; Moncure Conway, in *Harpers Magazine*, New York, July 1872, 273.

114 *Fraser's Magazine*, London, Aug. 1882, 244; *Ed. Naz. 80*, 224.

115 *Ed. Naz. 83*, 187; Richards, *3*, 64; *Journal of Modern History*, Chicago, June 1949, 110, 114, Marraro.

116 *Dark Blue*, London, May 1872, 314, Karl Blind; *Ed. Naz. 78*, 10–11; *ibid. 80*, 127.

117 Jane Addams, *Twenty Years at Hull House*, New York, 1928, 21; George D. Herron, *The Revival of Italy*, London, 1922, 15; *The Nation*, New York, 22 June 1905, 498, William Roscoe Thayer; Gaetano Salvemini, *Scritti sul Risorgimento*, ed. P. Pieri and C. Pischedda, Milan, 1961, 197–8.

118 *Notes and Queries*, London, Sept. 1922, 217; William Arthur, *Italy*

119   *in Transition*, London, 1860, 100.
      Corriere della Sera, Milan, 31 May
      1932, Luzio; *Rassegna*, Jan. 1924,
      180, Michel; *Ed. Naz. 78*, 21.

120   *Il Problema Veneto*, 2, 714–15;
      Royal Archives, Windsor, J. 36/
      134, 21 April 1864; *Lettere Inedite
      di Massimo d'Azeglio*, ed. N.
      Bianchi, Turin, 1883, 342–3;
      Lettere ad Antonio Panizzi, 480–2.

121   *Ed. Naz. 78*, 289; *Rassegna*, 1935,
      814, Onnis.

122   Derek Beales, 'Garibaldi in Eng-
      land: The Politics of Italian En-
      thusiasm', in *Society and Politics in
      the Age of the Risorgimento*, ed.
      John Davis and Paul Ginsborg,
      Cambridge, 1991, 198–9.

123   Herzen, *My Past*, 3, 1276–7.

124   *The Victoria Magazine*, London,
      May 1872, 5; *The Amberley Papers:
      The Letters and Diaries of Lord and
      Lady Amberley*, ed. Bertrand and
      Patricia Russell, London, 1937, *1*,
      518–19; L. Fagan, *The Life of Sir
      Anthony Panizzi*, London, 1880, *1*,
      186–7.

125   Muller, *Politica Segreta*, 48–9;
      *Carteggi e Documenti Inediti di E.
      d'Azeglio*, ed. A. Colombo, Turin,
      1920, *2*, 343–4; Lilla Lipparini,
      Minghetti, Bologna, 1947, *2*, 365.

126   *Politica Segreta*, 60; Saffi, *8*, 70.

127   *Ed. Naz. 78*, 142–3, 150, 173,
      305, 307; *Nuovi Documenti su
      Giuditta Sidoli*, ed. G. Marini, Pisa,
      1957, 113; A. Scirocco, *I
      Democratici Italiani da Sapri a Porta
      Pia*, Naples, 1969, 245; Bianca
      Montale, *Antonio Mosto: Battaglie e
      cospirazioni mazziniani 1848–1870*,
      Pisa, 1966, 114–17.

128   McAdam   Papers,   Glasgow,
      Mazzini's letter of 11 May 1864
      to McAdam; *The Life of Peter
      Stuart the Ditton Doctor*, London,
      1920, 22.

129   *Les Origines Diplomatiques de la
      Guerre de 1870–71*, Paris, 1910, *3*,
      344–6; *Carteggi di E. d'Azeglio*, *2*,
      347.

130   *Ed. Naz. 78*, 282; *ibid. 79*, 68.

131   *Ed. Naz. 78*, 254, 328; *Unità
      Italiana*, Milan, 25 Aug. 1864;
      Saffi, *8*, 61; *Le Carte di Lanza*, *3*,
      468.

132   *Ed. Naz. 79*, 132–3; *ibid. 83*, 3;
      Denis Mack Smith, *Italy and its
      Monarchy*, New Haven, 1989, 21–
      3.

133   *Ed. Naz. 80*, 199; *ibid. 85*, 337;
      Domus, *1981, 1*, 43, Monsagrati.

CHAPTER EIGHT. *The Later 1860s*

Venice acquired

1   *Ed. Naz. 60*, 38–9.

2   *Letters and Memorials of Catherine
      Winkworth*, edited by her sister,
      Clifton, 1883, *2*, 360, 363.

3   *The Roman Question: Extracts from
      the Despatches of Odo Russell from
      Rome 1858–1870*, ed. Noel
      Blakiston, London, 1962, 285,
      288; *Results of Victor Emanuel's
      Rule, by an eye-witness*, London,
      1863, 43.

4   *Ed. Naz. 79*, 192–3; A. Omodeo, *Il
      Senso della Storia*, 418; *Rivista
      d'Italia*, Jan. 1902, 14–15,
      Zanichelli.

5   *Ed. Naz. 79*, 159, 271; *ibid. 80*,
      160; *ibid. 81*, 185–6.

6   Federigo Sclopis, *Diario Segreto
      (1859–1878)*, ed. P. Pietro Pirri,
      Turin, 1959, 384–5; Saffi, *9*, 129.

7   *Ed. Naz. 79*, 219, 255–6; *ibid. 80*,
      4; *ibid. 83*, 34; Saffi, *8*, 108, 110,
      126–7; *Documenti del Risorgimento
      negli Archivi Trentini*, Rome,
      1938, 116; *Journal of Modern
      History*, Chicago, 1949, 113,
      Marraro.

8   *DDI ser. 1, 5*, 385.

9   *Ibid.* 277, 329, 332, 437, 559,
      564, 581, 686.

10   *DDI ser. 1, 6*, 19.

11   M. Cassetti, *Le Carte di Alfonso
      Ferrero Della Marmora*, Turin,
      1979, 637.

12   *Le Carte di Giovanni Lanza*, ed. De
      Vecchi di Val Cismon, Turin,

1935, *3*, 10, 38, 46, 60, 63; Luigi Federico Menabrea, *Memorie*, ed. L. Briguglio and L. Bulferetti, Florence, 1971, 55.

13   *Ed. Naz. 80*, 53, 65, 193, 292, 339.

14   *Le Carte di Lanza, 2*, 465; *ibid. 3*, 125, 143, 152, 382, 494.

15   *Ibid.* 130–1, 158, 160, 164, 191.

16   *Ibid.* 358–60.

17   *Ibid.* 445, 511, 548–9; Giuseppe Garibaldi, *Scritti e Discorsi Politici e Militari*, Bologna, 1935, *2*, 257.

18   *Le Lettere di Vittorio Emanuele II*, ed. F. Cognasso, Turin, 1966, *1*, 791.

19   Garibaldi, *Scritti, 3*, 486; *Discorsi Parlamentari di Francesco Crispi*, Rome, 1915, *1*, 537; *Discorsi Parlamentari di Agostino Depretis*, Rome, 1891, 7, 588.

20   *Ed. Naz. 80*, 130–1; *ibid. 81*, 256.

21   McAdam Papers, Glasgow University, MS General 530, 13 Nov. 1864, letter to McAdam.

22   *Ed. Naz. 73*, 194; Francesco Crispi, *Pensieri e Profezie*, ed. T. Palamenghi-Crispi, Rome, 1920, 113; Francesco Crispi, *Carteggi Politici Inediti (1860–1900)*, Rome, 1912, 81.

23   Francesco Crispi, *Repubblica e Monarchia: a Giuseppe Mazzini, lettera*, Turin 1865, 27, 54–5, 60–1.

24   *Ed. Naz. 80*, 161, 194–5; *ibid. 83*, 34, 40.

25   *Lettere Inedite di Massimo d'Azeglio al Marchese Emanuele d'Azeglio*, ed. N. Bianchi, Turin, 1883, 121; *Lettere e Documenti del Barone Bettino Ricasoli*, ed. M. Tabarrini and A. Gotti, Florence, 1891, 7, 340; Giuseppe Maranini, *Storia del Potere in Italia*, Florence, 1967, 190, 265; D. Mack Smith, 'Cavour and Parliament', in *Victor Emanuel, Cavour and the Risorgimento*, Oxford, 1971, 58–60.

26   *Ed. Naz. 79*, 163.

27   *Ed. Naz. 69*, 311; *ibid. 77*, 80; *ibid. 80*, 318; *ibid. 83*, 90.

28   *Ed. Naz. 75*, 17; *ibid. 83*, 110; *ibid.* 86, 41.

29   *Cavour e l'Inghilterra*, Bologna, 1933, *3*, 285; J. W. Mario, *Agostino Bertani e i Suoi Tempi*, Florence, 1888, *2*, 207.

30   Sidney Sonnino, *Diario 1866–1912*, ed. B. F. Brown and G. Spini, Bari, 1972, *1*, 41.

31   *Discorsi Parlamentari di Giuseppe Zanardelli*, Rome, *2*, 29–30; Giuseppe Sardo, *Dalla Convenzione di Settembre alla Breccia di Porta Pia*, vol. 6 of *Storia del Parlamento Italiano*, Palermo, 1969, 80.

32   *Carteggi di Bettino Ricasoli*, ed. S. Camerani and G. Arfè, Rome, 1968, *23*, 472.

33   *Carteggio tra Marco Minghetti e Giuseppe Pasolini*, ed. Guido Pasolini, Turin, 1924, *4*, 151.

34   *Ed. Naz. 79*, 57; *ibid. 80*, 4, 46; *ibid. 81*, 129.

35   *Ed. Naz. 80*, 260; *ibid. 81*, 32.

36   Morelli, *L'Inghilterra di Mazzini*, 203–18; *Ed. Naz. 81*, 208.

37   *The George Eliot Letters*, ed. Gordon Haight, London, 1956, *4*, 199–200.

38   *Ed. Naz. 80*, 291.

39   *Life of Frances Cobbe as told by herself*, London, 1904, 117; Leona Ravenna, *Il Giornalismo Mazziniano: Note ed appunti*, Florence, 1939, 217–21, 259; *Ed. Naz. 79*, 187; *ibid. 80*, 108–10.

40   *Carteggio e Bibliografia di Costantino Nigra*, Turin, 1930, 156–7.

41   *Ed. Naz. 81*, 289; *ibid. 82*, 157; *ibid. 83*, 182.

42   McAdam Papers, Glasgow, 19 June 1866, to McAdam.

43   Richards, 3, 67, 157–8; *Ed. Naz. 83*, 258–9, 262.

44   *Ed. Naz. 82*, 112, 123–4, 130, 149.

45   *Ed. Naz. 78*, 52; *ibid. 82*, 166, 218–20; *ibid. 83*, 256–7; D. Mack Smith , 'The King and the War of 1866', in *Victor Emanuel, Cavour and the Risorgimento*, London, 1971, 303–35.

46   *Ed. Naz. 82*, 198, 244, 266.
47   *Carteggi di Ricasoli*, 22, 113–14.
48   *Harper's New Monthly Magazine*, New York, July 1872, 289, Conway.

Final breach with the monarchy

49   Saffi, *9*, 7.
50   *Ed. Naz. 86*, 49.
51   *Ed. Naz. 82*, 324; *ibid. Appendice 6*, 356–8.
52   *Ed. Naz. 84*, 3–4.
53   *Rassegna*, Jan. 1963, 94–5, ed. Tamborra.
54   *DDI ser. 1, 7*, 320.
55   Mary Trauth, *Italo-American Diplomatic Relations 1861–1882*, Washington, 1958, 165; *Dublin Review*, Jan. 1867, 211–13.
56   P. Villari, *Saggi di Storia, di Critica, e di Politica*, Florence, 1868, 391–3; J. W. Mario, *In Memoria di Giovanni Nicotera*, Florence, 1894, 91.
57   Edoardo Pantano, *Memorie*, Bologna, 1933, *1*, 222; Livio Marchetti, *Il Trentino nel Risorgimento*, Milan, 1913, *2*, 107, 391–3.
58   *Ed. Naz. 84*, 7, 160; *DDI ser. 1, 11*, 431.
59   *Ed. Naz. 82*, 304; *ibid. 86*, 22; *Carteggi di Ricasoli, 22*, 56; Alfredo Comandini and Antonio Monti, *L'Italia nei Cento Anni del Secolo XIX*, Rome, 1924–8, *4*, 886.
60   *Ed. Naz. 84*, 179.
61   *Journal of Modern History*, Chicago, Mar. 1933, 67, Hoeing; *Nuovi Documenti su Giuditta Sidoli*, ed. G. Marini, Pisa, 1957, 117.
62   *Ed. Naz. 84*, 174, 218–19.
63   McAdam Papers, Glasgow, 18 April 1867; Giuseppe Guerzoni, *Garibaldi*, Florence, 1882, *2*, 479.
64   Saffi, *9*, 28, 35; Andrea Giannelli, *Aneddoti Ignorati ed Importanti: Brevi ricordi Mazziniani dal 1848 al 1872*, Florence, 1905, 42.
65   *Aspromonte e Mentana: Documenti inediti*, ed. Alessandro Luzio, Florence, 1935, 322–34; *Ed. Naz. 84*, 335.
66   Andrea Giannelli, *Cenni Autobiografici e Ricordi Politici*, Milan, 1926, 502; *Ed. Naz. 84*, 216–18, 254; *ibid. 85*, 108, 181, 193–4, 243, 291–2.
67   Paolo Alatri, *Lotte Politiche in Sicilia sotto il Governo della Destra (1866–74)*, Turin, 1954, 198.
68   *Ed. Naz. 86*, 84–8.
69   G. E. Curàtulo, *Il Dissidio tra Mazzini e Garibaldi: la storia senza veli*, Milan, 1928, 263; Guerzoni, *Garibaldi, 2*, 500; Gaspare Finali, *Memorie*, ed. G. Maioli, Faenza, 1955, 294–5; *Lettere del Ricasoli*, ed. Tabarrini, *10*, 8; *Discorsi Parlamentari di Urbano Rattazzi*, ed. E. Scovazzi, Rome, 1880, *7*, 209–14.
70   *Ed. Naz. 85*, 143–4, 205, 219, 237, 269; Richards, *3*, 187.
71   *Les Origines Diplomatiques de la Guerre de 1870–71*, Paris, 1926, *19*, 10, 22–4; *DDI ser. 1, 9*, 342; *Carteggio di Nigra*, 171; Renato Mori, *Il Tramonto del Potere Temporale 1866–1870*, Rome, 1967, 245–8; Luzio, *Aspromonte*, 405.
72   *Les Origines, 19*, 380; *Die Auswärtige Politik Preussens 1858–1871*, ed. H. Michaelis, Berlin, 1939, *10*, 5–6, Prince Friedrich Wilhelm; *Clio*, Rome, Jan. 1967, 44–5, Aquarone; Mori, *Tramonto*, 144.
73   *Ed. Naz. 85*, 277–8; *ibid. 86*, 96, 102; Mauro Macchi, *Almanacco Storico d'Italia*, Milan, 1870, *3*, 8–11; F. Cavallotti, *Storia della Insurrezione di Roma nel 1867*, Milan, 1869, 571–2; *Journal of Modern History*, June 1944, 119–21, Marraro.
74   Gustavo Sacerdote, *La Vita di Giuseppe Garibaldi*, Milan, 1933, 928; Giuseppe Garibaldi, *Scritti e Discorsi*, Bologna, 1937, *3*, 485; Saffi, *9*, 305.

75 *Le Memorie di Garibaldi nella Redazione Definitiva del 1872*, Bologna, 1932, 544–5; Guerzoni, *Garibaldi, 2*, 600–1; Jessie White Mario, supplementary third volume to the *Autobiography of Giuseppe Garibaldi*, London, 1889, 388–91; Giannelli, *Cenni*, 516.

76 PRO 30/22/16E, 1 Jan. 1868, Clarendon; *DDI ser. 1, 9*, 396; *Carteggi di Ricasoli, 26*, 139; Sclopis, *Diario*, 421; Genova di Revel, *Sette mesi al Ministero*, Milan, 1895, 229; Crispi, *Carteggi Politici Inediti*, 312; Mori, *Tramonto*, 567–70; Giuseppe Massari, *La Vita ed il Regno di Vittorio Emanuele II di Savoia*, Milan, 1878, *2*, 333.

77 *Ed. Naz. 86*, 107–8.

78 *La Civiltà Cattolica*, 26 April 1872, 360.

79 Alberto and Jessie White Mario, *Carlo Cattaneo: Cenni e reminiscenze*, Rome, 1884, 153; J. W. Mario, *Agostino Bertani, 2*, 343; Saffi, *9*, 87.

80 *Ed. Naz. 80*, 309; Lord Newton, *Lord Lyons*, London, 1913, *1*, 188.

81 *McAdam Papers*, Glasgow, 12 July 1868; *Ed. Naz. 87*, 57.

82 *Ed. Naz. 85*, 336–7.

83 *Domus*, 1981, *1*, 43, Monsagrati.

84 *Die Auswärtige Politik, 8*, 365, Usedom; note by Baron Karl Kübeck of 8 Feb. 1867, in Haus-, Hof- und Staatsarchiv, Vienna; *Rassegna*, Jan. 1963, 94–5, Tamborra.

85 Robert von Keudell, *Fürst und Fürstin Bismarck: Erinnerungen*, Berlin, 1901, 113–14; Felix Moscheles, *Fragments of an Autobiography*, London, 1899, 256.

86 *Ed. Naz. 87, 3*, 47.

87 *Ed. Naz. 83*, 243; *ibid. 86*, 107–10; *ibid. 87*, 182; *Risorgimento*, Brussels, 1982, 250–1, Jens Petersen.

88 Curàtulo, *Il Dissidio*, 326; Garibaldi, *Scritti e Discorsi, 3*, 497.

89 *DDI ser. 1, 10*, 433.

90 *Ed. Naz. 87*, 72, 120–1; J. W. Mario, *Della Vita di Giuseppe Mazzini*, Milan, 1886, 453.

Life in England

91 *Italia e Inghilterra nella Prima Fase del Risorgimento* (catalogue of exhibition at Italian Institute in London), ed. E. Morelli, Rome, 1952, 108.

92 *The Times*, 10 Sept. 1866; *Fortnightly Magazine*, 1 June 1868, 636–7; A. Gallenga, *Italy Revisited*, London, 1875, *2*, 206–7.

93 Terenzio Grandi, *Mazzini Aneddotico*, Turin, 1955, 158.

94 *The Letters of Elizabeth Barrett Browning*, ed. F. G. Kenyon, London, 1897, 277–9; Mountstuart Grant Duff, *Notes for a Diary 1851–1872*, London, 1897, *1*, 216–17; *ibid. 2*, 145; Henry Manning, *Rome and the Revolution*, London, 1867, 16; Henry Manning, *Christ and Antichrist*, London, 1867, 6.

95 *Letters of Lord Acton to Mary, daughter of the Rt Hon. W. E. Gladstone*, ed. H. Paul, London, 1904, 210.

96 *Blackwoods Magazine*, Edinburgh, April 1861, 416; John Vincent, *Disraeli, Derby and the Conservative Party*, London, 1978, 213.

97 *Ed. Naz. 80*, 267.

98 George J. Holyoake, *Sixty Years of an Agitator's Life*, London, 1892, *1*, 90; *Harper's New Monthly Magazine*, New York, July 1872, 287; *The Letters of William Lloyd Garrison*, ed. W. M. Merrill and L. Ruchames, Cambridge, Mass., 1981, *6*, 76; Herzen, *My Past, 3*, 1029; G. E. Curàtulo, *Garibaldi, Vittorio Emanuele, Cavour nei Fasti della Patria: Documenti inediti*, Bologna, 1911, 289–90.

99 *Fortnightly Review*, May 1878, 725, Myers; N. Colajanni, *Preti e Socialisti contro Mazzini*, Rome, 1971, 9; Richard Armstrong,

Makers of the Nineteenth Century, London, 1901, 137, 159.

100 W. J. Linton, *Memories*, London, 1898, 152.

101 Thomas Frost, *The Secret Societies of the European Revolution 1776-1876*, London, 1876, *2*, 140.

102 Bolton King, *Mazzini*, London, 1902, 179; Mrs Hamilton King, *Letters and Recollections of Mazzini*, London, 1912, 3.

103 *The Rossetti Papers 1862 to 1870*, ed. William Michael Rossetti, London, 1903, 208–9, 215, 248, 336; G. W. E. Russell, *A Pocketful of Sixpences*, London, 1907, 96.

104 *Macmillan's Magazine*, London, May 1867, 58; *The Life and Letters of Frederick Denison Maurice*, ed. F. Maurice, London, 1884, 58.

105 *Review of Reviews*, London, June 1895, 509.

106 *Fortnightly Review*, May 1891, 712; J. W. Mario, *Della Vita di Mazzini*, xii, 469.

107 Note by William Malleson in Bolton King Papers; Carl Wittke, *Against the Current: the life of Karl Heinzen (1809–80)*, Chicago, 1945, 120; Richards, *2*, v.

108 *The Nation*, New York, 9 Dec. 1909, 564.

109 *Daily News*, London, 12 Mar. 1872.

110 Richards, 1, 25.

111 *Murray's Magazine*, London, June 1891, 762; Domus, 1992, *1*, 106, Assing.

112 *Fifty Years of Fleet Street: Being the Life and Recollections of Sir John R. Robinson*, ed. F. M. Thomas, London, 1904, 341.

113 Moncure Conway, in *Harper's Magazine*, July 1872, 290–1; *Scritti Politici di Alberto Mario*, ed. G. Carducci, Bologna, 1901, 88; W. J. Linton, *European Republicans*, London, 1893, 163; M. J. Shaen, *Memorials of Two Sisters*, London, 1908, 59–60; J. W. Mario, *Mazzini*, 384; Richards, *1*, 25; *Murray's Magazine*, June

1891, 762; *Macmillan's Magazine*, April 1872, 519; *Dark Blue*, London, May 1872, 316; *Letters and Memorials of Catherine Winkworth*, Clifton, 1883, *1*, 416; Alessandro Levi, *Scritti Minori Storici e Politici*, Padua, 1957, *2*, 203.

114 Mrs King, *Letters and Recollections*, 116, 119, 123.

115 Facsimile letter in Edyth Hinkley, *Mazzini: The Story of a Great Italian*, London, 1924, 183; Moscheles, *Fragments of an Autobiography*, 250; Richards, *1*, 4; *ibid.*, *2*, 53, 267–70.

116 *Fortnightly Review*, May 1891, 702, 708–11.

117 H. M. Hyndman, *The Record of an Adventurous Life*, London, 1911, 59–66.

118 E. Castelar, *Semblanzas Contemporaneas*, Havana, 1872, *xi*, 62, 67.

119 Bolton King Papers; *Ed. Naz. 81*, 216–22.

120 *The London Review*, 17 Nov. 1860.

121 *Fortnightly Review*, May 1891, 702.

122 *Fifty Years of Fleet Street*, ed. F. M. Thomas, 336.

123 *Cosmopolis*, London, June 1897, 655–7.

124 *Daily News*, 12 Mar. 1872.

125 James Stansfeld, *The Italian Movement and Italian Parties*, London, 1862, 39; *Review of Reviews*, June 1895, 508–9.

126 Mrs King, *Letters*, 53; Justin McCarthy, *Portraits of the Sixties*, London, 1903, 323, 329–34.

127 Emilie Ashurst, introduction to Joseph Mazzini, *The Duties of Man*, London, 1862, vi; Petruccelli della Gattina, *I Fattori e Malfattori della Politica Europea Contemporanea*, Milan, 1881, *2*, 363.

128 *Ed. Naz. 87*, 165; Richards, *3*, 200, 223, 228, 232, 240, 280.

129 Shaen, *Memorials*, 11–12, 19.

130 *The Century Illustrated Monthly Magazine*, New York, Nov. 1891, 67; *American Historical Review*,

July 1929, 780.

131 Moncure Conway, *Mazzini: A Discourse Given in South Place Chapel, 17 Mar. 1872*, 3–4; Conway, *Autobiography*, London, 1904, *2*, 52–8.

132 S. Gwynn and G. M. Tuckwell, *The Life of Rt Hon. Sir Charles Dilke*, London, 1917, *2*, 238.

133 W. E. H. Lecky, *Democracy and Liberty*, London, 1896, *1*, 407–8.

134 *Ed. Naz. 81*, 224.

135 Adolf Friedrich von Schack, *Joseph Mazzini und die Italienische Einheit*, Stuttgart, 1891, 60; *Quaderni di Cultura*, Livorno, April 1952, 160, Barsali; Frederick Harrison, *Autobiographic Memoirs*, London, 1911, *1*, 95–9; *The Life and Letters of Frederick Denison Maurice*, *2*, 548; *The Spectator*, 3 Sept. 1870, 1062.

136 *The Works of John Ruskin*, ed. E. T. Cook and A. Wedderburn, London, 1903–12, *29*, 96; *ibid. 36*, 473.

137 MS in Bodleian Library, Oxford, quoted by G. Costa in *Rassegna*, July 1969, 441; *Ed. Naz. 58*, 143–4; *ibid. 71*, 301; *ibid. Appendice, 6*, 135.

138 *Ed. Naz. 82*, 173; *ibid. 90*, 312; *ibid. 91*, 169; Richards, *3*, 284; Augustus Hare, *The Story of My Life*, London, 1900, *4*, 305.

139 *George Eliot's Life as Related in her Letters and Journals*, ed. J. W. Cross, London, 1885, *3*, 156; Gordon S. Haight, *George Eliot: A Biography*, Oxford, 1969, 99; *Ed. Naz. 80*, 332; Richards, *3*, 76.

140 *The Letters of George Meredith*, ed. C. L. Cline, Oxford, 1970, *1*, 252, 331; *ibid. 3*, 1441; *The Letters and Memoirs of Sir William Hardman 1863–1865*, ed. S. M. Ellis, London, 1925, 160.

141 *The Letters of John Stuart Mill*, ed. Hugh Elliot, London, 1910, 269; *The Later Letters of John Stuart Mill 1849–1873*, ed. F. E. Mineka and D. N. Lindley, Toronto, 1972, *2*,

548, 713; *ibid. 4*, 1879; *Ed. Naz. 72*, 72–3.

142 *Ed. Naz. 76*, 78–9; *ibid. 81*, 8, 28; *ibid. 85*, 166–7, 230; *ibid. 87*, 54; *ibid. 89*, 152–3.

143 *Chamber's Journal*, London, 30 Sept. 1911, 695–7.

144 *The Economist*, London, 26 Mar. 1864, 283; *ibid.* 16 Mar. 1872, 323–4.

145 John Viscount Morley, *Recollections*, London, 1917, *1*, 75–9, 246; John Morley, *The Life of William Ewart Gladstone*, London, 1903, *3*, 478.

146 Chushichi Tsuzuki, *Edward Carpenter 1844–1929*, Cambridge, 1980, 16-18; Gwilym Griffith, *Mazzini: Prophet of Modern Europe*, London, 1932, 329; E. Gurney, *Phantasms of the Living*, London, 1886, *2*, 188; *Henry Sidgwick: A Memoir by A. S. and E. M. S.*, London, 1906, 165; *Ed. Naz. 91*, 343; F. W. H. Myers, *Essays Classic and Modern*, London, 1883, 1–69.

147 E. Abbott and L. Cambell, *The Life and Letters of Benjamin Jowett*, London, 1897, *2*, 10; Thomas Jones, CH, introduction to Mazzini's *The Duties of Man and other Essays*, London, 1955, xv; E. Morelli, *L'Inghilterra di Mazzini*, Rome, 1965, 206.

148 T. H. Green, *Lectures on the Principles of Political Obligation*, ed. P. Harris and J. Morrow, Cambridge, 1986, 86; *Undergraduate Papers*, Oxford, 1858, 96, 153–4; *The Works of Thomas Hill Green: Late Professor of Moral Philosophy at Oxford*, ed. R. L. Nettleship, London, 1888, *3*, xlii–xliii; Thomas Jones, *Welsh Broth*, London, 1951, 23; *Anglo-Italian Review*, July 1918, 264, Angelo Crespi; W. Knight, *Memoir of John Nichol, Professor of English Literature in the University of Glasgow*, Glasgow, 1896, 139–40.

149 Arnold Toynbee, *Lectures on the Industrial Revolution in England*,

London, 1884, 200.

150 Mrs Disney Leith, *The Boyhood of Algernon Charles Swinburne*, London, 1917, 90–93, 98, 213; Georges Lafourcade, *La Jeunesse de Swinburne*, Paris, 1928, *1*, 255–6; *ibid.* 2, 307; *The Letters of Algernon Charles Swinburne*, ed. E. Gosse and T. J. Wise, London, 1918, *1*, 29; *Rassegna*, Jan. 1962, 7, Daniels.

CHAPTER NINE. *Final Polemics*

Religion

1 E. Buonaiuti, *Storia del Cristianesimo*, Milan, 1951, *3*, 435; Giovanni Gentile, *Memorie Italiane e problemi della Filosofia della Vita*, Florence, 1936, 232; *Storia Illustrata*, Milan, Dec. 1961, 769, Spadolini; Richard Garnett, *A History of Italian Literature*, London, 1898, 372–3.

2 *Ed. Naz. 58*, 304; *ibid. 88*, 182–4, 275; Henry Hyndman, *The Record of an Adventurous Life*, London, 1911, 67; Mountstuart Grant Duff, *Notes for a Diary 1851–1872*, London, 1897, *1*, 282–3; Richards, *3*, 216.

3 *Ed. Naz. 69*, 23; *ibid. Appendice, 6*, 308–9.

4 *Ed. Naz. 80*, 83; *ibid. 88*, 108; *ibid. Appendice, 6*, 80.

5 *Ed. Naz. 65*, 146; *ibid. 69*, 5; *ibid. 75*; 115; *ibid. 89*, 50; *ibid. 93*, 99, 160; G. Mazzini, *I Doveri dell'Uomo*, ed. G. Macchia and G. Limiti, Rome, 1972, 4.

6 *Ed. Naz. 93*, 6, 120, 152–3.

7 *Ed. Naz. 60*, 255; *Hansard 166*, 946–7, 11 April 1862, Gladstone; *Massimo d'Azeglio e Diomede Pantaleoni: Carteggio inedito*, ed. G. Faldella, Turin, 1888, 249.

8 *Ed. Naz. 69*, 105; *ibid. 79*, 163; *ibid. 83*, 48, 51–2, 60–3; *ibid. 91*, 82; Richards, *3*, 216.

9 George Holyoake, *Bygones Worth Remembering*, London, 1905, *1*, 220–1; George Holyoake, *Sixty Years of an Agitator's Life*, London, 1892, *1*, 220–1; G. Garibaldi, *Scritti e Discorsi Politici e Militari*, Bologna, 1937, *3*, 519, 536; *Ed. Naz. 88*, 221, 224, 262; *ibid. 91*, 171.

10 *Ed. Naz. 79*, 75–6; *ibid. 81*, 326; *ibid. 85*, 90; *ibid. 87*, 140–1.

11 *Ed. Naz. 84*, 150–1; Giuseppe Leti, *Carboneria e Massoneria nel Risorgimento Italiano*, Genoa, 1925, 197–8.

12 *Ed. Naz. 26*, 69; Angelo Crespi, *Giuseppe Mazzini e la Futura Sintesi Religiosa*, Florence, 1912, 29–30.

13 *Letters and Memorials of Catherine Winkworth*, Clifton, 1886, *2*, 423.

14 Charles William Stubbs, *God and the People: The Religious Creed of a Democrat, Being Selections from the Writings of Joseph Mazzini*, London, 1891, and second edition in 1896; G. W. E. Russell, *A Pocketful of Sixpences*, London, 1907, 92.

15 *Ed. Naz. 78*, 350–2; *ibid. 81*, 49.

16 Hyndman, *The Record of an Adventurous Life*, 67; Joseph McCabe, *Life and Letters of George Jacob Holyoake*, London, 1908, *1*, 235; *Dark Blue*, May 1872, 317; A. H. Nethercot, *The First Five Lives of Annie Besant*, London, 1961, 75; *The Reasoner*, 10 June 1866; *Rassegna*, Dec. 1935, 898, Onnis.

17 Pellegrino Ascarelli, *Giuseppe Mazzini e il Problema Religiosa in Italia*, Rome, 1930, 39–40.

18 *Ed. Naz. 83*, 377; *ibid. 88*, 199–200; *ibid. 92*, 34; Daelli, *9*, xix; Felix Moscheles, *Fragments of an Autobiography*, London, 1899, 249.

19 Mrs King, *Letters and Recollections of Mazzini*, London, 1912, 113–14; *Ed. Naz. 3*, 19–20; *ibid. 91*, 244–5.

20 *Ed. Naz. 86*, 252–6.

21 *Ed. Naz. 83*, 95, 207; *ibid. 92*, 112; Mazzini, *Doveri dell'Uomo*, 30.

22 C. Pisacane, *La Rivoluzione*, ed. A.

Romano, Milan, 1957, 188; *Opere di Francesco de Sanctis*, ed. C. Muscetta and G. Candeloro, Turin, 1951, 60; G. Salvemini, *Mazzini*, Rome, 1920, 57, 101; Luigi Salvatorelli, *Prima e Dopo il Quarantotto*, Turin, 1948, 52; Elio Conti, *Le Origini del Socialismo a Firenze (1860–1880)*, Rome, 1950, 49; A. Omodeo, *Il Senso della Storia*, Turin, 1955, 409; *Corriere della Sera*, 2 Mar. 1972, Indro Montanelli.

23 *Fraser's Magazine*, Sept. 1882, 402; Domus, 1977, *2*, 210, de Cesare; G. Colamarino, *Il Fantasma Liberale*, Milan, 1946, 72.

24 *Ed. Naz. 92*, 33–4.

25 *Ed. Naz. 77*, 325.

26 *Ed. Naz. 83*, 218; *Doveri dell'Uomo*, 90; *L'Eco di Savonarola*, London, Aug. 1850, 121–3; *The National Review*, London, Jan. 1864, 28, Cobbe.

27 *Ed. Naz. 49*, 184; *ibid. 60*, 255–6; *ibid. 74*, 190–1; *ibid. 75*, 139; *ibid. 86*, 84–5, 186; *ibid. 92*, 29; *ibid. 93*, 257; Moscheles, *Fragments*, 247; J. W. Mario, *Mazzini*, 469–70, 485; Malvida von Meysenbug, *Memoiren einer Idealistin und ihr Nachtrag*, Stuttgart, 1922, *2*, 92.

28 Lord Bryce, *Modern Democracies*, London, 1921, *1*, 66.

Socialism

29 G. D. H. Cole, *A History of Socialist Thought*, London, 1953, *1*, 282; Gaetano Salvemini, *Mazzini*, London, 1956, 119–20.

30 Rosario Romeo, *Dal Piemonte Sabaudo all'Italia Liberale*, Bari, 1974, 290; Viscount Morley, *Recollections*, London, 1917, *1*, 78; Bryce, *Modern Democracies, 2*, 583.

31 *Ed. Naz. 34*, 102, 107; *ibid. 39*, 212; *ibid. 93*, 154, 251–2.

32 *Ed. Naz. 59*, 42; *ibid. 62*, 62; *ibid. 86*, 170; *ibid. 93*, 44.

33 P.-J. Proudhon, *La Fédération et*

l'Unité d'Italie, Paris, 1862, 28–9; P.-J. Proudhon, *Oeuvres Complètes*, ed. C. Bouglé and H. Moysset, Geneva, 1982, *15*, 242, 250; *Ed. Naz. 79*, 61.

34 *Ed. Naz. 63*, 150; *ibid. 93*, 151–2; *ibid. Appendice, 6*, 5–6.

35 *Doveri dell'Uomo*, Rome, 1972, 117–18, 122–3.

36 *Ed. Naz. 62*, 28; *ibid. 63*, 17–18; *ibid. 77*, 51–2; *ibid. 80*, 169; Marc Vuilleumier, *Autour d'Alexandre Herzen: Documents inédits*, Geneva, 1973, 34.

37 Holyoake, *Bygones, 1*, 221.

38 *Ed. Naz. 92*, 341–2; *ibid. 93*, 151–4.

39 *Doveri dell'Uomo*, 10–11.

40 *Ibid. 18*, 133; *Ed. Naz. 93*, 133.

41 *Ed. Naz. 64*, 164–5; *ibid. 69*, 163; *ibid. 71*, 274; *ibid. 92*, 329–30, 335; *Dark Blue*, May 1872, 323; Otto Vossler, *Mazzinis Politisches Denken und Wollen*, Munich, 1927, 72.

42 *Cosmopolis*, London, June 1897, 664–5.

43 *Ed. Naz. 83*, 157.

44 *Ed. Naz. 25*, 202; *ibid. 59*, 168; *ibid. 62*, 28.

45 *Fortnightly Review*, 1 April 1878, 527–8; *Ed. Naz. 25*, 204; *ibid. 58*, 32; *ibid. 81*, 326.

46 Mazzini to Palmerston, 14 May 1862, Palmerston Archives, Broadlands; *Ed. Naz. 69*, 381–407; *ibid. 78*, 302.

47 *Ed. Naz. 66*, 373–4.

48 *The Times*, 16 Oct. 1861.

49 *Ed. Naz. 72*, 218; *ibid. 79*, 257.

50 *Ed. Naz. 58*, 32–3; *ibid. 59*, 168; *ibid. 81*, 326.

51 *Rassegna*, July 1949, 165, Elio Conti; *Ed. Naz. 70*, 197; *ibid. 71*, 249; Nello Rosselli, *Mazzini e Bakounine*, Turin, 1927, 132–3; Delio Cantimori, *Studi di Storia*, Turin, 1959, 597.

52 A. Gramsci, *Il Risorgimento*, Turin, 1949, 104; Giuseppe Berti, *Russia e Stati Italiani nel Risorgimento*, Turin, 1957, 481; *Nuova Rivista*

Storica, Milan, Jan. 1964, 72, Della Peruta.

53 *Ed. Naz. 3*; 332–3; *ibid. 59*, 105–6; *ibid. 62*, 28; *ibid. 64*, 195; *ibid. 83*, 157, 174–5, 228.

54 *Ed. Naz. 74*, 47; *ibid. 87*, 244.

55 *Ed. Naz. 62*, 86; *ibid. 84*, 305, 310; *ibid. 87*, 77; A. Luzio, *Studi Critici*, Milan, 1927, 201.

56 *Ed. Naz. 59*, 103–4; E. Abbott and L. Campbell, *The Life and Letters of Benjamin Jowett*, London, 1897, *2*, 10–11.

57 *Ed. Naz. 27*, 7; M. d'Azeglio, *Timori e Speranze*, Turin, 1848; 15; Lord Malmesbury, *Memories of an Ex-Minister*, London, 1884, 503; Jack La Bolina, *Cronachette del Risorgimento Italiano*, Florence, 1920, 168; *Edizione Nazionale degli Scritti di Giuseppe Garibaldi*, Bologna, 1937, *2*, 412; *ibid. 9*, 62.

58 *Catechismo Popolare del Partito d'Azione*, London, 1859, paragraph no. 31; *Ed. Naz. 3*, 332–3, 335; *ibid. 51*, 41; *ibid. 59*, 106; *ibid. 62*, 28; *ibid. 64*, 194–7; *ibid. 70*, 292–3; *ibid. 72*, 57; *ibid. 75*, 38; *ibid. 83*, 157, 174–5, 228; *ibid. 85*, 298.

59 *Doveri dell'Uomo*, 134; *Ed. Naz. 86*, 210; *ibid. 92*, xxxi, 114; *ibid. 93*, 4, 133.

60 *Italia e Inghilterra nel Risorgimento*, ed. Istituto Italiano di Cultura, London, 1954, 37, Venturi.

61 Karl Marx and Frederick Engels, *Collected Works*, London, 1986, *15*, 485; *ibid. 16*, 354; *ibid. 41*, 517, 544; Giuseppe Berti, *I Democratici e L'Iniziativa Meridionale nel Risorgimento*, Milan, 1962, 123–4; *La Lettura*, Milan, Jan. 1915, 2–6, Luzio.

62 Arthur Lehning, *The International Association 1855–1859*, Leiden, 1938, 48, 90–1.

63 Marx and Engels, *Collected Works*, 42, 16; *Ed. Naz. 80*, 218; *ibid. 93*, 25, 135; Rosselli, *Mazzini e Bakounine*, 137–8, 148–9; V. Frosini, *Breve Storia della Critica al*

Marxismo in Italia, Catania, 1965, 16–17.

64 *Minute Book of the International*, Bishopsgate Institute, London, 44, 174–5.

65 *Ed. Naz. 79*, 81; *ibid. 81*, 326; *ibid. 86*, liv, 130; *ibid. 92*, 306.

66 *Ed. Naz. 27*, 258; *ibid. 72*, 167; *ibid. 74*, 268.

67 Arthur Lehning, *Archives Bakounine*, Leiden, 1961, *1*, xxiii, 72, 285; *Correspondance de Michel Bakounine: Lettres à Herzen et à Ogareff (1860–1874)*, ed. M. Dragomanov, Paris, 1896, 214; Michele Bakunin, *La Teologia Politica di Mazzini e l'Internationale (1871)*, ed. P. C. Masini, Bergamo, 1960, 1, 4, 37–9.

68 M. Nettlau, *Bakunin e L'Internazionale in Italia dal 1864 at 1872*, Geneva, 1928; 55; Lehning, *Archives Bakounine*, *1*, 283; *ibid. 2*, 235–7.

69 *Memorie di Giorgio Pallavicino*, edited by his wife, Turin, 1882, *2*, 300–1; Pallavicino, introduction to B. E. Maineri, *Il Piemonte nel 1850–2*, Milan, 1875, viii; E. Montecchi, *Mattia Montecchi nel Risorgimento*, Rome, 1932, 526; Nassau William Senior, *Conversations with Distinguished Persons during the Second Empire from 1860 to 1863*, London, 1880, *1*, 335.

70 Herzen, *My Past*, 3, 1462.

71 *Libertà e Giustizia*, 24 Aug. and 21 Sept. 1867, ed. Marcello Ralli, Salerno, 1977, 29–30, 126.

72 Cristina Trivulzio di Belgiojoso, *Osservazioni sullo Stato Attuale dell'Italia e sul suo Avvenire*, Milan, 1868, 52–7; A. Malvezzi, *La Principessa Cristina di Belgiojoso*, Milan, 1937, *2*, 308–10.

73 *Scritti Politici di Alberto Mario*, ed. G. Carducci, Bologna, 1901, 75, 87.

74 Carlo Cattaneo, *Scritti Politici*, ed. M. Boneschi, Florence, 1965, 4, 137–8.

75 *Archivio Triennale delle Cose d'Italia*

dall'Avvento di Pio IX all'Abbandono di Venezia, Capolago, 1850, 1, 641.

More conspiracy: 1868–70

76   Russell Papers, PRO, 30/22/16E; J. K. Laughton, Memoirs of the Life and Correspondence of Henry Reeve, London, 1898, 2, 135 (letter of 2 Feb. 1868, from Clarendon in Italy); R. Mori, Il Tramonto, del Potere Temporale, Rome, 1967, 567; The Roman Question, ed. N. Blakiston, London, 1962, 161, 218–21, 248, 285; Lettere del Barone Ricasoli, ed. Tabarrini, Florence, 1891, 6, 97–8.

77   Saffi, 9, 297; Ed. Naz. 87, 166.

78   DDI ser. 1, 10, 435; ibid. 11, 310; Luigi Menabrea, Memorie, ed. L. Briguglio and L. Bulferetti, Florence, 1971, 55; Mori, Il Tramonto, 352.

79   DDI ser.1, 10, 678, 743; G. Ferretti, Luigi Amedeo Melegari a Losanna, Rome, 1942, 354–5.

80   Moritz Hartmann, Gesammelte Werke, Stuttgart, 1874, 10, 176; Rossetti Papers 1862 to 1870, ed. William Michael Rossetti, London, 1903, 335; Domus, 1977, 2, 215, De Cesare; The Times, 18 Nov. 1868.

81   Ed. Naz. 87, 296, 306; ibid. 88, 21; 52, 175.

82   The Amberley Papers: The Letters and Diaries of Lord and Lady Amberley, ed. Bertrand and Patricia Russell, London, 1937, 2, 113.

83   Ed. Naz. 87, 292, 299, 313.

84   The Times, 18 Nov. 1868; S. Polenghi, La Politica Universitaria nell'Età della Destra Storica 1848–1876, 351–8.

85   DDI ser. 1, 10, 188; ibid. 11, 163, 274.

86   Clarendon Papers, Bodleian Library, Dep. c. 488/99, 27 May 1869, Paget.

87   Ed. Naz. 88, 13–14, 29.

88   Ed. Naz. 88, 13, 110; Schweizeri-

sches Bundesarchiv, E. 21/141, 10 May 1869.

89   Ed. Naz. 88, 21; Mrs Hamilton King, Letters and Recollections of Mazzini, London, 1912, 73; Bulletin of the International Institute of Social History, Amsterdam, Leiden, 1953, 32, Herzen.

90   Lettere di Giuseppe Mazzini ad Andrea Giannelli, Prato, 1888, 4, 412, 421.

91   Ed. Naz. 88, 240–1, 279; Annali Feltrinelli, Milan, 1961, 4, 316, Della Peruta.

92   Ed. Naz. 88, 148, 242; Mario Chini, Lettere di Giuseppe Mazzini a Giuseppe Riccioli Romano, Palermo, 1951, 154.

93   Ed. Naz. 89, 10–11, 23, 117.

94   G. E. Curàtulo, Il Dissidio tra Mazzini e Garibaldi, Milan, 1928, 326–7; Ed. Naz. 88, 224–5, 264; ibid. 91, 171.

95   Ed. Naz. 88, 311; ibid. 89, 5, 68, 116–17, 254–5, 272; Mrs King, Letters and Recollections, 73–4.

96   Diplomatische Dokumente der Schweiz, Berne, 1985, 2, 352; Le Carte di Giovanni Lanza, 5, 53; DDI ser. 1, 12, 383, 434, 522, 598.

97   Carte di Lanza, 5, 58, 71.

98   Saffi, 9, 191; Bollettino del Museo del Risorgimento, Bologna, 1973, 197, ed. L. Lotti; J. W. Mario, Della Vita di Mazzini, 453; Le Carte di Lanza, 5, 111.

99   Ed. Naz. 89, 94, 254.

100   Ed. Naz. 88, 307; ibid. 89, 11.

101   Annali Feltrinelli, Milan, 1961, 319–23, Della Peruta; Ed. Naz. 89, 109–10, 240.

102   Chini, Lettere a Riccioli, 173–4.

103   Paolo Alatri, Lotte Politiche in Sicilia sotto il Governo della Destra (1866–1874), Turin, 1954, 312–13, 326; Chini, Lettere a Riccioli, 144; Archivio Trimestrale, Rome, May 1975, 151, Schwarzenberg; E. A. V. (Emilie Ashurst Venturi), Joseph Mazzini, a Memoir, London, 1875, 159.

104   Giorgio Asproni, Diario Politico,

Milan, 1974, *5*, 565.

105 Norbert Miko, *Das Ende des Kirchenstaates*, Vienna, 1961, *2*, 16; G. Finali, *Memorie*, Faenza, 1955, 320; *Contemporary Review*, London, Mar. 1888, 391; *Fraser's Magazine*, Oct. 1879, 519; Marx and Engels, *Collected Works*, *42*, 361; P. Pietro Pirri, *Pio IX e Vittorio Emanuele dal loro Carteggio Privato*, Rome, 1961, *3*, part 1, 297–8.

106 Hermann Oncken, *Die Rheinpolitik Kaiser Napoleons III von 1863 bis 1870*, Berlin, 1926, *3*, 485; *DDI ser. 1, 11*, 467; *ibid. 12*, 449; *ibid. 13*, 147, 311; Mary Trauth, *Italo-American Diplomatic Relations*, Washington, 1958, 165.

107 *Carte di Lanza, 5*, 227, 233–7, 255; Stefano Castagnola, *Da Firenze a Roma: Diario storico-politico del 1870–71*, Turin, 1896, 15–16; F. E. Morando, *Mazziniani e Garibaldini nell'Ultimo Periodo del Risorgimento*, Genoa, n.d., 125.

108 *Carte di Lanza, 6*, 40.

109 *Ed. Naz. 90*, 24; Saffi, *9*, 90.

110 Edoardo Pantano, *Memorie*, Bologna, 1933, *1*, 388; Saffi, *13*, 114.

111 *Ed. Naz. 90*, 119–20; *ibid. 91*, 59, Chini, *Lettere a Riccioli*, 204; Pantano, *Memorie, 1*, 332; Saffi, *9*, 92; Castagnola, *Da Firenze a Roma*, 16.

CHAPTER TEN. *Failure and Achievement*

The capture of Rome

1 *Les Origines Diplomatiques de la Guerre de 1870–71*, Paris, 1932, *29*, 438; *DDI ser. 1, 13*, 286; Mme Rattazzi, *Rattazzi et son Temps*, Paris, 1881, *2*, 340; J. W. Mario, *Agostino Bertani e i Suoi Tempi*, Florence, 1888, *2*, 349–50; D. Mack Smith, *Italy and its Monarchy*, New Haven, 1989, 52–4.

2 *Rattazzi et son Temps, 2*, 349–50; Marco Minghetti, *La Convenzione di Settembre: Un capitolo dei miei ricordi*, Bologna, 1890, 214; *Discorsi Parlamentari di Francesco Crispi*, Rome, 1915, *3*, 642.

3 Raffaele Cadorna, *La Liberazione di Roma nell'Anno 1870*, Turin, 1889, 36.

4 *Le Lettere di Vittorio Emanuele II*, ed. F. Cognasso, Turin, 1966, *2*, 1488.

5 N. Miko, *Das Ende des Kirchenstaates*, Vienna, 1961, *2*, 550; *ibid. 3*, 135–6; *ibid. 4*, 172; *Neue Freie Presse*, quoted by A. Wandruska, *XLVI Congresso di Storia del Risorgimento Italiano* Sept. 1972, Rome, 481.

6 Domenico Farini, *Diario di Fine Secolo*, ed. E. Morelli, Rome, 1962, *1*, 552; Federigo Sclopis, *Diario Segreto (1859–1878)*, ed. P. Pietro Pirri, Turin, 1959, 449; S. Castagnola, *Da Firenze a Roma*, Turin, 1896, 131; S. Jacini, *Un Conservatore Rurale della Nuova Italia*, Bari, 1926, *2*, 47; F. Chabod, *Storia della Politica Estera*, Bari, 1951, 209, 315–18, 329–30; *Lettere Inedite di Massimo d'Azeglio*, ed. N. Bianchi, Turin, 1883, 356; Massimo d'Azeglio, *L'Italie de 1847 à 1865*, ed. E. Rendu, Paris, 1867, 206, 209.

7 *Dizionario Biografico degli Italiani, 10*, 758, 'Alberto Blanc', by R. Mori.

8 Miko, *Das Ende des Kirchenstaates, 3*, 6; Alessandro Guiccioli, *Quintino Sella*, Rovigo, 1887, *1*, 306; *Le Carte di Lanza*, Turin, 1935, *6*, 89.

9 Chabod, *Politica Estera*, 678.

10 Domus, 1972, *2*, 220, Gastaldi; *Rassegna*, April 1985, 190–2, Monsagrati.

11 *Ed. Naz. 90*, 42–3.

12 *The Victoria Magazine*, London, May 1872, 67.

13 Giacinto Fassio, *Mazzini a Gaeta*, Poggio Mirteto, 1912, 55, 59–

60, 74–6; U. Barengo, *Vincende Mazziniane e Garibaldine nelle Carte dei Carabinieri Reali*, Milan, 1942, 132–3; Giorgio Asproni, *Diario Politico*, Milan, 1974, 5, 621.

14 *Ed. Naz. 90*, 65; *ibid. 91*, 18, 39; *Le Carte di Lanza*, 6, 98–9, 215, 227–8.

15 *Ed. Naz. 90*, 99; Saffi, *9*, 211; E. A. V. (Emilie Ashurst), *Joseph Mazzini*, London, 1875, 160; *Rassegna*, April 1985, 199–200, Dagnino.

16 *Ed. Naz. 88*, 108; *ibid. 90*, 65, 151.

17 *Ed. Naz. 90*, 49–50.

18 *Ed. Naz. 91*, 102; *ibid. 93*, 187–8.

19 *Ed. Naz. 90*, 107; *ibid. 92*, 102; *ibid. 93*, 187–8; *Carteggio Politico di Michelangelo Castelli*, ed. L. Chiala, Turin, 1890, 2, 511; Chabod, *Politica Estera*, 328; D. Mack Smith, *Victor Emanuel, Cavour and the Risorgimento*, London, 1971, 367–8.

20 *Ed. Naz. 90*, 63, 111, 148.

21 Pellegrino Ascarelli, *Giuseppe Mazzini e il Problema Religioso in Italia*, Rome, 1930, 32; *Fortnightly Review*, 1 Mar. 1871, 289–90.

22 E. A. V., *Joseph Mazzini*, 47–8; *Ed. Naz. 92*, 81–2; *ibid. Appendice, 6*, 403.

23 *Ed. Naz. 86*, 206; *ibid. 87*, 311; *ibid. 92*, 92; *ibid. 93*, 241.

24 *The Victoria Magazine*, May 1872, 62; *Ed. Naz. 90*, 266, 299.

25 *Fortnightly Review*, 1 Mar. 1871, 289; *Ed. Naz. 90*, 195.

26 Moncure Conway, *Autobiography*, London, 1904, 2, 60.

27 George Holyoake, *Bygones Worth Remembering*, London, 1905, *1*, 204.

28 *Ed. Naz. 77*, 261–2; *ibid. 91*, 125; E. A. V., *Joseph Mazzini*, 64.

29 *Ed. Naz. 64*, 279; *ibid. 66*, 306; *ibid. 75*, 142–3; *ibid. 92*, 36; *ibid. 93*, 241–2; *ibid. 94*, 97; C. B. Furiozzi, *Da Mazzini a Bissolati*, Florence, 1988, 22.

A final year of journalism

30 Frau Förster-Nietzsche, *The Young Nietzsche*, London, 1912, 243–4; D. Halévy, *The Life of Friedrich Nietzsche*, London, 1911, 200–1; Malvida von Meysenbug, *Le Soir de Ma Vie*, Paris, 1908, 288; *Corriere della Sera*, 1 Sept. 1940, Luzio.

31 Miko, *Das Ende des Kirchenstaates*, 4, 103.

32 *Filippo Turati attraverso le Lettere di Corrispondenti (1880–1925)*, ed. Alessandro Schiavi, Bari, 1947, 38.

33 *Ed. Naz. 34*, 244–5; *ibid. 93*, 7–9, 132; Francesco Fiumara, *Mazzini e l'Internazionale*, Pisa, 1968, 14; Nello Rosselli, *Mazzini e Bakounine*, Turin, 1927, 295.

34 *Ed. Naz. 93*, 166.

35 *Ed. Naz. 92*, 185; *ibid. 93*, 9–10, 149, 158–9.

36 T. R. Ravindranathan, *Bakunin and the Italians*, Montreal, 1988, 101–4.

37 *Fortnightly Review*, 1 Mar. 1871, 298; Petruccelli della Gattina, *I Fattori e Malfattori della Politica Europea Contemporanea*, Milan, 1881, 2, 366.

38 *Ed. Naz. 91*, 87–8; *ibid. 92*, 20; *ibid. 93*, 37, 128, 162, 261.

39 Arthur Lehning, *Archives Bakounine*, Leiden, 1961, *1*, 283–5; *ibid. 2*, 242, 283, 297; *Annali Feltrinelli*, Milan, 1971, *14*, 183, A. Colombo.

40 Karl Marx and Frederick Engels, *Collected Works*, London, 1986, *22*, 598; *ibid. 23*, 497.

41 A. Omodeo, *Il Senso della Storia*, Turin, 1948, 417; Delio Cantimori, *Studi di Storia*, Turin, 1959, 79; Richards, *3*, 286.

42 *Ed. Naz. 92*, 153–4, 164–5.

43 Lord Bryce, *Modern Democracies*, London, 1921, *1*, 18.

44 *Ed. Naz. 34*, 225; *ibid. 91*, 317.

45 *Ed. Naz. 92*, 145, 262.

46 *Ed. Naz. 91*, 288–9; *ibid. 92*, 124;

Lettere Inedite di Giuseppe Mazzini all'Esule Carlo Blind, Naples, c.1927, 159–60.

47 *Ed. Naz. 87*, 107; *ibid. 92*, 88, 124, 126.

48 *Ed. Naz. 92*, 137–9, 143–4, 247.

49 *The Victoria Magazine*, May 1872, 68; Mazzini's letter of 7 Oct. 1870 to Kate Amberley; McAdam Papers, Glasgow, Mazzini's letter of 28 Jan. 1871; *Quaderni di Cultura*, Livorno, April 1952, 160–1.

50 L. B. Namier, 'Nationality and Liberty', in *Il 1848 nella Storia d'Europa*, conference (*convegno*) of Accademia dei Lincei, Rome, 1949, 170–1; R. Michels, *L'Imperialismo Italiano*, Milan, 1914, 106; A. Galante Garrone, *Salvemini e Mazzini*, Florence, 1981, 455, 468; E. Passerin d'Entreves, *L'Ultima Battaglia Politica di Cavour*, Turin, 1956, 169.

51 *Critica Fascista*, Rome, 1 Nov. 1932, 417; Giuseppe Bottai, *Incontri*, Milan, 1943, 128, 150; *Lo Stato*, Rome, Feb. 1937, 123; F. Ercole, *Dal Nazionalismo al Fascismo*, Rome, 1928, 199; Antonio Canepa, *Sistema di Dottrina del Fascismo*, Rome, 1937, 2, 194–5; Nazareno Mezzetti, *Mazzini Visto con Cuore Fascista*, Rome, 1933, 74, 122, 136–7; V. Cian, 'I precursori del Fascismo', in ed. G. Pomba, *La Civiltà Fascista*, Turin, 1928, 129–30; Giuseppe Calogero, *Il Pensiero Filosofico di Giuseppe Mazzini*, Brescia, 1937, 7 (preface by Orestano), 67, 295; *Lo Stato Operaio 1927–1939*, ed. F. Ferri, Città di Castello, 1964, 1, 472, Togliatti.

52 *La Critica*, Bari, 1903, 463–4.

53 *Educazione Politica*, Rome, Jan. 1926, 4; Giovanni Gentile, *I Profeti del Risorgimento Italiano*, Florence, 1923, 38–9; Giovanni Gentile, *Che Cosa è il Fascismo?*, Florence, 1924, 43; Giovanni Gentile, *Memorie Italiane e Problemi della Filosofia e della Vita*, Florence, 1936, 41.

54 G. Pini and D. Susmel, *Mussolini: l'Uomo e l'Opera*, Florence, 1955, 4, 494; Giuseppe Bottai, *Diario 1935–1944*, ed. Giordano Bruno Guerri, Milan, 1982, 149, 186, 468.

55 *Fortnightly Review*, April 1877, 561.

56 *Ed. Naz. 86*, 6–7; *ibid. 89*, 56; *ibid. 92*, 166–70.

57 *Ed. Naz. 28*, 92; *ibid. 75*, 118; *ibid. 83*, 164–5; *ibid. 93*, 92; *Pensiero ed Azione*, London, 15 Sept. 1858, 30; Otto Vossler, *Mazzinis Politisches Denken und Wollen*, Munich, 1927, 73.

58 *Westminster Review*, April 1852, 466; *Ed. Naz. 17*, 92.

59 *The Collected Works of Mahatma Gandhi*, Delhi, 1961, 5, 27–8; G. Srivastava, *Mazzini and his Impact on the Indian National Movement*, Delhi, 1982, 189, 277; Harold Schiffrin, *Sun Yat-Sen and the Origins of the Chinese Revolution*, Berkeley, 1968, 259; *Garibaldi, Mazzini e il Risorgimento nel Risveglio dell'Asia e dell'Africa*, ed. G. Borsa and P. B. Brocchieri, Milan, 1984, 152–3 (Ballhatchet), 173 (Borsa); *Rassegna*, April 1975, 258–9; *ibid.* July 1982, 297–300; *ibid.* July 1984, 262–4; S. Avineri, *The Making of Modern Zionism*, London, 1981, 45–6.

60 Renato Risaliti, *Movimenti del Realismo Russo*, Pisa, 1972, 194–6; G. Salvemini, *Scritti sul Risorgimento*, ed. P. Pieri and C. Pischedda, Milan, 1961, 197–8.

61 A. Omodeo, *Per la Riconquista della Libertà*, Naples, 1944, 83–5; Livio Zeno, *Ritratto di Carlo Sforza*, Florence, 1975, 322; *Movimento Operaio*, Oct. 1950, 416.

62 *Ed. Naz. 66*, 340; *ibid. 69*, 150; *ibid. 92*, 262; *ibid. 93*, 85–6.

63 *Macmillan's Magazine*, Mar. 1871, 440–3; *Doveri dell'Uomo*, Rome, 1972, 72; *Ed. Naz. 29*, 91–2; *ibid. 86*, 169; *ibid. 93*, 89–90.

64 C. E. Vaughan, *Studies in the History of Political Philosophy before and after Rousseau*, ed. A. G. Little, Manchester, 1925, *2*, 305, 321.

65 *La Critica*, Bari, Nov. 1938, 459–60; Benedetto Croce, *Pagine Sparse*, Naples, 1943, *3*, 383–4; Chabod, *Storia della Politica Estera*, 148, 157; *Contemporary Review*, London, Jan. 1950, 36, Gwilym Griffith; Graham Wallas, *Human Nature in Politics*, London, 1908, 278.

66 Holyoake, *Bygones*, *1*, 228.

67 *Fortnightly Review*, April, 1877, 570; *Ed. Naz. 92*, 157–8.

68 *The Papers of Woodrow Wilson*, ed. Arthur Link, Princeton, 1983, *41*, 530; *ibid. 53*, 613–15; F. Ruffini, *Il Presidente Wilson*, Milan, 1919, 64–5, 102; Felice Momigliano, *Giuseppe Mazzini e la Guerra Europea*, Milan, 1916, 7; *Corriere della Sera*, 25 April 1919; *The New Europe*, London, 9 May 1918, 7, 89.

69 *The Times*, 29 June 1922; Thomas Jones, *Whitehall Diary*, ed. K. Middlemas, London, 1969, *1*, xxi–xxii, 217; *Contemporary Review*, London, Nov. 1919, 560.

The end

70 Chabod, *Storia della Politica Estera*, 52, 261, 278–81, 328, 512.

71 *Fortnightly Review*, 1 March 1871, 299–301, 309.

72 *Ed. Naz. 91*, 112–13, 142–3.

73 *Ed. Naz. 91*, 10, 127, 141; *ibid. 94*, 95; *ibid. Appendice, 6*, 417.

74 *Ed. Naz. 91*, 224; *ibid. 92*, 276, 327; *ibid. Appendice, 6*, 410; Jessie White Mario, *Mazzini*, 485.

75 *Ed. Naz. 91*, 324–5.

76 *Ed. Naz. 91*, 268; Giuseppe Garibaldi, *Cantoni il Volontario*, Milan, 1870, 182; Giuseppe Garibaldi, *Scritti Politici*, ed. D. Ciàmpoli, Rome, 1907, *2*, 590–5; Marx and Engels, *Collected Works*, *23*, 29, 43–4.

77 Alessandro Levi, *Scritti Minori, Storici e Politici*, Padua, 1957, *2*, 209; Saffi. *9*, 262; J. W. Mario, *Agostino Bertani e i Suoi Tempi*, Florence, 1888, *2*, 232, 290.

78 Saffi, 7, 57; *Ed. Naz. 91*, 368; Mrs Hamilton King, *Letters and Recollections*, London, 1912, 124; Alexander Herzen, *My Past and Thoughts*, London, 1968, *3*, 1028.

79 *Dark Blue*, London, May 1872, 316, Karl Blind; *Daily News*, London, 12 Mar. 1872.

80 British Library Additional MS 40125/101, Emilie Ashurst letter to Blind, 20 Jan. 1872; Richards, *3*, 290.

81 *La Roma del Popolo*, Rome, 14 Mar. 1872, 218; *Ed. Naz. 91*, 354; *ibid. 93*, 120, 236, 259.

82 U. Barengo, *Vicende Mazziniane e Garibaldine nelle Carte dei Carabinieri Reali*, Milan, 1942, 139; *Le Carte di Lanza*, 8, 52, 56–7.

83 *Stansfeld Papers*, letter from Mrs King at Pisa, 17 May 1876.

84 Ferdinando Martini, *Confessioni e Ricordi 1859–1892*, Milan, 1929, 67–76.

85 Domus, 1958, *1*, 63, Carmignani; Tyne and Wear (Newcastle) MS 634, A. 933, 5 April 1872, Emilie Ashurst to Cowen; McAdam Papers, Glasgow, 4 June 1872, Garibaldi letter to McAdam.

86 *A Memoir of the Rt Hon. William Edmund Lecky*, by his wife, London, 1909, 87; *New York Times*, 14 April 1872; *Leisure Hour*, London, 16 Dec. 1876, 816; G. Asproni, *Diario Politico 1856–1876*, Milan, 1984, 7, 293.

87 *Camera dei Deputati, Discussioni*, 11 Mar. 1872, 113.

88 *Annali Feltrinelli*, Milan, 1972, *14*, 175, Colombo.

Epilogue

1 *Le Carte di Lanza*, Turin, 1935 *8*, 667; *Camera dei Deputati: Discussioni*, 24 May 1872, 2304; Andrea Giannelli, *Lettere di Giuseppe Mazzini ad Andrea Giannelli*, Prato, 1888, 4, 539; *Mazzini e i Repubblicani Italiani: Studi in onore di Terenzio Grandi*, Turin, 1976, 293–4, Morabito.

2 Felix Moscheles, *Fragments of an Autobiography*, London, 1899 268.

3 *New York Times*, 12 Mar. 1872.

4 *Discorsi Parlamentari di Felice Cavallotti*, Rome, 1914, *1*, 149; Jessie White Mario, *Mazzini*, Milan, 1886, 467; Alessandro Luzio, *Carlo Alberto e Giuseppe Mazzini*, Turin, 1923, 301.

5 *L'Opinione*, Turin, 11 Mar. 1872; *La Perseveranza*, 12 Mar. 1872.

6 *Camera dei Deputati, Discussioni*, 25 May 1872, 2333–4, Ferrari.

7 *La Rivista Europea*, Florence, April 1872, 209–11, Assing; *Revue Roumaine d'Histoire*, Bucharest, 1972, 978, Netea.

8 G. E. Curàtulo, *Il Dissidio tra Mazzini e Garibaldi*, Milan, 1928, 205–6; Ferdinando Martini, *Due dell'Estrema: Il Guerrazzi e Il Brofferio*, Florence, 1920, xi–xii.

9 *Bibliothèque Universelle et Revue Suisse*, Lausanne, 1877, *59*, 448–9; Marc Monnier, *L'Italia: è ella la terra de' morti?*, Naples, 1860, 382–4.

10 *The Reasoner*, London, April 1972, 241; *Victoria Magazine*, May 1872, 66; *The Athenaeum*, 16 Mar. 1872, 336; *Dark Blue*, May 1872, 316, 324; *The Nation*, New York, 14 Mar. 1872; *The Daily News*, London, 12 Mar. 1872; *The British Quarterly Review*, London, July 1873, 103–5; *The Economist*, London, 16 Mar. 1872, 323–4; *Punch*, 23 Mar. 1872, 122–5; *Saturday Review*, 16 Mar. 1872.

11 *The Nation*, 22 June 1905, 498–9.

12 *The Times*, London, 12 Mar. 1872; A. Gallenga, *Italy Revisited*, London, 1875, 2, 206–7.

13 *Macmillan's Magazine*, April 1872, 509–19.

14 *The Spectator*, 16 Mar. 1872, 325, 328.

15 *Ed. Naz. 91*, 53; *ibid. 94*, 99.

16 Rosario Romeo, in *La Repubblica*, Rome, 20 April 1977; Indro Montanelli, *L'Italia dei Notabili*, Milan, 1973, 154; *Corriere della Sera*, 2 March 1972; *Storia Illustrata*, Dec. 1971, 767–8; Domus, 1986, *1*, 95, Aiazzi.

17 *Camera dei Deputati, Discussioni*, 26 Mar. 1903, 6755–6; *ibid.* 11 May 1911, 13846, Colajanni; T. Grandi, *La Fortuna dei 'Doveri'*, Milan, 1961, 36–45; J. W. Mario, *Della Vita di Giuseppe Mazzini*, Milan, 1886, xii.

18 *Corriere della Sera*, 14 Jan. 1942; A. Ghisleri, *Giuseppe Mazzini e gli Operai*, Rome, 1946, 9; *La Critica*, Bari, 1915, *15*, 148, Gentile.

Index